THE CANON

First Published by
Elkin Mathews in 1897

This facsimile edition has been carefully scanned
and reprinted in the traditional manner by
THE LOST LIBRARY
5 High Street,
Glastonbury UK BA6 9DP

The LOST LIBRARY is a publishing house based in
Glastonbury, UK, dedicated to the reproduction
of important rare esoteric and scholarly texts for
the discerning reader.

Cataloguing Information
The Canon
William Sterling

ISBN 978 1 906621 15 5

Printed by Replika Press Pvt Ltd,
Haryana, India

**THE LOST
LIBRARY**

THE CANON ❧ ❧ AN EXPOSITION OF THE PAGAN MYSTERY PER: PETVATED IN THE CABA: LA AS THE RVLE OF ALL THE ARTS ❧

WITH A
PREFACE
BY R. B. CVNNINGHAME GRAHAM

PUBLISHED BY
THE LOST LIBRARY
GLASTONBURY, ENGLAND

THIS BOOK

IS DEDICATED

WITH EVERY FEELING OF REGARD

TO HIS FRIEND

H. W. H. D.

BY THE AUTHOR

PREFACE

TO

"SYMBOLISTS."

CONTEMPT of ancient learning is a sure sign of an enlightened mind.

We are the men.

Before our time, reason but little influenced mankind.

The demonstration of the above assertion being that in times gone by there were no railways, steamboats, torpedoes, or any of those anaesthetic inventions in regard to time and space on which we pride ourselves, and upon which we base our claim to have advanced the general welfare of mankind.

Marvels of science, mechanical improvements, increase of wealth (and income tax), and the perfection of all warlike apparatus, seem to blind us to the fact that abstract qualities of mind have shown no symptoms of progression. A rich barbarian, pale and dyspeptic, florid or flatulent, seated in a machine travelling at eighty miles an hour, with the machine luxuriously upholstered and well heated, and yet the traveller's mind a blank, or only occupied with schemes to cheat his fellows and advance himself is, in the abstract, no advance upon a citizen of Athens, in the time of Pericles, who never travelled faster than a bullock cart could take him, in all his life.

Science has no marvels; every so-called discovery heralded as marvellous (for men of science understand the power of bold advertisement to the full as well as scientists in clog dancing, in hair dressing, and tightrope walking), is not a marvel in the true meaning of the word.

The Röntgen Rays, the microphone, the phonograph, are all as simple in themselves as is the property of amber rubbed to take up straws. From the beginning there have been Röntgen Rays, and the principles of microphone and phonograph are coeval with the world. The wonder lies not in the discovery (so-called), but in the fact they have remained so long unknown. The real mystery of mysteries is the mind of man. Why, with a pen or brush, one man sits down and makes a masterpiece, and yet another, with the selfsame instruments and opportunities, turns out a daub or botch, is twenty times more curious than all the musings of the mystics, works of the Rosicrucians, or the mechanical contrivances which seem to-day so fine, and which our children will disdain as clumsy. The conquests of the mind never grow stale, let he who doubts it read a page of Plato and compare it with some *à la mode* philosopher.

I take it that one of the objects of the author of this work is to sustain, that in astronomy, in mathematics, and in certain other branches of learning, the ancients knew a good deal more than modern men of science care to admit.

Knowledge to-day is not diffused, as writers in newspapers, makers of almanacks, members of school-boards, and worthy men who see the means but cannot grasp the fullness of achievement, are never tired of stating, but on the contrary, goes almost contraband. The fact that all can read and write, cypher and scan the columns of a newspaper, can tell the latitude (the longitude more rarely) of Jella Coffee, can prattle innocently of literature, art, spiritualism, and chemistry, can make their pertinent remarks upon theosophy, discuss religion, say a word in season on lithotomy, and generally comport themselves as if their minds were fashioned after the pattern of a kaleidoscope, does not go far to prove the claim of wide extended knowledge.

When all write books and few have time to read, when thought grows rare and talking never ends, a serious book in which a man has put the labour of his life needs some apology for its appearance. Deal with sex problems (pruriently, of course), be mystic, moral, or immoral, flippant, or best of all be dull, success is sure. Still, in an age of symbolism, for everything we see is but a symbol, as kings, queens, dukes, lords, princes, barons, and sandwichmen, it must perforce be interesting to some to read of why the chief symbol of our present faith came to be held in veneration.

In modern times we use a word, merely to express a thing, and only rarely concern ourselves with the exact value that the word may have.

This may account to some extent for the loose
style of many English writers, but to examine into
that would be quite foreign to my purpose. Certain it is that in the ancient world, words and even
letters all had their value apart from what we, now-
a-days, call meaning. Thus it is that oriental
nations, and especially the Jews and Arabs, attach
to their particular alphabets not merely a divine
origin (for I suppose our alphabet is just as divine
as theirs), but a particular sense of sanctity. No
one supposes if a better alphabet than that we now
employ were to be found that we should still ad-
here from superstitious motives to our own. In the
ancient world, apart from letters, every ceremony,
each rite, and all the arts and sciences had some
peculiar canon which was supposed to govern them.
If, in his researches, the author has brought to light
some canon which may enlighten architects, and
so redeem us from the outrages our builders heap
upon us, if he can do even a little to stay the hands
of Deans and Chapters from destroying buildings
which, by the folly of the nation, have been committed to their care (like sheep to wolves), or put a
stop to the restorer, that arch-fiend, who in con-
suming thirst for unity tears down a fine Renais-
sance door-way in a Gothic church, and puts up in
its stead what he thinks Gothic, his labour will not
have been lost. Could he redeem us from Victorian
Queen Anne——but mitigate the horrors of plate-
glass, set bounds to all the Gothics, ranging from
Strangulated, through the degrees of Congrega-
tional and Convulsional down to Ebenezaresque,

could he but find a style in which our builders could express their thoughts, and help them build for us, our churches, houses, theatres, and bridges, without adhering slavishly to bygone styles, the twelve shillings which I understand his volume is to cost will be well spent.

Music and literature, with painting, surgery, and economics, with boxing, fencing, and others of the liberal arts, all have a style fit and peculiar to the times, but architecture yet remains a blot and a disgrace to those who live by it, and to all those who use the edifices which it makes, and pay the makers' bills.

But leaving architects bemired in stucco and happy in their "co-operation with the present system," let us return to the folly of the ancients.

Strabo and Celsus, with Diodorus Siculus, Ammianus Marcellinus, Maimonides, Raimundo Llull, with the Rabbi Jehudah ben Gabirol and others, whose names look well writ large in a quotation, have all remarked upon the symbolism not only of the Cross but of all ancient temples.

Pedro Mexia in his curious Silva[1] de Varia Leccion says that the Egyptians and the Arabians honoured the figure of the cross,[2] and thought so much of it, that the Egyptians drew it upon the

[1] "Madrid," por Joseph Fernandez de Buendía, Año de 1662.
[2] The Inca, Garcilaso de la Vega, in his "Comentarios Reales," vol. i., chap. iii., "Tuvieron los Reyes Incas en el Cozco, una Cruz de Marmol fino de color blanco y encarnado. . . . . No adoravan en ella, mas de que la tenian en veneracion; debia ser por su hermosa figura, ó por algun *otro respeto*, que no saben decir."

statue of Serapis, adored it, and held it as a god. To comprehend which it is necessary first to know the Arabians of old times were people very learned in the heavens, and in the phases of the stars . . . made images and statues . . . rings and other things, taking care to do so, at certain times and epochs when the planets and other stars were in a certain posture." And further on he says, "it is remarkable how the Egyptians esteemed the symbol of the cross above all other symbols."

It may be that, as Pedro Mexia says, the Egyptians looked upon the cross as something sacred, because it is "a perfect and most excellent figure geometrically considered." All things are possible, but a whole people lost in the admiration of a figure for geometric reasons seems improbable. Geometry is a most admirable science, but appeals little to imagination, and still less to any of the well rooted principles of folly inherent in mankind, which generally impel them to choose a subject to adore.

Again Antonio Llobera, in his book called "El Porqué de Todas las Ceremonias," printed at Figueras by Ignacio Porter in 1758, informs us that "all temples and churches are symbols or figures of the human body . . . the high altar is the head, the transepts are the arms, and the rest of the temple . . . is the body," so that he knew apparently, that churches were built according to a canon and had assumed the form in which we know them for a special reason. Many have known as much as did Antonio Llobera, and like him either have cared not, or have dared not, push their theory to its conclusion.

The author of the present work has not been so deterred, and argues out his case with much precision and a wealth of figures, proving most clearly that the external measurements of almost every ancient temple, the figures of the New Jerusalem, Holy Oblation, and other temples, real and imaginary, reveal the magnitudes of the sun, moon, and other planets, together with the distance of their orbits. And most ingeniously he argues that, as all these calculations were, of necessity, impossible of comprehension to the vulgar, they were typified by symbols, the principal of all these symbols being the cross. Therefore it follows, in his opinion, that the rage of the so-called Reformers of the church was not a blind unreasoning fury, blended with a dislike to beauty, but a reasoning fury against a symbol that they understood. And he remarks, when speaking of the Puritans, whom he most justly stigmatizes as both "ridiculous and ignorant," that it was curious that, having cast away the cross, they should still retain the Christ, as both are one.

We know the mystic letters I. H. S., familiar from our childhood on altar fronts, embroidered in gold thread by pious ladies, were used as symbols of Bacchus, and venerated in his temples by the unreasoning but faithful worshipper just as they are with us.

Thor's hammer was a cross; the ruins of Palenque bear sculptured on their lintels the mystic symbol, and Bernal Diaz tells us that, in

Cozumel, upon the altars of the temples, crosses were seen deep graven in the stone.

Thus it appears that almost every nation, every age, has had its Cross, and, if this is the case, what is the reason?

The writer of this work most plainly sets it forth, and, in so doing, connects conclusively our symbolism with that which seems inherent in mankind, and gently puts aside all our pretensions to the possession of a faith revealed to us alone.

Into these mysteries I shrink from entering, but watch him boldly walk amongst the Canon Laws which govern Architecture, Music, Religion, and other things, the laws of which I take on trust.

Unorthodox even in his unorthodoxy, he is sufficiently un-English to be logical and not to shirk, after the English fashion, the just conclusions towards which his reasoning leads.

Following his argument, it appears that, in "The Abbey" when the nave and aisles are packed with rich and pious *Iris de Florence* scented worshippers silently waiting for the circulating plate, they sit within a building built, like the ancient temples were, to typify the body of a man, and the chief symbol which the Romans held in honour they, too, venerate, when, in their pious contemplation, they lift adoring eyes towards the Cross which stands upon the altar or communion table.

R. B. Cunninghame Graham.

CONTENTS.

ERRATA.

Page 4, line 16, read *or* before "Rome."
Pages 48, 133, lines 33, 5, read "Tetragrammaton."
Page 65, line 27, read "1,110."
Page 102, line 26, insert *the* before "sequence."
Page 104, line 1, read *Greek* before "Zodiac."
Page 122, line 14, insert *is* after "2,047."
Page 128, line 3, read "592" for "562."
Page 142, line 4, read *of* before "notice."
Page 188, line 28, read *Dionysus* for "Dionysius."
Page 276, line 35, read "peoples."
Page 279, omit Note 1.
Page 288, line 23, insert *the* before "Mass."

THE CANON.

CHAPTER I.

INTRODUCTION.

" The wisdom of the Egyptians, what was it but principally astronomy ?"—St. Augustine, "City of God," bk. xviii., c. 39.

THE failure of all efforts in modern times to discover what constituted the ancient canon of the arts, has made this question one of the most hopeless puzzles which antiquity presents. It is discouraging in the extreme to approach the subject at all. The absence of all explicit information from the ancients themselves, combined with the complete ignorance of modern authorities, is sufficient to make one hesitate to lay before the reader any proposition, however plausible, on this obscure subject. It is hoped, however, that the investigation of what appears to be a clue to the method practised by the old architects in building the temples, may prove of some assistance in elucidating the principles, which were the common groundwork of the arts and sciences of the past. For it would appear, that there was an established canonical law underlying the practice of building as well as all other arts.

In a general way this has been felt by all competent students of antiquity ; and many traces of such an uniformity have been pointed out, but as the root of everything in the old world was

B

primarily centred in religion, it is to the ancient theology, that we must look for the foundation and basis of the old canon.

The priests were practically the masters of the old world. Everything and everybody was subservient to the ecclesiastical jurisdiction, and no work could be undertaken without its authority. That the priests were legitimately entitled to regulate the building of the temples of the gods, nobody will deny. And that they did exercise this control is beyond dispute. For we find that freemasons, or some body corresponding to the mediæval freemasons, with exclusive privileges and secrets required for building the temples, under ecclesiastical authority, have always existed. And the knowledge which we possess of the mediæval freemasons is sufficient to show that their secrets were the secrets of religion, that is, of mediæval Christianity.

It is these secrets of the old priests, carefully guarded by them, and only communicated to the authorized builders of the temples, that we propose to treat of in the following pages, and we shall endeavour to show that these secrets, comprising the esoteric doctrine of religion, have been transmitted in unbroken continuity, at least from the building of the Great Pyramid, down to recent times. It is, of course, far beyond the scope of this small work, limited to a single object of inquiry, to enter into a historical examination of the evidences of this continuity of idea, and since there are already in existence books dealing with this special investigation, it is superfluous to undertake it. It is only necessary to accept the testimony of the old Greek historians, who emphatically assert, that the essential doctrines of the Greek religion were imported into Greece from Egypt. We know that all modern civilization in Europe is of

Greek origin. The Gospel itself is indisputably as much a Greek as a Hebrew creation. It is written in Greek, and was first established among Hellenized peoples, and wherever it was accepted in succeeding generations, it brought with it the ideas of Greece. As there is no reason to doubt the assertions of the Greek historians, as to the indebtedness of their nation to the Egyptians for instruction in the arts and sciences, there has clearly been, through the Greeks, a direct communication of Egyptian ideas to the Hellenized portions of the world, to which we ourselves belong.

Just as Pythagoras and Plato, and other Greek philosophers, visited Egypt to study the religion and sciences of that country, so every educated man of a subsequent age studied the religion and philosophy of Greece with the same object, namely, to perfect themselves in that knowledge, of which the Greeks were known to have been the recipients. To us the Egyptians are only a step further off; but fundamentally the doctrines which we are now investigating were the same both in Greece and Egypt. How much, the original religion and philosophy of the Egyptians may have been improved by filtering through the refining influence of Greece, must be decided when Egyptologists come to have a deeper knowledge of Egyptian things, than they have at present. But whatever changes may have been added by Greeks and Christians to the original Egyptian theology, it is insisted, that the central mysteries were accepted by all priests and philosophers, as the only possible basis of religion. And more than that (for we must not always be content with a sensible reason for anything in human affairs) the absolute conservatism, always observed in religious matters, would scarcely admit that any received doctrine, once established, should be removed.

It must be borne in mind, that only the vaguest ideas at present prevail as to the mystical secrets[1] of the old priests. Everybody knows that the Egyptians, Greeks, and other Eastern nations concealed the vital doctrines of their theology from the ignorant and vulgar, and it was only by a gradual process of initiation that the meaning of the sacred writings and ceremonies were explained. And then, after this preparation, the initiates were allowed to be full partakers in the religious rites. It is a misfortune that all the ritual of the older religions has been destroyed, and it is particularly regretable that no scrap of the sacred writings, or temple ritual of pagan Greece of Rome, has survived to our time. We do not even know whether the Hebraized or Christianized version of the Masonic ritual, as we now know it, has anything more than a faint resemblance to its primitive form. Besides the ordinary services in the pagan temples, it is well known that there were in certain periods especially mysterious celebrations of the nature of dramatic shows or plays, in some cases apparently intended to form the concluding spectacle of the initiations. A few ancient authors have alluded to these shows, but when everything is collected from their works, it amounts to very little indeed. Plutarch, St. Clement of Alexandria

---

[1] To avoid misunderstanding, it may be stated here, that throughout the present inquiry the doctrine of the mysteries is assumed to have been a defined scientific tradition, communicated orally to the initiates or mystics, who secretly passed it on from generation to generation. Therefore, mysticism being synonymous with gnosticism, it must not be confounded with the speculative mistiness which is cultivated by certain dreamy philosophers of our day. The mystic ($\mu\acute{\upsilon}\sigma\tau\eta\varsigma$) in the old sense has naturally become extinct, together with the gnosis which formerly instructed him.

(who had been initiated at Eleusis before he became a Christian), Lucian, Apuleius, Macrobius and other writers give some slight information, directly or indirectly, on these mystical ceremonies. Besides these, there is a treatise by Jamblichus pretending to expound the whole subject of the mysteries, but this work has been composed with such careful and scrupulous obscurity, that few people have found themselves much the wiser after reading it. There is also the Jewish Cabala, containing an explanation of the priestly secrets and mysteries of the Hebrews, but no one at the present day can fully understand it. There are the works attributed to Hermes Trismegistus preserved by the Neo-Platonists, written in the same philosophical jargon used by Jamblichus and the rest; and there are the references to the doctrines of the heretical Christians called Gnostics, preserved in the controversial works of the early fathers. These are some of the most direct sources of information on the mystical doctrines common to the Egyptian, Greek, Hebrew, and Christian religions.

But turning from these obscure and fragmentary references, the law of the Hebrew Scriptures and the extensive commentaries of the Talmud, the Gospel with the offices and ritual of the Church, are each an epitome, in its most complete form, of those mysteries for the expounding of which they were severally created; if these works were clearly understood the difficulty would be cleared up. The deplorable fact, which we have now to regret is, that the priests who ought to be able to tell us the meaning of the Scriptures, which they undertake to expound, know nothing whatever of their real significance. It is probable, that there is not a single Christian priest who knows what the Canon of the Church is, or why a certain office or literary ar-

rangement is canonical or what makes it so. He
would deny that the Old Testament and the Gospel
are allegorical books, but has no explanation to
offer for the absurdities, which occur in these works,
if taken literally. In fact, the modern priest, to
whom we naturally turn for instruction in the mysteries of the Church, is the very last person from
whom we are likely to get any information. Let
us therefore leave this man, who does not seem to
be aware that his office was created that he might
receive the canonical tradition from the mouth of
a pre-ordained teacher, and by its light impart the
spirit to the letter of the law.

We shall assume, that at the building of the
Great Pyramid, the first principles of all later
theology were already established and fixed, and it
would seem, notwithstanding the modern belief to
the contrary, that at that early period the Egyptians had arrived at some elementary knowledge of
astronomy and cosmography; that they knew the
measures of the earth, and the distance of the
planets, and had observed the recurrent cycles of
the sun and moon in their several orbits, and many
other simple astronomical phenomena; that from
these ascertained facts, they derived a scheme embodying, in the persons of certain hypothetical
gods, a symbolical image of the created universe,
and the invisible powers which regulate it. The
deity in this scheme was conceived according to
the exact forms manifested in the phenomena of
nature. The whole physical and material universe
was symbolized by the seven revolving planets
and the sphere of the fixed stars, while the agent,
or mover, who inspires all bodies with life, was
personified by the figure of a man. Thus the philosophers constructed a system, which attributed
to God a body composed of all the matter of the
world, and a soul, which was diffused through all

its parts. The creed of the philosophers, however, was never openly avowed in the popular religion, but was concealed in the parables of which the old theology was composed. For the old priests never scrupled to believe. that history and philosophy " sufficed but for the chosen few," while the populace were carefully instigated to the practice of morality by being instructed in that kind of fiction which, in this country, emanates from Exeter Hall. Strabo admirably expresses the attitude of an educated man to the religion of his day. He says, " The great mass of women and common people cannot be induced by mere force of reason to devote themselves to piety, virtue, and honesty; superstition must therefore be employed, and even this is insufficient without the aid of the marvellous and the terrible. For what are the thunderbolts, the aegis, the trident, the torches, the dragons, the barbed thyrses, the arms of the gods, and all the paraphernalia of antique theology, but fables employed by the founders of states as bugbears to frighten timorous minds?" (Strabo's "Geography," bk. i., ch. ii, § 8).[1] Again, the difference between Moses, and Linus, Musæus, Orpheus, and Pherecydes, is well defined by Origen, who says, that the Greek poets " display little concern for those readers who are to peruse them at once unaided, but have composed their philosophy (as you term it) *for those who are unable to comprehend its metaphorical and allegorical signification.* Whereas Moses, like a distinguished orator, who meditates some figure of rhetoric, and who carefully introduces in every part a *language of twofold meaning*, has done this in his five books; neither affording,

---

[1] Cicero, who was an Augur as well as an Advocate, did not seem to have taken his duties very seriously, for he is reported to have said that he could never understand how two Augurs could look each other in the face without laughing.

in the portion which relates to morals, any handle
to his Jewish subjects for committing evil ; nor yet
giving to the few individuals who were endowed
with greater WISDOM, and *who were capable
of investigating his meaning*, a treatise devoid
of material for speculation." (Origen " Against
Celsus," bk. i., ch. xviii). That is to say, the
Hebrew delivered his fictions in the guise of moral
precepts, while the pagan Greeks were not so particular.

It is well known to many people that certain
numbers had an important place in the philosophical and theological system of the ancients.
The Pythagoreans concealed their doctrines in a
numerical and geometric system, which was the
only form of their philosophy given to the outer
world. The Jewish priests also elaborated an extensive system of numeration in the Cabala, and
the Rabbis frequently make use of it in the Talmudic commentaries on the Scriptures. The early
fathers of the church have preserved considerable
expositions of the system in their books con-
troverting the heretical opinions of the various
sects of Christian Gnostics. But the purport of
all these theories of numbers has ceased to be
understood, together with the greater part of the
doctrines of the ancient mysteries of which this
numerical philosophy formed a part.

The oldest use of numbers as symbols of an
esoteric doctrine is to be found in Egypt, from
whence it was derived by the Greeks, and transmitted by them to the modern world. Although
we have, unfortunately, no direct evidence of how
the mysterious people of Egypt actually made
use of their numbers, it would appear that their
numerical system formed a part of the dogma in
those laws, referred to by Plato as having been
ten thousand years old, and was perpetuated, as one

of the bases of religion and art by all subsequent peoples. The words of Plato are : " Long ago they appeared to recognize the very principle of which we are now speaking—that their young citizens must be habituated to forms and strains of virtue. These they fixed, and exhibited patterns of them in their temples ; and no painter or artist is allowed to innovate upon them, or to leave the traditional forms, or invent new ones. To this day no alteration is allowed, either in those arts or in music, at all. And you will find that their works of art are painted or moulded in the same forms that they had ten thousand years ago (this is literally true, and no exaggeration), their ancient paintings and sculptures are not a whit better, or worse than the work of to-day, but are made with just the same skill." ("Laws," 656. Jowett's translation, vol. v., p. 226). What this canon of art actually was is now unknown, but it is possible to discover the traces of it in the religion and art of the Greeks and Christians.

Theology, in its various forms, has always been the epitome of art, and constituted the law for its guidance. From the times of ancient Egypt this law has been a sacred arcanum, only communicated by symbols and parables, the making of which, in the ancient world, constituted the most important form of literary art ; it therefore required for its exposition a priestly caste, trained in its use, and the guilds of initiated artists, which existed throughout the world till comparatively recent times, were instructed in it. Now-a-days, all this is changed. Theology has dropped her secrets ; her symbols have become meaningless ornaments, and her parables are no longer understood. The artist in the service of the Church no longer repre- sents her mysteries in metaphorical shapes, and the priests have as little skill in the old art of

myth-making, as they have in interpreting the
Scriptures.

Few people have an adequate appreciation of
this lost principle—the art, that is, of working
symbolically. To us, who have now nothing to
conceal, such a practice has naturally gone out of
fashion, and the symbol, as a means of concealing
rather more than it was intended to explain, has
become gradually obsolete. We still write or paint
symbolically, but only to make that, which is obscure, more plain. In the hands of the old priest,
or artist, on the contrary, the symbol was a veil
for concealment, beautiful or grotesque, as the case
might be. A myth or parable, in their hands,
subtly conveyed a hidden truth, by means of a
more or less obvious fiction; but it has come to
pass, that the crude and childish lie on its surface
is ignorantly believed for the whole truth, instead
of being recognized, as the mere clue to its inner
meaning. All theology is composed in this way,
and her two-fold utterances must be read with a
double mind. Thus, when we read in the Scriptures of the Church, or in the saintly legends, a
fiction showing more than ordinary exuberance of
fancy, we may be sure, that our attention is being
specially arrested. When miraculous events are
related of the gods, or when they are depicted in
marvellous shapes, the author gives us to understand, that something uncommon is being conveyed. When singular and unearthly beasts are
described, such as Behemoth and Leviathan, the
unicorn, or the phœnix, it is intended, that we
should search deeply into their meaning: for such
are some of the artifices, by which the ancients
at once concealed and explained their hidden
mysteries.

When everything was mystical and metaphorical,
it was only natural that numbers should have

been brought to the service of Art. Geometry also provided a symbolical code, which may some day be understood. These geometrical symbols enabled the mathematicians to import the secret mysteries into their works, and also gave to the builders a means of applying a numerical system to the temples, which, as Plato says, exhibited the pattern of the laws in Egypt. Considerable traces of this symbolical geometry survive in the arcana of Freemasonry. Most of the practical secrets of the old mediæval architects, who built the cathedrals according to the mysteries of the church, have perished with the old craft lodges, which preceded the establishment of the modern theoretical masonry. Nevertheless it is possible to gather out of the early architectural and technical books some clue to the old practice of building. All old writers on architecture, as well as freemasons, insist that geometry is the foundation of their art, but their hints as to its application are so obscure, that no one in recent times has been able to explain how it was used.

Philosophy must have been equally dependent upon some system of geometry, for Plato wrote over the door of his academy " LET NONE IGNORANT OF GEOMETRY ENTER HERE," and in the " Republic" (bk. vii. 527), he says, " You must in the utmost possible manner direct the citizens of your beautiful city on no account to fail to apply themselves to GEOMETRY "—a science which, he says, " flatly contradicts the language employed by those who handle it." From this it may be concluded, that Plato meant to inform us, that no one could understand his philosophy without knowing the geometrical basis of it, since geometry contained the fundamental secret of all the ancient science.

It is known both to freemasons and architects, that the mystical figure called the Vesica Piscis, so

popular in the Middle Ages, and generally placed
as the first proposition of Euclid, was a symbol
applied by the masons in planning their temples.
Albert Dürer, Serlio, and other architectural writers
depict the Vesica in their works, but presumably
because an unspeakable mystery attached to it
these authors make no reference to it.   Thomas
Kerrich, a freemason and principal librarian of the
University of Cambridge, read a paper upon this
mystical figure before the Society of Antiquaries
on January 20th, 1820. He illustrated his remarks
with many diagrams illustrating its use by the
ancient masons, and piously concludes by saying, " I
would by no means indulge in conjectures as to the
reference these figures might possibly have to the
most sacred mysteries of religion." [1]   Dr. Oliver,
(" Discrep." p. 109) speaking of the Vesica, says,
" This mysterious figure Vesica Piscis possessed
an unbounded influence on the details of sacred
architecture ; and *it constituted the great and enduring secret of our ancient brethren*.   The plans
of religious buildings were determined by its
use ; and the proportions of length and height
were dependent on it alone." [2]   Mr. Clarkson (In-
troductory Essay to Billings' " Temple Church ")
considered that the elementary letters of the
primitive language were derived from the same
mystical symbol.   He says that it was known
to Plato and " his masters in the Egyptian
colleges," and was to the old builders " an archetype of ideal beauty."   The Vesica was also
regarded as a baneful object under the name of

---

[1] The west is the feminine end of a Christian church, and
the western gables of Gothic cathedrals are often lighted by a
rose-window, or one in the shape of the Vesica Piscis, as at
Dunblane.

[2] See also the article in Gwilt's " Encyclopædia of Archi
tecture " (1876), p. 968.

the "Evil Eye," and the charm most generally employed to avert the dread effects of its fascination was the Phallus (J. Millinger "Archæologia," xix). In Heraldry the Vesica was used as the feminine shield. It was interchangeable with the Fusill, or Mascle (Guillim's "Display of Heraldry," 4th ed. 1660, § iv., ch. xix., p. 354), and was also figured as a lozenge or rhombus. In the East the Vesica was used as a symbol of the womb, and was joined to the cross by the Egyptians forming the handle of the Crux ansata.

Geometrically, the Vesica is constructed from two intersecting circles, so that it may be taken as

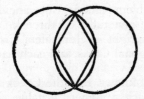

FIG. I.—THE VESICA PISCIS.

having a double significance. Edward Clarkson says that it " means astronomically at the present day a starry conjunction ; and by a very intelligent transfer of typical ideas a divine marriage," or the two-fold essence of life, which the ancients supposed to be male and female. To every Christian the Vesica is familiar from its constant use in early art, for not only was it an attribute of the Virgin, and the feminine aspect of the Saviour as symbolized by the *wound*[1] in his side, but it commonly surrounds the figure of Christ, as His Throne when seated in Glory. As a hieroglyph the combination

[1] All the early writers declare that this mystic wound emitted blood and water at the Crucifixion, and it is never omitted in the works of the early masters.

of Christ with the Vesica is analogous to the Crux ansata of the Egyptians.

Besides the Vesica Piscis the old philosophers and freemasons were accustomed to use as symbols all the plane geometrical figures. The Pythagorean emblem, the Pentalpha, or five-pointed star, and the Hexalpha, or Solomon's Seal, have been used in the church from time immemorial as symbols of Christ and the Trinity, and have a variety of emblematic associations. The Hexagon was the common symbol of the Masonic Cube or Cubical Stone, while the Triangle, and Square had each their use as geometrical symbols. The Cross has also been from the remotest times a potent mystical emblem among all ancient peoples. Crosses were generally of three kinds, the Tau Cross, the upright or Jerusalem Cross, and the Saltire or diagonal Cross, and each had its peculiar significance.

Everybody knows, that the Greek and Hebrew letters had each a numerical value, so that every word in these languages may be resolved into a number, by adding together the value of each letter of which it is composed.

A	B	Γ	Δ	E	ϛ	Z	H	Θ	I	K	Λ	M	N
1	2	3	4	5	6	7	8	9	10	20	30	40	50

Ξ	O	Π	P	Σ	T	Υ	Φ	X	Ψ	Ω
60	70	80	100	200	300	400	500	600	700	800

ע	ס	נ	מ	ל	כ	י	ט	ח	ז	ו	ה	ד	ג	ב	א
70	60	50	40	30	20	10	9	8	7	6	5	4	3	2	1

ץ	ף	ד	ר	ם	ת	ש	ר	ק	צ	פ
900	800	700	600	500	400	300	200	100	90	80

Thus the word IESOVS = 888, CHRISTOS = 1,480, LOGOS = 373, the Hebrew word, Messiah = 358, IHVH (Jehovah) = 26, ZEUS = 612, MITHRAS = 360, and ABRAXAS = 365. Of course no one supposes now, that the numerical value of the name CHRISTOS has any particular significance, or that the number 1,480 is anything but an accidental number, produced by adding together the letters which form the Greek word for "Anointed;" nevertheless, we believe, that the word CHRISTOS was carefully selected by the Greeks, who constructed the Christian theology, in order to exemplify the old Gnosticism, which forms the basis of Christianity in common with every other old religious system. This number 1,480, as will be shown further on, accurately exhibits an important measure of the Cosmos, and was, apparently, chosen to be the foundation of the scientific pantheism upon which the Christian theology is built, and was a part of the Gnosis, primarily derived from those laws of the priestly astronomers of ancient Egypt, who first devised the canon, which became a fundamental principle in the Greek, Jewish, and Christian Law.

But there is no *apparent* evidence, that the Jews and Christians possessed a sufficiently exact knowledge of the Cosmic scheme, to introduce any of its dimensions into the names of the Deity. And so it would appear. But the meaning of those works which make up the canon of the Scriptures are no longer understood, and although the knowledge of which we are speaking is carefully preserved in these Scriptures, so unintelligible have they become, that no one at the present day appears to be aware of its existence.

CHAPTER II.

THE HOLY OBLATION.

"Perusing the nine last chapters of Ezekiel's prophecy, whilst I hoped to find, and feel a solid body, I only grasped the flitting aire, or rather a meer spirit; I mean instead of a literall sense I found the Canaan *by him described no* Geography, *but* OURANOGRAPHY."—THOMAS FULLER, "Pisgah-sight of Palestine" (1650), bk. v., p. 189.

THE publication by Copernicus of the measures of the universe, which are at once straightforward and accurate, was coincident with the Reformation, and the breaking-up of the old mysticism of the Middle Ages. His scheme was printed in 1543 in his celebrated work, "De Revolutionibus Orbium Cœlestium," the first copy of which was placed in his hands a few hours before his death; but the Pythagorean doctrine of the diurnal motion of the earth, and its revolution round the sun, was taught by him during his life, and received a considerable amount of attention at the beginning of the sixteenth century. In the above work, according to Newcomb ("Pop. Astron.," p. 60), the relative distances of the planets are recorded with fair accuracy, the unit of measurement employed being the interval of the earth's distance from the sun.

The measures are :

	According to Copernicus.	According to Newcomb.
☿	0·326	0·308
♀	0·709	0·718
⊕	1·000	1·000
♂	1·373	1·382
♃	5·453	5·454
♄	9·760	10·070

The moon's distance he computed at $60\frac{1}{3}$ semi-diameters of the earth.

At this time it was a dangerous innovation to publish any but the vaguest astronomical facts, and as Copernicus had some anxiety as to how his statement would be received, his friend Rheticus published a volume, giving a preliminary account of the Copernican theory. Although the Papal authorities did not like the work of Copernicus, it only received their qualified disapprobation, for they put it on the index "subject to correction." However, although Copernicus stands as the first of the modern astronomers, he wrote very much in the same mystical strain as his predecessors, and was by no means like an astronomer of the nineteenth century. What he really appears to have done was to establish a precedent for the open publication of genuine observations, which even the gentle discouragement of the inquisitors was unable to suppress. Whether the measures of the planetary system, which he published, were derived from his own observations, or were only the revelation of an existing tradition, it is difficult to determine. But as he is said to have died without ever seeing his planet Mercury, presumably he could have made no observations as to the distances of this planet, and consequently must have received his data from some one else. This would imply, that the astronomers before his time knew the distances of the other planets, as well as that of Mercury. Again, if it were possible for Copernicus to arrive at the correct proportions of the universe without a telescope, and unaided by any previous observations beyond those which were published, we can see no reason for disbelieving, that the ancients, who are alleged to have gazed at the stars for thousands of years, were incapable of coming to a similarly accurate conclusion.

C

In the next century the fact, that the diameter
of the earth's orbit round the sum is 220 diameters
of the sun, is, so far as we know, mentioned for the
first time—a statement which implies a true knowledge of the earth's magnitude. This statement is
to be found in Galileo's "System of the World,"
the work which was condemned by the Inquisitors,
and for the publication of which he was arraigned,
and prohibited from continuing his astronomical
researches, or at least from publishing them. The
passage in which the measurement of the sun's
distance is given, is such as to make it doubtful if
the calculation were made at that time.   The con-
text is as follows:—" I suppose with the said
Copernicus, and also with his opposers, that the
semi-diameter of the grand orb, which is the distance of the earth from the sun, containeth 1,208
scmi-diamctcrs of the said earth. Secondly, I
premise with the allowance aforesaid, and of truth,
that the apparent diameter of the sun, in its mean
distance, to be about half a degree, that is 30 *min.
prim.*, which are 1,800 seconds, that is, 108,000
thirds.   And because the apparent diameter of a
fixed star of the first magnitude is no more than 5
seconds, that is, 300 thirds, and the diameter of a
fixed star of the sixth magnitude, 50 thirds (and
herein is the greatest error of the anti-Coper-
nicans), therefore the diameter of the sun containeth the diameter of a fixed star of the sixth
magnitude 2,160 times. . . .

 "The diameter of the sun is 11 semi-
diameters of the earth, and the diameter of the
grand orb contains 2,146 of these same semi-
diameters, by the assent of both parties ; so that,
the diameter of the said orb contains the sun's
diameter 220 times very near. And because the
spheres are to one another as the cubes of their
diameters, let us make the cube of 220, which

is 106,480,000, and we shall have the grand orb
106,480,000 times bigger than the sun, to which
grand orb a star of the sixth magnitude ought to
be equal, according to the assertion of this author.

"The error, then, of these men consisteth in
being extremely mistaken, in taking the apparent
diameter of the fixed stars." (Salusbury's Translation, tom. i., p. 325.)

The first assumption in this remarkable passage,
namely, the distance from the earth to the sun
called the grand orb, is enormously deficient.
The distance according to modern calculations is
$\frac{91,404,000}{3,959} = 23,086$ semi-diameters at the least,
or about 10 times the number stated in the text,
that is, if Galileo had given the number at 12,000
instead of 1,200 (12,080), it would have been approximately correct. Again, the diameter of the
sun is nearly 110 diameters of the earth, not 11
semi-diameters, as stated. Whether, in face of
this error, it was possible to compute the earth's
distance correctly by diameters of the sun, is a
question for astronomers to decide. It seems most
extraordinary, that, holding such erroneous conceptions of the magnitude both of the earth and
the sun, he should yet bring out the correct result
in his final calculation of their distance, measured
by the diameter of the sun. It is also curious,
that by multiplying the two numbers 1,208 and 11
by 10 we get a real dimension of the sun's diameter
and distance. It is true that we have to take the
last in diameters instead of semi-diameters to make
it right. But, if the whole thing is a mystification,
this would be quite sufficient for the purpose, and
make detection more difficult. We know that
Galileo was delayed for a considerable time before
he obtained his privilege to publish this work,
and no one knows what alterations he may have

been required to make before the Inquisitors, who first sanctioned the book and then condemned it, were satisfied. It is tolerably certain, from what we know of Galileo's stated opinions, that if there had been no censorship he would have published his work in a more direct form, notwithstanding his obliging complacence to the wishes of the priests, when they used their Procrustean persuasion to make him change his mind, and take their view as to how astronomical matters ought to be announced to the world. His non-resistance on this occasion, as well as the obscure and mystical language in which his four tedious dialogues are written, rather favours the idea, that his views differed very little from those of the Inquisitors after all. This tribunal merely disliked the idea of accurate astronomical knowledge becoming common property, and Galileo showed no serious objection to gratify them. Kepler and Tycho Brahe, the contemporaries of Galileo, always kept their disclosures within the bounds of ecclesiastical license, and Kepler never pretended that he spoke otherwise than in parables in his "Mysterium Cosmographicum"—an obviously mystical work, written entirely as an exposition of the old doctrines which we find in the "Timæus" of Plato.

All these mystifications resorted to by the astronomers of the sixteenth and seventeenth centuries suggest, that there was no real desire on their part to allow the true facts of their science to become generally known, and a sentence of John Hutchinson's implies, that their was nothing new in the disclosures of Copernicus. For he says: "Such as believe that the motions of the orbs were never known before Copernicus, nor philosophy before, or that it was understood by Sir Isaac Newton, let them study their books."[1] Again, the

----

[1] "The Religion of Satan, or Antichrist delineated," 1749.

assertion, which is so frequently made, that Galileo was the first astronomer who used a telescope, is unsubstantiated by any certain evidence. From a passage in the "Clouds" of Aristophanes we know that the Greeks used burning glasses, and consequently must have known their magnifying powers. Roger Bacon in the thirteenth century alludes to his use of a telescope and microscope. Cornelius Agrippa ("Vanity of the Arts and Sciences") alludes to experiments with hollow, convex, and other glasses, which make little things appear great, and things afar off near. J. B. Porta (1598) also makes a similar statement: "Concave lenses show distant objects more clearly, convex those which are nearer, whence they may be used to assist the sight. . . . If you know rightly how to combine one of each sort, you will see both far and near objects larger and clearer. . . . I shall now endeavour to show in what manner we may contrive to recognize our friends at the distance of several miles, and how those of weak sight may read most minute letters from a distance. It is an invention of great utility, and grounded on optical principles, nor is it at all difficult of execution ; *but it must be so divulged as not to be understood by the vulgar and yet be clear to the sharp-sighted*." (Life of Galileo, p.) The English mathematician, Leonard Digges, who died about 1573, is supposed to have possessed a telescope which he used in private. The accusers of Galileo called him plagiarist, liar, and impostor, as well as heretic, so his "Invention" may have been merely the disclosure of what everybody up to his time had concealed. At best Galileo only imitated or improved upon the instruments made by the Dutch, a specimen of which was in the possession of Cardinal Borghese before the year 1609. The great interest taken in Galileo's telescope at Venice is certainly in favour of its novelty, and bears out the received opinion, that the telescope first made its appearance openly at the beginning of the seventeenth century.

Since so much uncertainty exists as to the origin of exact astronomical observations, and considering that the ancients devoted such extraordinary attention to the heavenly bodies, it is reasonable to suppose that the Egyptians and Chaldæans, who are said to have observed the stars for countless generations, must have arrived at something more than a vague and absurdly inadequate knowledge of a science to which they had been so long addicted. It is incredible that their knowledge of the magnitude of the planetary system should have been so erroneous as we are generally expected to believe. The fact appears to be, that this science was a part of the hidden doctrine of the mysteries, and was consequently withheld from the uninitiated. The practice of astronomy among the Egyptians is repeatedly alluded to by Herodotus, Diodorus, and all early authorities. Strabo saw at Heliopolis "The houses of the priests and the residences of Plato and Eudoxus . . . Eudoxus came here with Plato, and according to some writers, lived thirteen years in the society of the priests, for the latter were distinguished by their knowledge of the heavenly bodies, but were mysterious and uncommunicative, yet after a time they were prevailed upon by courtesy to acquaint them with some of the principles of their science, but the barbarians concealed the greater part of them." He says further, that the later Greek astronomers derived much knowledge from the records of the priests and the Chaldæans.

It is also certain that the myths and fables of all early peoples contain veiled allusions to astronomical facts, and could afford us definite information, if we had the key to their interpretation, and they are in fact the only records which it was then considered desirable to preserve. Sir Isaac Newton, for instance, who was not likely to be deceived in astronomical matters, deduces the date of the Argonautic Expedition from the sphere of Musæus ("Chron.," pp. 82, 95). He entirely accepts the reality of this primitive sphere, constructed by a mythical person, the master of Orpheus, and further proves his date from the observations of Thales, Meton, and Hipparchus. To Sir Isaac Newton this story of the Argonauts is quite real, as regards the astronomy, and is apparently regarded by him as the ordinary mythological manner of recording a date. He never questions its accuracy beyond saying that the observations of the ancients were coarse. That this is the true attitude to be taken towards such early writings we have no doubt, and until these are systematically read with a view of ascertaining their hidden meaning, all ancient history must remain as at present a grotesque absurdity.

The Christians, from the outset of their existence, seem to have deliberately destroyed all the early works on astronomy. The New Sect had no doubt the same reason for this course of action as for the persecution of astronomers in later times. Nevertheless, out of the fragments of the classical writers, we get some idea of what was known in their time. The following passage from Strabo (bk. ii., ch. v.) gives some notion of what he knew, or rather what he cared to tell on this subject : " The earth and heaven are spheroidal. The tendency of all bodies having weight, is to a centre. Further, the earth, being spheroidal, and having the same centre as the heavens, is motionless as well as the axis, which passes through both it and the heavens. The heavens turn round both

the earth, and its axis from east to west. . . .
While the planets, the sun, and the moon describe
certain oblique circles comprehended within the
Zodiac. Admitting these points in whole or in
part, astronomers proceed to treat of other matters
[such as] the motions [of the stars], their revolutions, eclipses, size, relative distance, and a thousand similar particulars. . . . The heavens and
the earth must be supposed to be divided each into
five zones, the celestial zone to possess the same
names as those below. . . . These zones may be
distinguished by circles drawn parallel to the
equator on either side of it. Two of these will
separate the torrid from the temperate zones, and
the remaining two the temperate from the frigid.
. . . Likewise the torrid zone, which is divided
into two halves by the equator, is distinguished
as having a northern and southern side." In
a general way, this is substantially what a
modern astronomer would tell us, with the exception that in the old system the earth took the
place of the sun, and it is noticeable, that Strabo
says, that it is the business of an astronomer to
ascertain the size and relative distances of the
heavenly bodies.

Several ancient computations of the measures
of the universe, claiming to be accurate, have survived to our time. Such as the distances of the
planetary orbits recorded by Ptolemy, and the
calculation of the earth's circumference made by
Eratosthenes. Ptolemy's measurements are very
obviously wrong, and curiously enough this seems
to be well known to Hippolytus, who, after quoting
the figures, thus concludes an ironical passage:
" Oh pride of vain-toiling soul, and incredible
belief, that Ptolemy should be considered pre-
eminently wise among those who have cultivated
similar wisdom " ("Refutation of all Heresies,"

bk. iv., c. xii.). Eratosthenes gives the earth's circumference at 250,000 stadia; but it is impossible to decide whether this was a true estimate, since we have no positive information as to the value of the stadium he used. He made his observations in Egypt, and arrived at his result according to the methods practised at the present day. He had the advantage of using the astronomical appliances anciently established at Alexandria, and as librarian to the great library he had access to all the available astronomical knowledge of the Egyptians. He was, moreover, in every way qualified for the task, so that it must be almost a certainty that his calculation was substantially correct. Little or nothing being now known about the Alexandrian standard measures, speculations based upon any hypothetical value of the stadium of Eratosthenes can only lead to doubtful results. Nevertheless it is not an unreasonable supposition that the Egyptians and Greeks had accurately computed the measurements of the earth.

To discover the precise knowledge of the ancients as to the measures of the universe, it is first necessary to determine the standards of measurement which were generally in use. Unfortunately our ignorance on this essential point makes all inquiries on the subject extremely hazardous and difficult. If the British standard measure of length be examined, it would appear that the division of its component parts has been derived from the ascertained diameter of the earth. It is well known that the modern French standard constructed in the last century, was deduced from a fraction of the earth's circumference, possibly in accordance with a more ancient precedent. The antiquity of our English standard is unknown, there being apparently no allusion to it before the time of Elizabeth. The Druids were credited by Julius Cæsar, and other writers, with a considerable knowledge of astronomy, and must consequently have possessed a set of measures, but whether the original British standard of the Druids was preserved during the Roman and subsequent invasions, and is that which now survives, is uncertain. In any case the following coincidences may be pointed out, and need not be regarded as being purely accidental. The number of British miles in the mean diameter of the earth is in round numbers 7,920. The polar diameter is 7,899, and the equatorial diameter is 7,926, giving 7,918 as the exact mean. But 7,920, being a more convenient number, may be accepted as the reputed amount. Now the British furlong contains 7,920 inches. It also contains 220 yards and 110 fathoms, which are respectively the diameter and radius of the earth's orbit measured by the diameter of the sun. A mile contains 1,760 yards, and an equilateral triangle, inscribed within in the orbit of Saturn measured by the diameter of the sun, measures about 1,760 diameters on each of its sides. Therefore the British standard records three important measures of the cosmic system. Assuming that these coincidences are the result, not of accident but of design, we are led to the conclusion that at some time, possibly very remote, the dimensions of the cosmos were ascertained, and introduced into the standard measures inherited by the English people. Another coincidence, lately discovered, is that the English quarter measure is exactly a quarter of the capacity of the coffer of the Great Pyramid, which suggests a connection between our measures and those of the builders of Egypt. There are other reasons for supposing that this coincidence between the English standard and that of the Great Pyramid is not accidental, but these must be discussed further on. For the present the reader must be asked to assume that a standard measure, corresponding to that in use in England, was known to the Egyptians, Hebrews, and Greeks, and was mystically employed to register the facts of astronomy in the several scriptures of these peoples.

The first measures are said to have been derived from the body of a man, "according to the similitude whereof God formed the world . . . . in such sort, that the one is called the greater world, and the other the lesser" (Lomazzo on "Painting," p. 109). Therefore man having been made in the image both of God and the world, God, the world, and man are synonymous terms, and the human body becomes the standard measure of the world. According to Vitruvius a man's height is four cubits $= 6$ feet $= 24$ palms $= 96$ digits. Now, taking the earth's distance from the sun at 10, the radius of the sphere of the zodiac becomes about 96, so that the number of digits in a man's height may have been supposed to measure the seven orbits of the planets, surrounded by the fixed stars. In that case, when Vitruvius lays it down that all temples are to be designed according to the proportions of the human body, he may mean that the temples were to conform to the measures of the universe.

The astronomical science of the Hebrews seems to be mystically concealed under the figures of Noah's ark, the Tabernacle, the Temple of Solomon, and the Holy Oblation of Ezekiel, while the Christians added to these the mystical city of the New Jerusalem, described in the two last chapters of the Revelation. Each of these mystical structures appears to exhibit a particular aspect of the heavens, and constitutes a scientific record of certain known facts of astronomy, which formed the true basis of the ancient theology.

The cosmos of the Christians, according to late writers, but presumably derived from the tradition of the ancient church, consisted of three principal divisions: First, there were the three

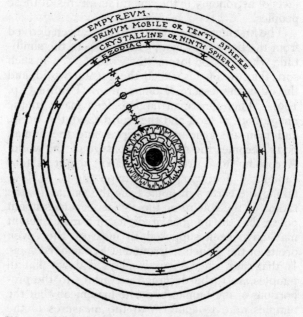

FIG. 2.—CONVENTIONAL PLAN OF THE UNIVERSE HAVING THE SEVEN ORBITS OF THE PLANETS INSTEAD OF THE SEVEN INTERVALS GENERALLY SHOWN ON THE OLD DIAGRAMS.

circles of the empyreum; secondly, the sphere of the fixed stars, together with the seven planets; and, lastly, the sublunary, or elementary world. In Greek the names of the three divisions of the universe are EMPYREION, AITHER, and STOICHEIA, whose numerical values, as will be seen, correctly set forth the measures of the system for which

they stand. This scheme appears in many of
the illustrated works of the sixteenth and seventeenth centuries, but the intervals between the
orbits of the planets are never correctly drawn.
To make a diagram accurately showing the
relative distances of the seven planetary orbits, it
will be found that the sun's diameter, the interval
between the earth and the moon, called the Tone
by Pliny, or the earth's diameter, are convenient
units of measurement. All these units, as well as
the British mile, appear to have been employed
by the ancients. If the orbits of the planets are
measured by the length of the sun's diameter,
taken at 852,584 British miles, the distances
are :

				Diam. of the sun.
From the sun to	☿	35,392,638 miles		$41\frac{1}{2}$
,,	,,	♀	66,131,476 ,,	$77\frac{1}{2}$
,,	,,	⊕	92,500,000 ,,	$108\frac{1}{2}$
,,	,,	♂	139,312,226 ,,	$163\frac{1}{2}$
,,	,,	♃	475,693,149 ,,	558
,,	,,	♄	872,134,583 ,,	1,023

According to the old Egyptian system, the earth
stood in the centre, the sun was supposed to
occupy the earth's orbit, while Mercury and Venus
revolved round the sun as satellites. Even modern
astronomers, with all their appliances, are uncertain as to the exact distance of the earth from the
sun. It has been computed to be from 108 to 110
of its own diameters. Galileo called it 110, and
the ancients seem to have usually taken it at this
amount.

Origen ("Against Celsus," bk. vi., ch. 23),
after describing the cosmic ladder of the Mithraic
mysteries, and the harmonic arrangements of the
stars, continues : " If one wished to obtain means
for a profounder contemplation of the entrance of

souls into divine things . . . . let him peruse at
the end of Ezekiel's prophecies the visions . . . .
and let him peruse also from the Apocalypse of
John what is related of the city of God, the
heavenly Jerusalem, and of its foundations and
gates. And if he is capable of finding out also

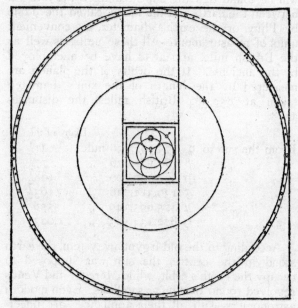

FIG. 3.—THE HOLY OBLATION.

the road, which is indicated by symbols . . . ., let
him read the book of Moses entitled 'Numbers,'
and let him seek the help of one who is capable of
initiating him into the meaning of the narratives
concerning the encampments of the Children of
Israel. . . . He will distinguish in the encampments certain things relating to the numbers that
are enumerated, and which are especially adapted

to each tribe, *of which the present does not appear to be the proper time to speak.*" [1] The vision referred to at the end of Ezekiel's prophecies is the mystical description of the land of Canaan (Ezekiel, ch. xlviii). The city of Jerusalem is there described as being surrounded by a four-square figure, called the Holy Oblation, which is said to be 25,000 reeds on every side. The suburbs of the city are enclosed by a square whose sides are 5,000 reeds, and the city in the middle measures 4,500 reeds on every side. Beyond the suburbs on the north and south a space of 25,000 × 10,000 reeds was allotted to the priests and Levites. Now, if the sides of the three squares be divided by 12—the number of the tribes—

$$\left(\frac{25,000}{12} = 2,083\tfrac{1}{3},\ \frac{5,000}{12} = 416\tfrac{2}{3},\ \text{and}\ \frac{4,500}{12} = 375\right),$$

it will be found that the city exactly contains the sun's orbit, together with the orbit of Venus, shown in the four quarters according to the Egyptian system, and probably represents the wheels of the four living creatures, seen in the first vision of Ezekiel. The orbit of Saturn, being about 2,046 diameters of the sun, is contained within the outer square, whose sides are 2,083⅓. The square surrounding the suburbs of the city has no direct affinity with the orbits of the planets, but a circle whose area is equal to this square has a circumference of 1,480. For various reasons it would seem that the measure 2,083⅓ is a mean between the numbers 2,093 and 2,073. Let it therefore be taken for granted that the Holy Oblation is a square enclosed by two lines, which are represented by the mean dimension 2,083⅓. The outer line, which measures 2,093, is the side of a square having an area double that, which has a side of

---

[1] This last sentence is a very good specimen of Patristic equivocation.

1,480. That is to say, a circle inscribed within
the square 2,093 exactly contains a square whose
sides are 1,480; and this circle will be assumed to
be the sphere of the zodiac or firmament. The
side of the inner square, again, measuring 2,073,
is $\frac{1}{12}$th of the earth's circumference measured
in miles. The numerical value of the name
CHRISTOS is 1,480, and the mystery of this number
appears to be that it supplies the measure of
God's body extending crosswise throughout the
whole universe. The wisdom of the number 666
conveys the same theological secret, for 666 is the
diameter of a circle having a circumference of
2,093.

The Greeks appear to have concealed a similar
knowledge in the names of the planets, as recorded
in the Epinomis of Plato, who calls the five planets
ΧΡΟΝΟΣ, 1,090, ΖΕΥΣ, 612, ᾿ΑΡΗΣ, 309, ᾿ΑΦΡΟΔΙΤΗ,
993, and ᾿ΕΡΜΗΣ, 353; if the sun, ῾ΗΛΙΟΣ, 318,
and the moon, ΣΕΛΗΝΗ, 301, be included, the sum
of the numbers obtained from the seven names is
3,976, a number which is one less than the radius
of a circle 25,000 in circumference. Now the side
of the Holy Oblation, according to Ezekiel, is

25,000 reeds $\left(\frac{25,000}{12} = 2,083\frac{1}{3} \right)$.

But a far more striking coincidence arises from
the addition of the numbers deduced from the
names ᾿ΕΜΠΥΡΕΙΟΝ, 760, ᾿ΑΙΘΗΡ, 128, and
ΣΤΟΙΧΕΙΑ, 1,196, for the sum of these amounts
to 2,084, or the mean length of the side of the
Holy Oblation.

In the same way the geometrical figure called
the New Jerusalem in the Apocalypse will be
found to contain the sun's orbit and that of
Mercury. Francis Potter, who published a book
on "the number 666" in 1647, alludes to the mys-
teires of this celestial city. He tell us, that the

144 cubits ascribed to the wall are to be taken as the area of its section—the wall being 12 cubits high and 12 cubits broad. The other measurement given is that in ch. xxi., v. 16 : "And the city lieth four square, and the length is as large as the breadth ; and he measured the city with the reed 12,000 furlongs. The length, and the breadth, and the height of it are equal." Francis Potter explains, that the 12,000 furlongs ($\sigma\tau\acute{a}\delta\iota a$) are to be taken as the contents of a cube, but his calculations as to its size are obscure. However 12,000 furlongs = 7,920,000 feet (12,000 × 660 = 7,920,000), and the cube root of this number is about $199\frac{1}{3}$, or roughly 200, which gives the length of one side of the cube. The area of the city is therefore a square nearly 200 feet on every side, surrounded by a wall 12 cubits, or 18 feet wide, which increases the outside dimensions to $235\frac{1}{3}$ feet. This figure appears to be a Christian variation of the Hebrew city of Ezekiel, and so it is interpreted by Francis Potter. For it will be found, that it incloses the sun's orbit together with that of Mercury, drawn in each of the four corners of the square. It is well known that the four beasts, which appear in the midst of the four wheels in Ezekiel's vision, are identical with the four symbols of the Evangelists, and the devices upon the four standards of the Camp of the Israelites, where they stand for the four corner signs of the Zodiac—Taurus, Leo, Scorpio, and Aquarius. In a thirteenth century manuscript of the Apocalypse in the British Museum (MSS. Add. 18,633), there is a miniature of the city of the New Jerusalem, showing the three persons of the Trinity, in the midst of a square having the four symbols of the Evangelists depicted in the four corners, corresponding to the four orbits of Mercury. This peculiar arrangement constantly recurs in early Christian art. Usually the Christ is surrounded

by the Vesica, and it is a remarkable fact, that a Vesica, whose length is equal to that of the city in the preceding diagram, coincides with the four circles of Mercury's orbit, and consequently produces a geometrical figure exactly resembling the common method of representing Christ in Glory. The circumferences of the two circles which form the Vesica being nearly 360, they may be taken to represent the two intersecting circles of the equator and the ecliptic. Some interpreters, according to Francis Potter, take the 12,000 furlongs to be the area of the city, and therefore he says, "that the

FIG. 4.—THE NEW JERUSALEM.

perimeter or compass of such an area must be 436 furlongs at the least," the side being about 109 furlongs. And since 109 is roughly the radius of the sun's orbit measured by the sun's diameter the New Jerusalem is doubly shadowed forth as a vision of the city of the Sun.   In ch. xxi., v. 9, " that great city, the holy Jerusalem descending out of Heaven " is called " the Bride the Lamb's wife, and her light was like unto a stone most precious, even like a jasper stone, clear as crystal." The bride of the Cabala was called ADNI or THORA, and it is evidently she whom St. John is describing under the figure of the heavenly city. The name Tarot has been derived from the Hebrew word THORA, the law; and it is a further confirmation of the cosmic import of this diagram that the hieroglyph of the twenty-second card of the Tarot-pack, called " Le Monde," represents the four symbols of the Evangelists surrounding a Vesica, inclosing the figure of a young virgin. Moreover the circle which surrounds the city has a circumference of 888, the numerical value of the name Jesus.

Again, Francis Potter constantly connects the New Jerusalem with the number 666, and this may be explained by the fact that its diagonals measure $(333 \times 2 =)$ 666, and the cross thus formed symbolized what he calls the Antichrist.

If the inferences just drawn from the numbers ascribed to the Holy Oblation and the New Jerusalem be correct, it is obvious that these diagrams afford a positive evidence of the knowledge possessed by the Hebrews and Christians concerning the magnitude and distances of the heavenly bodies. The position of these figures in the Canonical Scriptures also conclusively demonstrates a connection between theology and cosmic science. For while the extent of the ancient knowledge of astronomy has still to be proved, no one can reasonably doubt that the old theological systems were largely concerned with, if not actually founded upon, the order of the universe, which in its entirety supplies the only comprehensible manifestation of the Deity evident to the senses of mankind.

In the statement of Origen, already quoted, he refers to the Camp, as well as the Holy Oblation, and hints that a similar interpretation applies to both. The description, of which he speaks, occurs in the second chapter of Numbers, where it is said that the Israelites pitched their camp round the Tabernacle. They were grouped in four companies composed of three tribes, each under a standard. The standard of Judah was set at the east, that of Reuben at the south, that of Ephraim at the west, and that of Dan at the north. Judah's standard bore a lion, Reuben's bore a mandrake, Ephraim's a bull, and Dan's a serpent. The total number of the whole army distributed under the standards was 603,550 (v. 32).

Villalpanda ("In Ezek." vol. ii., p. 470) gives a diagram of the camp (reproduced by Kircher "Œdip." tom. ii., pars 1, p. 21, and Sir W. Drummond, "Œdipus Judaicus," plate 15) in the form of a square, with the signs of the zodiac arranged round it, three on every side. Each of the twelve tribes is identified with one of the signs, and the standards are allotted to the four tribes which occupy the corners of the square, whose corresponding signs are Leo, Aquarius, Taurus, and Scorpio. The four corner signs of the Zodiac were afterwards assigned as the symbols of the four evangelists, beginning with Aquarius (Matthew), Leo (Mark), Taurus (Luke), and Scorpio, changed to an eagle (John). Villalpanda's diagram contains, besides the Zodiac, the symbols of the seven planets and four elements, thus comprising the whole cosmic system which has been supposed to be included in the Holy Oblation. The arrangement of the squares in which the symbols are placed suggests that if the solution of the mystery is a geometrical one, it depends upon the problem of squaring the circle. For the old method of finding the diameter of a circle whose area was equal to a given square was to divide the diagonal of the square into ten parts, and to take eight for the diameter of the circle. The division of the camp in Villalpanda's diagram is into ten equal squares, the space between each of the squares bearing the symbol of the Zodiac upon it, being a double square. Therefore, a circle touching the inner angle of the four corner signs has an area equal to the area of the camp. Now, by dividing 603,550, the number of the Israelites, by 12, we get 50,295$\frac{5}{6}$, which is nearly equal to the length of the two diagonals of the square, whose area is

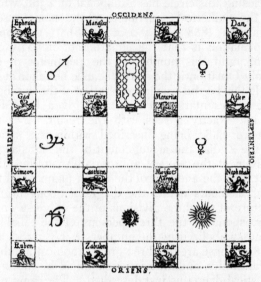

FIG. 5.—THE CAMP OF THE ISRAELITES (VILLALPANDA, "IN EZEK. EXPLANATIONES," 1596, TOM. II., P. 470.)

half of that of the Holy Oblation. The diagonal of this square being $\left(\dfrac{50,295}{2}=\right)$ 25,147$\frac{1}{2}$, and taking, as in the case of the Holy Oblation, $\frac{1}{12}$ of this number to be the length required, we get $\dfrac{25,147}{12}=$ 2,095$\frac{7}{12}$, or very nearly the diagonal of a square whose sides are 1,480. The diagonal of such a square is about 2,093, which has been suggested as the extreme measure of the Holy Oblation. Now a circle having an area equal to that of a square whose sides are 1,480, and whose diagonal is 2,093, has a diameter of 1,674 $\left(\dfrac{2,093}{10} = 209\tfrac{3}{10} \times 8 = 1,674\tfrac{2}{5}\right)$. And the square inclosing this circle has a diagonal of 2,368, which is the numerical equivalent of the name IESOVS CHRISTOS (888 + 1,480 = 2,368). A simpler explanation is that the square root of 603,550 is 776$\tfrac{8}{9}$, and this number is the perimeter of the Holy Oblation if the sun's distance be taken at 10.

If this be the true interpretation of the numbers, the representation of the camp given by Villalpanda exactly agrees with the result. For the square 1,480 being inscribed within the sphere of the Zodiac the arrangement of the signs as the border of the square appropriately notifies that fact, and the addition of the seven planets and the four elements makes the diagram a conventional picture of the three divisions of the universe which correspond to the three persons of the cabalistic triad symbolized by the numbers 2,368, 1,480, and 888. These are the three great canonical numbers of antiquity, and they are exemplified by the three mystical diagrams just described. The camp may be said to symbolize the number 2,368 (IESOVS CHRISTOS), the Holy Oblation may be referred to the number 1,480, CHRISTOS, and the Heavenly City of the Bride, being inclosed in a circle 888 in circumference, may be accepted as the symbol of the number 888 (IESOVS). Generally the third person of the Trinity represented the sublunary world or four elements only, but in the Pythagorean system she also personified the sun, whose orbit, as has been shown, is contained in her city described by St. John.

CHAPTER III.

THE CABALA.

" The Jews, in imitation of the Pythagorean Institutes, made the Cabala their codex or Canon Law."—" Court of the Gentiles," vol. iii., p. 216.

" The Church of Rome persisted obstinately in affirming, though not always with the same imprudence and plainness of speech, that the Holy Scriptures were not composed for the use of the multitude, but only for that of their spiritual teachers."—Mosheim, " Eccl. Hist.," vol. ii., sect. iii., ch. i., p. 25.

IN order that what follows may be better understood, we must now attempt to elucidate the principal doctrines of the Cabala. This singular work is known to have formed an important part of the Masonic traditions, and undoubtedly contains the nearest approach to a direct revelation of the ancient canonical secrets of the old world ; and however obscure it may be, those parts which are intelligible provide us with a few fundamental facts, which are indisputably the basis of the old esoteric philosophy. The books of the Cabala which have come down to us are said to have been first written by Simeon Ben Jochai at the time of the destruction of the second temple, and afterwards expanded by his disciples. Mr. Mathers, in the introduction to his translation of the " Zohar," tells us that the mysterious science of the Cabala was said to have been communicated by angels to Adam after his fall. From Adam it passed to Noah and the Patriarchs. " Moses, who was learned in all the wisdom of the Egyptians,

was first initiated into the Cabala in the land of
his birth, but became most proficient in it during
his wanderings in the wilderness, where he not
only devoted to it the leisure hours of the
whole forty years, but received lessons in it from
one of the angels." Although statements of this
kind are merely philosophic fictions, we may safely
accept the antiquity of the Cabala as being very
great. The legends of its origin are not made
without a purpose, for underneath their fictitious terms a truth is concealed. For instance,
the communication of the Cabala was said to be
coeval with the Fall, because this event, allegorically understood, symbolizes the transmission of
the mystical doctrine as an emblem of the divine
essence or life existing in the universe. The
Cabala was the emblem of the soul of the world,
and, as all human art was created in the imitation
of nature, the secret tradition symbolized the invisible soul, which inspired the letter of the Scriptures. And since it was a postulate of the philosophers, that the tradition or passage of the spirit
or soul of God from heaven to earth was effected
through the Zodiac and seven planets, so they
alleged that the Cabala was transmitted through
the mouths of the Patriarchs and the Messiah
Christos, who personified the planetary system.
According to the old cosmic arrangement, the
universe consisted of three stages, the Empyreum,
the seven planets, and the earth in the centre.
This order we may call God, the Universe, and
Man, and the cabalistic steps or degrees, embracing
these three divisions, may be said to express the
hypothetical agency through which the spirit flowed
down to earth, and was first incarnated in the human
body of the hypothetical creature, Adam.

The cabalistic theology, representing the endless
reasoning of countless generations of ingenious

men, is the epitome of man's first efforts to grasp
the problems connected with the cause and continuance of life, the inscrutable mystery which has
baffled the understanding of all inquirers alike.
They reasoned concerning all the phenomena of
existence by their analogy to human creation, and
it was supposed that the universal creation took
place after the manner of human creation, and
that the generative attributes of a man and a
woman were those of God and the universe, and
finally that all the bodily functions of a human
being had their counterpart in the macrocosm or
greater world.

The theoretical system based upon these ideas
constituted the secret doctrine, which was taught
orally, and was never written. All the old
canonical writings are an exposition of its teaching, but these works are composed, so that only
those persons, who are instructed in the rules of
the hidden wisdom could discover their meaning.
There was a mystical doctrine taught in all the old
schools of philosophy. In the case of the Pythagoreans, a long and severe period of probation
was required on the part of an aspirant, before the
ultimate truths of the system were communicated.
Although the true interpretation of the Jewish law
depends upon a knowledge of these cabalistic
mysteries, it is possible, that not a single human
being at the present day understands their meaning or application. Menasseh Ben Israel, a Jewish
writer at the beginning of the seventeenth century,
has recorded some valuable observations on this
mystical science, and has given the thirteen rules
for practical use in interpreting the myths of the
prophets. He says, " God delivered to Moses
the written law, and the commentary called the
oral law ; the latter was to be retained mentally
and to be transmitted by tradition ; it is therefore

termed 'Cabala' (received). Accordingly the two texts (Exodus, xxxiv. 27) are presumed to allude to the two laws, so denominated from one being an exposition of the other. . . .

"All the known languages of the world, excepting the Hebrew only, owe their origin to human construction and art; but the Hebrew had the Lord for its author and framer, and is thence called the 'holy tongue,' as it proceeded from that consummate Wisdom, which is infinite; *each word in itself contains the profoundest mysteries.* . . . for which reason R. Simeon Ben Jochai says in the 'Zohar,' '*Woe to him who imagines that the Law only contains the superficial structure of its narration*'. . . . 'and he, who supposes it has no soul comprised within its veiled mysteries, has no portion in the world to come.' 'Its body only,' he continues, 'the ignorant enjoy, but sages, who are the gifted servants of the Sublime and Most High King, look to its soul as its superior portion, and others still more learned to the soul of that soul. . . .'

"The least instructed are those who . . . . occupy themselves in the endeavour to learn how things happen according to the literal record; these are rewarded for their pious application (although they do not properly understand it) yet acquire salvation by virtue of their good intention.

"Others employ themselves in studying the explanations of the precepts and ceremonies, that is, knowledge of the 'Mishna,' called by some the oral law, from having been formerly retained in the memory of sages, and conveyed verbally to their disciples.

"And lastly, many aspire to the highest contemplation of the mysteries contained in the words, letters, points, and musical accents used in the construction of the text of the law.

"R. Simeon Ben Jochai termed the first of these, Masters of the Reading; the second, Masters of the Second or Double Lecture; and the third, Masters of the Cabala, that is, of Tradition (or the Received), it being an explanation of the divine law, received from the mouth of God by Moses, revealed by him to the sages or elders, and by them handed down to posterity. . . . 'As Moses was a hundred and twenty days on the Mount, on three different occasions of forty days each, it is highly probably he learned them all during these three studies, dedicating forty days to each, and as all beginnings are the most difficult, he was gradually prepared, and rendered capable of attaining the highest contemplation of the Cabala, in the same period of forty days as he had employed in mastering the lesser ones, from being thus gradually instructed. Hence it may be understood what "Cabala" is, and how it is divided into two parts. . . .'

"A demonstration will now be attempted, for the information of the curious, as to the means employed by the 'Cabalists' to discover the highest mysteries of the Law. . . . They have thirteen methods of discovering the mystery they attribute to the whole Law in a logical sense, and the secret meaning of its words. Brief examples of these rules will clearly explain their nature. . . .

"The second rule is called Transposition, that is, the letters of a word being transposed, and joined different ways, form various words. . . . This rule also seems to be derived from scripture, as it says in Genesis, 'Noah found grace in the sight of the Lord.' The letters in the name NCн, Noah, being transposed, form CнN, grace." By this change the numerical value of the word becomes 708, instead of 58. . . .

"The third rule is called Gematria or Numera-

tion, and is performed by numbers, being a mathematical mode of comprehending the Scripture, for
*as the Hebrew letters are numerals they contain
everything*. Pythagoras said, God created the
world by numbers, as did Plato (See Question
71); so the word BRASHITH amounts numerically
to the same as ITSR BTHVRH (He formed the
Law), thus drawing the conclusion, that the Law
was the instrumental cause of the creation of the
world. To this question, Why does the Law
begin with a B? They answer, To signify the
two Laws—the written and oral, or justice and
mercy, and similar things. This rule is used in
different modes, as explained in 'Pardes Ria-
monim'; they often add a unit to the amount of
the letters in a word, which is called Colel, as to
the word (Covenant) numerically 612, they add
this Colel making it 613, saying, this word signifies the Law, which contains 613 precepts. This
mystery of numbers also appears stated in Holy
Writ; for in the case of the idolatrous priests of
Baal, who accepted Elijah's challenge, it says, that
Elijah took 12 stones, according to the number
of the sons of Jacob; his taking this number, for
the special purpose of invoking the Lord, was
not merely that 12 was the number of Israel's
sons, but because those sons were 12 in consequence of that special number in Scripture covering a profound mystery. The Talmudists also use
this rule in various passages in the Talmud, and
modern authors much more so; as R. Solomon
Molcho, R. Jacob ben Habib, R. Mordecai, R.
Sabatai and others deducing great mysteries there-
from." [1]—" Conciliator," vol. i., p. 206.

The Christian equivalent to the word Cabala

---

[1] These statements are corroborated by Diodorus, who says,
"the Chaldeans preserve their learning within themselves by a
continued tradition from father to son."

was *Gnosis, knowledge*, and from innumerable references in the writings of the Fathers, it is evident
that the new sect, in the construction of the Gospel
and ritual of the Church, perpetuated the same
mystical tradition which they had received from
the Hebrews. The nature of the Knowledge is
explicitly stated by Clement of Alexandria, in the
following words : "And the GNOSIS itself is that
which has descended by transmission to a few,
having been imparted unwritten by the Apostles"
("Miscell." bk. vi., ch. 7). St. Basil also alludes to
it thus : "They [the Fathers] were well instructed
to preserve the veneration of the mysteries by
silence. For how could it be proper, publicly to
proclaim in writing the doctrine of those things,
which no unbaptized person may so much as look
upon ?"—"De Spiritu Sancto," c. 27.

From expressions of this kind it becomes apparent
that the importance, attached to the unbroken
continuity of the Apostolic succession, was due to
the necessity for securing the transmission of the
oral Tradition or Gnosis unimpaired, in order that
the true interpretation of the Gospel might be
insured to succeeding generations. The works
of Irenæus, Hippolytus, and Epiphanius have
numerous references to the Gnostic practices of
the Christians, and particularly to the Cabalistic
process of Gematria. The fact, that the numerical
system of the Cabalists and Gnostics is generally
condemned by the Fathers, appears to be no more
than a priestly artifice, intended to deceive the
vulgar, and prevent inquisitive people from prying
too deeply into the mysteries, which were retained
as the exclusive property of the few, referred to by
St. Clement. That the Greek philosophy rested
upon the same secret tradition, which was accepted
and retained as the basis of the Christian theology,
in common with other religious and philosophical

systems, seems to be borne out by another passage from the "Miscellanies": "Peter says in his 'Preaching,' Know that there is one God, . . . who made all things by the 'Word of His power,' that is, according to the Gnostic Scripture, His Son. Then he adds: 'Worship this God, not as the Greeks'—signifying plainly, that the excellent among the Greeks *worshipped the same God as we*, but that they had not learned by perfect knowledge that which was delivered by the Son. 'Do not then worship,' he did not say the God whom the Greeks worship, but 'as the Greeks'—changing the manner of the worship of God, NOT ANNOUNCING ANOTHER GOD. . . . Neither worship as the Jews; for they, thinking that they only know God, do not know Him, adoring as they do angels and archangels, the month, and the moon. . . . For what belonged to the Greeks and the Jews is old. But we, who worship him in a new way, IN THE THIRD FORM, are Christians" ("Miscell." vi., ch. 5).

Theophilus Gale, one of the most learned Puritans of the seventeenth century, says, that "The Jews, in imitation of the Pythagorean Institutes, made the Cabala their codex or Canon-Law" ("Court of the Gentiles," vol. iii., p. 216); and again on page 217, he repeats, "As for the Jewish Cabala or Cabalistic mythologie it seems to me exactly framed in imitation of the Grecian Mythology and symbolic mode of philosophizing. It's true the Jewish Church had even from its first institution, its choicest mysteries delivered in Symbols, Parables, Enigmes, and other terrene shadows." He speaks further of the Jewish Talmud or system of traditions, called the oral Law, which, he says, the Jews "equalize unto, yea prefer before the Scriptures. For they say (just as the Papists of their *Traditions*) 'that we cannot arrive at a perfect explication of the Divine precepts, but by the traditions of the ancients; again, that without the oral Law, the whole written Law is wrapped up in darknesse.'" This is corroborated by Lightfoot, probably the most competent Rabbinical scholar of the English Church, who declares, "That the Jews venerate the oral Law as the foundation of the written Law, and scruple not to say, 'the words of the Elders are weightier than the words of the Prophets.'"

The Jews were not the only people who possessed a mystical tradition, for the Neo-Platonists of the Alexandrian School claimed to have had a "sacred succession," by which the inner doctrines of the school were received and perpetuated. The Christians also had their Gnosis, said to have been received from Christ, by whom it was transmitted to the Apostles, and successively to the heads of the churches.[1] It is explicitly stated

---

[1] St. Clement declared that the barbarian Scriptures were all symbolical, and to be understood required "an interpreter and guide. For they considered that, receiving truth from those who knew it well, we should be more earnest and less liable to deception;" and speaking of his own tenets, he says (bk. v., ch. x.), "Rightly, therefore, the divine Apostle says, 'By revelation the mystery was made known to me,' for without a guide or interpreter to reveal the meaning of the Scriptures, the mysteries are hidden and dark." Such a revelation was given by St. John, only his "Revelation" is as obscure as the Parable which it is supposed to lay bare. A plain explanation of the Gospel was handed down by oral tradition only, as St. Clement intimates, for "fear of the swinish and untrained hearers." "Even now I fear, as it is said, 'to cast pearls before swine, lest they tread them under foot, and turn and rend us!' . . . . For scarcely could anything which they would hear be more ludicrous than those to the multitude." ("Miscell.," bk. i., ch. i.) Thus without disguise he gives the reason why "the mysteries of faith are not to be divulged to all." All old philosophers and priests, Christian or otherwise, had the same dread of the vulgar and profane, and had the same motive for concealing their mystical doctrine from the people, namely, lest it should be turned into ribaldry.

by Mosheim (" Ecc. Hist.," ii., p. 57) that "the religion of Rome . . . . is derived, according to the unanimous accounts of its doctors, from two sources, the written Word of God and the *UN-WRITTEN;* or, in other words, from scripture and tradition." By the Apostolic succession the true elucidation of the mysterious wisdom of the Gospel was secured, and presumably is still retained in the unreformed churches. After the Reformation the Protestants discarded the original traditions of the Church, and eventually ceased to regard the Papal authority, received uninterruptedly from St. Peter, as being of paramount importance. Thus the teaching of the traditions having been dropped, the veneration of the Pope, as the representative of the Apostolic succession, gradually lapsed, and the traditional knowledge intrusted to him has ceased to be known. Whether any part of the Gnosis, alluded to by St. Clement, is still received and transmitted by the modern Popes cannot be easily discovered, but judging from the Papal nervousness at present exhibited towards Freemasonry, it may be surmised that some faint remnant of the ancient knowledge is even now in the keeping of the Vicar of Christ.[1]

As the practice of Gematria, defined by Menasseh ben Israel, will be constantly used throughout the present work, the following instances will explain the method of its application in the works of the philosophers. In Hebrew the word THORA, the law, and Adonai, the bride, whose name was generally used as a substitute for the tetragammaton, or IHVH, have each the numerical value

---

[1] The reason why his holiness has declared the ordinations of the reformed Church of England to be invalid, is presumably because the Protestants, when they broke with the Church, declined to acknowledge or teach the unwritten word.

of 671, therefore, by the rule of Gematria, they have the same signification. In Greek ΠΑΡΑ-ΔΕΙΣΟΣ (Paradeisos) has the same numerical value, and is equivalent by Gematria to Ο ΚΟΣΜΟΣ, 670 + 1 = 671; and ΚΟΣΜΟΣ being numerically equal to 600, implies the number 1,040, which is the radius of the sphere of the Zodiac contained within the Holy Oblation for a vesica 600 broad is 1,040 long. ΜΑΚΡΟ-ΚΟΣΜΟΣ, 831, was the name given to the Father, or the first three steps forming the upper triad of the Cabala. These three steps form a triangle at the crown of the diagram. And ΠΥΡΑΜΙΣ, a pyramid or tri-angle, has also the value of 831. By Gematria these two words are equivalent to ΦΑΛΛΟΣ (Phallos), 831, and according to the proportion of the figure of Cesarino, 831 multiplied by 9½ gives the height of a man, stretched crosswise in a square enclosing a circle 7,899 in diameter, or the length of the polar diameter of the earth measured by British miles. Again Ἡ ΓΝΩΣΙΣ (the Gnosis), 1,271, and ΣΤΑΥΡΟΣ, a cross, have each the same numerical value; therefore the Gnosis of the Christians may be said to be the knowledge of the cross. ΤΕΛΕΤΑΙ, 651, one of the names applied to the Greek mysteries, yields the same number as ᾽ΕΠΙΣΤΗΜΗ, science, and 651 is the diameter of a circle 2,046 in circumference, and 2,046 is the diameter of Saturn's orbit, measured by the diameter of the sun. Therefore both the mystic rites, and science of the Greek religion signified the knowledge of the cosmos. And ᾽ΕΚΚΛΗΣΙΑ, the Church, who was called the Spouse of Christ, is equivalent numerically to ῬΟΔΟΝ, a rose, the emblem of the Rosicrucians, and was regarded by them as the antithesis of the Cross.

The doctrine of the Cabala was reduced to a geometrical diagram, in which the ten steps were grouped according to a progressive scheme, so that the emanations of the Spirit of the Elohim issues from the first step called the Crown, and after passing through the whole figure is carried through the ninth step, and finally reaches the tenth or last of the series. The theory of the Cabala teaches that these ten steps symbolize a trinity of persons, whose function consists in receiving and transmitting the spirit of life in its passage from heaven to earth. The first three steps shadow forth the first person of the trinity, called "Long face," the Macrocosm, or the Father. The next six steps are assigned to "Small face," who is called the Microcosm, the King or Son, the second person of the trinity. The tenth and last step is personated by the third person, called Malchuth, the Bride or Mother. Each of these ten symbols is associated with one of the heavenly bodies, so that the whole diagram is an epitome and image of the universe.

The ideas which the ancients connected with these three persons, combined into this figure of ten progessive steps, appear to form the basis of all their philosophy, religion, and art, and in it we have the nearest approach to a direct revelation of the traditional science, or Gnosis, which was never communicated except by myths and symbols. A very little knowledge is required to recognize the identity of the cabalistic doctrine with that of the Gospel, for the Christian Trinity is clearly derived from the geometrical disposition of the ten steps. Kircher ("Œdipus," tom. ii., pars 1, p. 289) has given one of the most complete illustrations of the diagram which is now available. And it is specially valuable from the fact that he has placed the symbols of the temple in its various parts, so that he makes the temple synonymous with the universe, and identifies its furniture with the three

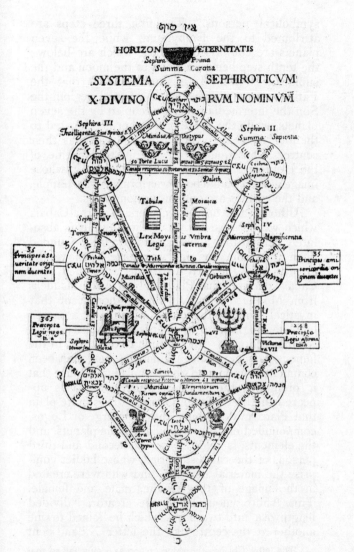

FIG. 6.—THE CABALISTIC DIAGRAM FROM KIRCHER'S "ŒDIPUS."

symbolical persons. The first three steps are
attributed to the Empyreum, while the seven
planets are comprised in those which are below ;
the tenth step being assigned to the moon and the
sublunary world. It is thus apparent that the
Father represents the super-celestial region, the
Son the intermediate space occupied by the seven
planets, while the Bride or Mother is relegated to
the four elements, which have the earth as their
centre. Consequently we see in the scheme of
the Hebrew philosophy, that the Deity—in whose
image man's twofold body was formed—the temple,
and the cosmos are one and synonymous.

Although the only direct version of the Cabala
which we possess is that of the Jews, it is absolutely certain that a similar oral tradition founded
upon the same doctrine was current among the
Greeks. All the early Christians, who knew their
Cabala, declared that Plato had borrowed his ideas
from Moses. Nor was Plato ignorant of that
mystical symbol, the cross, which was a sacred
emblem long before it emerged from obscurity in
the first century. The allusion to the cross, in the
famous passage in the " Timæus," has often been
commented upon, and there can be no doubt that
it prefigures the Mythos, which afterwards appeared in the Christian Gospel. It is quite plain
that Plato, in describing the Demiurge or Logos,
compounded out of the Zodiac, all the planets, and
the elements, is referring to the second and third
persons of the cabalistic triad, whose bodies comprise the material universe, and who were created
in the image of the Elohim, male and female.
This Androgynous being the creator, " divided
lengthwise into two parts, which he joined to one
another at the centre like the letter X,[1] and bent

[1] The letter Chi has the value of 600 as a numeral, so that
it is the numerical equivalent to the word cosmos, and a vesica

them into a circular form, connecting them with themselves and each other at the point opposite their original meeting point." The two limbs of the cross symbolize the double sex of this "heavenly creature," whom we find in the Apocalypse standing amidst the seven candlesticks or planets, or as the image of Daniel, and again as

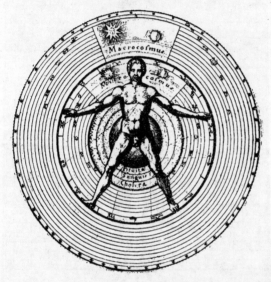

FIG. 7.—THE MACROCOSM. FROM THE FRONTISPIECE TO ROBERT FLUDD'S "UTRIUSQUE COSMI MAJORIS ET MINORIS HISTORIA." 1617.

the Man in Ezekiel's vision, and, above all, as CHRISTOS extended crosswise in the Holy Oblation. This was the cross which Constantine saw in the sky, and his conversation meant that he was enlightened and instructed in the Christian Gnosis, and saw with his spiritual eye the crucified

600 wide is 1,040 long, or the radius of the circle 2,080 in diameter which is contained in the Holy Oblation.

man stretched across the heavens, and believed in the verity of the visionary Christ.

The architect Cesariano, who edited an Italian

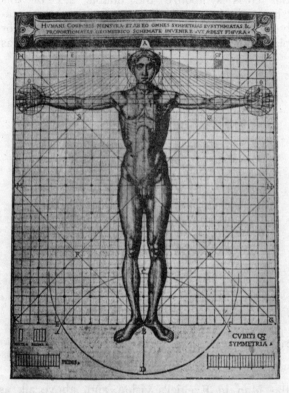

FIG. 8.—THE MACROCOSM.   FROM CESARIANO'S EDITION OF "VITRUVIUS" (COMO, 1521), FOLIO XLIX.

translation of Vitruvius published in 1521, has drawn the two figures, intended by Vitruvius to embody the proportions of temples, with an anatomical exactness not to be found elsewhere. The first glance at these two figures shows us, that they are each disposed in the form of a cross.[1] The man whose body forms the Jerusalem cross is relatively bigger than the other, whose limbs describe the St. Andrew's cross or saltire, their proportions being so arranged as to exemplify the

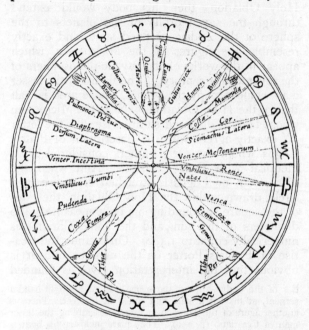

FIG. 9.—THE MICROCOSM. FROM ROBERT FLUDD'S "HISTORIA MICROSMI," P. 113.

duplication of the square. The square inclosing the greater man is divided horizontally and vertic-

[1] Cornelius Agrippa ("Occulta Philosophia," Parisiis, 1567, p. 237) has depicted the figure of the Microcosm standing within a circle, on a quadrangular stone, with his arms stretched out to the circumference. In each hand is placed a five-pointed star, the emblem of the firmament. On page 238 he has represented the Macrocosm in a square like the figure of Cesariano. Four symbols are drawn opposite the four extremi-

ally into thirty parts, thus dividing the area into 900 small squares. His height being 96 digits, the perimeter of the square is 384 digits—the number of the soul of the world according to Plutarch—and if he were were drawn within the Holy Oblation, then his body would extend through the seven orbits of the planets to the sphere of the Zodiac or fixed stars, and exactly resemble the figures of the Macrocosm, which appear in the works of the mystic philosophers of the seventeenth century. The figure of the lesser man would occupy the square, whose area is half that of the Holy Oblation.[1] Now the Microcosm whose body is disposed saltire-wise, like the letter X, exactly agrees with the description of Plato's Logos, whom the early Fathers considered to be identical with their Christos. And when the Microcosm or Logos is stretched crosswise in a circle, drawn within the Holy Oblation, the sides of the square surrounding his body measure 1,480 diameters of the sun, and the name Christos is numerically equal to 1,480. On reading the treatise of Francis Potter on the number 666, it is obvious that the interpretation given is founded

ties of the body—an eye above his head, at his right hand a serpent, at his left a staff, and shield at his feet. There is another figure of the Microcosm exactly resembling the lesser man of Cesariano (p. 240). The square inclosing his body is surrounded by the twelve signs of the zodiac. There are also two other figures (pp. 239, 241), each drawn within a circle having one of the seven planets corresponding to some member of their bodies.

[1] The duplication of the square illustrated by the relative sizes of these two figures is minutely explained by Plato in the " Meno." par. 82 (Jowett's translation, p. 43). The old Masonic writers declare that the true system of the universe, and the foundation of all geometrical proportion is to be found in the forty-seventh proposition of Euclid, as expounded by Pythagoras, and communicated in writing by Plato, because, apparently, the ratio which those two figures bear to one another is calculated by it.

upon some knowledge of the true meaning of the
number, which it was not the intention of the
author to reveal. For the " explanations " are very
often mere verbal quibblings, which mean little or
nothing. However, he occasionally commits himself to a direct statement, as when he says—following the interpretations of Rupertius and P. Bongus
(" De Numerorum Mysteriis ")—" that the number
666 is not only the number of the Beast's name, *but
also the number of God*, that is, it is a number which
God hath pleased to name and reveal to men, that
by counting of this number, they might find out
that other number, which it pleased not God expressly to name in this place, but rather mystically
to conceal, etc." (p. 60). From this we learn that
" by counting " the number 666 we may discover
the number of God. The term " counting " might
very properly be used here to describe the process
of finding the circumference of a circle 666 in
diameter, that is, 2,093—the diagonal of a square
whose sides are 1,480, the numerical equivalent
of Christos, the name of God.

Francis Potter does not count the number in
this way. He extracts the square root of 666
which he computes at $25\frac{41}{51}$, or $25\frac{25}{31}$, or $25\frac{806}{1000}$,
remarking, that " however the number of the frac-
tions be variable, yet the number 25 is always constant and the same." The fractions curiously introduced may possibly give us an indication of the
methods of those cryptic writers. For 41 multiplied by 51 produces 2,091, a number which is only
one and a fraction less than the side of the Holy
Oblation containing the square 1,480, the numerical
equivalent of Christos. The next fraction is $\frac{25}{31}$,
and the product of the two numbers is 775, or the
perimeter of the Holy Oblation, taking the Sun's
distance at 10. It is, in fact, another way of expressing the number 2,093. The third fraction is

apparently the true one : but the square root of 666 is more nearly 25·807 than 25·806.

The two figures include three persons, for the Microcosm or lesser man represents the double sexed creature, whose bride, or the feminine half of his body, is fixed to his back. According to the Cabala, they were not always conjoined in this way, but were sometimes separated. In Cesariano's figure only the masculine half is visible.

In the case of the temples, it is difficult to see how these figures of Cesariano's could have been used, unless they were associated with specific measures ; therefore we may conclude that they formed the canon or rule of measurement in architecture. Any measure of the universe could be identified with their bodies and applied to a temple, and it would thus become possible to canonize a certain number of figures which for convenience and use could be recognized, as the sanctioned patterns for the practice of the architectural arts. Originally the builders must have been instructed by the priests, and the rule of Vitruvius could only have resulted from a theological system based upon cosmic science. An illustration by Cataneo the architect (" Architectura," p. 37), who wrote in 1554, gives the plan of a Christian church disposed crosswise according to the figure of the Macrocosm, or, as he calls him, Jesus Christ.

What Hippolytus (" Refutation," bk. v.) tells us of the doctrines of the Nasseni seems to show that their creed was derived from the Cabala, and is a valuable illustration of its meaning. The Nasseni were a sect of Christian Gnostics, who worshipped the Logos under the name and image of the Serpent. They appear to have been of Hebrew origin, for they took their name from the Hebrew word *nachash*, a serpent.[1] "These Nasseni magnify, as the

---

[1] "For the serpent is called *naas* [in Hebrew]". The

originating cause of all things else, a Man, and a
Son of man. And this Man is a hermaphrodite,
and is called among them Adam" (p. 127): and a
hymn addressed to him begins thus: "From thee
[comes] Father, and through thee [comes] Mother"
. . . . "And they say of this Man, that one part

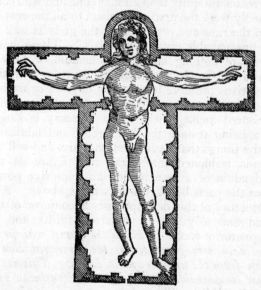

FIG. 10.—THE PLAN OF A CHRISTIAN CHURCH DISPOSED ACCORD-
ING TO THE FIGURE OF VITRUVIUS. CATANEO, P. 37.

is rational, another psychical, another earthly.
And they suppose that the knowledge of him is
the beginning of the knowledge of God. And the
Samothracians worship that Adam as the primal
man, and in their temples "there stand two images
of naked men having both hands stretched aloft
towards heaven, and their pudenda turned up-

numerical value of NChSh (serpent) is 358; it is therefore
equivalent by Gematria to MShICh, Messiah.

wards, as the statue of Mercury on Mount Cyllene "
(p. 140). " And the Nasseni affirm concerning
the spirit of the seed that it is the cause of all
existing things and is the secret and unknown
mystery of the universe concealed and revealed
among the Egyptians, who, after the Phrygians, are
of greater antiquity than all mankind, and who confessedly were the first to proclaim to all the rest of
men the rites and orgies of all the gods as well as
the unspeakable mysteries of Isis." These, however, are nothing but the pudendum of Osiris.
" And the Greeks deriving this mystery from the
Egyptians preserve it unto this day. For we behold the statues of Mercury of such a figure
honoured among them. For Mercury is Logos
who, being at once the interpreter and fabricator
of the things that have been, that are, and will be,
stands fashioned into some such figure as the
pudendum of a man having an impulsive power
from the parts below towards those above. And
a Mercury of this description is a conjuror of the
dead and a guide of departed spirits and an
originator of souls. *This is the Christ who in all
who have been generated is the portrayed Son of
Man from the unportrayable Logos. This is the
great unspeakable mystery of the Eleusinian rites
HYE CYE.*" [1] (The above quotation is given in
the words of Hippolytus, but it is condensed, and
is not quite consecutive.)

From the foregoing quotation it is plain, that
the Logos or soul of the world, according to Plato,
the Greek Hermes, and the Christ, according to the
Christian Gnostics, are all one and the same as the
Hebrew Adam Kadmon, who is the second person
of the cabalistic triad. The Cyllenian Hermes,
described by Hippolytus, so exactly resembles the

---

[1] The numerical value of 'ΥΕ ΚΥΕ is 830, or one less than
that of φαλλός.

lesser man found in Cesariano's edition of Vitruvius, that they may be justifiably considered to be identical. According to the masonic traditions the initiated architects, who preceded the Collegia Fabrorum of the Romans, and the Freemasons of the Middle Ages, were called Dionysiac architects. They were said to have been instructed in the rites and mysteries of Dionysus, and to have constructed the temples according to the secrets thus imparted to them. And it is a remarkable verification of this tradition, that the lesser man of Cesariano is depicted with vine leaves in his hair and an upright phallus, both well known attributes of Dionysus. No one can look at these two figures of Cesariano without seeing that they are something more than mere anatomical patterns. In later editions they become so, but here we have clearly and distinctly a curious survival of the cosmic deity of Greece, copied and disfigured by the crude draughtsmen of the Middle Ages, but faithfully preserved, and recognizable to the last.

There is still a further means of connecting the figure of Vitruvius with the Christ, and the Microcosm. From a passage in the Cabala we learn the following very curious fact as to the body of the King : "Longitudo autem membri hujus 248 mundorum." Now this is the only measurement of the body of the Microcosm recorded in the Cabala, so that it is of the highest importance as a means of identification. The fact that the measurement is given in " worlds " is also remarkable. By the proportions of Cesariano's figure, we can find the height of the whole body by multiplying 248 by $9\frac{1}{2}$. But by adding colel or unity to 248 we get 249. And 249 and a fraction multiplied by $9\frac{1}{2}$ gives 2,368, the numerical value of the name Jesus Christ.

In the " Book of Concealed Mystery" (p. 46) the

following interpretation of the first verse of Genesis
occurs. "In the beginning the Elohim created
the substance of the heavens, and the substance of
the earth (the sense is : six members were created,
which are the six numerations of Microprosopus—
viz., *Benignity*, as his right arm : *Severity*, as his

FIG. 11.—THE MICROCOSM. FROM CESARIANO'S EDITION OF
"VITRUVIUS," FOLIO L.

left arm : *Beauty* as his body : *Victory*, as his
right leg : *Glory*, as his left leg : and the *Foundation*, as reproductive)." For instead of "in the
beginning," it may be read " He created the six."
Upon these depend all things, which are below
(principally the Queen)." From this it is plain,
that the heavens and the earth are here supposed

to take the form of man, and it is no wonder that the Christian mystics of the Middle Ages saw in the " Timæus" of Plato the same doctrine of creation, which they found in the Mosaic Law. Jowett, in his introduction to the " Timæus," says, " The Neo-Platonists, believing that Plato was inspired by the Holy Ghost and had received his wisdom from Moses, seem to find in his writings the Christian Trinity, the Word, the Church, and the Creation of the World in a Jewish sense."

The Microcosm seems to have been used as a pattern in the practice of all the arts. Geofroy Tory introduces it in some of the letters of the " Champ Fleury," 1529, and Silvanus Morgan, the heraldic painter, shows it on a shield intended to symbolize the charges of the sixth day of creation. It stands on the shield as the image of Mercury, *i.e.*, Adam. He is surrounded by a lion, a hart, a horse, and a dragon, apparently corresponding to the four cosmic beasts of the Gospels (" Armilogia," 1666, p. 188).

Geometrically, the diagram containing the ten steps of the Cabala is shown by Kircher and other authorities in the form ascribed by Freemasons to what they call the " Double Cube," that is to say, an irregular hexagon, which will exactly enclose a Vesica. Consequently its length and breadth are of the proportion of 26 to 15. It is said that the ten cabalistic steps, in their entirety, symbolize the aspect of the Deity expressed by the four mystic letters IHVH, whose numerical value is 26. This number was said by the Jews to comprise the most sacred mysteries of the Law. No explanation, however, has ever been given showing how the number 26 afforded a key to all the science of the Israelites. It is now suggested that the Vesica, whose proportion is in the ratio of 26 to 15, was the symbol of the hidden rule or canon, by which the synthesis of nature was reduced to a comprehensible figure, capable of demonstrating to initiates the truth and knowledge which constituted the secret wisdom of antiquity.

Bryant, quoting from Eusebius, refers to a very singular fish, which, described in the language of hyperbole, is probably no other than the Vesica piscis. Eusebius copied his account of it from Berosus, a priest of Belus, and a native of Babylonia, who lived in the time of Alexander the Great. After declaring that writings were preserved at Babylon containing "a history of the heavens and

FIG. 12.—DOUBLE CUBE.

the sea" for fifteen myriads of years, he says, that in those ancient times the Chaldæans lived *without rule and order*, when "there made its appearance from a part of the Eruthrean sea, which bordered upon Babylonia, an animal endowed with reason, who was called Oannes. According to the accounts of Apollodorus the whole body of the animal was like that of a fish; and had under a fish's head another head, and also feet below, similar to those of a man, subjoined to the fish's tail. His voice, too, and language was articulate and human; and there was a representation of him to be seen in the time of Berosos. This Being, in the day-time, used to converse with men; but took no food at that

season ; and he gave them an insight into letters
and science, and every kind of art. He taught
them to construct houses, to found temples, to
compile laws, and explained to them the principles
of geometrical knowledge. He made them distinguish the seeds of the earth. . . . When the sun
set it was the custom of this Being to plunge again
into the sea, and abide all the night in the deep."
(Bryant, "Myth." vol. iv., p. 129). Apollodorus
called this animal Μυσαρος, 1,011. Now the two
vesicas whose perimeters are respectively 671 and
676 are each formed by the intersection of two
circles, 1,006½ and 1,014 in circumference, therefore 1,011 would be a mean between the last two
numbers. And the diameter of a circle whose
circumference is 1,011, is 321¾, or the numerical
equivalent of ΚΑΛΟΣ, beautiful, and ΝΑΟΣ, a
Temple.

A vesica formed of two such circles measures
about 482 across. And 482 is the numerical equivalent of the name of ῬΟΜΒΟΣ, and if two intersecting circles, 1,011 in circumference, be inclosed
in a greater vesica, the latter will be inclosed in
a square contained within the orbit of Saturn.
Moreover, the English word Truth has the value
of 1,011, and ᾺΝΝΗΣ, 1,109, is 1 less than the numerical equivalent of ΜΙΚΡΟΠΡΟΣΟΠΟΣ, 1,101, the
second person of the cabalistic triad. Finally, the
names of the three persons of the Hebrew Cabala,
Macroprosopos, 1,101, Microprosopos, 1,110, and
Malchuth, 496, yield the number 2,707, which is
the perimeter of a rhombus whose sides are 676,
the square of 26, the length of the Vesica, and
the numerical equivalent of the unspeakable name
of God, IHVH.[1]

[1] The following statement of Plutarch may be compared with
this of Eusebius. "Anaximander concludes that men were
first generated in the bellies of *fishes*, and being there nourished

Another fish remarkable in antiquity is the whale which swallowed Jonah. It is called τό κῆτος,[1] (370 × 598 =) 968, and if two circles 968 in diameter are formed into a vesica, their circumferences are equal to the two diagonals of a square whose sides are 2,151; and 597 is the circumference of Saturn's orbit if the sun's distance be taken at 10.

The Rabbis pretended that the mystery of the name ihvh (translated Jehovah in the English version of the Scriptures) lay in its proper pronunciation, and no pious Jew ever attempts to utter it, the High Priest alone being privileged to pronounce it once a year, in the Holy of Holies of the temple. Much philosophy may be extracted from the combination of these four Hebrew letters, which need not be discussed here, but it may be mentioned that the numerical values of the two Greek names of the Deity, ZEΥΣ,[2] 612 and 'ΑΠΟΛΛΩΝ,[3] 1,061, bear the proportion of 26 : 15 to each other, and the numbers, produced from the two spellings of the name Dionysos are in the same ratio to one another. It is also probable that this ratio was used as a means of expressing one number by another. For example, the word ΠΟΛΙΣ, a city, used as the name of the Bride in the Apocalypse, has the value of 390, and a vesica 390 broad is 676 long, and 676 is the square of 26, therefore the Greek word for a city may be taken to be equivalent to 26 ihvh, the Tetragammaton.

Again, the name iesous yields 888, a number which is the length of a rhombus having a perimeter of 2,048, the diameter of Saturn's orbit. And the number of the Hebrew name Messiah,

till they grew strong, and were able to shift for themselves, they were afterwards cast out upon the dry land."—CUDWORTH'S "Intellectual System of the Universe," vol. i., p. 189.

[1] Matthew, xii. 40.   [2] Zeus.   [3] Apollo.

358, is the width of a vesica 620 long, and 620 is the value of Kether, the first step of the Cabala.

And 666 is the length of a vesica, whose width is 384, or the sun's radius measured by the tone.

If the Greek numerals from one to ten be arranged so as to correspond to the cabalistic steps and their numerical values computed, we find that ἙΙΣ, 215, ΔΥΟ, 474, ΤΡΕΙΣ, 615, yield 1,304, which is one less than the length of a vesica which will contain a circle having a circumference of 2,368, and this triad represents the three steps of the Macrocosm.

The next six numerals are ΤΕΤΡΑΣ, 906, ΠΕΝΤΕ, 440, ἙΞ, 65, ἙΠΤΑ, 386, ὈΚΤΩ, 1,100, and ἘΝΝΕΑ, 111—the sum of the numbers being 3,098—and if this be taken as the perimeter of a cubical stone, or hexagon, the perimeter of its upper face would be 2,065, the mean number between 2,083, the side of the Holy Oblation, and 2,046, the diameter of Saturn's orbit; it is consequently an appropriate number for the Microcosm who personates the Zodiac and seven planets.

ΔΕΚΑ, the tenth numeral, has the value of 30, and this number denoting the distance from the earth to the moon, measured by the earth's diameter, symbolizes the sublunary world—the cosmic counterpart of the Bride. Again, if the numbers of the second and third persons of the Triad be added together, their sum is 3,128, which is the width of two circles 2,083 in diameter, formed into a vesica. And thus are represented the two circles of the ecliptic, and the equator on a celestial sphere.

CHAPTER IV.

NOAH'S ARK.

"After they had all entered into the Ark, if any one had beheld the entire collection, he would not have been wrong if he had said that it was a representation of the whole earth."—PHILO JUDÆUS, "Life of Moses," bk. ii., ch. xii.

"God also created man after his image; for as the world is the image of God, so man is the image of the world."—CORNELIUS AGRIPPA, "Occult Philosophy," bk. iii., p. 458.

THE Ark of Noah has had an absorbing attraction for most people at one time of their life, but it is to be regretted that after a certain period in their career the interest gradually fades into a mere reminiscence of the nursery. How or when it happened that the ship which miraculously saved the just Noah and his family and the beasts of the earth came to be manufactured into a toy for children, is a question which it would be difficult to answer; but it may be accepted that the Hebrew elders, who constructed the curious and ingenious parable of the flood, and all the details of the voyage and salvation of Noah, had probably other intentions than the invention of a plaything for their grandchildren. In the ages preceding the nineteenth century this seems to have been quite well understood, and the references to the Ark found in the works of early writers show that the story was received in an allegorical sense; by the early Christians it was evidently regarded as a myth analogous to that related of the Greek Deucalion,

for in the Clementine Homilies there is a reference to Noah as "Him who amongst you is called
Deucalion" ("Clem. Hom.," ch. xvi.), implying
that both the Patriarch and the Greek hero were
fictitious personages, created to suit the variations
of a similar allegory.

Philo declares that the Ark was prepared in
imitation of the human body, and this view is
followed by Cornelius Agrippa, who says, "Seeing
man is the most beautiful and perfect work of
God, and His Image, and also the lesser world;
therefore he by a more perfect composition, and
sweet harmony, and more sublime dignity doth
contain, and maintain in himself all numbers,
measures, weights, motions, elements, and all other
things, which are of his composition; and in him,
as it were, is the supreme workmanship. From
hence all the ancients in time past did number by
their fingers, and showed all numbers by them.
And they seem to prove, that from the very joints
of man's body all numbers, measures, proportions,
and harmonies were invented; hence according to
the measure of the body they framed and contrived
their temples, palaces, houses, theatres; also their
ships, engines, and every kind of artifice, and
every part and member of their edifices, and
buildings, as columns, chapiters, and pillars, bases,
buttresses, feet of pillars, and all of this kind.
Moreover God Himself taught Noah to build the
Ark according to the measure of man's body, and
He made the whole fabric of the world proportion-
able to man's body.

Therefore some who have written of the Microcosm, or of man, measure the body by 6 feet, a
foot by 10 degrees, every degree by 5 minutes;
from hence are numbered 60 degrees, which make
300 minutes, to the which are compared so many
geometrical cubits by which Moses describes the

Ark ; for as the body of man is in length 300
minutes, in breadth 50, in height 30 ; so the Ark
was 300 cubits long, 50 broad, and 30 high ; that
the proportion of the length to the breadth be six-
fold, to the height tenfold, and the proportion of
the breadth to the height about two-thirds.   In
like manner the measures of all the members are
proportionate and consonant, both to the parts of
the world, and the measures of the Archetype, and
*so agreeing, that there is no member in man, which
hath not correspondence with some sign, star, intelligence, divine name, and sometimes in God Himself
the Archetype"* ("Occult Philosophy," p. 263, Engl.
Trans., 1651).

Lomazzo ("Art of Painting," Oxf., 1598) says
the same thing, but adds, "by this rule the
Grecians afterwards framed their stately Argo-
navis." And Montanus ("Antiq. Judaic.," plate L.)
gives a diagram of the Ark [1] containing the body
of Christ within it, thus indicating the stature and
measure of the Saviour.

Josephus (bk. i., ch. iii.), speaking of the long
life of Noah (950 years) and the Patriarchs, says,
that God prolonged their life, on account of the
"good use they made of it in astronomical and
geometrical discoveries, which would not have
afforded the time of foretelling [the period of the
stars], unless they had lived 600 years ; for the
great year is completed in that interval." According to the Hebrews Noah was 600 years old when
the Flood commenced. This hint of Josephus, that
Noah was an astronomer, suggests the conclusion,
that the Ark had a cosmic significance, and what
it represents is probably indicated by the following
passage in the Book of Enoch : "*In those days
Noah saw that the earth became inclined.*"   We

---

[1] Reproduced on p. 214.

believe that astronomically the rectangular figure
of the Ark recorded the invention of the measures
of the ecliptic, mythically attributed to Noah.
This conclusion is borne out by an examination of
the numbers introduced into the story. According
to the Hebrew chronology Noah was born in the
year 1056 from the creation of the world. He
built the Ark in 1656, and he died 2006, aged
950.

There were canons of chronology in the ancient
world, as of everything else, and the dates which
appear in canonical works were presumably recorded to exemplify the mystical facts of the
numerical philosophy, along with all the other
circumstances of the narrative. The numbers
connected with the events of Noah's life have
been evidently devised in accordance with this
canonical rule, for the number 1,056, being the
length of a vesica 609 [1] broad, expresses the
dimensions of the Holy Oblation, the canonical
figure, to which we have supposed that all the
cosmic measures of the Scriptures are referred
back. Then, 1,656 records the altitude of the
sun's course measured upon a terrestrial globe.
For every "degree of latitude on any meridian is
about 69 miles everywhere, that is, 69·4 in high
latitudes, and 68·8 near the equator" (Denison's
"Astronomy," p. 9) ; and Vitruvius calculated in
his time that the ecliptic was inclined to the
equator at an angle of 24 degrees, therefore the
distance of the tropics from the equator measured
on the earth's circumference would be (69 × 24 =)
1,656 British miles. Supposing the ancients to
have discovered the true proportions of the sun's
path in the ecliptic, and seeking to publish the

[1] The circumference of a circle 194 in diameter is 609, and
194 is the width of the Holy Oblation if the sun's distance be
taken at 10.

fact according to their mystical custom, they would look for a symbol whose shape would agree with the space they had measured in the heavens. A city would obviously be unsuitable for the purpose. A temple would hardly meet the case, so they not unnaturally hit upon the form of a ship as a means of expressing the measures of their discovery, and proceeded to devise a myth which would at once explain and conceal the facts. The story of Noah is the Hebrew version of a mythos, which was universal in antiquity, having been probably invented by the Eygptians. Faber, one of the last of the old school of mythologists, says, " not content with making the sun sail over the ocean in a ship, they considered the whole solar system as one large vessel ; in which the seven planets act as sailors, while the sun as the fountain of ethereal light presides as pilot or captain. These eight celestial mariners, who navigate the ship of the sphere, are clearly the astronomical repre- sentatives of the eight great gods of Egypt " (" Origin of the Pag. Idol," bk. iv., p. 218). The ancients, however, counted only seven planets, including the sun, so that the pilot must really be the personification of the eighth sphere or zodiac, who is here called Noah by the Hebrews, while the seven members of his family, saved with him, correspond to the seven planets.

The numerical value of the name applied to a ship by the Greeks gives it a cosmic meaning. For the word ΝΑΥΣ yields the number 651, the diameter of a circle whose circumference is 2,046, the diameter of Saturn's orbit. By Gematria, it is equivalent to Plato's favourite word, ΈΠΙΣΤΗΜΗ, science, and ΤΕΛΕΤΑΙ, mystic rites. It is prob- ably for this reason that the Church was called a ship (Ναός and Navis), since the temple was designed as an image of the universe. Again,

ʽΗ ΝΑΥΣ has the value of 659, or $\frac{1}{12}$ of the earth's diameter in miles $\left(\frac{7,913}{12} = 659\frac{5}{12}\right)$.

The observations of Theophilus Gale are always instructive; in a passage on the building of the Ark, he says, "We need no way doubt, but that Noah had been fully instructed by Church-Tradition from his godly predecessors Methuselah, Enoch, and Seth, touching the creation of the world by God, and particularly touching the excellent fabric of the heavens, the nature of the celestial bodies, their harmonious order and motion; that the sun was made to govern by day, and the moon by night. . . . And it is the opinion of some (which is not without probable grounds), that the whole story of the creation, written by Moses, was conveyed down even from Adam to his time, by a constant uninterrupted tradition, to the holy seed and Church in all ages. . . . That the people of God were, in the infant state of the Church, much ravished with holy contemplations of the glory of God, that shone so brightly in those celestial bodies, their order, government, motion, and influence is evident in many philosophic, yet gracious meditations, we have to this purpose in the psalms."

The measures of the Ark, as recorded in Genesis, are 300 cubits in length, 50 cubits in breadth, and 30 cubits in height, or when rendered in feet, 450 × 75 × 45 feet. Its proportion was therefore that of a long narrow box, roughly agreeing with the measures of a man's body, and very much like a coffin, as the figure of Montanus shows. At one end there was a small window of the size of a cubit. But there seems to have been a doubt among the Rabbis whether the word translated "window" really was a window. The word in the Hebrew means "brightness," or "splendour," and it was said to have been a precious stone, brought from the river Pison in Paradise. Altogether it may be said that both as regards size and ventilation, the Ark was decidedly deficient for its ostensible purpose, and quite unlike the comfortable-looking house-boat with which we are familiar in the nursery.

The Vesica, by its intersecting circles, formed a geometrical representation of the crossing of the two circles of the ecliptic and equator, and perhaps by the aid of this figure we may arrive at the reason for the choice of 300 cubits, as the length of the Ark. For a vesica whose width is 300·48 is 520·84 long, and 520·84 is the side of a rhombus having a perimeter of 2,083⅓—the length of a side of the Holy Oblation; and 2,083⅓ being the mean number between 2,092 and 2,075, which is $\frac{1}{12}$ of the earth's circumference in miles, the 300 cubits may be taken to give the length of the sun's orbit, measured on a terrestrial globe.

Assuming that our English word Ark (called in Hebrew Thebah, by the Seventy κιβωτός in the Vulgate, Arca) preserves the meaning of the Greek word ἀρχή and ἀργώ, it would mean that which was at the beginning, the first original pattern or rule of things. That by which the ἀρχιτέκτων worked, and the rule of the ἀρχιερεύς, the High Priest, or Archbishop. It would be a canonical measure of the universe and the Creator ; exhibiting, by the proportions of the human body, the numbers and measures of time and space. For the sun in his journey measures a definite space in the heavens, and a recurrent period of time.

The following geometrical process will illustrate the agreement between proportions of the Ark, and the measures of the ecliptic. If a rectangle, having a ratio of 6 to 1, be drawn, so that its length is equal to the sun's course, as delineated upon a terrestrial globe, the length of the Ark would be equal to the circumference of the earth, and the line drawn through its centre would represent the equator. And if the oblique course of the sun be described by two straight lines, cutting the equator, so as to produce the exact declination of the sun's orbit, it will be found that the rectangle contains a representation of the solar path, leaving a sufficient margin all round to provide a wall. The sun's course is thus inclosed inside a long narrow coffer, and appears in the form of a bridge or pediment, marking the tropics by the solstitial signs of Cancer and Capricorn, at its apex and base—the equinoctial points being marked on the equator by Aries and Libra. When the rest of the signs are drawn at their proper intervals, it is quite an allowable figure of speech to say, that the Ark contains all the beasts of the earth.

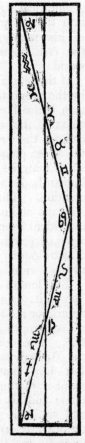

FIG. 13.—NOAH'S ARK.

The equatorial circumference of the earth is 24,900 miles, therefore an ark enclosing the sun's course, taking the obliquity of the ecliptic at 24°, as computed by Vitruvius, measures externally 24,900 by 4,150 miles. Internally it is 24,048 by 3,223. If these measures be divided by 12, as in the case of the Holy Oblation, they become, for the exterior $2,075 \times 345\frac{5}{6}$, and for the interior $2,004 \times 268\frac{7}{12}$.

Now if such an Ark be drawn upon the Holy Oblation, so that it is crossed by the orbits of the seven planets, then, when Noah's body is introduced according to the diagram of Montanus, it is easy to understand how the facts of this geometrical figure might be mystically converted into the story of Noah, and the seven members of his family, who took a year's voyage in the Ark, together with all the animals of the world.

If this explanation be correct, we must conceive, by the proportions of the Ark, the vast figure of a man, in the likeness and image of God, whose body contains the measure of the sun's path in the ecliptic, the circuit of the earth, and the orbits of the seven planets. We are, in fact, to imagine the whole material universe, accurately epitomized in a human body, symbolizing the Creator reflected in creation. That the human body was used as a means of illustrating the parts of the universe, is evident from the figures surrounded by the 12 signs, depicted on old almanacks, and by the custom of astrologers, who allocate the signs and planets to the various members of the body.

The length of the sun's orbit amounts to about 690 of its own diameters ($220 \times 3\frac{1}{7} = 691$), and an ark, or rectangular box, as previously described, whose length outside is 690, measures internally 666. The notorious allusion to this number in the Apocalypse is as follows : " Here is wisdom. Let him that hath understanding count the number of the beast ; for it is the number of a man ; and his number is six hundred, three score, and six." It is possible that the wisdom mysteriously referred to by St. John, may have reference to the sun's boat, which accurately measured the extent of his course in the heavens. It is generally admitted that the revealed wisdom of the Apocalypse is concerned with astronomy, and that the vision of St. John was a sight of heaven, such as astronomers see, but set forth in the mystical language of prophecy. Victorinus, who was Bishop of Petau at the end of the third century, in a treatise on the Revelation, alluding to the number 666, speaks thus : " As they have reckoned from the Greek characters, as they find it among many to be TEITAN, for *Teitan* (666) has this number, which the Gentiles call Sol and Phœbus." This statement of the bishop explicitly connects the number 666 with the sun, and the statement in the text, that " it is the number of a man," further associates it with the Ark of the sun, which contained the figure of the Microcosm. In some early manuscripts of the Apocalypse the number 616 is substituted for 666. And 616 is the perimeter of a square, enclosed by the sun's orbit, so that both numbers record the same measure in a different way. When Eratosthenes took his observations for determining the circumference of the earth, he is said to have been informed that when a pit was dug at Syene in Egypt, the sun's rays at the summer solstice shone perpendicularly into it. This place was consequently considered by the Greeks to mark the northern tropic. Can it be a purely accidental coincidence, that the Greeks should have called the place which measured the sun's course in the ecliptic by a name which has the value of 666 ? Assuming that it was the custom to give names an appropriate number, and that it was known that the sun's orbit was contained in an ark whose internal length was 666 of its own diameters, it must be admitted that Syene, 666, was a very fitting name for a place which indicated the boundary of the sun's path.

Similarly, the length of an ark of the sun, which is measured by the tone, or interval between the earth and the moon, is 2,406 long (766 × 3·1416

= 2,406) and 401 broad. Its internal length is 2,318, and its width is 311.

According to St. Clement, "there are some who say that 300 cubits [Tau, 300] are the symbol of the Lord's sign" ("Miscel.," bk. vi., ch. ix). Now every scholar knows that the letter Tau,[1] or cross, was the emblem of the Phallus. And the word ΣΗΜΕΙΟΝ (sign), used here, yields the number 383, or the radius of the sun's orbit measured by the tone. In classical Greek ΣΗΜΕΙΟΝ was written ΣΗΜΑ, 249, and 249 and a fraction multiplied by $9\frac{1}{2}$, in accordance with the proportion of Cesariano's figure, produces the number 2,368, the numerical value of the name Jesus Christ, who was a personification of the Logos or Microcosm. The reason why the ark was considered to symbolize the generative power in the universe may be thus explained. The diameter of the sun's orbit being about 216 times its own diameter, and the diameter of Saturn's orbit being 2,046 of these diameters, the two orbits roughly stand to each other in the ratio of $9\frac{1}{2}$ to 1 $(216 \times 9\frac{1}{2} = 2,052)$. The sun is thus identified with the creative principle of the universe on account of a geometric ratio, as well as for the more obvious qualities which mark him as the fertilizing or impregnating power of the earth.

The width of an ark 216 long is 36 broad, and Philo (vol. iv., p. 453, Yonge's Transl.) says: "It was by the employment of this number [36] that the Creator of the universe made the world;" now the sum of the numbers from 1 to 36 is 666, the internal length of the sun's boat.

Cornelius Agrippa perceived a parallel between the ark of Noah and the ship Argo. According to the Greek legend, the ship of the Argonauts

---

[1] In Hebrew the word ThBH 407 (Ark) is equivalent by Gematria to ThV 406 (Tau).

was built by ΆΡΓΟΣ, 374. Supposing the number 374 to represent the length of an ark of the ratio of 6 to 1, its width would be 62, and $62\frac{1}{3} \times 9\frac{1}{2} = 592$, by which we get the size of a man inclosed within a square having a perimeter of 2,368 ($592 \times 4 = 2,368$). And 62 squared, if we increase the fraction, gives the number 3,956, the number of miles in the earth's radius. The name ΆΡΓΩ yields 904, which is the circumference of the two circles which produce a vesica $249\frac{1}{4}$ long, and $249\frac{1}{4} \times 9\frac{1}{2} = 2,368$.

Deucalion, the name of the Greek Noah, has the numerical value of 1,320, which is the length of an ark 220 wide, and 220 is the diameter of the sun's orbit. And a cross drawn within a vesica 1,321 long, measures 2,083, the length of a side of the Holy Oblation. His ark was called ΛΑΡΝΑΞ, 242; if colel be deducted the number becomes 241, which is the width of an ark 1,446 long, and 1,446 is side of a square inscribed within the orbit of Saturn; therefore the vessel of Deucalion may be conceived as signifying the body of a man surrounded by the seventh and outermost sphere of the planets.

In the early writings of the Church, Noah, by his voyage in the Ark, and Christos, by His death on the Cross, fulfilled the same mystic sacrifice for the salvation of the human race, and their respective symbols in each case represented the creative agent, whose function is to transmit the divine essence, which they supposed was received through the sun's rays, animated by the spirit of life, flowing round the universe in the milky way.

The diagram of the Ark given by Montanus shows the body of Christ laid in it. Now the numerical value of the Hebrew name Messiah is 358. If we take the number $358\frac{1}{2}$ to be the side of an ark, then its length will be 2,151 ($358\frac{1}{2} \times 6$), the number of years occupied by the sun in each of the 12 signs of the Zodiac, during the cycle of the procession of the equinoxes, or the great year. And this space of time constitutes the great month or Messianic period. In a series of thirteenth century designs in the South Kensington Museum painted on ivory, there is a measure of Christ's body among other emblems of the passion. It is in the form of an oblong enclosure resembling the Ark.

The proportions of the Ark being accepted as the measures of a human body, the following application of them to the body of truth as revealed to Marcus the Gnostic, may explain the meaning of an otherwise incomprehensible passage. The description is recorded by Hippolytus (Ref., bk. vi., ch. xxxix.). "The Tetrad, after having explained these things, spoke as follows : ' Now I wish also to exhibit to you Truth herself, for I have brought her down from the mansions above, in order that you may behold her naked, and became acquainted with her Beauty; nay, also that you may hear her speak, and may marvel at her wisdom. Observe then first the head above, Ἄλφα and Ω ; the neck, B and Ψ ; shoulders, along with hands, Γ and X ; breasts, Δέλτα and Φ; diaphragm, EΥ ; belly, Z and T ; pudenda Ἦτα and Σ ; thighs, Θ and P ; knees, ΙΠ ; calves, KO ; ankles, ΛΞ ; feet M and N.' . . . And he styles this element Man, and affirms it to be the source of every word, and the originating principle of every sound." The numbers of all these letters, when added together, amount to 6,166. And if we suppose this to be the length of the body of Truth, according to the proportions of the Ark, the width would be 1,027 $\left(\frac{6,166}{6} = 1,027\right)$, a number, which is at the same time the radius of Saturn's orbit, and the length of a

rhombus (1,027 : 592) which has a perimeter of
2,368. The height of this Ark is 616, which is the
perimeter of a square inscribed within the sun's
orbit.

The numerical value of the name 'ΑΛΗΘΕΙΑ,
Truth, is 64, and the sum of the numbers from 1 to
64 is 2,080, the side of the Holy Oblation. Therefore to the Greeks Truth meant the whole cosmic
system, accurately and truly delineated. This idea
seems also to have been transferred to the Christian
Virgin, for ΜΑΡΙΑΜ has the value of 192, which is
the width of the two intersecting circles, which form
a vesica 64 wide.

And it was also the doctrine of the Gnostic
Marcus, that the soul of the visible universe consisted of seven powers, which glorify the Logos by
uttering seven notes. " The first heaven sounds
Ἄλφα, and the one after that Ε, and the third Ἦτα,
and the fourth, even that in the midst of the seven,
the power of Ἰῶτα, and the fifth Ο, and the sixth Υ,
and the seventh and fourth from the central one, Ω.
And all the powers, when they are connected together in one, emit a sound and glorify that being
from whom they have been projected" (" Ref."
bk. vi., ch. xliii). It is noticeable, that in the
text of Hippolytus some of the letters are written
in full, while others are written with a single letter
only. When these are added together, as they
stand, they amount to 3,227, which is the length
of an Ark having a width of 538, which is the
side of a rhombus whose perimeter is 2,151, the
number of years in the great month. And 3,223
is the width of an Ark containing the sun's course
measured on a terrestrial globe.

CHAPTER V.

NAMES OF THE GODS.

"*Pythagoras thought, that he, who gave things their names, ought to be regarded not only the most intelligent, but the oldest of the wise men. We must then search the Scriptures accurately, since they are admitted to be expressed in parables, and from the names hunt out the thoughts which the Holy Spirit, propounding respecting things, teaches by imprinting His mind, so to speak, on the expressions; that the names used with various meanings, being made the subject of accurate investigation, may be explained, and that which is hidden under many integuments may, being handled and learned, come to light and gleam forth. For so also lead turns white as you rub it, white lead being produced from black. So also knowledge (gnosis), shedding its light and brightness on things, shows itself to be in truth the divine wisdom, the pure light, which illumines the men whose eyeball is clear, unto the sure vision and comprehension of truth.*"—"Selections from the Prophetic Scriptures," xxxii., "Ante-Nicene Library," vol. xxiv., p. 127.*

"*The Names declare the glory of Al; and the firmament showeth his handiwork.*"—Psalm xix. 1.

WITH respect to the early history of the world, we are at present in the hands of a school of teachers whose attention is divided between the deductions of science and the traditions of antiquity; and since there is much doubt about the primitive condition of man, so there is no certainty about the origin of language. Amongst the nations of Christendom, the "traditions" generally affirm that the Elohim spoke in the Hebrew tongue, and taught the letters of that language to Adam, who was the first, and, owing to his nearness to divine inspiration, the most perfect philologist. Theo-

philus Gale admirably expresses the ancient view
in his "Court of the Gentiles" (vol. ii., p. 6):
"The first created divine institutor of all philo-
sophie was Adam, who without all peradventure
was the greatest among all mere mortals that ever
the world possessed; concerning whom the Scripture tells us (Gen. ii. 19, 20), that "he gave names
to every 'living thing,'[1] which argues his great
sagacity and philosophic penetration into their
natures . . . for Adam could, by his profound
philosophy, anatomize and exactly prie into the
very nature of things, and then contemplate those
glorious ideas, and characters of created light
and order, which Divine Wisdom had impressed
thereon. And that Plato had received some
broken tradition, touching this philosophy of
Adam, is evident from what he lays down in his
"Politicus," and elsewhere, touching the golden
age or the state of innocence, wherein he says
our first parent was the greatest philosopher
that ever was. And Baleus ('De Script. Brit.
Cent. X.,' Præfat.) tells us, 'That from Adam all
good arts and human wisdom flow, as from their
fountain. He was the first that discovered the
motions of the celestial bodies, the nature of plants,
of living, and all other creatures; he first published the forms of Ecclesiastick Politie, œco-
nomick government. . . . From whose school
proceeded whatever good arts and wisdom were
afterwards propagated by our Fathers unto Man-

---

[1] This is also repeated in the Koran (ch. ii.) God "taught
Adam the names of all things, and then proposed them to the
angels, and said, Declare unto me the names of these things if
ye say truth. They answered, Praise be unto thee, we have no
knowledge but what thou teachest us, for thou art knowing and
wise. God said, O Adam, tell them their names. And when
he had told them their names, God said, Did I not tell you
that I know the secrets of heaven and earth, and know all that
which ye discover and that which ye conceal?"

kind. So that *whatever Astronomie, Geometrie, and other Arts contain in them, he knew the whole thereof.*'" The Hebrew letters were carefully transmitted by him to posterity, and religiously preserved, till after the addition of new languages at the fall of the Tower of Babel.

On the other hand, if we turn to the legend of science, we learn a totally different account of the creation of the world. The affair, we are told, took place at a time incredibly remote, and in a manner both vague and uncertain. The very name of the Elohim, who created and instructed our father Adam, is not even mentioned. For the primitive man, according to science, was not born of great stature, nor endowed with pre-eminent faculties, which made him at once fit to receive a profound and abstruse philosophy from the mouth of a paternal God. Instead of which, he was merely an animal who had risen from very small beginnings, and had gradually improved himself, as his opportunities permitted, till, probably to his own surprise, he discovered that he was a man. And then, still retaining his old faculty of getting from worse to better, he ultimately learned to speak, to write, and to practise all other arts. This history, as far as it goes, is plausible and probable enough, but it lacks the fulness, which is the strong point about the traditions. There everything is specific and defined ; the story is complete ; the very generations from the creation of the world are counted and the years recorded ; while science, on all these highly interesting points, has nothing but a few guesses to offer.

The traditions, when received according to the letter, are crude, childish, and unquestionably fabulous ; but since science has so little to tell us, we are compelled to fall back upon them, and

make the most of their information.   In fact, it
must be admitted that authoritative knowledge of
the archaic history of man does not exist.   All
that is known of human affairs is confined to a late
and recent period.   This will be most apparent
when it is remembered how little has been ascertained about the Egyptians, who lived only a few
thousand years before our own time, and who represent the culmination of a vastly remote civilization, of which we know little or nothing.   Indeed,
such is the scantiness of our knowledge of still more
recent times, that it cannot now with certainty be
ascertained whether Plato or Moses is the older
writer.[1]

Although the scientist is justified in disregard-
ing the traditions when these are offered as literal
facts, he is nevertheless himself quite as much at
fault in his attitude towards them as the serious
people, who have brought discredit upon all
ancient history.   For his misconception as to the
value of the traditions is due to his entire ignorance of their meaning, and since this ignorance has
come about through the neglect of those critical
methods formerly in use among the old interpreters, if we are to understand the ancients at all,
it is clear that we must return to the old manner of
criticism.   The absence, at the present day, of an
illuminated class, and the consequent lapse of the
old traditional knowledge, has left us without the
guidance which was required for the explanation
of the mystical compositions of the old poets and
law-givers.   Therefore, our only course must be

[1] According to Josephus, Apion thought that Moses led the
Israelites out of Egypt in the seventh Olympiad (749 B.C.), but
this date is uncorroborated, and agrees with no other account.
The LXX. declare that he lived A.M. 3839, while the Hebrews
put the year of the exodus at A.M. 2423.   None of these dates,
however, can be supported by any evidence whatsoever.

to try and recover that knowledge which could transform an apparently stupid fable into the statement of some intelligible, and, more or less, important fact.

The oldest treatise upon names which has come down to us from antiquity is Plato's "Kratylos." This dialogue was written to illustrate the origin of words, and to account for the reasons and motives which influenced the ancients in imposing their names upon gods and things, and it consequently affords us the most reliable information available as to the views of the Greek philosophers upon this subject. But we are at once confronted with the difficulty as to how this treatise is to be interpreted. Mr. Jowett, for instance, says : " I am not one of those who believe Plato to have been a mystic, or have had hidden meanings ; " and, again : " Plato was not a mystic, nor in any way affected by the eastern influences which afterwards overspread the Alexandrian world . . . but one who aspired only to see reasoned truth, and whose thoughts are clearly expressed in his language." If Mr. Jowett's emphatic opinion could only settle the difficulty, we should have no further trouble in the matter, but unfortunately this opinion, so far as we know, is unsupported by the testimony of a single ancient author ; at any rate it would be easy to bring forward innumerable assertions to the contrary, which are quite as credible as any statement of Mr. Jowett's. The Neo-Platonists claimed to have had a secret tradition, which had been received from Plato himself, and handed down by the successive members of the school ; and by this knowledge they professed to interpret the works of the Master. According to St. Clement of Alexandria, " It was not only the Pythagoreans, and Plato, that concealed many things, but the Epicureans, too, say that they have things which may not be uttered, and do not allow all to peruse those writings. The Stoics also say, that by the first Zeno things were written which they do not readily allow disciples to read, without their first giving proof whether or not they are genuine philosophers. And the disciples of Aristotle say, that some of their teachings are esoteric and others common and exoteric. Further, those who instituted the mysteries, being philosophers, buried their doctrines in myths, so as not to be obvious to all." It is evident, therefore, if St. Clement was not mistaken, that all the Greek philosophers expressed their doctrines mystically. And it must be remembered that the Greeks, amongst whom St. Clement lived at Alexandria, were the sons and grandsons of the men who had learned their philosophy in the schools at Athens, and there is no reason to suppose that the mere change of locality brought about such an entire change in the method of philosophizing as Mr. Jowett would have us believe. Admitting that about this time the influence of what remained of the ancient Egyptian wisdom was affecting the current of thought, it is still ridiculous to suggest that the allegorical and mystical method had not been practised by the old philosophers in Greece. Besides, the Alexandrian Greeks were only going back to the fountain-head of all their original speculations ; for, according to the evidence of their own historians, their entire theology and philosophy was first learned among the Egyptians. All the Christian Fathers declared for the symbolical, and not the literal interpretation of ancient philosophy, which they regarded in the light of their own Scriptures. They believed that Plato had had access to the Hebrew law, and had based his philosophy upon it. This view was held by all Christians, down to the nineteenth century. St.

Clement quotes Aristobulus to that effect: "And Plato followed the Laws given to us, and had manifestly studied all that is said in them." And Numenius, the Pythagorean philosopher, expressly writes: "For what is Plato, but Moses speaking in Attic Greek?" This latter statement, that Plato had borrowed his ideas from the Hebrew Scriptures, may have been a mere fiction, invented by the fathers to give greater authority to the new Gospel. But whether they really believed it or not, there is no doubt that all educated Christians, down to within quite recent times, recognized the identity of the Greek and Hebrew philosophy, and throughout the Middle Ages even went so far as to make the works of Plato and Aristotle the text-books of theology. Now, making every possible allowance for delusion and stupidity on the part of the Fathers, is it likely that, living as they did in the midst of the Pagan world, with the opportunity of being instructed by the Sophists, and even being initiated into the Eleusinian mysteries, as St. Clement was, they could have made a mistake, which involves the misunderstanding of every philosophical and theological system that had ever been propounded? No doubt the Christian Fathers were not the most skilful of philosophers, but neither can we regard them as being the hopeless imbeciles which we should be compelled to do if we are to believe Mr. Jowett. And it must not be forgotten, that skilful or otherwise, these Christian philosophers were skilful enough to prevail against all their rivals, and establish their system as the permanent creed of subsequent ages.

Having chosen to follow the united voice of the ancients as to the mystical nature of the Platonic philosophy, it now remains to show what mysterious facts may be elicited from the discussion about names in the Kratylos.

The bulk of the argument is put into the mouth of Socrates, who undertakes to instruct the others, as to the derivation of the various words. He speaks throughout in a distinctly flippant tone, and as usual, need not to be taken too seriously. There are the inevitable allusions to the geometrical mysteries, and apparently the aim of the whole piece is directed to play upon the numerical values of the different words, without arousing the suspicion of the uninstructed.

The opening paragraph has been numbered by Stephanus 383, and it begins by Hermogenes saying, " Our friend Kratylos [1,121] has been arguing about names ; he says . . . that there is a truth or correctness in them, which is the same for Hellenes as for Barbarians. Whereupon I asked him, whether his own name of Kratylos is a true name or not, and he answers 'Yes.' And Socrates [1,629] 'Yes.' Then every man's name, as I tell him, is that which he is called. To this he replies —' If all the world were to call you Hermogenes, that would not be your name.' And when I am anxious to have a further explanation, he is ironical and *mysterious*, and seems to imply that he has a notion of his own about the matter, *if he would only tell*, and could entirely convince me *if he chose to be intelligible.'*

"Socrates replies 'Son of Hipponicus, there is an ancient saying, that ' Hard is the knowledge of the Good.' And the knowledge of names is a great part of knowledge.' "

---

[1] The Sophists appear to have been the Pagan gnostics or cabalists, as Plato explains : " *Soc.* And what is the nature of this truth or correctness of names ? That, if you care to know, is the next question. *Her.* Certainly I care to know. *Soc.* Then reflect. *Her.* How shall I reflect ? *Soc.* The true way is to have the assistance of *those who know*, and you must pay them well, both in money and thanks—these are the Sophists." —KRATYLOS.

Thus at the very outset, there is more than a hint given us, that Kratylos knew more than he was willing to reveal on this subject, and the statement of Socrates, that knowledge is greatly concerned with names, may be taken mystically, for since the word ONOMA, a name, yields 231, and TO ONOMA, *the* name, is numerically equivalent to 601,[1] he means, that those who know all that is contained in that number have a great part of knowledge, and further, when the opinions of Plato are examined, they will be found to be entirely consistent with the supposition that the Greeks were in the habit of regarding names as numbers, and connecting these with the measures of the universe, and the cabalistic or traditional order of the Canon. We are told, that "the first imposers of names were philosophers," and legislators. By legislators, we suppose he means the men who formulated the Law, as the Jews use the expression, when applied to the five books of Moses, which constitute the exposition of the rule or Canon. And it is said, " Naming is an art, and has artificers ; " and again, " he who by syllables and letters imitates the nature of things, if he gives all that is appropriate, will produce a good image, or in other words, a name." At another time Socrates is made to say, " By the dog of Egypt, I have not a bad notion, which came into my head only this moment ; I believe that the primæval givers of names were undoubtedly like too many of our modern philosophers, who in the search after the nature of things are always getting dizzy, from constantly going round and round, and

---

[1] The number 601 is the width of a vesica 1,041½ long, or the radius of the circle of the zodiac contained in the Holy Oblation, and is equivalent by Gematria to cosmos, 600. In Hebrew SHMIM (names) is synonymous with, and is generally translated, Heavens, in the Authorized Version of the Scriptures.

then they imagine, that the world is going round and round, and moving in all directions; and this appearance, which arises out of their own internal condition, they suppose to be a reality of nature; they think there is nothing stable or permanent, but only flux and motion, and that the world is always full of every sort of motions and change. The consideration of the names I mentioned has led me into making this reflection. . . . Perhaps you did not observe, that in the names, which have been just cited, the motion, or flux, or generation of things is most assuredly indicated."

The above passage may reasonably be taken to mean, that the names referred to, in setting forth the three laws of the universe, " motion, flux, and generation " are symbols of the powers of creation and the world.

Again, he says, " A name rightly imposed ought to have the proper letters. And the proper letters are those which are like the things." In another place, in reply to a statement of Kratylos, that a name wrongly spelt is not a name at all, he says, " I believe what you say may be true about numbers, which must be just what they are, or not be at all." This last sentence is the only open suggestion, in the whole dialogue, that names have a numerical value. But in the following passage, we are able to put this supposed allusion to numbers to the test, and discover Plato's method of disclosing his numerical philosophy. " *Soc.* No more could names ever resemble any actually existing thing, unless the original elements of which they are compounded bore some degree of resemblance to the objects of which the names are an imitation; and the original elements are letters. . . . Were we not saying, that all things are in motion, and progress, and flux, and that this idea of motion is expressed by names? Do you not conceive that to be the meaning of them ?

"*Kratylos.* Yes, that is assuredly their meaning, and their true meaning.

"*Soc.* Let us revert to ΈΠΙΣΤΗΜΗ [651] (knowledge), and observe how ambiguous the word is, seeming rather to signify stopping the soul at things, than going round with them ; and therefore we should leave the beginning as at present, and not reject the E, but make an insertion of an I instead of an E (not πιστημι but ἐπιστήμη). Take another example : ΒΕΒΑΙΟΝ [140] (sure) is clearly the expression of station, and position, and not of motion. Again, the word ΊΣΤΟΡΙΑ [691] (inquiry) bears upon the face of it the stopping of the stream ; and the word ΠΙΣΤΟΝ [710] (faithful) certainly indicates cessation of motion ; then again ΜΝΗΜΗ [146] (memory), as any one may see, expresses rest in the soul, and not motion. Moreover words such as ΆΜΑΡΤΙΑ [453] and ΣΥΜΦΟΡΑ [1311], which have a bad sense, viewed in the light of their etymologies, will be the same as ΣΥΝΕΣΙΣ [1,065] and ΈΠΙΣΤΗΜΗ [651], and other words which have a good sense ; and much the same may be said of ΆΜΑΘΙΑ [62], and ΆΚΟΛΑΣΙΑ 333."

If the foregoing passage is to be taken literally, it can scarcely be said to have very much point or sense, but if it is to be taken equivocally—each name being chosen for the sake of its numerical value, which gives it a double sense, then it is evident, that the derivations are merely used to give a facetious meaning to the word, in contradistinction to its numerical significance. Regarded in this light, it becomes, in fact, a specimen of philosophic wit, intended for the amusement of the Sophists. This will become clearer when the numbers of each name are examined.

The first word to which he draws attention is
ΈΠΙΣΤΗΜΗ, 651. It occurs several times in the
course of the dialogue, and is used for knowledge,
in the same way that Ἡ ΓΝΩΣΙΣ, 1,271, was afterwards used by the Christians. Clement of Alexandria (" Misc." bk. vi. 18) says, "For real science
(ἐπιστήμη), which we affirm the Gnostic alone possesses, is a sure comprehension (κατάληψις, 1,270)
leading up through true and sure reasons to the
knowledge (ἡ γνῶσις, 1,271) of the cause." He
refers to it again thus : " If then we are to give
the etymology of ἐπιστήμη, knowledge, its significance is to be derived from στάσις, 911,[1] placing "
(*Ibid*. bk. iv. 22). The motion attributed by
Plato to this word appears to be the motion of the
universe, for 651 is the diameter of a circle, whose
circumference is equal to the diameter of Saturn's
orbit, measured by the diameter of the sun ($651 \times 3\frac{1}{7}$
$= 2,046$). It is therefore, numerically, the name for
cosmic science. On the same principle BEBAION,
140, if a fraction be added, is the breadth of a
vesica formed by two intersecting circles 422
wide ; and a square 422 is enclosed by a rhombus
whose sides are 666. Further, a circle 141 in
diameter has a circumference of 443, the numerical
equivalent of Ὁ ΛΟΓΟΣ. The next word, ἹΣΤΟΡΙΑ,
has the value of 691, the length of the sun's orbit
measured by its own diameter. The word ΠΙΣΤΟΝ
yields 710 ; and 709, less a fraction, is the side of
a square whose diagonals are $(1,002 \times 2)$ 2,004,
the numerical equivalent of the four Greek names
of the elements. The number 709 is also the
measure of a cross ($354\frac{1}{2} \times 2 = 709$) expressing
the number of days in the Lunar Year. More-
over, by Gematria ΠΙΣΤΟΝ is equivalent to ΠΝΕΥΜΑ
ἍΓΙΟΝ, the Holy Ghost, or Third Person of the

---

[1] $912\frac{1}{2} \times 4 = 3,650 =$ radius of Saturn's orbit by Tonos.

Christian Trinity. MNHMH, 146, is equivalent by
Gematria to ΠΑΝΑΓΙΑ, an epithet applied to the
Virgin in the Greek Church.　A vesica 48⅔ wide
is produced by two intersecting circles, whose
width is 146, and 48⅔ is the square root of 2,368,
the numerical value of the name Jesus Christ.
Ἡ MNHMH has the value of 154, which is the side
of a square enclosed by the sun's orbit—the perimeter of this square being 616, a mystical number,
which appears in some early manuscripts of the
Apocalypse instead of the number 666.　The word
ἉΜΑΡΤΊΑ, again, brings out the number 453, and a
cross, whose limbs are each 226½, makes up the
length 453 (226½ × 2 = 453), and 226½ × 9½ =
2,151.　ΣΥΜΦΟΡΑ, 1,311, has the same numerical
value as Tetragammaton, whose numerical significance is dealt with elsewhere.　ΣΥΝΕΣΙΣ yields
1,065, which is about three times the number of
days in the Lunar Year ; and Ἡ ΣΥΝΕΣΙΣ, if colel
be added to each word, gives 1,075½, or the limb of
a cross which measures 2,151, the number of years
in the Great Month.　ἈΜΑΘΙΑ has the value of
62, and 62 × 9½ = 592 ; it is also the side of a
rhombus whose perimeter is 248, while ἈΚΟΛΑΣΙΑ
gives the number 333, a number equal to the
diagonal of the New Jerusalem, and the limb of a
cross which measures 666.

It may be said, that all these words by their
numerical value refer to motion, in having an
agreement with the measures of the celestial
bodies, in spite of the assurances of Plato that they
express rest and not motion.

The recurrence of the word ἐπιστήμη, and the
introduction of so many other words, which produce numbers representing important measures of
the heavenly bodies, and their orbits may very
reasonably justify the conclusion, that here, as in
so many other places, there is an allusion to the

scheme of the universe, and that, in the discussion of the origin of words, there is a mystical reference to their use, as symbols of the cosmic system, by means of their numerical value. The arguments as they stand are not convincing, and it is not likely that Plato would have written such a work as the "Kratylos," if it is to be taken unequivocally, as Mr. Jowett imagined, and without mystery of any kind. Neither Plato nor the Hebrew philosophers who declare that Adam was taught the Hebrew tongue that he might converse with God in Paradise, wrote those things, as we nowadays write a philological work, but both seem to have thought their story good enough for any one who knew no better than to believe it.

Clement of Alexandria, whose testimony has been already quoted, is said to have died A.D. 220, so that he lived about five hundred years after Plato. He was the first considerable writer of the Christian School, which was the final development of the philosophic eclecticism of the Greeks, and his opinions may be supposed to accurately reflect the prevailing views of the later theologists. He, along with the other Fathers, refers to the signification of names, and treats the subject exactly as Plato did. But while Plato was satisfied to indicate the measures of the universe simply as the thing to be known (ἘΠΙΣΤΗΜΗ, 651), the Christians intimated that the science of Nature was to be reached through the knowledge of the Cross, for Ἡ ΓΝΩΣΙΣ and ΣΤΑΥΡΟΣ have the same numerical value.

Gregory Thaumaturgus, Bishop of Neo-Cæsareia, an early Christian writer, called a near successor of the Apostles, speaking of the quality of names, ingeniously introduces a series of mystical numbers by means of certain words in his discourse upon the Trinity. " I see," he says, " in

all, three essentials—substance, genus, name. . . .
We speak of Father, Son, and Holy Spirit; these,
however, are not names, which have only super-
vened at some after period, but they are substances. Again, the denomination Man is not in
actual fact a denomination, but a substance common to men, and is the denomination common to
all men. Moreover, names such as these—'Αδάμ
[46], 'Αβραάμ [145], 'Ισαάκ [232], 'Ιακώβ [1] [833];
these I say are names. But the Divine Persons
are names indeed, and the names are still the
Persons; and the Persons then signify that which
is and subsists, which is the essence of God. . . .
The vocable word (logos) belongs to these three
genera of words, which are named in Scripture,
and which are not substantial, namely, the word
conceived ('ENNOIAN, 236), the word uttered (ΠΡΟ-
ΦΟΡΙΚΟΝ, 1,080), and the word articulated ('ΑΡΘΡΙ-
ΚΟΝ, 360)." The names of the Patriarchs we shall
speak of elsewhere, so it is only necessary to draw
attention to the three words emphasized at the end
of the paragraph. The first number, 236, is the
length of the side of the New Jerusalem. The
second number is 1,080, which is the number of
miles in the moon's radius. The third number,
360, is both the degrees in the circumference of
the earth, and the number of days in the Greek
year.

Origen also testifies as to the mysterious properties of names. He begins with a quotation
from Celsus in these words :—" Those herdsmen
and shepherds who followed Moses as their leader
had their minds deluded by vulgar deceits, and so
supposed that there was one God, named either
the Highest, or Adonai, or the Heavenly, or
Sabaoth, or called by some other of those names,

---

[1] Adam, Abraham, Isaak, Jacob.

which they delight to give this world; and they
knew nothing beyond that! And in a subsequent part of his work he says that 'it makes no
difference whether the God who is over all things
be called by the name Zeus, which is current
among the Greeks, or by that, *e.g.*, which is in use
among the Indians or Egyptians.' Now, in answer
to this, we have to remark, that this involves a
deep and mysterious subject, that, viz., respecting
the nature of names ; it being a question whether,
as Aristotle thinks, names were bestowed by
arrangement, or, as the Stoics hold, by nature. . . .
If, then, we shall be able to establish, in reference
to the preceding statement, the nature of powerful
names, some of which are used by the learned
among the Egyptians, or by the Magi among the
Persians, and by the Indian philosophers, called
Brahmans, or by the Samanæans, and others in
different countries ; and shall be able to make out
that the so-called magic is not, as the followers of
Epicurus and Aristotle suppose, an altogether
certain thing, but is, as those skilled in it prove, a
consistent system, having words which are known
to exceedingly few. Then, we say that the name
Sabaoth, and Adonai, and the other names treated
with so much reverence among the Hebrews, are
not applicable to any ordinary created things, but
belong to a secret theology which refers to the
Framer of all things" ("Against Celsus," bk. i.,
ch. xxiv.).

That the reader may follow the next section
with a clear mind, we now quote the exposition of
the Christian faith, defined with such perfect
lucidity by St. Athanasius: "And the Catholic
faith is this : that we worship one God in Trinity,
and Trinity in Unity ; neither confounding the
persons, nor dividing the substance. For there
is one Person of the Father, another of the Son,

and another of the Holy Ghost. But the god-
head of the Father, of the Son, and of the Holy
Ghost is all one ; the glory equal, the majesty co-
eternal. Such as the Father is, such is the Son :
and such is the Holy Ghost."

These being the opinions of the Fathers, we
are, at any rate, safe in judging their writings by
what Mr. Jowett calls "oriental ideas," for the
Gospel appears to have emanated directly from
the Alexandrian influences. It is, moreover, de-
monstrable that the threefold unity worshipped as
God by the new theologists merely exemplified
afresh the conceptions of the older philosophies of
Egypt and Greece finally brought together by the
conquests of Alexander the Great. Before the
Christian era, the Greeks had been in the habit of
summing up their theology in a Triad, or Tetrad
of symbolical persons, who, it appears, were always
analogous to the great Triad of the Cabala. Many
such combinations of names are to be found in
Plato's writings. In the "Timæus" the divine
Triad is called Θεός, Λόγος, and Ψυχή—God, the
Word, and the Soul. The Christian Fathers
identified these with their own Trinity, the
Father, the Son, and Holy Ghost. And when
the various names are reduced to numbers, it
will be evident that Plato and Moses, as the
Fathers declared, established their theology upon
a similar cosmic basis, each deriving the divine
names from the numbers which occur in the Holy
Oblation, the New Jerusalem and the other
canonical figures.

The three names of the Platonic Triad have the
following values :

$$\Theta\text{EO}\Sigma \quad \ldots \ldots \quad 284 + 1$$

$$\Lambda\text{O}\Gamma\text{O}\Sigma \quad \ldots \ldots \quad 373 + 1 \left.\right\} \; 2,083$$

$$\Psi\text{Y}\text{X}\text{H} \quad \ldots \ldots \quad 1,708 + 1$$

$$2,365 + 3 = 2,368$$

$$\Theta\text{EO}\Sigma \quad \ldots \quad 284$$

$$\Lambda\text{O}\Gamma\text{O}\Sigma \quad \ldots \quad 373$$

$$657 - 1 = 656 \; \text{ME}\Sigma\Sigma\text{IA}\Sigma.$$

It would, perhaps, be impossible to illustrate the doctrine of the Trinity more ingeniously than by those names and their corresponding numbers. For 284, representing the first person, the Father, or Macrocosm, is the diameter of a circle 892 in circumference, and 891 is the numerical equivalent of 'OYPANOΣ, Heaven. Accordingly the numbers deduced from those two words being each the measure of one circle, God and Heaven are presented to us as one and the same—a conception admirably set forth by the rest of the numbers. Then 284 is the width of a vesica $492\frac{4}{5}$ long, and this is the width of a vesica 853 long, which in its turn is the width of another 1,480 long. So the name, Theos, the god of the Pagan and Christian Greeks, expresses, in a roundabout way, the same number and the same meaning, as the name Christos, 1,480.

The second and third persons, called Logos and Psyche, represent the twofold body of the Microcosm, and are appropriately symbolized by the number 2,083, the side of the Holy Oblation containing the seven planets and the sublunary world.

The sum of the three numbers, when colel is added to each, is the ever-recurring 2,368, which the Christians afterwards adopted as the complete name of God, expressed by the letters 'IHΣOYΣ XPIΣTOΣ, Jesus Christ.

It is plain that the threefold deity of Plato embodies in the persons of the Triad the three parts of the universe called :

			ἘΜΠΥΡΕΙΟΝ .	760
ἘΜΠΥΡΕΙΟΝ .	760		᾽ΑΙΘΗΡ . . .	128
᾽ΑΙΘΗΡ . . .	128			———
ΣΤΟΙΧΕΙΑ . .	1,196			888
	———			
	2,084		ΘΕΟΣ . . .	284
			ΣΤΟΙΧΕΙΑ . .	1,196
				———
				1,480

And since the sum of these numbers is 2,084, it was unnecessary for a Greek to specify the measures of the cosmos otherwise than by repeating the three names.

According to some of the old cosmographers there was a region beyond the Empyreum. This was called by the Cabalists Ain Soph, or limitless expansion, an impossible conception usually ascribed as an attribute of God. If, therefore, we add the word Θεός, God, as symbolizing this infinite region, beyond the three lower and nearer divisions, which manifest the Deity to us in a more comprehensible manner, we shall extend the universe to four parts. And 284 (Θεός) added to 2,084 makes 2,368 as the numerical value of the Tetrad. Again, the sum of 760 and 128 is 888, and 1,196 + 284 = 1,480, so that from the names of the four divisions of the universe there are produced the numbers which, as will now be shown, determined the names of the great gods of antiquity, and thus labelled them as personifications of specific parts of the cosmic system.

The Christian Trinity, composed in like manner, yields the number 2,047 (when colel is deducted from each name), which is the diameter of Saturn's orbit measured by the diameter of the sun.

Ό ΠΑΤΗΡ . . . .   559 − 1
Ο ΎΙΟΣ . . . . .   750 − 1
ΚΑΙ ΠΝΕΥΜΑ ʽΑΓΙΟΝ   741 − 1
─────────
2,050 − 3 = 2,047.

In works of art the Trinity was most often represented by Jesus on the cross, supported by John
and Mary. The three names combined thus bring
out 2,151, the number of years occupied by the sun
in each of the twelve signs, during the precession
of the equinoxes, or great year,

ʼΙΗΣΟΥΣ . .   888
ʼΙΩΑΝΗΣ . .   1,069 + 1 $\Big\}$ 1,263 = 2,163
ΜΑΡΙΑΜ . .   192 + 1

─────────
2,149 + 2 = 2,151

and exhibit the Messiah stretched within the
Holy Oblation containing the sphere of the
Zodiac and seven planets.

It has already been explained that the value of
the name Christos, 1,480, being the side of a square
inscribed within the Zodiac or fixed stars, gives
the measure of his body, extended in the form
of a cross throughout the whole universe. Surrounded thus by the twelve signs, he represents
the Messiah, or periodic Divinity, connected with
the cycle of the great precessional period of 25,816
years. A month of this great year is 2,151 years
$\left(\dfrac{25,816}{12} = 2,151\right)$, and it is supposed that the
ancients accepted the particular sign, in which the
sun rose at the vernal equinox, during this cycle,
as the symbol of the Messiah. It is thought to
be on this account that the Egyptians worshipped
the black and white bulls, Apis and Mnevis, as
emblems of the Deity, when the sun was in
Taurus, while the Greeks probably called their

Zeus, 'ΑΜΜΩΝ (Ammon), and gave him the head
of a ram, when the sun entered the sign Aries.
For Ammon has the value of 931, and 932·10 is
the length of a rhombus having a perimeter of
2,151. This heralding of a new Messiah, every
month of the Great Year, had a peculiarly mystical
meaning. For having conceived the universe in
the likeness of a woman, they made their image or
type to conform literally to the original or archetype, and looked forward with joyful expectation
to the fulfilment of time, when a new Saviour
would come, and symbolically purge the sins of
the world, and accomplish its renewal and regenera-
tion.[1]

We have seen that the twelve signs of the
Zodiac, according to Villalpanda's diagram of the
camp were identified with the twelve tribes of the
Israelites. The twelve tribes were considered by
the old theologians to prefigure the twelve apostles,
who were also said to be analogous to the signs of
the Zodiac. In the first century the sun had
passed from the Ram to the sign of the Fishes.
Now, taking the order of the apostles as it is given
by St. Mark (ch. iii.), and supposing Petros, the
fisherman, to correspond to Ἰχθύες (the fishes) the
names of the apostles represent sequence of the
signs in the new epoch, as follows :

March	Ram	Κριός	400	♓	Πέτρος	755
April	Bull	Ταῦρος	1071	♈	Ἰακωβος	1103
May	Twins	Δίδυμοι	538	♉	Ἰωανης	1069
June	Crab	Καρκίνος	471	♊	Ἀνδρέας	361
July	Lion	Λέων	885	♋	Φίλιππος	980
August	Virgin	Παρθένος	515	♌	Βαρθολομαῖος	603
September	Scales	Χηλαί	649	♍	Ματθαῖος	340
October	Scorpion	Σκορπίος	750	♎	Θωμας	1050
November	Archer	Τοξευτής	1343	♏	Ἰακωβος	1103
December	Goat	Ἀιγοκερως	1209	♐	Θαδδαῖος	299
January	Waterman	Ὑδροχόος	1514	♑	Σίμων	1100
February	Fishes	Ἰχθύες	1224	♒	Ἰούδας Ἰσκαριώθ	1835
			10,569			10,598

[1] Consult Mr. Massey's "Natural Genesis" on this subject.

Accordingly, when the Logos is stretched cross-wise in the Zodiacal circle, so that the Ram occupies the vernal equinox, his hands and feet, extended to the four corners of the circumference, are in the signs of the Bull, the Lion, the Scorpion, and the Waterman—the four signs which correspond to the four beasts symbolizing the evangelists. The names of the apostles analogous to these in the new cycle are, Ἰάκωβος, Φίλιππος, Θώμας, and Σίμων. The name δώδεκα (twelve), so frequently applied to the disciples in the New Testament, very fitly expresses their true significance by the number 834, which is the side of a rhombus 1,446 long, or the side of the square contained in the orbit of Saturn, encircled by the twelve signs.

The number deduced from the twelve pagan names of the Zodiac, is the perimeter of a rhombus 2,642 wide, which is produced by two intersecting circles with a united width of 7,926, or the number of miles in the equatorial diameter of the earth. Accordingly, the number 10,569 affords the means of correctly determining the distance of the twelve signs on a terrestrial globe.

The apostles, again, belonged to the theological system of the Gospel, which presents the mythos in the third manner (St. Clement), and on that account they set forth the measure of the sublunary world, the symbol of the third person of the Triad. For the sum of the twelve names is 10,598, or the circumference of the moon's orbit divided twice by twelve ($3,372 \times 3\frac{1}{7} = 10,597$).

The Greek Zodiac, therefore, may be said to denote the solar year, while the apostles of Messiah, 656, signify a lunar month, or lunar year.

Moreover, by the cabalistic process of trans-position, the number 10,569 may become 10,596 $+ 1 = 10,597$ and is equal to $10,598 - 1 = 10,597$,

therefore the great Zodiac and the twelve disciples
of Christos are analogous to one another.

ΊΗΣΟΥΣ (Jesus) yields the number 888, which is
the length of a rhombus having a perimeter of
2,046, the diameter of Saturn's orbit. And a circle,
whose circumference is 888 contains the square of
the New Jerusalem.

The Holy Ghost, the third person of the Christian Trinity, corresponds to the Bride of the
Cabala, and properly personifies the sublunary
world or four elements, and as the embodiment of
the receptive and reproductive principle in generation, she symbolized the earth, the mother of all
living creatures. Now, ΤΟ ΠΝΕΥΜΑ ʹΑΓΙΟΝ (the
Holy Ghost) has the value of 1,080, which is the
number of miles in the moon's radius. She is
thus also a personification of the moon, whom the
ancients regarded as the wife or sister of the sun.
Again, ΠΝΕΥΜΑ ʹΑΓΙΟΝ, without the article, yields
(deducting colel from each name) 708, and a
saltire drawn within a square, whose sides are
708⅔, measures (1,002 × 2 =) 2,004, the numerical
value of the Greek names of the elements.[1]   The
number 708 is also the measure of a cross whose
limbs are 354 long, the number of days in the
lunar year.   The name was also sometimes written
ΤΟ ʹΑΓΙΟΝ ΤΟ ΠΝΕΥΜΑ, which gives the number 1,450: and, if colel be deducted from each
word, the remainder is 1,446, the side of a square
contained within the orbit of Saturn. By this
number she is manifested as an image of the whole
material universe, and corresponds to the ψῦχή τοῦ
κόσμου, the Soul of the World, described by Plato.
The Bride, likened by St. John in the Apocalypse
to the Heavenly City, the new Jerusalem, is
another figure of the Holy Ghost, and 710 (Πνεῦμα

---

[1] See chapter vi.; p. 142.

Ἅγιον) is the length of a vesica 409⅔ broad, and 409$\frac{1}{15}$ is the length of a second vesica whose breadth is 236, the length of the wall in each of the four sides of the celestial city. Robert Flood has beautifully illustrated the figure of this heavenly woman, standing in the midst of the cosmos with her feet upon the elements, and her head reaching up to the firmament ("Utriusque cosmi majoris scilicet et minoris . . . historia," 1617).

There were also various other names applied to the Christian Trinity singly or collectively. The word Κυριος, Lord, for instance, has the value of 800, which is the perimeter of the New Jerusalem, within the wall (200 × 4 = 800). None of the names given to Christ was more often used than that of the Saviour and ὁ Σωτηρ, if colel be added to each word, yields 1,480. Jesus was said to be a Nazarite, and he is frequently called Jesus of Nazareth. Now the word Ναζυραῖος yields 1,239, which is the width of a vesica 2,151 long.

It is evident that the numbers obtained from all these names are simple cosmic measures derived geometrically from the canonical figures of the Holy Oblation, the city of Ezekiel, and the New Jerusalem, identifying the Deity with the measures of the universe.

To return to the "Kratylos," an analysis of the statements which are made there with reference to the names of the Greek Deities suggests, that the same mystical principle of naming the Gods existed among the Greeks. Plato says, that there was reason in the Athenians calling "the essence of all things ΕΣΤΙΑ, 516." Now the numbers 511·5 and 520·83 are respectively the sides of rhombi whose perimeters are 2,046, the diameter of Saturn's orbit, and 2,083·33 the side of the Holy Oblation. And the 516·16 being the mean number between the two, may be very properly said to represent the sphere of the fixed stars, which was supposed by the old philosophers to contain the vital essence of all existing things, and was symbolized by the Christians in the name Christos, 1,480, who was supposed to be extended crosswise within this sphere.

The name 'HPA, 109, he says, "may have been given, when the legislator was thinking of the heavens, and may be only a disguise of the air ($\dot{\alpha}\acute{\eta}\rho$), putting the end in place of the beginning. You will recognize the truth of this, if you repeat the letters of 'HPH, 116, several times over." Now 109 is the mean radius of the sun's orbit, its distance from the earth being from 108 to 110 of its own diameters. 'HPH again has the value of 116. And $116\frac{1}{2}$ is the diameter of a circle 365, the number of days in a year. And when he tells us to repeat the letters several times over, he apparently means the numbers, which are the equivalents of the letters, for all the following multiples of 116 are mystical numbers. $116 \times 2 = 232$, $116 \times 6 = 696$, $116 \times 7 = 812$, $116 \times 8 = 928$, and $116 \times 9 = 1,044$. These numbers will be referred to, and explained further on. For the present, it is enough to say that Hera was the wife or feminine part of the androgynous Zeus, whose name we shall now proceed to examine. To use Plato's own words, "the name of Zeus has an excellent meaning although hard to understand, because really like a sentence which is divided into two parts; for some call him ZHN, and use one half, and others who use the other half call him ZEYΣ; the two together signify the nature of the God." And he further declares, that these names are appropriate to, and symbolize "the God, through whom all creatures always have life." The numerical value of this double name is 677, that is, ZHN, 65, + ZEYΣ, 612 = 677, and we have

been told that its meaning is "hard to understand."
Nevertheless, by the help of geometry, it may be
possible to discover Plato's intention. The division of the God into two is evidently intended to
exhibit his androgynous nature, the double name
Zen-Zeus being equivalent to the Hebrew Elohim,
the twofold Deity of creation. The number 677,
when colel is added and abstracted, produces the
numbers 676 and 678. The first of these is the
square of 26, the value of Tetragammaton, while
678 is the length of the sun's orbit ($216 \times 3\frac{1}{7} =$
678), the former number having a feminine and
the latter a masculine significance.

The four letters, which compose the name ΖΕΥΣ,
have been supposed to be analagous to the Tetragammaton of the Jews, accordingly it may be
received, in a geometrical sense, as an illustration
of the square or rhombus. Among the Romans
and Italians of the Middle Ages, Zeus was identified with the planet Jupiter, and we find in the
series of the planets, designed by Baldini, that
Jupiter sits in his chariot on a cube, or square
seat. He is also depicted thus, in the edition of
Hyginus, printed at Venice in 1488. This quadrangular form, as an attribute of Zeus, is traceable
to the number 612, for a square, whose sides are
153 ($153 \times 4 = 612$), is just contained within the
sun's orbit, so that the great God of the Greeks,
by the numerical value of his name, in exemplifying
the measure of the sun's course, may fitly be received as the symbol of that animating power,
which flows from the sun, and gives life to all
things. Apparently in imitation of this, the Christians afterwards perpetuated the same conception,
by similarly placing Christos in a square, within
the sphere of the firmament. Such a striking
geometrical parallel between the two great gods
of antiquity is not likely to be an accidental cir-

cumstance, exhibiting no community of purpose
on the part of the legislators, as Plato calls them,
who devised and established the Greek and Christian theological systems. The number 612 was
also a mystical number among the Hebrews, who,
by adding colel, produced the number 613. There
are 354 days in the lunar year, and a vesica 354
wide is 613·6 long; the two intersecting arcs of
which it is composed measuring 741·417. The
diameter of the two circles is 708, and their united
width is 1,062. The numbers produced from this
diagram are certainly remarkable. In the first
place 354 is the number of days in the lunar year,
and the equivalent of ὁ Θεος; secondly, 708 is the
side of a square whose diagonals are 2,004, the
numerical equivalent of the names of the four
elements (see p. 142), and also of the Holy Ghost,
Πνευμα Ἁγιον; thirdly, 741·416 is the circumference
of a circle whose diameter is 236, the side of the
New Jerusalem; lastly, the circumference of the
vesica is 1,482·832, or with a small reduction, 1,480.

"The meaning of the name ᾽ΑΠΟΛΛΩΝ, 1,061,
will be moving together, whether in the poles of
heaven, as they are called, or in the harmony of
song, which is termed concord, because he moves
altogether by an harmonious power, as astronomers
and musicians ingeniously declare." By the
numerical value of the name ᾽Απόλλων, the Sun God
appears to be the counterpart of Zeus, for a vesica
612 wide is 1,061 long; therefore each brother
appears to be the complement of the other, and the
sum of their names is (612 + 1,061 =) 1,673 or 1 less
than the side of a square whose diagonal is 2,368.

The name ᾽ΑΡΤΕΜΙΣ yields 656. The moon was
of course regarded as the wife as well as the sister
of the sun, but in either case the two together
represent the double potency in generation. The
sides of a triangle whose perimeter is 656 are 218⅔,

or the diameter of the sun's orbit. This triangle, being a symbol of the sun, or the male power of the universe, may possibly account for the worship of Artemis under the name of Orthia at Sparta. Artemis was also specially regarded as the protectress of cities and streets, presumably because the geometricians found out that a rhombus whose sides are 656·85 contains a square 416⅔, or the city of Ezekiel. Again, by Gematria, Artemis is equivalent to Messias, one of the names applied to Christos in the gospel. "The name of the Muses (Μοῦσα) and Music would seem to be derived from their making philosophical inquiries (μόσθαι), and ΛΗΤΩ, 1,138, is called by this name, because she is such a gentle goddess, and so willing (ἐθελημόν) to grant our requests; or her name may be Λнθω, as she is often called by strangers: they seem to imply by it her amiability and her smooth and easy-going way of behaving. Artemis is named from her healthy (ἀρτεμής) well ordered nature, and because of her love of virginity, and perhaps because she is proficient in virtue (ἀρετή). Numerically the names, Leto and Artemis, would seem to have a similar significance, for a rhombus 656·85 broad is 1,138·68 long, and this rhombus contains the city of Ezekiel, which may be referred to in the legend of the birth of Leto's twins on the floating island called Asteria, the starry. It is said that the island suddenly stood still, being borne up by four pillars, which possibly refer to the four orbits of Mercury inclosed within the mystical city. By Gematria Leto is equivalent to ΔΕΛΦΥΣ, 1,139, the womb, and would thus appear to be the goddess who personates the cosmic mother, or the feminine essence of creation, and was worshipped as an embodiment of the matter of the universe. The legend of her retreat to the floating island of Delos, 312 (vesica 312 : 540 × 4 =

2,160), appears to identify her with the tenth step of the Cabala, for this step is hung to the figure containing the other nine steps by a chain, or properly a canal, so it might be legitimately likened to an island.

When Hermogenes asks, "What is the meaning of Dionysos and Aphrodite?" Socrates answers, "Son of Hipponicus, you ask a solemn question; there is a serious and also a facetious explanation of both these names; the *serious explanation is not to be had from me*." The mysterious explanation which Socrates declines to divulge, may possibly lie in the following geometrical problems, derived from the numbers of the names. Dionysos was spelt in two ways, ΔΙΟΝΥΣΟΣ, 1,004, and ΔΙΩΝΥΣΟΣ, 1,734. Now these two numbers are to one another in the ratio, or very nearly so, of 26 to 15, for a rhombus 1,001 wide is 1,734 long; accordingly they afford a parallel to the names Zeus and Apollo, and Leto and Artemis. The rhombus was one of the attributes of Dionysos, carried in the processions at the celebrations of his orgies; for although his usual attribute was the phallus, he was a masculo-feminine god. It has been shown that the number 1,002 may be taken to be one of the limbs of a cross measuring 2,004, or the numerical value of the four elements, so that the name Dionysos implies that he was a personification of the Logos described in the "Timæus." Another reason why he may be appropriately symbolized by a cross is given in the following chapter, p. 148. He was the wine-god of the Greeks, being called by Plato "giver of wine;" and Ὁ ΟΙΝΟΣ yields 470, the diameter of a circle whose circumference is 1,480. This seems to bear out the identity of this god with the Christos, recognized by the Gnostics, and his identification with the seasons of the year, and the equinoxes may also be attributed to the numbers of his name.   By Gematria, Dionysos is equivalent to ΣΑΒΑΩ, 1,004.

The value of the name Aphrodite is 993, and Plato connects her with Dionysos, 1,004, possibly because 1,004 added to 994 makes 1,998, the width of the two intersecting circles, which produce a vesica 666 broad.   Again 994 is the perimeter of a rhombus 248½ wide, and the vesica enclosing it has a circumference of 1,041⅓, or the radius of the sphere of the firmament inscribed within the Holy Oblation.   As the personification of the great feminine principle of nature, she ought to be connected with the earth.   This is expressed in the number 991, which is the side of a rhombus having a perimeter of 3,964, the radius of the earth measured in miles.   But Aphrodite had also a masculine significance ; for while she was adored as the essence of all beauty, grace, and feminine fruitfulness, there was also strangely worshipped under her name a masculine power.   Her image, which in her feminine aspect personated every womanly perfection, was set up in Crete and elsewhere in the form of a crude stake, roughly carved into the semblance of a human body, and her face disfigured with an unsightly beard.   This monstrous idol may also be referred to the number 248 (see "Cabala," Greater Holy Assembly, 968). Hesiod derived the name from Ἀφρός, 871 (foam), which is the perimeter of a square whose sides are equal to the diameter of the sun's orbit.   By Gematria ἀφρός is equivalent to χάος, the primæval matter from which all things were generated.

With respect to Athene, Plato says : " Modern interpreters . . . assert, that Homer meant by Athene mind and intelligence. . . . This is she, who has the mind of God, Θεοῦ (484), νόησις (538)." These two words both bring out mystical numbers, 484 being the width of a vesica formed by the

intersection of two circles whose circumferences
are 3,042 the diagonal of a square 2,151 (968 ×
$3\frac{1}{7} = 3,042$), and 538 is the side of a rhombus
having a perimeter of 2,152. The name Pallas, he
says, "is derived from armed dances. For the
elevation of one's self or anything else above the
earth . . . we call dancing (πάλλειν)." ΠΑΛΛΑΣ
has the value of 342, and a rhombus having a
perimeter of 1,368 is 342 on its sides, and 1,368
is the width of a vesica 2,368 long. Again 341 ×
6 = 2,046, the diameter of Saturn's orbit. ᾿ΑΘΗΝΗ
yields 76, which is the square root of 5,776, or the
limb of a cross which measures 11,552, or the
sun's distance measured by the diameter of the
earth; and 76, with the addition of a fraction, is
the square root 5,920, or the perimeter of the
square 1480. It will be enough to notice here
that the name of this mysterious goddess of the
Athenians exhibits those numbers which afterwards are found so prominently in the Christian
theology. Some other characteristics of this
goddess will be considered, in reference to her
great temple on the Acropolis.

Hermogenes asks, " But what is Σελήνη (moon)?
Soc. That name is rather unfortunate for Anax-
agoras. *Her.* How so? *Soc.* The word seems to
forestall his recent discovery, that the moon receives
her light from the sun." Now ῾Η ΣΕΛΗΝΗ has the
numerical value of 309, which is the diagonal of a
square inclosing the sun's orbit, which is possibly
what Socrates refers to; and a rhombus, 309
broad, is 535 long and 535 is the value of ΚΤΕΙΣ,
a word used for the womb by the Greeks (Clement
of Alexandria); and 309 is $\frac{1}{7}$ of the moon's diameter
in miles (309 × 7 = 2,163). " Then surely Pan,
who is the declarer of all things (πάν), and the
perpetual mover (ἀεί πολων, 1,046) of all things, is
rightly called ᾿Αιπόλος, 461 (goatherd), he being the

two-formed son of Hermes, smooth in his upper part, and rough and goat-like in his lower regions. And as the son of Hermes he is speech, or the brother of speech, and that brother should be like brother is no marvel." The name Pan, everything, has the value of 131, and a square, which has a perimeter of 130 is $32\frac{1}{2}$ on its sides, and 32·35 is the square root of $1{,}046\frac{1}{2}$, the radius of the circle containing the square 1,480 within the Holy Oblation. Then 130 is the diameter of a circle having a circumference of 408·4, which is the length of a vesica whose width is 235·3, the length of the wall on each side of the New Jerusalem.

Hermes yields the number 353, or one less than the number of days in the lunar year. Again, 353 is the perimeter of a square whose sides are $88\frac{1}{4}$, or the space between the tropics measured by the diameter of the sun. And 353 is the diameter of a circle whose circumference is 1,110, which is the numerical value of the name Microprosopos, the second person of the cabalistic triad. Therefore Hermes appears to symbolize the lunar year, and the measure of the ecliptic, thus symbolizing the masculo-feminine nature of the Logos. From ἙΡΜΑΙΟΣ, another spelling of the name, the number 426 is obtained. A square whose sides are 426 is contained in a rhombus whose sides are 671, the numerical equivalent of Adonai; and $425 \times 3 = 1{,}275$.

Ares has the value of 309, which is the diagonal of a square inclosing the sun's orbit; and $309\frac{3}{4}$ is the side of a rhombus having a perimeter of 1,239, and this number is the width of a vesica 2,151 long.

Poseidon yields the number 1,219, which is the circumference of a circle whose diameter is 388, the numerical equivalent of ὁ Ἥλιος, the sun; and a vesica 388 wide is 672 long, or one more than the value of ΤΗΟRA. A vesica formed of two circles 1,219 in circumference contains the sphere

of the Zodiac, taking the sun's distance at 10
(194 : 335$\frac{11}{20}$). This god was also called ΠΟΤΕΙΔΑΝ,
520, or one less than the side of a rhombus whose
perimeter is equal to the side of the Holy Oblation ; and the length of this rhombus is 901, the
number of ὁ φαλλός. By Gematria, ΠΟΣΕΙΔΩΝ is
equivalent to ΊΧΘΥΣ, a fish.

The value of ΠΕΡΣΕΦΟΝΕΙΑ is 1,026, which is the
length of a rhombus whose perimeter is 2,368.
And 1,024 is the radius of Saturn's orbit. She
is sometimes called ΚΟΡΗ, 198, or ΚΟΥΡΗ, 598 ;
198 is equivalent to $\frac{2,368}{12} = 197\frac{1}{3}$, and 598 is the
circumference of Saturn's orbit, taking the sun's
distance at 10. Persephone is therefore the
feminine counterpart of the deity representing the
number 2,368.

Heracles yields 370, or the side of a rhombus
whose perimeter is 1,480.

Before the final establishment of the Christian
religion, when its ultimate form was still uncertain,
some of those who had severed themselves from
the old pagan cults worshipped the deity under
the name of Iao. And it was probably a doubtful
question, for some time, whether the votaries of
Iao would prevail over those who advocated the
claims of Christos. However, the popularity of
Iao did not last very long, and it is now many
centuries since altars were raised to this god. The
numerical value of ΙΑΩ is 811, and this is found to
be the circumference of a circle 258$\frac{1}{3}$ in diameter.
Now the Greek name of the tenth step of the
Cabala was Βασιλεία, the kingdom, a word of very
frequent occurrence in the New Testament, as,
for instance, in the Lord's Prayer, " Thy Kingdom
come." And ΒΑΣΙΛΕΙΑ yields 259, and Ἡ ΒΑΣΙΛΕΙΑ
has the value of 267. And 266$\frac{2}{3}$ is the diameter
of a circle whose area is equal to that of the New

Jerusalem, so that this name may appropriately stand for the Bride whom St. John saw coming down from heaven. But Iao has still other significations, for $811\frac{2}{3}$ is the diameter of a circle whose circumference is 2,550, and this is the measure of the limbs of a cross 1,275 long ($1,275 \times 2 = 2,550$). Again, the three letters written in full bring out the number 2,492, which is the perimeter of a triangle whose sides are 831, the numerical value of Macrocosmos.

ΣΑΒΑΩΘ is a name sometimes found in conjunction with ʼΙΑΩ. It is a translation of the Hebrew word which means "armies," and has the value of 1,013, which is also the number of the name Πρωτόγονος, the Orphic Adam, or first man. Now $1,014 \times 3 = 3,042$ the diagonal of a square 2,151. Protogonos was produced from an egg, which Bryant declares was an emblem of the Ark. At any rate an Ark whose perimeter is 2,368 is 1,014 long. The names IAO SABAOTH yield 1,824, which is the measure of a cross whose limbs are 912 $\left(\dfrac{1,824}{2} = 912\right)$.

As it would require a Hebrew scholar to deal properly with the names and words of that language, very little can be said here with respect to the Jewish scriptures. It is possible, however, to mention a few facts which seem conclusively to support the principle of numeration which has been pointed out in the case of the Greek writings.

Whatever doubt may exist as to the knowledge of the Cabala among other peoples, there can be no question as to its use among the Jews. This circumstance makes the Jewish law the chief source of mystical knowledge, on account of its completeness, for supposing the Homeric poems to be earlier in point of time, the Law of Moses, being accompanied by the ancient traditional commentaries preserved in the Cabala and Talmud, is provided with the key which is required to unlock its secrets, while all similar aids to the understanding of the Greek poems are lost. In this respect the Hebrew writings stand alone, but it may be that there is in the Romish and Eastern Churches some remnant of the old oral tradition which is still handed down and preserved in silence.

When, therefore, the same analysis, already applied to the names of the Greek gods, is extended to those given to the Deity by the Hebrews, it would appear that both peoples regarded the universe as the emblem of God, and each formulated a theology, founded upon the same numbers and symbols. In view of the entire lack of reliable evidence, it would be useless to attempt to decide whether the Greeks borrowed from the Hebrews, as the Fathers declare, or whether the Hebrews borrowed from the Greeks. It is more probable that each derived their knowledge from the Egyptians independently. And it will be enough to remember that the Jews, who make such pretensions to antiquity, have absolutely nothing to show in support of such an ancient origin.

The name of God, most highly venerated amongst the Jews was that written with the four letters IHVH. The name was considered to be too holy and sacred to be spoken. Its communication to Moses, upon the Mount, was regarded as the supreme revelation of the secret and mysterious nature of the Deity, and the knowledge of its pronunciation was the great *arcanum* of the Jewish Church, only known to the high priest. The pious Jew was taught to pause when he came to this name in reading the Law, or to say the name Adonai in its stead. By Christians it was generally called Tetragrammaton, or the Tetrad. The numerical value of IHVH is 26; but the number

of the letters gave it the value of the number 4.
According to the ancient computation, 4 was
equivalent to 10 because $1 + 2 + 3 + 4 = 10$, and
10 was equivalent to 1, because $1 + 0 = 1$.
Regarded as the number 4 it typified the elements
and cardinal points of the universe, and conse-
quently the Cross or Omphalos at the centre of
the world; it also denoted the Logos, and the
Bride or tenth step of the Cabala—she who was
the great mother, the earth, and the city of the
New Jerusalem, called Adonai by the Hebrews.
Finally, the number 26 connects this aspect of the
Deity with that mysterious symbol, the Vesica
Piscis, for the proportion of this figure is 26 to 15.
The number 26 is also the square root of the
length of the sun's orbit ($26^2 = 676$ and $216 \times 3\frac{1}{7} =$
678). This name was considered to be the same
as the Tetractys of the Pythagoreans, which they
regarded as the foundation of all things. In fact, by
its various aspects, the IHVH of the Jews epitomized
the whole mystery of the old theology, and represents
the body and soul of creation. It may be viewed
as the symbol of God, seen in the sun, the earth, the
whole universe, or as the powers of creation, symbolized by the three persons of the cabalistic triad.

It has been already pointed out that the ten
steps of the Cabala are jointed together according
to the proportion of a vesica, the symbol of Tetragrammaton, 1,311. Now the whole ten names, if
reduced to numbers and added together, amount
to 2,868, which is the circumference of a circle 912
in diameter. The number 912 is the value of the
name Prometheus, who is an exact counterpart of
the Hebrew Adam Kadmon, or supernal Adam,
in whose person the ten steps were symbolically
manifested. By comparing the character and adventures attributed to Prometheus by the Greeks,
it will be seen that he was to them what the

Messiah was to the Hebrews and Christians. The Messiah, of course, was the philosophical creation of the cabalistic sages, personified as a historical person for the benefit of the populace, and this being, as portrayed in the drama of Æschylus, is the Greek conception of the Mediator, who brings life and salvation to mortals, under the symbol of Fire. The Greek play is essentially religious in its purpose, and is a kind of dramatic gospel, corresponding to the Mystery Plays, acted by Christians in the Middle Ages. It is written in lofty language, calculated to inspire the audience with a religious awe, in spite of the singular nature of the myth. The attitude of the poet appears to be reverent and sincere. Like Christ, Prometheus was made to suffer innocently at the hands of the Father. For Jesus was crucified to expiate the crime of Adam, who disobeyed the Elohim, while Prometheus was chained to the rock, on the pretext of his having brought down the divine fire to mortals against the will of Zeus. Both were blameless in their lives, and devoted themselves to instruct and aid mankind. In the play Prometheus is made to say, "And verily I discovered for them Numbers, the surpassing all inventions." And he bestowed the benefit of fire upon men by means of the Narthex (Fennel-rod), "which has shown itself a teacher of every art to mortals, and a great resource." It was the counterpart of the cross of Christ. The numerical value of Νάρθηξ is 228, or the side of a rhombus whose perimeter is 912, which seems to trebly accentuate this number, which is again found in the name Kaukasos, 912, where the giant was bound over a great cleft in the rocks. Now 228 by $9\frac{1}{2} = 2,166$, or very nearly the number of miles in the diameter of the moon. The artificer of the gods, to whom was imputed an exquisite and marvellous skill in smith-work and other crafts, was named Hephaistos, 1,289, a number which is the diagonal of a square whose sides are 912. He only differed from Prometheus (912) in that he guided the hand of the artisan, in contradistinction to the god, who taught men letters and the intellectual arts. His wife, too, was called 911 (Χάρις), so we may suppose that all artistic handiwork was inspired by the wisdom of this number.

The point of the myth appears to be that Prometheus, or the hollow reed, was the mediator between heaven and earth who transmitted the mystic fire from the moon, which is the lowest heaven. The fire, being the highest of the elements, reached up to the lunar orb, and was therefore made to symbolize the celestial essence or spark of divine life, conveyed to mortals by the deity. But a more comprehensive meaning may be attached to the number 912, for if the sun's distance be taken at 10, the radius of Saturn's orbit measures 95, and $95 \times 9\frac{1}{2} = 902$, or 1 more than the value of ὁ φαλλός, and the radius of a circle inscribed within the Holy Oblation measures, to the same scale, 97, and $96 \times 9\frac{1}{2} = 912$; thus Prometheus personifies the radius or rod, which measures the whole world. The Hebrews, like the Greeks, attributed the act of mediatorship to many persons, each of whom was a personification of the Messiah, in some aspect or another. Thus Adam, Noah, Abraham, and Moses are all conspicuous embodiments of some fact in the Jewish philosophy. The Christian mythologists recognized an affinity between Prometheus and Noah as may be seen from the opinions of Vossius (see Gale, "Court of the Gen." vol. i., p. 185) and Bryant ("Myth." vol. iii., p. 7, etc.). Bochart and Stillingfleet, again, discover an analogy between Magog and Prometheus (Gale, p. 187), and many other similarities of this kind could be pointed out.

The identification of these persons can only be perceived from a knowledge of the philosophical ideas which gave rise to the myths, and this recognition of identity, between seemingly diverse deities, is not the result of ignorance on the part of the mythologists, as people nowadays imagine, but is due to a knowledge which we moderns no longer possess, for persons as well as things may be used as symbols, and such persons were symbolically introduced into the old histories to embody the ideas of the philosophical theology.

The names, by which the ten steps of the Cabala were known, are as follows :

$$689 \begin{cases} 1 & \text{KThR} & . & 620 \\ 2 & \text{ChKMH} & . & 73 \\ 3 & \text{BINH} & . & . & 67 \end{cases} \Big\} 760 - 3 = 757$$

$$\begin{cases} 4 & \text{ChSD} & . & . & 72 \\ 5 & \text{GBVRH} & . & 216 \\ 6 & \text{ThPAPTh} & 1,081 \\ 7 & \text{NTzCh} & . & 148 \\ 8 & \text{HVD} & . & . & 15 \\ 9 & \text{ISUD} & . & . & 80 \end{cases} \Big\} 1,612$$

$$10 \quad \text{MLKVTh} \quad 496$$

$$2,868 = (913 \times 3\tfrac{1}{7}).$$

KThR .	620
ChKMH	73
BINH .	67
ChSD .	72

$$832 \times 9\tfrac{1}{2} = 7,904.$$

As pointed out by Menasseh ben Israel, BRASHITH, the first word of the Mosaic Law, has the value of 913, and by Gematria, this is equivalent to the Hebrew expression, " He created the Law," therefore 2,868, the sum of the numbers deduced from the names of the ten cabalistic steps, being the circumference of a circle whose diameter is nearly 913 $(913 \times 3\tfrac{1}{7} = 2,869)$, the word BRASHITH by its numerical value implies, that the Law was founded upon the ten steps. A rhombus whose perimeter is 2,868 is 717 on each of its sides, therefore the perimeter of each of the equilateral triangles of which it is formed, amounts to 2,151, the number of years in the great month.[1]

The first two names numerically amount to 689, or the length of the sun's orbit measured by its own diameter.

The first three names forming the upper Triad, called Long-face or the Macrocosm, yield 760, which is the side of a square whose diagonals measure 2,151.

The first four names have the value of 834: and $834 \times 9\frac{1}{2} = 7,923$, the number of miles in the earth's diameter; and the length of a vesica 834 broad is 1,446, which is side of a square contained in Saturn's orbit.

And the ten steps, besides the names enumerated above, were called as follows:

Crown	. .	AHIH .	.	21 ⎫
Wisdom	. .	IH . .	.	15 ⎬ 57
Understanding		IHV .	.	21 ⎭
Majesty .	. .	AL . .	.	31
Severity	. .	ALHIM .		86
Beauty .	. .	IHVH .	.	26
Victory ⎫ Glory ⎭	. .	TzBAVTh		499
Foundation	.	ShDI .	.	314
Kingdom .	.	ADNI .	.	65

1,078

"Book of Concealed Mystery," ch. iii., p. 88 (Mathers).

[1] A further reason for the choice of the number 2,868 is explained in the following chapter.

The number 1,078 is the limb of a cross which measures 2,156, which is the mean between 2,151 and 2,161. The number of the names may be therefore said to represent the Logos, in the form of a cross, symbolizing the month of the great year, and the space between the earth and the moon.

The Greek names of the first and second persons of the great cabalistic triad are Macroprosopos or Long-face, Microprosopos or Short-face, and Basileia the kingdom.

ΜΑΚΡΟΠΡΟΣΟΠΟΣ	.	1,101		1,101
ΜΙΚΡΟΠΡΟΣΟΠΟΣ	.	1,110	} 1,369	1,110
ΒΑΣΙΛΕΙΑ	. . .	259		
				2,211
		2,470		

The sum of the three names is 2,470, which by transposition becomes 2,047, the diameter of Saturn's orbit, and 2,407 the length of the sun's orbit measured by the tone. It is also the perimeter of a rhombus whose sides are $617\frac{1}{2}$, the mean between 616, the number of the Beast, and 619, the numerical equivalent of Helios and Selene, the sun and the moon ($318 \times 301 = 619$). The number 1,101 (Macroprosopos) is the perimeter of a square containing a vesica 666 in circumference ($275\cdot34 \times 4 = 1,101$). This vesica is formed by two intersecting circles 318 ($317\cdot99$) in diameter, and the cross inscribed within it measures $434\frac{1}{3}$, the numerical equivalent of Diotima the priestess, who is said to have instructed Socrates. And 109 (Hera) $\times 4 = 436$; and the circumference of the two intersecting circles is 999, or one more than the 998, the number of *Nymphe*, the name of the Bride in the Apocalypse. This vesica, with its circuit of 666, appears to have been one of the fundamental figures of the old theology, and to

have been the source of many names, including
the Trinity itself; for the square, inclosing the
two circles, has a perimeter of 1,907·28.

$$\begin{array}{ll}
\text{ΠΑΤΗΡ} \quad . \quad . \quad . \quad . & 489 - 1 \\
\text{ΥΙΟΣ} \quad . \quad . \quad . \quad . & 680 - 1 \\
\text{ΚΑΙ ΠΝΕΥΜΑ-}\text{'ΑΓΙΟΝ} & 741 - 1
\end{array}$$

$$1,910 - 3 = 1,907.$$

This requires the insertion of καί, but the three
names, without the "and," appear to be derived
from the number 666 in another way.

$$\begin{array}{ll}
\text{ΠΑΤΗΡ} \quad . \quad . \quad . & 489 + 1 \\
\text{ΥΙΟΣ} \quad . \quad . \quad . & 680 + 1 \left.\begin{array}{l}\end{array}\right\} \, 1,390 \\
\text{ΠΝΕΥΜΑ-}\text{'ΑΓΙΟΝ} & 710 + 2
\end{array}$$

$$1,879 + 4 = 1,883.$$

The number now becomes 1,883, and the diagonals
of a square whose sides are 666, measure 1884
($= 942 \times 2$). Macroprosopos may also be identified with the number 2,368 in a very simple manner, as will be shown in the following chapter,
p. 155.

If Malchuth, 496 be substituted for Basileia,
the three names yield 2,707, the perimeter of a
rhombus whose sides are $676\frac{3}{4}$, the square of 26,
and the length of the sun's orbit.

The first and second persons of the Triad were
otherwise called Macrocosmos and Microcosmos.
By Gematria, Macrocosmos is equivalent to φαλλός,
831 ; and Microcosmos, 840, represents the
measure of a man's body derived from the space,
between the tropics measured by the sun's diameter
for $88\frac{1}{2} \times 9\frac{1}{2} = 840$. The sum of the two names,
if colel be added to each, amounts to 1673, or
1 less than the side of a square whose diagonal

is 2,368. Together, with that of the bride, the numbers (831 × 840 + 496) amount to 2,167 — 3 = 2,164, the number of miles in the moon's diameter. The three great canonical numbers 888 ('Ιησοῦς), 1,480 (Χριστός), and 2,368 ('Ιησοῦς Χριστός) are to each other in the ratio of 3, 5, and 8, their greatest common measure being 296 $\left(\frac{888}{296} = 3, \frac{1,480}{296} = 5, \frac{2,368}{296} = 8\right)$. Now these three numerals, 3, 5, and 8, if converted into a single number, become 358, which is numerically equal to the Hebrew name, MSʜICʜ, Messiah. And $358\frac{1}{2} × 6$ equals 2,151, therefore a stone or hexagon, having a perimeter of 2,151, is a geometrical symbol of the Hebrew Messiah. In the Apocalypse the Messiah is called the Alpha and the Omega (τό Ἄλφα καί τό Ὠμέγα), 2,152. And a hexagon or stone, described round a circle having a circumference of 2,151, has a perimeter of 2,368, and is therefore the equivalent of 'Ιησοῦς Χριστός. The period of 2,151 years, besides being the length of a month of the great year, during which time it was alleged that the world was regenerated, has also the peculiarity that it is the sum of the two numbers 1,480 (Christos), and 671 (Thora the Bride) ; it is therefore the symbol of the masculo-feminine nature of the Messiah. And a vesica 358 broad is 620 long, and 620 is the value of Kether, the first step of the Cabala. And a rhombus 359 long is $207\frac{1}{4}$ broad, and $207\frac{1}{4}$ is the diameter of a circle having a circumference of 651, the diameter of a circle 2,046 in circumference.

We learn from the Cabala that Adam Kadmon was the father of the earthly Adam. He was the being, analogous to Christos in his super-mundane state, when he personates God's essence before it reaches the earth. He is the Hebrew Demiurge or Logos. The numerical value of Adam Kadmon is 245, or counting the values of the M and N as finals, the number is 1,455. Now a rhombus whose sides are 245 contains a square drawn within the sun's orbit and having a perimeter of 612, the value of the name ZEUS; and a saltire $(122\frac{1}{2} \times 2 =)$ 245 is contained within the space of the tropics measured by the diameter of the sun. The name Kadmon, 200, exemplifies the measure of the Heavenly Jerusalem, and must surely have an affinity with the Greek Kadmos, 335 ($335\frac{1}{2} \times 2 = 671$) who built the mystical city of Thebes, with its seven cosmic walls and seven gates, guarded by the seven heroes, whose shields bore the symbols of the planets. The number 335 is so near the diagonal (333) of the city of the New Jerusalem, that it may be reasonably connected with that measure.

The name Adam has the value of 45; and this number, with a fraction added, is the square root of the diameter of Saturn's orbit. The name Eve has the value of 19, which is the square root of 361. The value of the two names $(19 + 45) = 64$, and the sum of the numbers from 1 to 64 equals 2,080, the side of the Holy Oblation. In the Talmud it is said that Adam's body stretched from one end of the world to the other. At the request of the angels God reduced it to 1,000 cubits, meaning, perhaps, that he also personates the distance between the equinoxes. Counting the M, final, as 600 ADM (Adam) yields 605; and by deducting $1\frac{1}{4}$ it becomes $603\frac{3}{4}$, which is half of $1,207\frac{1}{2}$, the side of a vesica 2,093 long. And 2,093 is the diameter of the circle containing the square 1,480. Again, $605 + 19 = 624$, the length of a vesica 360 wide. The sum of the numbers from 1 to 9 is 45, so that Adam may be said to symbolize the power of the ninth step

called Yesod the foundation; it is the reproductive principle, and applies to Adam as the
progenitor of the human race. A cross whose
beams are 45·53 broad is 1,275 high, and will
crucify a man within a square whose perimeter is
2,368.

The name Malchuth, the Bride, who, together
with Macrocosmos and Microcosmos, completes
the great Triad, has the value of 496. She is
possibly a personification of the earth, for $495\frac{3}{8} \times 8$
equals 3,963, the earth's radius in miles. In the
"Greater Holy Assembly" (ch. xxxiv., par. 800),
the Bride is called THORA, 671, the gate, and the
numerical value of THORA is equivalent to the name
Adonai, when it is written in its plenitude." This
means that when ADNI is spelt ALP, DLTH, NUN,
IUD, the value of the letters, written thus, make
up 671 instead of 65, its simple value. The
number 671 is exactly the mean between 666 and
676. The name ADNI also gives 65, which, with
a fraction added, is the square root of 4,326,
or 2,163 × 2, which is the measure of a cross
whose limbs are equal to the moon's diameter.
Adonai is the great mother of the Jews, who was
worshipped as elsewhere under the image of the
earth, the moon, and the material universe. She
symbolized the Omphalos, with its cross indicating
the cardinal points, for she marked the central
point of the world.

It will be instructive to make a comparison in
this place between the Virgin Mary of the Gospel,
and the Bride of the Old Testament. For the
Mother of Jesus, like the Spouse of the Hebrew
Messiah, appears with all the attributes generally
assigned to the feminine deities of the ancients.
In the New Testament her name is spelt MAPIAM,
192, and occasionally MAPIA, 152. But in the
Latin Church she was called MARIA, 252. Her

symbol in the early Church was usually the vesica ;
and she is frequently depicted in early Christian
art surrounded by this figure. Now a vesica 192
broad is 332⅖ long, which is the diagonal of the
New Jerusalem. And 'H MAPIAM (192+8) equals
200, or the length of a side of the same mystical
city. Therefore, like the Hebrew Bride, she is
the personification of the heavens, and agrees with
the Greek Aphrodite Ourania. And it is noticeable that 496 × 2 equals 992, one less than the
value of the name Aphrodite. The vesica again,
which is 192 broad, is formed by two intersecting
circles 384 in diameter (192 × 2 = 384), and their
breadth is 576 (192 × 3) ; and 576 is the square of
24, the number of letters in the Greek alphabet,
and one less than the numerical value of the word
Evangelion, the " Good News," or Gospel. Again,
the sum of the numbers 1,480 (Christos), and 192
(Mariam) with colel added to each is 1,674, the
side of a square, whose diagonal is 2,368. She
accordingly expresses the feminine aspect of the
Gospel, while by the number 384 is indicated the
amount of the sun's distance measured by the
tone, and indirectly also the number 666, for 384
is the width of a vesica 666 long. Then the
perimeter of the rhombus formed from the previous figure is 768 (192 × 4), which identifies her
with the cross of Christ. For, regarded as the
instrument of His Passion to which He was
nailed, this symbol seems to have had a feminine
aspect. The cross, 769 broad, is 1,656 high, and
2,366⅔ measured to its full extent. Like the
cross, the cubical stone had also a feminine significance. And a hexagon whose sides are 192
has a perimeter of 1,152, which is about a tenth
of the sun's distance measured by the diameter
of the earth, and the length of a rhombus 666
wide is 1,154 long. And the number 192 is

the diameter of a circle whose circumference is 593, or 1 more than the side of a square whose perimeter is 2,368 (562 × 4 = 2,368). In this last number we see her as the mystical spouse who represents the feminine aspect of the twofold Logos—she whom the Greeks personified as Psyche, the Bride of Love. The name Ἡ ΠΑΡΘΕΝΟΣ ΜΑΡΙΑΜ, the Virgin Mary, has the value of 675, or 1 less than the number 676, the square of 26, so she thus becomes the Christian version of the unspeakable Jewish Tetrad, called ιηυη. And the numerical value of Μαρίαμ Παρθένος is 707, or 1 less than the side of a cross whose diagonals measure 2,004, the value of the names of the four elements. And by Gematria, this name is equivalent to Pneuma Hagion, Holy Ghost. Lastly, if the sun's distance be taken at 10, the mean diameter between the sphere of Saturn and the Zodiac is 192, so that the person of the Virgin answers to the whole cosmic system.

From the statements of theologians on the translation of the Scriptures, it is made evident that the mysteries of the originals were not always retained when the text was transferred to another language. Philo Judæus, speaking of the seventy translators says : "Just as I suppose the things which are proved in geometry and logic do not admit any variety of explanation, but the proposition which was set forth at the beginning remains unaltered, in like manner I conceive did those men find words precisely and literally corresponding to things . . . for if Chaldæans were to learn the Greek language, and if the Greeks were to learn Chaldæan, and if each were to meet with the Scriptures in both languages, namely, the Chaldæan and the translated version, they would admire and reverence them both as sisters, or rather as one and the same, both in their facts and their language; considering these translators not mere interpreters but hierophants and prophets."—(" Life of Moses," bk. ii., c. 7.)

Again, Origen says that " when those names, which in a certain language were possessed of natural powers, were translated into another, they were no longer able to accomplish what they did before, when uttered in their native tongues. . . . Nay, even if we translated into the Greek language the name of an individual who had been originally invoked in the Roman tongue, we could not produce the result which the incantation professed itself capable of accomplishing, had it preserved the name first conferred upon him. And if these statements are true when spoken of the names of *men*, what are we to think of those which are transferred, for any cause whatever, to the *Deity?* For example, something is transferred from the name Abraham when translated into Greek, and something is signified by that of Isaac, and also by that of Jacob; and accordingly, if any one, either in an invocation or in swearing an oath, were to use the expression, ' the God of Abraham,' and ' the God of Isaac,' and ' the God of Jacob,' he would produce certain effects, either to the nature of these names or to their powers, since even demons are vanquished and become submissive to him who pronounces these names; whereas if we say, ' the God of the chosen father of the echo, and the God of Laughter, and the God of him who strikes with the heel,' the mention of the name is attended with no result, as is the case with other names possessed of no power. And in the same way, if we translate the name ' Israel' into Greek or any other language, we shall produce no result; but if we retain it as it is, and join it to those expressions to which such as

K

are skilled in these matters think it ought to be united, there would then follow some result from the pronunciation of the word, which would accord with the professions of those who employ such invocations. And we may say the same also of the pronunciation of 'Sabaoth,' a word which is frequently employed in incantations; for if we translate the term into 'Lord of Hosts,' or 'Lord of Armies,' or 'Almighty' (different acceptations of it having been proposed by the interpreters), we shall accomplish nothing; whereas if we retain the original pronunciation we shall, as those who are skilled in such matters maintain, produce some effect. And the same observation holds good of 'Adonai.' If, then, neither 'Sabaoth' nor "Adonai," when rendered into what appears to be their meaning in the Greek tongue, can accomplish anything, how much less would be the result, among those who regard it as a matter of indifference, whether the highest being be called Zeus, Jupiter, or Zen, or Adonai, or Sabaoth!"—("Against Celsus," bk. v., ch. xlv.)

It is difficult to understand the meaning of the preceding passage, unless the changes which names undergo, when translated into another language, refer to *numerical* changes. The words of Origen seem to be capable of a satisfactory explanation upon this principle, as will be seen when those names are examined which are said to signify something when translated into Greek. For instance, Abraham in Hebrew yields 248, a number already discussed. In Greek the name becomes (Ἀβραάμ) 145, which, by adding and subtracting colel gives 144 and 146: and $144 \times 9\frac{1}{2} = 1,368$, the width of a vesica 2,368 long; and 146 is the width of two intersecting circles which produce a vesica $48\frac{2}{3}$ long, and $48\frac{2}{3}$ is the square root of 2,368. Ἰσαάκ has the value of 232, or the side of a rhombus having a perimeter of 924, the square root of the sun's diameter in miles. Ἰακώβ is numerically equal to 833, and $833 \times 9\frac{1}{2} = 7,923$, the number of miles in the diameter of the earth. Then "the God of Abraham" and "the God of Isaak" and "the God of Jacob" yield the following numbers:

Ὁ	. .	70 – 1		Ὁ	. .	70
Θεός	. . .	284 – 1		Θεός	. .	284
Ἀβραάμ	. .	145 – 1		Ἰσαάκ	.	232
		499 – 3 = 496				686 – 1 = 685

Ὁ	. . .	70 – 1
Θεός	. . .	284 – 1
Ἰακώβ	. .	833 – 1
		1,187 – 3 = 1,184.

Of these 496 is equivalent to Malchuth : 685 is the diameter of a circle 2,151 in circumference : and $1,184 \times 2 = 2,368$.

We are told that the name Israel, when translated into Greek, produces no result, although it possesses certain powers in the original. Now the word ISHRAL (Israel) in Hebrew yields 541, the side of a rhombus having a perimeter of 2,164, the number of miles in the moon's diameter; whereas 349, the numerical value of Ἰσραήλ, has no obvious analogy with any measure of the universe.

Although the reformers were responsible for the more modern translations of the Scriptures, they pretended to acknowledge none but the originals. Accordingly, we find Dr. Featly, an English divine of the seventeenth century, in a report of a disputation with some Anabaptists,[1] declaring that

[1] "Dippers Dipt" (1651), p. 17. Although these early Dissenters appear to have especially asserted the claims of the "Laver," they disapproved of the "Steeple-houses" of the king, who is accused of making "an Idoll of the Church."

his opponents, who were confessedly unlearned men, could not "convince any Jew, Pagan, or Mahometan, out of their translated bible, *without other aids of learning*." Again, he says, " If you will dispute in Divinity you must be able to produce the Scriptures in the original languages," and he calls it blasphemy to deny the LETTER of of the text to be Scripture. John Hutchinson is even more emphatic, for he asserts that " the Scriptures have been buried in a load of filthy translations " (" Religion of Satan or Antichrist delineated," p. 112).

Assuming that these writers are alluding to the numerical value of names, in their appreciation or condemnation of the translations, it is obvious that to re-introduce into a translation the appropriate numbers, as well as the sense of the original, would certainly add a serious difficulty to the task, and if this were successfully accomplished in the Septuagint version, it might well call forth the admiration of Philo. But no translation ever does or can reproduce the peculiarities of another language. Thus, Mr. Mathers points out that, "in Isaiah, ix. 6 and 7, the word LMBRH, for multiplying, is written with the character for M final in the middle of the word, instead of the ordinary initial and medial M. The consequence of this is that the total numerical value of the word instead of being 277 is 837." It is obvious that nobody could translate a singularity like this into another tongue. Yet it must have an important meaning, which is probably connected with the fact that 837 is the diagonal of a square whose perimeter is 2,368.

Another objection to the translations is that they are not always accurate, even as regards the outward sense. For example, the English translation of the eighteenth verse of the fourteenth chapter of Numbers very inadequately renders the real meaning of the words. In the authorized version the verse runs, "The Lord is long-suffering and of great mercy:" but the literal interpretation is, "Tetragammaton (IHVH) is long of nose (ARK APIM) and of great mercy" (Mather's "Cabala," p. 213). The term "Long Nose" is a variation of the ordinary name, "Long-face" (Macroprosopos), generally applied to the Father in the Cabala. In the "Lesser Holy Assembly" it is said (572), "The Nose of the Most Holy Ancient One is long and extended, and he is called Long of Nose." In the "Greater Holy Assembly" the nose is mentioned in paragraph 173: "From the nose is the face known;" and again in 175, "This nose is as a mighty gallery, whence his spirit rusheth forth upon Microprosopos." Now ARK APIM yields 832, which is 1 more than the numerical equivalent of φαλλός.

Italian is one of the modern languages invented, or at least reduced to writing, in comparatively recent times. Dante was the first great poet to use it, and did for the Italian what Robert Langlande, the author of "Piers Ploughman," in a lesser degree did for the language of England. Nothing had been written in the spoken or vulgar tongue till within 150 years of Dante's time ("Vita Nuova," p. 71, Rossetti's translation). Before that all the literature of the Roman Empire had been composed in Greek or Latin. But from thenceforth the modern languages began gradually to supersede those of the classical era, both for speech and writing. Their grammar, spelling, and construction were fixed and regulated by rules similar to those observed in the older languages; and presumably the grammarians, who wrote in the vulgar tongues for the first time, transferred to the newly-appointed names an appropriate number, such as

they had been accustomed to in the earlier literature. At any rate, if the letters of the Latin
language, and the languages derived from it, be
supposed to have the same numerical value as in
Hebrew, it will be found that the numbers deduced
from the new words agree with the sense of the
name previously established. This will be evident from the following translations of the name
Ἰησοῦς Χριστός.

Latin.		Italian.		French.		English.	
J	10	G	3	J	10	J	10
E	5	E	5	E	5	H	5
S	60 } 141	S	60 } 74	S	60 } 141	E	5
V	6	V	6	V	6	S	300 } 325
S	60			S	60	V	5
C	3	C	3	C	3	C	3
H	5	R	200	H	5	R	200
R	200	I	10	R	200 } 287	I	10
I	10 } 353	S	300 } 592	I	10	S	300 } 913
S	60	T	9	S	60	T	400
T	9	O	70	T	9		
V	6						
S	60						

The Latin name yields 494, or $\frac{1}{8}$ of the earth's
radius in miles; and if colel be added to each
name, it is by Gematria equivalent to Malchuth,
the personification of the sublunary world. Again,
141 (Jesus) is the width of a vesica formed by two
circles whose united width is 423, or the side of a
square inclosed by a rhombus whose sides are
666. And $353 + 1 = 354$, the number of days in
the lunar year.

In Italian the name has the value of 666, being
the sum of 74 (Gesu) and 592 (Cristo): 74 is a
common multiple of the 888, 1,480, and 2,368 and
592 is the side of a rhombus having a circumference
of 2,368.

The French name is the same as the modern
English, and yields 428. Jesus is retained as in
the Latin, and Christ has the value of 287: and
287 is the diameter of a circle having a circum-

ference of 901 (ὁ φαλλός). Again, if colel be deducted from each word, the remainder is 426, which is the side of a square inclosed by a rhombus whose sides are 671, the mean number between 666 and 676.

The spelling of the English name is taken from the allegory of "Piers Ploughman." The double name yields with the addition of colel 1,239, or the length of a rhombus having a perimeter of 2,151. The numbers $325\frac{1}{2}$ (Jhesu) is the limb of a cross which measures 651, and 913 (Crist) is the equivalent of Brashith (beginning), the first word of the Hebrew bible.

It only remains, now, to examine the names of the Egyptian deities, and to show that the numbers deduced from them exactly agree with the numerical values obtained from the gods of the Hebrews, Greeks, and Christians. The names of the great Egyptian triad, written in Greek letters, are ΟΣΙΡΙΣ, or ΥΣΙΡΙΣ, ΙΣΙΣ, and ΩΡΟΣ. These are the names under which these deities were worshipped in Greece and Rome. Osiris has the value of 590, which may be taken to be the side of a rhombus 2,368 (it ought to be 592). The spelling Husiris yields 920, or the numerical equivalent of the Greek word κανών (Canon) ; and 97 the radius of the sphere of the Zodiac, if the Sun's distance be taken at 10, multiplied by $9\frac{1}{2}$, produces 921. Isis, again, who is well known to have been identical with Cybele, Athene, and the other feminine deities of the Greeks, has the value of 420 ; and a cross inscribed within a vesica 421 long measures 663, the diameter of a circle whose circumference is 2,083, the side of the Holy Oblation. She is thus the counterpart of the Bride of the Cabala, and an image of the whole universe. Horus yields 1,170, which is one-twelfth of the side of a square 14,035, equals ($1,169\frac{1}{2} \times 12$), whose area is equal to the surface of the earth, measured in miles. The sum of the numbers, deduced from the three names, is 2,180, which is the circumference of a circle 694 in diameter; and a vesica formed of two such circles is 1,041 across, and 1,041⅔ is the radius of the sphere of the Zodiac contained within the Holy Oblation.

ΦΘΑΣ (Phthas), 710, is the Egyptian Phtha, called by Suidas the Hephaistos of Memphis. The numerical value of his name is equivalent to Pneuma Hagion, the Holy Ghost.

ΤΥΦΩΝ (Typhon) has the value of 2,050, or about the diameter of Saturn's orbit.

The Greeks all affirmed that their knowledge of astronomy was derived from the Egyptians, and an analysis of the numbers attributed to the Hill of Bat, in the Book of the Dead (bk. ix., ch. cviii.), shows that these statements are not necessarily unfounded, and its measures seem to be the Egyptian prototype of the descriptions of the ark, the temples, and cities found in the Hebrew scriptures; for they anticipate, in a most remarkable manner, the geometrical results obtained from the mystical fabrics of the Bible.

"There is the Hill of Bat, the heaven rests on it. It is in the east of the heaven about 370 cubits long, 140 cubits broad. Sabak, Lord of the Bat [cavern] in the east is on the hill in his temple upon its edge. There is a snake on the brow of that hill, about 30 cubits long, 10 cubits broad; 3 cubits in front of him are of stone? [hard]. I know the name of that snake on his hill, Eater of Fire is his name."

The parallelogram here ascribed to the Hill of Bat has a perimeter of 1,020 cubits, or nearly the radius of Saturn's orbit, measured by diameters of the sun. Again, this parallelogram is exactly inclosed by the rhombus, 613 by 354, described

under the names Zeus and Apollo. Further, the
square containing the hill has a perimeter of 1,480
cubits (= 370 × 4), and 1,480 is the numerical
value of the name Christos, and the side of a
square contained within the Holy Oblation. Then
370 cubits = 6,660 inches ; and 140 cubits = 2,520
inches, and this number is the diameter of a circle
whose circumference is 7,920 (= 2,520 × $3\frac{1}{7}$), or
the number of miles in the diameter of the earth.
The measure of the serpent is 30 × 10 cubits,
giving an area of 300, which is the width of a
vesica 520 long, which is the side of a rhombus
having a perimeter of 2,080, the side of the Holy
Oblation, and the length of that rhombus is 888.
When converted into feet these measures become
45 × 15, and 45 with a fraction added is the
square root of the diameter of Saturn's orbit, and
15 cubed equals 3,375, the diameter of the moon's
orbit, and if they are multiplied together they give
675, or the side of a rhombus 1,170 long. Now,
$1,169\frac{1}{2}$ is $\frac{1}{12}$ the side of a square, whose area
equals the surface of the earth. And 676 is the
square of 26, the number of the Tetrad. Again,
45 feet = 540 inches, and 540 is the side of a
rhombus having a perimeter of 2,160, or the
moon's diameter in miles. It appears, therefore,
that this mystical hill, upon which "the heaven
rests," is a figure of the mound, mundus, or world
composed of the earth, the seven planets, and the
Zodiac.

It is universally admitted that the Mohammedan
religion was imitated from that of the Hebrews
and Christians, and since the scriptures and gospel
were acknowledged as sacred books by the prophet
himself, the matter is placed beyond dispute. But
it is perhaps not generally known, at least amongst
Christians, that the identity of the two systems is
quite so close as it appears to be. Numerically

the god of Islam is an exact counterpart of the
pantheistic deity of the old pagan philosophers.
For Alla, according to Kircher ("Arithmologia,"
p. 153), has the value of 66, and is equivalent by
Gematria to Zen, one of the names of Zeus, and
to Adonai, the ordinary Jewish substitute for the
unspeakable Tetragammaton. This number is the
diameter of a circle $207\frac{1}{3}$ in circumference, which
is the diameter of a second circle whose circumference is 651, which is the diameter of a third
circle having a circumference of 2,046, the diameter of Saturn's orbit. It is true that Alla is
three stages removed from the god comprising
the whole planetary system, but he is evidently
no more than a new aspect of the old cosmic
god.

CHAPTER VI.

THE HOLY ROOD.

*"Now an account must be taken of the Cross itself, and its
meaning must be related. . . . For whatever sufferings He under-
went . . . . had a figurative meaning and great significance. . . .
In his suffering He stretched forth His hands, and measured
out the world."*—LACTANTIUS, "Divine Institutes," bk. iv., ch.
xxvi.

ST. CYRIL of Jerusalem, in his fourth lecture,
addressed the following words to the Catechumens :
" Let us not then be ashamed of the Cross of
Christ ; but though another hide it do thou openly
seal it on thy brow." The cross, long before the year
350 A.D., when St. Cyril delivered his lectures, had
been a mystical emblem among the old pagan races
of Egypt and Greece. St. Cyril, if not a Greek by
birth, at least wrote in the Greek tongue, and
living as he did at Jerusalem, was stationed
between the Egyptian influences of Alexandria on
the one hand, and those of Greece on the other.
His reference to the custom of concealing the cross
probably refers to the Greeks, since the Egyptians
had openly displayed the cross as a sacred symbol
from the remotest times.

Owing to the fact that the Greeks, as implied
by St. Cyril, were accustomed to hide the cross, we
have very few references to it by the early Greek
writers ; that of Plato in the " Timæus " is probably
the best known, and by its obscurity bears out the
suggestion of concealment. The two figures of
Vitruvius already described probably denote the

peculiar mysteries attached to the cross by the
Greeks and Romans, while the reverence paid
to it by the Christians was apparently no more
than the expansion of the old pagan ideas more
openly expressed. Plato's cross was the saltire, or
St. Andrew's cross, like the letter X, and was the
shape attributed by him to the Logos. The corresponding figure, described by Vitruvius, shows a
man with his legs and arms stretched out in this
form, so that the tips of his fingers and toes
touch the four corners of a circle, having its centre
upon the navel or omphalos. The other figure of
Vitruvius forms a cross, by stretching his arms out
horizontally, so that he measures the same distance
across the arms as from head to foot. In some of
the earliest works of Christian art, the Christ is
represented in this form, standing against a cross,
but without any appearance of being nailed to it,
and is probably represented according to the old
classical manner.[1]

In the old Greek market-place, which was the
centre or omphalos of the town, there generally
stood an upright Hermes to mark the crossing of
the two lines, which indicated the four quarters of
the universe, and which meet at its centre. The
earth, being in the centre of the cosmos, was
symbolized by a cross of this kind $\oplus$, and represented, in the old astronomical system, the omphalos or navel of the universe. Delphi, as is
well known, marked the supposed crossing of these
imaginary lines in Greece, while Jerusalem occupied
a similar position in Palestine ; and the same
practice existed in Egypt, Thebes being an omphalos in that country. In Italy the Romans
called the crossing place the cardo, from which we
derive the name, cardinal points. In England we

[1] See Mrs. Jameson, "History of our Lord."

THE HOLY ROOD. 141

call the middle of our towns simply the cross, and until comparatively recently, a crucifix or other suitable erection always occupied this position.

In the old temples, which were microcosms or little worlds, there was always an omphalos, although it was not always marked by any architectural feature.   In the temple of Apollo at Delphi, the tripod stood over the omphalos, and near the centre of the church of the Holy Sepulchre at Jerusalem there is a stone which was called the "Compass of our Lord."   In a Christian cathedral, which is cruciform in plan, the cardo or compass is marked by the crossing of the transepts and nave.

Procopius has left us an account of how the plan of a Christian church was laid out in the sixth century.   He says :

"In ancient times there was one church at Byzantium dedicated to all the Apostles, but through length of time it became ruinous, and seemed not likely to stand much longer.   Justinian took this entirely down, and was most careful not only to rebuild it, but to render it more admirable in size and beauty ; he carried out his intention in the following manner.   Two lines were drawn in the form of a cross, joining one another in the middle, the upright one pointing to the rising and setting sun, and the other cross line towards the north and south wind.   These were surrounded by a circuit of walls, and within by columns placed both above and below ; at the crossing of the two straight lines, that is, about the middle point of them, there is a place set apart, which may not be entered except by the priests, and which is consequently termed the sanctuary.   The transepts which lie on each side of this, about the cross line, are of equal length ; but that part of the upright line towards the setting sun is built so much

longer than the other part as to form the figure of
the cross."—Procopius, "Sacred Buildings of Justinian," Aubrey Stewart's transl., p. 20. It is
worthy notice of that the method, described here
by Procopius, is exactly similar to that employed
by the Roman Augurs, in setting out a Templum.
In the latter case, the cross-lines were called
Cardo, and Decumanus.

We are told by Plato in the " Timæus" that
" the Creator compounded the world out of all the
fire, and all the water, and all the air, and all the
earth, leaving no part of any of them, nor any
power of them outside . . . in the centre, he put
the soul. . . . This entire compound he divided
lengthways into two parts, which he joined to
one another at the centre, like the letter X,[1] and
bent them into a circular form, connecting them
with themselves and each other at the point opposite their original meeting point." This cross was
a symbol of the Logos, or invisible soul of the
world, and his body being compounded of the
four elements, the size of the cross may be taken
to be 2,004, the numerical value of the four Greek
words, ΠΥΡ, 580, fire, 'ΑΗΡ, 109, air, 'ΥΔΩΡ, 1,304,
water, and ΓΗ, 11, earth. The limbs of the cross
would therefore measure 1,002 $\left(\dfrac{2,004}{2} = 1,002 \right)$.
After the Creator had divided the elements into
two strips, in the form of a cross, he bent them
into two circles one within the other. The circumferences of these two circles being 1,002, their
diameters would be 318·94 (318·94 × 3·1416 =
1,002). The two circles, crossing each other thus,
are generally thought to refer to the circles of the

[1] The letter Chi as a numeral = 600, which is the numerical
equivalent to the word cosmos. And 601 is the width of a
vesica 1,041⅔ long, or the radius of the sphere of the zodiac
contained in the Holy Oblation.

equator and the ecliptic on the sphere of the world. And the number 2,004 is the internal length of an ark containing the ecliptic, measured on a terrestrial globe. Consequently, by the measure of his cross, Plato was enabled indirectly to introduce the actual space of the sun's path, as an attribute of the Logos. If these two circles again be made to form a vesica, the rhombus inscribed within it has a perimeter of 1,275 (318·94 × 4 = 1,275·76). And 1,276 is the numerical value of the name Achilleus, the hero of the "Iliad." While the united width of the two circles forming the rhombus is 956·82, which is 1 and a fraction less than the numerical value of 'Ο ΙΗΣΟΥΣ, 958, the divine Being whose life forms the subject of the gospel.

In the oldest representations of the crucifixion, the four elements are constantly depicted at the foot of the cross, while the sun and moon are placed above the two arms. This invariable arrangement exhibits the main features of the cosmos, surrounding the body of the elemental god, prefigured in the "Timæus."

The elements were represented in the east by three geometrical figures—a square, a circle, and a triangle—surmounted by a crescent the symbol of the moon, the emblem of the upper region, called Æther, occupied by the planets. The earth was assigned to the square or cube, water and air to the circle or sphere, while the triangle or pyramid was the symbol of fire. This figure is analogous to the cross of the Christians, and may be taken to symbolize the three parts of a man's body, his head, his middle, and his legs; and the height of his body, being the amount of the moon's distance from the earth, is a symbol of the measure called the tone.

Sanford (De decen. Chri.) tells us that, "by the

four children of Chronos, there is supposed to be a reference to the first elements of things. By Zeus was understood fire ; by Hera, air ; by Poseidon, water ; and Hades, earth." The numerical value of these four names is 2,163, which is exactly the number of miles in the moon's diameter. The four elements being assigned to the space between the earth and the moon, this measure may be taken to express the whole sublunary world, and to explain the assertion of Sandford.

The reason for connecting the Logos with the elements, or the interval between the earth and the moon, may be explained thus : the moon being the lowest heaven, a mediating power was required to convey the divine essence, diffused throughout the region of the stars, to the earth. The mediator, who personified the vital fluid, was invariably associated with a cross, the symbol of the generative power. And this cross, standing upon the earth, passing through the elements, and reaching up to heaven, seems to have symbolized the agent of creation in the cosmic system.

The early crucifixes always show the upright beam of the cross very much longer than the transverse piece ; and seeing that the treatment of the subject, in the hands of the old artists, was reduced to a stereotyped or canonical form, it might be expected that a rule for the proportion of the cross had existed also. The only measurements attributed to the cross of Christ which we have been able to find are those given by Sir John Maundeville. In the second chapter of his " Travels," he says, " And zee schulle undirstonde, that the Cros of oure Lord was eyght cubytes long, and the overthwart piece was of lengthe thre cubytes and a half." Now $8 \times 3\frac{1}{2}$ cubits are equal to $12 \times 5\frac{1}{4}$ feet, or 144×63 inches. In practice the proportions of crucifixes vary, but they keep

approximately to this ratio.   There is a working
drawing of a cross, which might establish the existence of a rule among the old craftsmen in making
their crucifixes, given by Juan de Arphe, a Spanish
goldsmith of the sixteenth century, who published
a book in 1589 called "Varia Commensuracion
para le Esculta y Arquitectura;" this is a pro-
cessional cross, with a reliquary forming the lower
part of it.   Arphe divides the height into eight,
and the cross beam measures rather more than $3\frac{3}{4}$
of these parts, so it is very nearly of Sir John's
proportion.   Dr. Oliver gives a cross, used by the
Freemasons, of the proportion of 14 to 5 ; but the
clue to the proportions of the cross, which has an
analogy with the cosmos, is probably to be found
in the name "Holy Rood."   It is well known that
the crucifix set over the screen, which separated
the sanctuary from the nave of a church, was called
the Holy Rood, but there is no explanation to be
found why it was so called.   The natural supposition is, that it had some reference to the rood
measure and, in fact, we believe that it originated
from the proportions of a cross composed of this
measure.

The rood is a quarter of an acre, and is composed of forty square perches—a perch being $16\frac{1}{2}$
feet square—and 40 perches (long measure) make
a furlong of 660 feet, containing 7,920 inches, the
number of miles in the diameter of the earth.   The
Iconostasis is, in the Greek church, what we should
call the Rood Screen.   And Ἡ ʼΕΙΚΟΝΟΣΤΑΣΙΣ
yields the number 1,144, which is the length of
a vesica 660 wide.   And 660 being $\frac{1}{12}$ of 7,920,
it may be taken to represent the diameter of
the earth.   Now, if the 40 square perches composing the rood measure be arranged in the form
of a cross, as nearly as possible according to
Sir John's proportion for the cross of Christ, it

will be found that such a cross has a ratio of 28 to 13.

If the orbits of the planets (taking the interval of the earth's distance from the sun at 10) be arranged upon a cross of this proportion, the sun's orbit, together with the orbit of Mercury, will

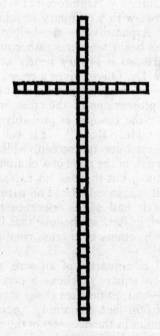

FIG. 14.—THE ROOD-CROSS.

measure 28 parts, equal to the height of the cross. And if the greater man of Vitruvius be crucified upon it, so that his arms stretched out occupy the centre of the transverse beam, and the tips of his fingers touch its extremities, then the top of his head will reach to the summit of the sun's orbit. This may account for the fact that, on the figure of Cesariano, there are a series of rays, drawn from a point corresponding to the position of the sun, in the said figure. When the lesser man is made to take the place of the greater man, according to the proper proportion, the top of the square inclosing his body is found to be on a line with the top of the cross beam, and his hands occupy a position similar to those of Christ in an ordinary crucifix. Justus Lipsius, in his treatise on the cross, gives an illustration of a man crucified in this manner—his legs being kept in position by two pieces of wood hung from the transverse beam (" De Cruce," 1593, p. 117). There are many reasons for believing that this method was the canonical way of crucifying the Logos in the midst of the universe, and that the earlier representations of the crucifixion were based upon this secret rule, which was traditionally handed down in the early church, and communicated to the craftsmen and freemasons who were employed to manufacture the ecclesiastical ornaments.

In the legend of the crucifixion of Christos in the Gospel, we are told that the tragedy took place on the spot called in Hebrew, Golgotha, which means a skull. By later writers it was called a mount, and according to "the tradition" it was the centre of the world. The Hebrew word, BGVLGLTHA (Golgotha), has the value of 475. And a rood cross 475 high will crucify a man whose body is inclosed by a circle equal to the sun's orbit. For if the upright beam measure 475, by the ratio of 28 to 13 the transverse beam will measure 220, which is the diameter of the sun's orbit. And the extreme length of the cross being 678, we get the length of the orbit, computing the diameter at 216 ($216 \times 3\frac{1}{7} = 678$).

Golgotha was also spelt without the B, and consequently yields the number 473; and 473 is

the side of a pentalpha having a perimeter of
2,368, the numerical value of the name ΙΗΣΟΥΣ
ΧΡΙΣΤΟΣ.

It is also spelt GLGLTHA, $467 - 1 = 466$: and a
cross whose height is 466 has some very remarkable cosmic analogies. Its transverse beam is
216, or the diameter of the sun's orbit measured
by its own diameter. Its extreme measure is 666,
the length of the sun's ark. From the bottom to
the centre of the cross beam is 358, the number of
the name Messiah, while the height to the top of
the cross beam is $366\frac{2}{3}$. And 466 is the side of a
square having a diagonal of 660, $\frac{1}{12}$ of the earth's
diameter in miles. This may explain the tra-
dition that Golgotha, 467, was in the middle of
the earth.

A cross of the proportion of 28 to 13, having an
area equal to a rood, is ($28 \times 16\frac{1}{2} =$) 462 feet
high, while the transverse beam is ($13 \times 16\frac{1}{2} =$)
$214\frac{1}{2}$, and its full extent being 660 feet, it measures
the diameter of the earth.

There is no reason to doubt that the early
Christians regarded the cross, in its symbolical
sense, otherwise than the rest of mankind, and it
appears to be used by Sir John Maundeville
according to the ordinary mystical acceptation.
Accordingly, the length of a cross (and we have
seen that Sir John describes the cross of Christ as
being 144 inches high) affords a means of measuring
a man's body ; now by the proportion of the lesser
figure of Cesariano, $144 \times 9\frac{1}{2} = 1,368$, and 1,368 is
the width of a rhombus 2,368 (ΙΗΣΟΥΣ ΧΡΙΣΤΟΣ)
long. Therefore Sir John's measure is equivalent
to the number $249\frac{1}{4}$ (248 + 1), recorded in the
Cabala, "Greater Holy Assembly," par. 968.

If the lesser man of Vitruvius be crucified on a
rood cross, in a square whose diagonals are 1,002
($1,002 \times 2 = 2,004$, the numerical value of the four

elements), the height of the cross will be 2,156, the
mean number between 2,151 and 2,160, the number
of miles in the moon's diameter. A more accurate
measure of the moon's diameter is 2,162·44, and
the transverse beam of a cross 2,162·44 is 1,004,
the numerical value of the name Dionysus, who
was identified with the Logos by the Greeks and
Christians, and whose rites constituted the mysterious knowledge of the old Greek architects,
called Dionysiacs.

The numbers deduced from the Hebrew names
of the elements, like those of the Greeks, set forth
the distance between the earth and the moon, as
well as the altitude of the ecliptic; for ASH, 301,
RVCH, 214, MIM, 90, and OPR, 350, amount to
955. And a vesica 956·769 broad is 1,658 long, and
1,658 is equal to the moon's distance in miles
divided by 12 twice $\left(\frac{238,828}{12} = \frac{19,902}{12} = 1,658 \right)$.
Again, the length of a vesica 955·38 broad is 1,656,
the number of miles from the equator to the tropics,
measured on the earth's circumference (69 × 24 =
1,656). And a rood cross which measures 1,657,
the mean number between 1,656 and 1,658, contains
three measures, found in the names of the hypothetical being, deified by the ancients. A cross
1,657 high measures 2,367·12 in its full extent,
which may be taken at 2,368, the value of the
name IESOUS CHRISTOS. The cross beam measures
769·314, which is nearly the circumference of a
circle having a diameter of 245 (245 × 3·1416 =
769·682), the value of the Hebrew Adam Kadmon,
while a vesica 769·314 long is 443·835 broad, and
443 is the numerical value of Ὁ ΛΟΓΟΣ, The
Word.

If we may accept the authority of Sir Thomas
Browne, the cross seen by the Emperor Constantine
in his vision was a quincunx, that is to say, the

saltire of five points. The inscription on the
Labarum, or standard, was "'ΕΝ ΤΟΥΤΟ ΝΙΚΑ,"
" In this thou shalt conquer." Now, the numerical
value of these three Greek words is 1,276, a number
which is a fraction less than the height of a rood
cross capable of crucifying a man whose body is
inclosed by a square having a perimeter of 2,368,
the numerical value of *Iesous Christos*. The Latin
version of the inscription was " In hoc vince," and
it yields the number 212, if the letters be computed
according to the Hebrew valuation (60+78+74 =
212). Now 212 is the diameter of a circle whose
circumference is 666, and that number, being the
diameter of another circle whose circumference
is 2,092·3, represents the diameter of the sphere of
the Zodiac, containing the square 1,480 (Christos).
Therefore the translation has transferred to the Latin
the meaning, as well as the words, of the original,
for the circle of the Zodiac bears the mystical ratio
of $9\frac{1}{2}$ to 1 to the sun's orbit ($220 \times 9\frac{1}{2} = 2,090$), and
thus expresses the hidden significance of the cross.
The name Labarum does not appear in classical
Latin. It was presumably invented by the Christians, and has a value of 840, according to the
Hebrew value of the letters, which makes it by
Gematria equivalent to Microcosmos. The number
1,276,[1] therefore, unites the cross of the " Timæus "
with that of Jesus Christ, and was an appropriate
number to be borne upon the standard of the
pagan Emperor who became a convert to Christianity, and was the first imperial supporter of the
new cult.

The diagonal of a square whose sides are 901 is
1,275, and the number 901 is the numerical equivalent of ὁ φαλλός. Since the Hebrew word ΤΗΒΗ,

---

[1] It is a peculiarity of the number 1,275, that it is the diameter of a circle the length of whose circumference is twice
2,004, the numerical value of the names of the elements.

407 (Ark), is equivalent by Gematria to TнV, 406
(Tau), and since 406 is the diameter of a circle
whose circumference is 1,276, or the height of a
rood cross which will crucify a man within a square
whose sides are 2,368 (Jesus Christ), there seems
to be good reason for accepting the testimony of
St. Clement, that the sun's ark and the cross were
used synonymously. In the dimensions attributed
to the ark, 300 is equivalent to Tau, and the sum of
the numbers from 1 to 50 is 1,276, and from 1 to 30,
465, or 1 less than 466.

The word Ἥ︢ΛΙΟΣ (Sun) has the value of 318,
and by transposing the numerals, it may become
831 (φαλλός). A curious commentary on this
mystical number occurs in the Epistle of Barnabas
(ch. ix.) : " For Scripture says, that Abraham cir-
cumcised 318 men of his house. But what was
the mystery that was made known unto him ?
Mark, first, the 18, and next, the 300. For the
numerical letters of 10 and 8 are IH. And these
denote 'IH(ΣΟΥΣ), Jesus. And because the cross
was that by which we were to find grace, therefore he adds 300; the note of which is T (the
figure of his cross). Wherefore by two letters he
signified Jesus, and by the third his cross. He
knows this, who has put the engrafted gift [1] of his
doctrine within us. No one has learned a more
genuine word from me than this, but I know that
ye are worthy of it."

The genuine word of Barnabas may be explained
thus : the word σταυρός (cross) has the value of
1,271, and 1,272 is the perimeter of a rhombus
whose sides are 318. And it has just been shown
that the circles formed from the limbs of Plato's
cross were 318·94 in diameter. From this it may

[1] "This is rendered in the Latin, 'the more profound gift,'
referring as it does to the *gnosis* of the initiated."—*Ante-Nicene
Library*, vol. i., p. 117.

be inferred that the cross of Jesus was intended to
measure the space between the earth and the
moon occupied by the four elements, and that he
was consequently analogous to the Logos of Plato.
But this number has still deeper mysteries, and by
a further geometrical process the " genuine word "
may be still more fully unfolded ; for 318·756 is
the side of a rhombus whose circuit is equal to the
height of a cross which will crucify a man in a
square having a perimeter of 2,368 (Jesus Christ).
Again, 318 is the diameter of the two circles which
produce a vesica 666 in circumference.   Lastly,
the circumference of a circle 318 in diameter is
999·028, and 999·75 is the side of a rhombus
having a perimeter of 3,999, the sum of the numbers deduced from the twenty-four letters of the
Greek alphabet—a fact which may account for
the name Logos (speech) being applied to the
Microcosm.

The commentary of the Rabbis on the circum-
cision of the 318 members of Abraham's house-
hold is quite as curious as that of Barnabas.   The
name of Eliezer (ALIOZR), Abraham's steward, has
the value of 318.   " Now, say the Jews, the
numerical letters of Eliezer, making just 318, the
number of servants which Abraham armed, we
learn hence that Abraham did the business, and
got the victory with Eliezer alone, who was equal
to all of them, and that he left the rest at home "
(Jeremiah Jones' "Canon of New Testament,"
vol. ii., p. 386).

The cruciform Man being double-sexed and
being composed of soul and body, his soul or masculine half was diffused through the Æther, that
is, the Zodiac and seven planets, while it was his
body, which was feminine or material, that properly
belonged to the elements.   Therefore, since the
complete Being, male and female, represented the

two lower divisions of the cosmos, the numbers with which he was identified connected his body with the ascertained measures of the sun and the planetary system as well as the moon and the elements. And this double nature had its counterpart in the two limbs of the cross.

There can be little doubt that the cosmic significance of the cross was acknowledged in Greece long before the time of Plato.[1] For instance, the name 'ΟΡΦΕΥΣ has the value of 1,275, and the mysterious doctrines of the Orphic system presumably had reference to the cross. At any rate, in the earliest efforts of Christian Art, it is not uncommon to find Christos depicted playing upon a lyre in the character of Orpheus. No reason is known for this singular impersonation, but the number 1,275, deduced from the name Orpheus, suggests the reason why the two gods had a similar identity.

'ΑΧΙΛΛΕΥΣ, 1,276, and 'ΟΔΥΣΣΕΥΣ, 1,479, the heroes of the two Homeric poems which formed the Bible of the Greeks, were apparently regarded as personifications of the Logos, for if 1 is subtracted from 1,276 and is added to 1,479, we get the numbers 1,275 and 1,480—the first being equivalent to 2,368 (Jesus Christ), and the latter being the exact value of the name Christos. And 'Ο ΤΡΙΠΤΟΛΕΜΟΣ, a kindred deity, has the value of 1,275 ; without the article and with the addition of colel the name yields 1,206½, the side of a vesica 2,093 long.

Plato declared that the moon received her light from the sun. He may have had a further geometrical reason for saying this than that already suggested, for a rood cross 666 high has a transverse beam 309 ('Η ΣΕΛΗΝΗ) long, consequently

---

[1] See Schlieman, " Ilios," p. 349, etc.

the sides of the square which encloses the lesser man, crucified on such a cross, measure nearly 220, the diameter of the sun's orbit, and the fact that the ark, a symbol analogous to the cross,[1] was regarded by the old mythologists as a type of the moon, may have had something to do with the above numbers.

Hippolytus (" Refut.," bk. iv., ch. xliv.), continuing an account of the Egyptian theory of numbers as applied to the nature of God, says : " And moreover they make this assertion, that they have calculated the word ΘΕΙΟΝ, deity, and found that it reverts into a pentad with an ennead subtracted. Now this name is an even number, and when it is written down they attach it to the body and accomplish cures by it." Servius, on the Eclogues of Virgil (viii. 75), and Pliny (Hist. Nat. xxxviii. 2), make similar statements. The numerical value of the word ΘΕΙΟΝ is 144, and 144 — 9 = 135, and if 135 be converted into a pentad, we get (135 × 5=) 675, or 1 less than the square of 26, the mystical vesica. What they appear to mean is, that the particular aspect of the deity for working cures may be symbolized by a combination of the cross and the vesica.

It is unlikely that the conjunction of the names Rose and Cross, as the emblem of the Rosicrucian order, was an accidental circumstance arrived at without reason. In Greek the words yield, Rodon 294 and Stauros 1,271 ; and the sum of the two numbers is 1,565. Now, if 2 be deducted, there remains 1,563, which is the length of a vesica 901 broad, and 901 is the side of a square whose diagonals are 1,275, the height of a rood cross which will crucify a man in a square having a perimeter of 2,368. And 1,565 is the perimeter

[1] See p. 78.

of a rhombus 678 long, or the extent of the sun's orbit. Again, 1,565 is the perimeter of a triangle whose sides are 521, a quarter of the side of the Holy Oblation. Finally, 1,565 is the circumference of a circle 495 in diameter, a number which is 1 less than the numerical value of Malchuth, the Bride, and is $\frac{1}{16}$ of the earth's diameter in miles.

The numerical value of the name φαλλός is 831, and a cross 831 high has a transverse beam 385·71 long, and its full extent is 1,186·8. It has already been pointed out that the number 831½ gives the height of a man, equal to the polar diameter of the earth in miles. But that is not the only cosmic measure to be observed in this cross. For the transverse beam is about the sun's distance, computed by the tone, and the extreme measure is the length of a vesica whose width is 684·6, the diameter of a circle 2,151 in circumference, or the number of years occupied by the sun in each of the signs during the period of the precession of the equinoxes, or Great Year. Again, 831 is the numerical equivalent of Macrocosmos, who was also called by the cabalists Macroprosopos, Long Face. The value of the latter name is 1,101, and a cross 1,101·688 high will crucify a man in a square having a perimeter of 2,046 (511½ × 4), the diameter of Saturn's orbit. The sum of the numbers of Macroprosopos and Microprosopos is 2,211, or the length of a rhombus 1,275 broad. And 1,275 is the height of a cross which will crucify a man in a square having a perimeter of 2,368.

Again, a cross which is 248[1] high has a transverse beam 115·05 long, and measures 354 over all. The diameter of a circle 360 in circumference being 114·59, this cross roughly combines in its

---

[1] See "Greater Holy Assembly," par. 968.

measures the length of the solar and lunar years, and thus acquires a masculine and feminine significance. Consequently it expresses the twofold character of the symbol, exemplified by the fact that Stauros and Omphalos are equal to one another by Gematria.

The height of a cross whose transverse beam exactly measures the diameter of a circle 360 in circumference, is 246·792, or in a round number, 247 ; and this is equivalent to the name ΘHPION, the Beast of the Apocalypse. Since there is an allusion in the text to the Beast's name, it may be supposed that some mystery lies in the word. It was certainly the received opinion, that the Beast's mark was the cross, so the mystery may have had reference to the figure of the Microcosm crucified in a circle having a circumference of 360, the number of degrees in the earth's circuit.

Finally, if the Logos be crucified, saltirewise, so that his body measures 666 (333 × 2), the square which contains him is 236 on each of its sides— the measure of the New Jerusalem — then the extreme measure of the cross is 1,024·63, the radius of Saturn's orbit ; while the height of the cross is 717·248, or a third of 2,151, the number of years in the Great Month. And the square enclosing this cross (717 × 4) has a perimeter of 2,868, the sum of the numbers deduced from the names of the ten cabalistic steps, the canonical synthesis of the Jewish theology.

$$\Sigma TAYPO\Sigma = 1,271.$$
$$ʽH\ \Gamma N\Omega\Sigma I\Sigma = 1,271.$$
$$ʽH\ \Gamma E\Omega METPIA = 1,272.$$

CHAPTER VII.

TOWER OF BABEL.

"Oh reverend arthists of times past, what despite hath gotten the upper hand of your cunning that the same is buried with you, and none left for us to inherit in this age."—"Hypnerotomachia" (English translation), fol. 18.

It is written that the sons of Noah journeyed from the east to the land of Shinar, and having settled to dwell there, they said, "Go to, let us build us a city and a tower, whose top may reach unto heaven; and let us make us a name, lest we be scattered abroad upon the face of the whole earth." But the Elohim were displeased with the children of men, saying also, "Go to, let us go down, and there confound their language" (Genesis, xi. 4-7). Henceforth on this account the place was called Babel (BL), which has the numerical value of 34, the square root of 1,156. Now 1,156 is the length of a vesica 2,004 long, and 2,004 is the numerical value of the four Greek names of the elements.

The fall of the Tower of Babel commemorates to the believer the dispersal of mankind throughout the world and the origin of many languages. The Freemasons also connected the building of this tower with the origin of architecture. And after the confusion of tongues, new alphabets must obviously have been invented, so it was also associated with the institution of letters. Kircher, who of all late writers has preserved the most detailed account of the old mysticism, depicts the

Tower ("Turris Babel," p. 38) as reaching up
to the moon, the lowest heaven, a distance of
238,828 miles, or, as he measures it, 52 semi-
diameters of the earth.   It is not related that the
builders succeeded in their preposterous attempt,
nor is it credible that any race of madmen could
ever have projected or commenced such a work ;
but that does not prevent our assuming that the
fable may have some point.   It is clear that
the myth-writers have made the attempt to span
the distance from the earth to the moon, coincident with the commencement of all earthly
languages, so that by joining this astronomical
invention with the formation of new alphabets
and words, the story may be a metaphorical
intimation of the first bestowal of cosmic values
upon names.   If that were so, the Freemasons
would obviously see in such a fable the consequent beginning of that practice in building which
made a temple, like a name, an imitation of the
universe, and, more particularly, that part of the
universe symbolized by the Logos composed of
the elements.   And since the Tower, if it had
been completed, would have accurately measured
the sublunary world, the languages of the dispersed nations are probably contrasted with the
divine language of the Elohim, which was spoken
in the heavens above.   In Paradise Hebrew was
the only language known ; Noah also, whose ark
has been supposed to represent the Zodiac and
seven planets, knew no other, and it was not till
the building and collapse of the Elemental Tower,
that the speech of the gods was dispersed to the
four corners of the earth.   The other mysteries
underlying the myth need not concern us.   But it
may be said, in a word, that the allegory describes
the speech of Macrocosmos and Microcosmos being conveyed to Basileia.

The next important structure, erected by the Jews, was the Tabernacle, or Tent of Tetragammaton. Though trifling in size, being neither comparable in its accommodation to the Ark, nor to the Towel of Babel in height, it has great interest, as being the first Hebrew shrine or temple of which there is any description in the Canonical Scriptures. We learn from Philo Judæus that Moses "Speedily learnt arithmetic, and geometry, and the whole science of rhythm, and harmony and metre, and the whole of music by means of the use of musical instruments, and by lectures on the different arts, and by explanations of each ; and lessons on these subjects were given him by Egyptian philosophers, who also taught him the philosophy which is contained in symbols, which they exhibit in those sacred characters or hieroglyphics, as they are called, and also that philosophy which is conversant about that respect which they pay to animals which they invest with the honours due to God.

All other branches of the encyclical education he learned from the Greeks ;[1] and the philosophers from the adjacent countries taught him Assyrian literature, and the knowledge of the heavenly bodies, so much studied by the Chaldæans. And this knowledge he derived also from the Egyptians, who study mathematics above all things, and he learnt with great accuracy the state of that art among both Chaldæans and Egyptians, making

---

[1] The Fathers, as we have seen, all declared that the Greeks learnt their philosophy from Moses, but it is remarkable that his earliest biographer should exactly reverse the position. The importance of Philo's statement is enormous, from its implication of Hellenic influences having affected the Hebrew Scriptures, producing the alleged agreement between the writings of the two peoples. Of course we are assuming that Philo is not giving us a picture of Moses otherwise than as a mythical personage.

himself acquainted with the points in which they agree with, and differ from, each other" (" Life of Moses," bk. i., c. v.).

All this knowledge was said to be contained in the five books of Moses, and the Ark, Camp, and Tabernacle are the embodiment of the mathematical and astronomical part of it. Besides the account in the Scriptures, the Tabernacle is fully described by Philo, Josephus, and Clement of Alexandria; in recent times Sir William Drummond ("Œdipus Judaicus," 1811, p. 119) has pointed out all that can be said in a general way, as to the cosmic symbolism of the Tabernacle and Temple. From all these sources it is made evident that this structure was a mystical image of the universe, intended as a shrine for the Pantheistic deity, whose nature is enigmatically shadowed forth in the Law.

Moses, we are told, " having gone up into the loftiest and most sacred mountain in the district . . . which was very difficult of access and very hard to ascend," was there " initiated into the sacred will of God," and received the pattern from which the Tabernacle was to be built, and all the measures of its parts. The court, in which the tent was set up, was 100 cubits long, by 50 cubits broad. The vesica containing this parallelogram is 83×144, and the circumference of the two circles from which it is produced is 521, the side of a rhombus 2,081 in circuit. It has been already pointed out that $144 \times 9\frac{1}{2} = 1,368$, the side of vesica 2,368 long. Then if the court be surrounded by a rhombus, its sides are 107·55, say 108, the radius of the sun's orbit.

The Tabernacle itself was placed in the court towards the west, but with its front to the east, that " when the sun arose it might send its first rays upon it" (Josephus). Its measures are

30 cubits = 45 feet = 540 inches by 10 cubits =
15 feet = 180 in. Now the moon's distance is
30 diameters of the earth; and 10 may be taken
to be the sun's radius. Then 45, with the addition
of a fraction, is the square root of the diameter of
Saturn's orbit measured by the diameter of the
sun. The number 15 is, in round numbers, the
square root of 3,960, the number of miles in the
earth's radius, and is the width of the mystical
vesica, 26 to 15. The length of the Holy Place
is 360 inches, and its perimeter is 1,080 inches,
the radius of the moon's diameter in miles. While
the perimeter of the whole tent is 1,440, or 6 less
than the diagonal of the square contained in the
mean orbit of Saturn measured by the diameter of
the sun.

The building is formed of three cubes; a double
cube being assigned to the Holy Place, and a
cube to the Holy of Holies. Now the Holy of
Holies is 15 feet square, and 15 cubed = 3,375 feet,
or the diameter of the moon's orbit twice divided
by 12 $\left(\frac{485,576}{12} = \frac{40,464}{12} = 3,372 \right)$. And the
Holy Place contains 6,750 cubic feet. Josephus
says that "this proportion of the measures of the
Tabernacle proved to be an imitation of the system
of the world" ("Antiq.," bk. vi., chap. vi.).

If it be open to question whether the preceding
measures relate to the structure of the universe,
there can, at least, be no doubt that the furniture
of this mystical shrine is symbolical of the heavenly
order. In the Holy Place there stood on the
north side a table "like those at Delphi" (Josephus), upon which were placed twelve loaves,
arranged in two heaps of six each, typical of the
twelve months of the year. And opposite the
table, on the south side, stood the golden candlestick having seven branches, which "carried seven

M

lamps, one by one, in imitation of the number of the planets" (Josephus, "Antiq.," bk. iii., chap. vi.). And the candlestick was set obliquely, like the ecliptic (*ibid*.). "The altar of incense was placed in the middle, between earth and water, as a symbol of gratitude which it was fitting should be offered up on account of things that had been done for the Hebrews on both these elements, for these elements have had the central situation of the world allotted to them. The candlestick was placed on the southern side of the Tabernacle, since by it the maker intimates, in a figurative manner, the motions of the stars, which give light; for the sun and the moon, and the rest of the stars, being all at a great distance from the northern parts of the universe, make all their revolutions in the south. And from this candlestick there proceeded six branches, three on each side, projecting from the candlestick in the centre, so as altogether to complete the number seven; and in all the seven there were seven candles, and seven lights, being symbols of those seven stars, which are called planets by those men who are versed in natural philosophy; for the sun, like the candlestick, being placed in the middle of the other six, in the fourth rank, gives light to the three planets which are above him, and to those of equal number which are below him, adapting to circumstances the musical and truly divine instruments. . . . For the symbols of heaven and earth are placed side by side, as the Holy Scripture shows, the candlestick being the symbol of heaven, and that which is truly called the altar of incense, on which all the fumigatory offerings are made, being emblems of things of earth" (Philo, "Life of Moses," bk. iii.).

Clement of Alexandria considered both the altar of incense and the table to be symbols of the earth. He says, "But the table, as I think, signifies the image of the earth; it is sustained by four feet, answering to the summer, autumn, spring, and winter, by which the year proceeds" ("Miscell.," bk. vi., chap. ix.). He also says, "the golden lamp conveys another enigma, as a symbol of Christ" (bk. vi., chap. vi.), alluding apparently to the number 1,480, which is the measure of the whole planetary system.

The most sacred and mysterious object of the Tabernacle was the Ark, containing the two stones of the Law. It measured $2\frac{1}{2}$ cubits long, or $3\frac{3}{4}$ feet, or 45 inches; its breadth and height were $1\frac{1}{2}$ cubits, or $2\frac{1}{4}$ feet, or 27 inches. Its perimeter was therefore the mystic number of 144 inches. If the Ark were rather more than an inch thick, which would be sufficient for a box of this size, its contents would amount to 24,860 cubic inches, or the number of miles in the circumference of the earth.

The Tables of the Law preserved in the Ark appear to have had a cosmic significance, for Clement of Alexandria, speaking of the Decalogue, says that "ten is a sacred number, it is superfluous now to say. And if the Tables which were written were the work of God, they will be found to exhibit physical creation. For by the 'finger of God' is understood the power of God, by which the creation of *heaven* and *earth* is accomplished; both of which the Tables will be understood to be symbols. For the writing and handiwork put on the Table is the creation of the world. And the Decalogue, viewed as an image of heaven, embraces sun, moon, and stars, clouds, light, wind, water, air, darkness, fire. This is the physical decalogue of the heaven. And the representation of the earth contains men, cattle, reptiles, wild beasts, etc. . . . And the Ark, which held them, will then be the knowledge of divine and human things, and wisdom " (" Miscell.," bk. vi., ch. xvi.).

If the Ark be enclosed in a rhombus, its perimeter is 211·80 inches, or say 212 inches ; and 212 is the diameter of a circle whose circumference is 666. It may also be enclosed in another rhombus having a perimeter of 241·80 inches ; and this is the diameter of a circle with a circumference of 759·94, which is the side of a square whose diagonals measure 2,151. The united width of the circles which produce the rhombus is 181·35, or very nearly the width of the Holy of Holies, and it may be that these two circles were shadowed forth in the figures of the cherubim which were placed upon the mercy seat over the Ark. Philo quotes the opinion " that these two cherubim are the symbols of the two hemispheres, placed opposite to and fronting one another, the one beneath the earth, and the other above the earth, for the whole heaven is endowed with wings " (" Life of Moses," bk. iii.). Josephus describes them as flying creatures unlike anything seen by men, " though Moses said, he had seen such beings near the throne of God." Clement gives a fuller description. " Those golden figures, each of them with six wings, signify either the two bears, as some will have it, or rather the two hemispheres. And the name cherubim meant *much knowledge*. But both together have twelve wings, and by the Zodiac, and time, which moves on it, point out the world of sense. It is of them, I think, that Tragedy, discoursing of Nature, says :

> " ' Unwearied Time circles full in perennial flow
> Producing itself. And the two bears
> On the swift wandering motions of their wings,
> Keep the Atlantean pole.'

" And Atlas, the unsuffering pole, may mean the

fixed sphere, or, better perhaps, motionless eternity." By this St. Clement seems to hint, that the Holy of Holies was the receptacle of the twofold principle of life, which was symbolized in the heavens by the two bears, the two hemispheres, and the starry firmament, or fixed sphere from which the germinating powers of God the Elohim were supposed to flow. Nor are the Ark, with the two stones of the Law, and the Schekinah above it without a meaning, but it was thought fit to conceal the real import of all these symbols for reasons given by Origen: " I might have mentioned what is said of those beings which are called seraphim by the Hebrews, and described in Isaiah, who cover the face and feet of God, and of those called cherubim, whom Ezekiel has described, and the postures of these, and of the manner in which God is said to be borne upon the cherubim. But since they are mentioned in a very mysterious manner, on account of the unworthy and the indecent, who are unable to enter into the great thoughts and venerable nature of theology, I have not deemed it becoming to discourse of them in this treatise" ("Against Celsus," bk. vi., ch. xviii.).

Before the door of the Holy of Holies was the veil symbolizing the four elements. The holy place, 360 inches long, the number of degrees in the earth's circumference, symbolized the mystic ship, which measured the sun's course, and corresponds to the Naos ($\nu\alpha\tilde{\upsilon}\varsigma$) of a Greek temple or nave (navis) of a Christian church. Thus the mystic triad, the ancient emblem of God, invisibly ordered the proportions of this sacred tent (see Arius Montanus, "Antiq. Jud.," Plate G).

The name of the Tabernacle in the Hebrew (Ex. xxv. 9) is MSHKN, and yields 1,060, one less than the length of a vesica 612 broad, two numbers which are found in the names Apollo and

Zeus—612 being the perimeter of a square enclosed in the sun's orbit. The number 1,060 is
also the diagonal of a square whose sides are $749\frac{1}{2}$,
and this square is contained within a rhombus inscribed in Saturn's orbit. By counting the final
N as 50, we get 410, one and a fraction more than
the length of a vesica 236 broad, the side of the
New Jerusalem. The word AHL, 36, was also
applied to the tent, and the sum of the numbers
from 1 to 36 equals 666. The Ark was called
ARUN, 907, or 257 if the final N be taken at 50.
Now 908 is the perimeter of a rhombus whose
sides are 227, which, multiplied by $9\frac{1}{2}$, gives 2,156,
the mean number between 2,151 and 2,161. And
$257 + \text{colel} = 258$, which is the diameter of a
circle whose circumference is 811, a number already
discussed under the name Iao. The name Moses
given to the leader of the Israelites, and the
builder of the Tabernacle yields 345 (MShH).
Now 345 is at once the diameter of a circle whose
circumference equals the moon's radius ($345 \times 3\frac{1}{7}$
$=1084$), and is half the length of the sun's orbit,
and consequently measures half the year, or the
interval between the equinoxes ($345 \times 2 = 690 =$
$220 \times 3\frac{1}{7}$). Then if colel be added $345 \times 1 = 346$,
which is the length of a vesica 200 broad, the side
of the New Jerusalem; and $346 \times 6 = 2,076$, or
$\frac{1}{12}$ of the earth's circumference. Further, by
Gematria the name Moses is equivalent to Shiloh
(ShILH, 345), which was regarded as a prophetic
name of the Messiah (Gen. xlix. 10). Moses,
according to the Talmud, was 10 ells high. Taking
the ell at 3 feet 9 inches, his height would be $37\frac{1}{2}$
feet, or 450 inches. A square whose sides are
450 contains a figure of the Logos, measuring
$635\frac{1}{2} \times 2 = 1,271$, the numerical value of the word
Stauros, the symbol of the Messiah. Again 37 is
the square root of 1,369, the width of a rhombus

2,368 long. And Moses was born, according to the Hebrew and Samaritan chronologies, in the year of the world 2,368, the numerical value of the name Jesus Christ (Kircher, " Œdip.," tom. ii., par. 2, p. 270). The craftsmen who were engaged in the construction of the Tabernacle were Bezaleel (BTZLAL), 153, and Aholiab (AHLIAB), 49. The first number, 153, is the side of the square contained within the sun's orbit, and has a perimeter of 612 ; the second number, 49, may be taken to represent 48⅔, the square root of 2,368. Without attempting to expound the allegory of Moses' life, it is sufficient to infer from the preceding numbers that Moses was conceived as an incarnation of the Messiah, created by the myth-writer in the semblance of a historical personage, exactly parallel to the heroes of the Greek traditions, or the saints of the Christian church.

Following the description of the Tabernacle is the account of the vestments of Aaron, the High Priest. The symbolical meaning of these garments harmonizes with the cosmic significance of the shrine, in which it was the duty of the high priest to minister. We are told by Philo, that the priestly dress " in its whole is a copy and representation of the world ; and the parts are a representation of the world " (" Life of Moses," bk. iii., c. xii.). " The High Priest, then, being equipped in this way, is properly prepared for the performance of all sacred ceremonies, that, whenever he enters the temple to offer up the prayers and sacrifices in use among his nation, all the world may likewise enter in with him, by means of the imitations of it which he bears about him, the garment reaching to his feet being the imitation of the air, the pomegranate of the water, the flowery hem of the earth, and the scarlet dye of his robe being the emblem of fire " (*Ibid.*, c. xiii.).

And Josephus summarizes the import of the robes and their ornaments thus : " Now the vestment of the High Priest being made of linen, signified the earth ; the blue denoted the sky, being like lightning in its pomegranates, and in the noise of the bells resembling thunder. And for the ephod, it showed that God had made the universe of four [elements] ; and as for the gold interwoven, I suppose it related to the splendour by which all things are enlightened. He also appointed the breastplate to be placed in the middle of the ephod, to resemble the earth, for that has the very middle place of the world. And the girdle which encompassed the High Priest round, signified the ocean, for that goes round about and includes the universe. Each of the sardonyxes declares to us the sun and moon, those, I mean, that were in the nature of buttons on the High Priest's shoulders. And for the twelve stones, whether we understand by them the months, or whether we understand the like number of the signs of that circle which the Greeks call the Zodiac, we shall not be mistaken in their meaning. And for the mitre, which was of a blue colour, it seems to me to mean heaven ; for how otherwise could the name of God be inscribed upon it ? " (" Antiquities," bk. iii., c. vii.).

Philo's account substantially agrees with this, but he adds that the long robe reaching down to the feet, with a fringe of pomegranates, flowers, and bells, exhibits the emblems of the three elements, air, water, and earth. There were 360 bells, which were a type of the year, according to St. Clement. The twelve stones on the breastplate, called the Logeion by Philo, were set in four rows, to distinguish the four seasons of the year. He says it was made double to agree with the twofold nature of the world, " for the Logos is

double," and the Logeion is a symbol " of that
reason which holds together and regulates the
universe." Now, the High Priest being regarded
as the type of the world, the Logeion, that is, the
place of the Logos, is evidently the type of the
Microcosm stretched crosswise on his breast,
and this is what is apparently meant by Philo
when he says : " It was indispensable that the man,
who was consecrated to the Father of the world,
should have as a paraclete His Son, the Being
most perfect in all virtue, to procure forgiveness of
sins and a supply of united blessings . . . so that
he shall be in a manner changed from the nature
of a man into the nature of the world, and, if one
may say so, become a little world himself " (*Ibid.*,
c. xiv.).

It is noticeable that this Jew's ideas as to the
Logos are exactly those, afterwards formulated by
the Christians. The Logeion or breastplate is
called by Josephus Ἐσσηνη, 471. And 471 is the
diameter of a circle whose circumference is 1,480,
the numerical value of the name Christos. The
name λογειον, 238, has numerically the same mean-
ing, for $238\frac{1}{2}$ is the diameter of a circle $749\frac{1}{2}$ in
circumference, and $749\frac{1}{2}$ is the side of a square
enclosed by a rhombus inscribed within Saturn's
orbit. Therefore the Logeion exhibits the Christ
or Logos in the midst of the twelve signs symbolized by the twelve precious stones.

The mystic inscription on the Mitre, QDNSh
LIHVH, " Holiness to the Lord," has the value
of 510, and is one and a half less than the side of
a rhombus whose perimeter is equal to the diameter
of Saturn's orbit.

The altar of the Tabernacle was 5 cubits broad
by 5 cubits long, by 3 cubits high, which is equal
to $7\frac{1}{2} \times 7\frac{1}{2} \times 4\frac{1}{2}$ feet, or $90 \times 90 \times 54$ inches. The
perimeter of its base was therefore 360 inches, and

the perimeter of one of its sides 288 inches, and $288\frac{1}{2}$ is the side of a square having a perimeter of 1,154, or the length of a vesica 666 broad.

In the "Ion" of Euripides mention is made of a tent or tabernacle at Delphi, whose area was 10,000 feet. If this tent were built of the proportions of the Hebrew Tabernacle, its width would be 57·74, and its length 173·22 feet (57·74 × 3 = 173·2), giving an area of 10,001 sq. feet. Its perimeter would consequently be 462 (actually 461·92) the height of the cross of the holy rood, whose extreme measure is 660. The length of the tent would be 2,078·64, or the mean number between the side of the Holy Oblation and $\frac{1}{12}$ of the earth's circumference. The perimeter of the Holy of Holies would be almost 230·96 feet, which is the side of a square whose diagonals measure 651, the diameter of a circle 2,046 in circumference; and $230\frac{1}{4} \times 4 = 921$, the numerical equivalent of the word κανών (Canon). The perimeter of the Holy Place would be 346·44, which is the length of a vesica 200 broad, and 200 is the side of the cube of the New Jerusalem. Then a square containing the whole building would have a perimeter of 692 ($220 \times 3\frac{1}{7} = 691$), the length of the sun's orbit.

The description of the Temple built by Solomon, the King, is less minute than that of the Tabernacle, but the principal measurements are given without ambiguity. The oldest plan which has any serious pretensions to accuracy, is that of Villalpanda, the Jesuit ("In Ezekielem Explanationes," 1596). It is, in fact, thoroughly workmanlike and practical, and has all the appearance of being a copy from some traditional drawing, probably preserved by the old Freemasons. According to all information at present available, there is no reason to suppose that the Temple of Solomon ever existed as a

building. Like all the other fabrics of the Old
Testament, it seems to be a purely theoretical
structure, described as the canonical pattern for
the guidance of architects, in the design of real
temples or churches. If it were ever actually
built, a glance at the plan will show that it must
have been a very substantial work, its main walls
being 9 feet thick; such a building would necessarily require considerable foundations, and, if they
exist at Jerusalem, it would be easy to recognize
them, since all the measurements of the building
are known. However, until actual traces of its
walls are brought to light, it may be reasonably
supposed that its description has a place among
the canonical books for the same mystical reason
that the ark of Noah, the Tower of Babel, the
Tabernacle, and the Holy Oblation are found
there.

The legends connected with the construction of
the Temple are certainly not in favour of its having
had an earthly origin, as the following story from
the Talmud clearly shows. " And the house,
when it was building, was built of stone, made
ready before it was brought thither. For before
the operations commenced, Solomon asked the
Rabbis, ' How shall I accomplish this, without
using tools of iron?' And they, remembering of
an insect, which had existed since the creation of
the world, whose powers were such as the hardest
substances could not resist, replied, ' There is the
Shameer, with which Moses cut the precious stones
of the ephod.' Solomon asked, ' And where, pray,
is the Shameer to be found?' To which they
made answer, ' Let a male demon, and a female
come, and do thou coerce them both; mayhap
they know and will reveal it to thee.' He then
conjured into his presence a male and female
demon, and proceeded to torture them, but in vain,

for, said they, 'We know not its whereabouts and cannot tell; perhaps Ashmedai, the king of the demons, knows.' On being further interrogated, as to where he in turn might be found, they made this answer: 'In yonder mount is his residence, there he has dug a pit, and after filling it with water, covered it over with a stone and sealed it with his own seal. Daily he ascends to heaven and studies in the school of wisdom there, then he comes down and studies in the school of wisdom here; upon which, he goes and examines the seal, then opens the pit, and, after quenching his thirst, covers it up again, reseals it and takes his departure.'

"Solomon thereupon sent Benaiah, the son of Jehoiada, provided with a magic chain and ring, upon both of which the name of God was engraved. He also provided him with a fleece of wool, and sundry skins with wine. Then Benaiah went and sank a pit below that of Ashmedai, by means of which the pit was filled with the wine he brought. After levelling the ground, so as not to rouse suspicion, he withdrew to a tree close by to watch the result. After a while Ashmedai came and examined the seal, when, seeing it all right, he raised the stone, and to his surprise found wine in the pit. For a time he stood muttering, it is written, 'Wine is a mocker, strong drink is raging, and whosoever is deceived thereby is not wise;' but, being thirsty, he could not long resist the temptation. He proceeded to drink, therefore, when becoming intoxicated, he lay down to sleep. Then Benaiah came forth from his ambush, and, stealthily approaching, fastened the chain round the sleeper's neck. Ashmedai, when he awoke, began to fret and fume, and would have torn off the chain that bound him, had not Benaiah warned him, saying, 'The name of the Lord is upon thee.'

Having thus secured him, Benaiah proceeded to lead him away to his sovereign master.

"On arriving at the royal city, he was in due course introduced to the king; when, measuring off four cubits on the floor with the stick he held in his hand, he said to Solomon: 'When thou diest thou wilt not possess in the world (he referred to the grave) more than four cubits of earth. Meanwhile thou hast conquered the world, yet thou art not satisfied until thou hadst overcome me also.' To this the king quietly replied: 'I want nothing of thee, but I wish to build the Temple, and have need of the Shameer.' To which Ashmedai at once answered: 'The Shameer is not committed in charge to me, but to the prince of the sea, and he entrusts it to no one except the great wild cock, and that upon oath that he return it to him again.' Whereupon Solomon asked: 'And what does the wild cock do with the Shameer?' To which the demon replied: 'He takes it to a barren rocky mountain, and by means of it he cleaves the mountain asunder, into the cleft of which, formed into a valley, he drops the seeds of various plants and trees, and thus the place becomes clothed with verdure and fit for habitation.' This is the Shameer (Levit. ix. 19), Nagger Tura, which the Targum renders mountain splitter.[1]

"They therefore searched for the nest of the wild cock, which they found contained a young brood. This they covered with a glass, that the bird might see its young but not be able to get at them. When, accordingly, the bird came and found his nest impenetrably glazed over, he went and fetched the Shameer. Just as he was about

[1] The name ShMIR (Shameer) yields 550, which is the length of a rhombus having a perimeter of 1,271, the numerical equivalent of Stauros, a cross.

to apply it to the glass in order to cut it, Solomon's messenger gave a startling shout, and this so agitated the bird, that he dropped the Shameer, and Solomon's messenger caught it up, and made off with it. The cock thereupon went and strangled himself, because he was unable to keep the oath by which he had bound himself to return the Shameer.

"Having once acquired a power over Ashmedai, Solomon detained him till the building of the Temple was completed."

A temple constructed without iron tools, and by means of an insect whose powers were such as the hardest substances could not resist, must have obviously been a structure of no ordinary kind. And when we find that the Freemasons, whose ritual chiefly revolves round the building of this mysterious fabric, regarded it as a peculiar symbol, rather than a real building, we cannot be altogether wrong in adopting their view. Solomon, too, was no less extraordinary, and according to all the legends about him, was exactly the kind of prince who would build such a remarkable temple ; for his splendour and riches were so great, that he made gold and silver as common in Jerusalem as stones in the streets. The name Solomon (SHLMH) has the numerical value of 375, a number which is at once the side of the city of Ezekiel, and the width of a vesica 651 long, and 651 is the diameter of a circle having a circumference equal to the diameter of Saturn's orbit. The rabbis declare that certain horses were kept in the court of the Temple, and that they were every morning harnessed to the chariots dedicated to the sun ; and that the king got up and rode to meet the sun at its rising, as far as from the eastern gate of the Temple to the suburbs of Jerusalem (Calmet). By a figure of speech, therefore, Solomon might be said to be king of the city of the sun, and all the world beside. And this may account for the romantic stories of his glory, and suggest the motive for ascribing the erection of this golden temple to him.

The internal measures of the Temple are just double those of the Tabernacle, the Holy of Holies being 20 cubits, or 360 inches square, with a perimeter of 1,440 inches, while the Holy Place is 720 by 360 inches, having a perimeter of 2,160, the number of miles in the moon's diameter; its width being 20 cubits, it just contains the sun's orbit, taking the sun's distance at 10; and its diagonal is $63\frac{1}{3}$ cubits, which is nearly the circumference of the sun's orbit $(20 \times 3\frac{1}{7} = 62\frac{6}{7})$. The rhombus, which contains the Holy of Holies and Holy Place, has a perimeter of 217·80 cubits, or the diameter of the sun's orbit.

The measures of the porch are 180 × 360 inches, which gives a perimeter of 1,080, the number of miles in the moon's radius. The internal length of the Temple, from east to west, including the porch, is 76 cubits, or 1,368 inches, and $144 \times 9\frac{1}{2} = 1,368$, and a vesica 1,368 broad is 2,368 long. The perimeter of the Temple externally is 471 feet, or the diameter of a circle having a circumference of 1,480 (Christos); and its length externally, from east to west, is 98 cubits, which is about the radius of Saturn's orbit, if the sun's distance be taken at 10. The width of two intersecting circles forming a vesica 98 broad is 294, the number of the name ecclesia, the Church. The width of the front is 59 cubits, or 88 feet, or 1,062 inches, and 88 is the amount of the sun's declination in the ecliptic measured by its own diameter. The length, from the outside of the eastern wall to the outside of the western wall of the Holy of Holies, is 88 cubits. The external width of the cell is 576 inches, the width, including the side chambers, being 756 inches, the height of the cross, whose extreme length is 1,080.

The three divisions of the Temple were called DBIR, 216, HKL, 55, or HIKL, 65, and AVLM, 637. The name of the Holy of Holies, DBIR, has the value of the diameter of the sun's orbit; the numbers 55 and 65, deduced from the names of the Holy Place, express the number of miles in the earth's diameter divided by 12 twice, and the side of the Holy Oblation (the sum of the numbers from 1 to 64 = 2,080); whilst the name of the porch, AVLM, denotes the cross ($637\frac{1}{2} \times 2 = 1,275$). The three numbers evidently symbolize the persons of the great cabalistic triad, the macrocosm being represented by the sun, the microcosm by the Holy Oblation, and the Bride by the elemental cross.

$$216 + 1$$
$$\left.\begin{array}{c} 55 + 1 \\ 637 + 1 \end{array}\right\} 692 \qquad \begin{array}{c} 216 + 1 \\ 65 + 1 \\ 637 + 1 \end{array}$$
$$\overline{908 + 3 = 911} \qquad \overline{918 + 3 = 921.}$$

According to the first valuation, the sum of the three numbers, with the addition and subtraction of colel, is either 905 or 911. The number 905 is the circumference of the two circles, producing a vesica having a perimeter of $603\frac{1}{2}$, which is the side of another vesica 1,046 long, or the radius of the circle which contains the square 1,480. The same vesica measures $249\frac{3}{13}$ by 144, and 249·264 × 9·5 = 2,368. Again, 55 + 637 = 692, or one more than the length of the sun's orbit; and 216 + 637 = 853, the side of a vesica 1,480 long. Then 911 is the perimeter of a rhombus whose sides are $227\frac{1}{2}$, which gives the height of a man 2,160 high ($227\frac{1}{2}$ × $9\frac{1}{2}$ = 2,160). And 911 is the numerical equivalent of RASHITH, Beginning.

In the second case, the sum of the numbers, with the addition of colel to each, is 921, the numerical equivalent of the Greek word, ΚΑΝΩΝ (canon). The Temple is designed in a peculiar form, being in fact in the shape of the ithyphallos, the appropriate symbol of the great triad, and 97 (the radius of the Holy Oblation, taking the sun's distance at 10), multiplied by $9\frac{1}{2}$, produces 921, the sum of the three names.

It is not proposed to enter minutely into the measures of the last temple of the Jews, described by Josephus and the Rabbis. But the altar of that temple has been so fully commented upon by old writers, and its measures having been carefully recorded, it may be profitably examined here. The altar was situated in the court in front of the temple, its height was 10 cubits, and it was arranged in three stories. The foundation was 32 cubits square and 1 cubit high; it therefore contains 1,024 solid cubits ($32^2 = 1,024$) which is the radius of Saturn's orbit. The next storey is 30 cubits square by 5 cubits high, and contains 4,500 solid cubits. The third storey is 28 cubits square by 4 cubits high, and contains 3,136 solid cubits. Now, 1,024 + 4,500 + 3,136 = 8,660, and this number is the perimeter of a square whose sides are 2,165 $\left(\dfrac{8,660}{4} = 2,165\right)$, the number of miles in the moon's diameter. This calculation bringing out the moon's diameter, seems to account for the horns, which were fashioned upon its corners, and for which there is no satisfactory explanation extant.

There is a further peculiarity about the foundation of this altar noticed by Oliver ("Landmarks," vol. ii., p. 431). He says 5 and 7 are the nearest

N

roots of two square numbers, one of which is double the other, or, in other words, 5 is very nearly the side of a square whose diagonal is seven. Therefore, if the area of the one square $(5 \times 5 = 25)$ be double the area of the other square $(7 \times 7 = 49)$, and if in both these squares we make all the stones we can double squares, we get all the stones but one in each square of the proportion of the Holy Place, that is, a double square ; but the corner one being square, or of the proportion of the Holy of Holies, was called the chief corner stone ; and the one wanting to the 49 to make the double square was identified with the Logos or Messiah. The lesser square has twelve stones and the holy one, and symbolizes the Messiah and the twelve prophets or apostles ; while the greater one contains twenty-four stones corresponding to the twenty-four elders : " thereby making the future glory and perfection of the Mosaic or Christian dispensation analagous to the duplication of the square." The holy corner stone is placed in the south-east angle (" Bab. Talmud "). Now the Rabbis, in their description of the altar, say, " the length of the foundation on every side of the square was 32 cubits . . . but in the southeast angle it wanted somewhat, to make the corner a perfect angle " (Lightfoot, "Temple," p. 195). And 32 cubits are equal to 48 feet. But if the foundation were 49 on every side, its area would be $(2{,}368 + 33 =) 2{,}401$, therefore this square must have a piece deducted from it to make it exactly 2,368 square. If this be the mystery referred to by Oliver, it is necessary to suppose that the altar was composed of 49 such cubes as he describes, each 7 feet square, then the area of the upper face of the odd stone being 33 and its thickness being 7, its cubical contents would be 231, and this odd piece is apparently to be taken from the south-east angle. The reason for calling the rejected stone the chief corner stone may be due to the extraordinary number of cosmic measures found in the multiples of 231.

For instance, $231 \times 2 = 462$, which is the height of a rood cross whose extreme length is 660 or $\dfrac{7,920}{12}$.

Then $231 \times 3 = 693$, which is nearly the length of the sun's orbit ($220 \times 3\frac{1}{7} = 691$). And $231 \times 4 = 924$, which is the square root of the sun's diameter in miles. Again, $231 \times 5 = 1,155$, which is one more than the length of a vesica 666 broad. And $231 \times 9 = 2,079$, which is nearly $\frac{1}{12}$ of the earth's circumference, divided by 12. And a square whose sides are $230\frac{1}{5}$ has a diagonal of $325\frac{1}{2}$; therefore the two limbs of a cross drawn within it measure 651 ($= 325\frac{1}{2} \times 2$), and 651 is the diameter of a circle having a circumference of 2,046, the diameter of Saturn's orbit. A circle whose area is equal to that of a square whose sides are 231 has a diameter of 260 and a circumference of 817, and 817 is the length of a vesica 471 broad, and 471 is the diameter of a circle having a circumference of 1,480. Thus it would appear that the stone which the builders rejected became the head stone of the corner, because it contained the number 231, the measures of the earth, the sun, and the universe. This number 231 seems to have been one of the great canonical numbers. In the cabalistic book " Yetsirah " we hear of 231 gates or combination of letters, which, together with the 10 sephiroth are called " the foundation of all things." And 231 is the sum of the numbers from 1 to 21 ; and this may have occasioned the omission of the number 22 from the cards of the Tarot, their sum being 231. The Greek word, ὄνομα, a name, has the numerical value of 231, and the perimeter of the lid of the pyramid coffer is 231 inches.

It was said that the square whose area was 49 was double that which was 25. Francis Potter, in his work on the number 666, has pointed out the importance attached to the number 25 in the Romish Church. The sum of the numbers from 1 to 25 is 325, and $325\frac{1}{2}$ is the diagonal of a square whose sides are $230\frac{1}{5}$. He gives a diagram of the altar of St. Peter, in St. Peter's Church at Rome, which he says was a cube 25 feet on every side. The area of one of the sides of the altar would therefore be $25^2 = 625$, and its solid bulk would be $25^3 = 15,625$ feet. According to Archimedes a circle which has a circumference of 15,625 (actually between 15,610 and 15,620) is 4,970 in diameter; now, if the number be increased to 15,635, the square which incloses this circle has a perimeter of $4,975 \times 4 = 19,902$, and 19,902 feet $= 238,828$ inches, or the number of miles in the moon's distance from the earth. Therefore, the altar of St. Peter has the same numerical significance as the altar described by the Rabbis. This cubical stone or altar is evidently a symbol of the rock Petros. The number 5, the square root of 25, was further accentuated by the stamping of the 5 wounds of Christ in 5 places in every altar.

Another mystical statement about Herod's temple, which may be mentioned, is that of Josephus with respect to the stones used in its construction. He says, "Now the temple was built of stones that were white and strong, and each of their length was 25 cubits, their height was 8, and their breadth *about* 12" ("Antiq.," bk. xv., chap. xi.). And $25 \times 8 \times 11\cdot84 = 2,368$, the numerical value of the name Jesus Christ. Again, 25 cubits $= 37\frac{1}{2}$ feet, and 12 cubits $= 18$ feet, and $37\frac{1}{2} \times 18 = 675$, therefore, the area of the top of these stones, if we add colel, was 676, the square of 26, the number of Tetragammaton. Further,

the area of the side of one of these stones is
$18 \times 12 = 216$ feet, the diameter of the sun's
orbit.

The temple described by Ezekiel is so much
more magnificent in scale than that of Solomon,
and so disproportionately large for a city of the
size of Jerusalem, that the commentators have been
obliged to acknowledge it as a visionary structure.
In fact, the precincts are stated to be so great that,
when drawn upon the site, they nearly cover the
whole area of the city. Each side of the temple is
given at 500 cubits of 21 inches, that is, the cubit
and handbreadth or palm, which is $\frac{1}{6}$ of an ordinary
cubit of a foot and a half. Now 500 of these
great cubits are equal to $583\frac{1}{3}$ common cubits.
The peribolus is given at 125 reeds, or 750 great
cubits, while the outer wall measures 500 reeds.

The courts of Ezekiel's temple, like the camp,
are formed into a diagram illustrating the squaring
of the circle (see p. 37). And the diagonal of a
square whose side is $583\frac{1}{3}$ being 825, the diameter
of the circle whose area is equal to that of the
temple is 660 $\left(\dfrac{825}{10} = 82 \cdot 5 \times 8 = 660, \right)$ or $\frac{1}{12}$ of the
earth's diameter in miles.

Again, a vesica formed of two circles whose
united width is $583\frac{1}{3}$ measures 194·4 broad, and
therefore contains the circle of the Zodiac, the
sun's distance being taken at 10.

Moreover the peribolus being 750 cubits square
is enclosed by a rhombus inscribed within the
orbit of Saturn.

The outer square of 500 reeds may indicate the
lunar year, for the diagonal of a square 354 is $500\frac{1}{2}$.
And the diagonals of a square 501 amount to 1,002,
or half the number 2,004, the numerical equivalent
of the Greek names of the elements.

"Strange and uncouth," says Samuel Lee, "is

the fancy of Villalpanda stating the temple's typical similitude in proportion to and with the body of our Blessed Lord upon the cross, with His arms stretched out and His legs conjoined together, in such a manner; as that His head should possess the sanctuary, and his breast the altar, His feet the eastern gate; in His hands the two gates on the north and south side of the temple, so that as the passage or way to the altar and sanctuary lay open through those principal gates, in like manner should the path to the sanctuary be made plain and easy, through the wounds of His feet and hands. Whence it is, that the brazen sea, which was situated on the south side of the temple, near the altar, should prefigure the water and blood issuing out of the right side of the Lord." (" Solomon's Temple," 1659, p. 189).

It has already been explained that a rood cross inscribed within the square contained by the circumference of the earth divided by 12 has many analogies with the measures of the universe. A man crucified on such a cross would be enclosed by a circle equal to the sun's orbit, and the extreme length of the cross is 666. From the preceding analysis of the measures of the temple it appears that the fancy of Villalpanda is not so strange as Samuel Lee pretends, nor is it more strange than some of his own "fancies," which any one may read in the work just quoted.

These coincidences are perhaps enough to show the mystical nature of the Biblical structures, and the purely allegorical character of the descriptions.

CHAPTER VIII.

THE TEMPLES.

> " *The frame thereof seem'd partly circular,*
> *And part triangular : O work divine !*
> *Those two the first and last proportions are ;*
> *The one imperfect, mortal, feminine !*
> *Th' other immortal, perfect, masculine ;*
> *And twixt them both a quadrate was the base,*
> *Proportioned equally by seven and nine ;*
> *Nine was the circle set in heaven's place :*
> *All which compacted, made a goodly diapase.*"
>   Description of the Castle of Temperance, " Faerie
>   Queen," bk. ii., canto ix., stanza 22.

> " *When the proportions are adjusted, and the dimensions found*
> *by calculation, then it is the part of a skilful architect to consider*
> *the nature of the place, the purpose of the building, and the beauty*
> *of it.*"—VITRUVIUS, bk. vi., c. ii.

THE beauty of the old temples and cathedrals,
and the veneration in which they were held present a striking contrast to the insignificant churches
of modern Christendom, and the indifference shown
towards them by priests and peoples alike. A few
centuries ago the mysticism of theology used to
make every feature of ecclesiastical architecture a
hieroglyph, which all could read except the totally
blind. But new times bring new manners, and so
we notice the English Puritans of the Seventeenth
Century—intent upon boastful reformations of the
old worship—busily converting the " idolatrous
Steeple-House " into a place where decent people
could invoke the Logos free from offensive symbols.
Since then purity has given place to ignorance. So

now, instead of a church pervaded by some of that sublimity, seen in universal nature, and faithfully imitated by reverent and skilful artists, we find the significant measures and consecrated proportions of antiquity succeeded by the meaningless emptiness of mere cant and cheapness.

The beginning of the sixteenth century, when Cesariano was editing Vitruvius, was the beginning of that time of severance. It marks the decadence of the old ideas, preserved and continued under various conditions from an origin reaching back thousands of years, and inaugurates the birth of the new and necessarily crude doctrines, which have, ever since, been gradually replacing the accumulated store of achievement which the art of countless generations of men had brought to a marvellous perfection.

Amongst other changes, and coincident with the decay of so much else, we notice at this time the gradual disappearance of the old order of practical Freemasons, and a corresponding decline in all the architectural arts. The change of religious opinions affecting the whole basis of theology, necessarily extended to the design of the churches, entrusted during the Middle Ages to the Freemasons who had worked according to the ancient rules received in continuity from their predecessors, who had worshipped the older gods of earlier systems, whose rites still survived and accorded with the primitive Christianity of the mediæval Church.

It was when this old conception of religion began to be superseded at the Reformation, that the need or desire for a body of architects instructed in theological mysteries no longer acknowledged, ceased to exist, and the secret methods of all previous temple builders left in the hands of the Freemasons fell into disuse and were gradually forgotten.

Out of the records of the modern lodges, and other collateral sources, it is possible to derive a clue to the mysterious rules which constituted the canonical method of building churches, according to ecclesiastical use and practice. It is an unquestionable fact that there was a canonical art of building, just as there was a canon of the Mass, canonical books, canonical robes, canonical hours, canons of chronology, and canonized saints. All these canonical forms appear to depend upon one fundamental mystery, which we shall now only attempt to explain in its architectural aspect.

It is stated by J. S. Hawkins ("Origin of Gothic Architecture," p. 183) that during the erection of the dome of Sienna, in 1321, the five gentlemen appointed to inspect the building objected to the continuance of the work, " because if completed as it had been begun it would not have that measure in length, breadth, and height, which the rules of a church require. And they further added that the old structure, to which as it seems the new adjoined, was so justly proportioned, and its members so well agreed with each other in breadth, length, and height, that if in any one part an addition were made to it under the pretence of reducing it to the right measure of a church, the whole would be destroyed." (Quoted from a document dated 1321, published by Della Valle, " Lettere Senese," vol. ii., p. 60).

One of the most direct evidences of the old mystical rule of building is found in Cesariano's edition of Vitruvius, published at Como, in 1521. In this valuable and remarkable book there are a plan and sections of Milan Cathedral, drawn with the geometrical forms, which are said to have determined the proportions of the building. It would appear that this so-called German method of fixing the measures of a cathedral does partly reveal the canonical methods of the masons, and that it also applies to the classical temples described by Vitruvius, otherwise it would scarcely find a place as an illustration in this work. Nor would an architect of the Renascence, who built by the rules of Vitruvius, and who must have been instructed in the German manner of design, make the mistake of claiming a common basis for classical and mediæval architecture, if such an agreement had not existed. During the fifteenth and sixteenth centuries in Italy, the book of Vitruvius was held in the highest esteem, and societies were even instituted for its study and interpretation (Addington Symonds). This appreciation must have been due to some cause unknown to modern critics, for this work is no longer read, and does not form, as it used to do, the one text book on the art of building, revered as much by an architect as the canonical Scriptures are by a priest. And it is not surprising to find that modern architects, who do not know that the treatise of Vitruvius is a mystical book, and do not understand the rules which he teaches, have considered the introduction of the plan of Milan Cathedral as an irrelevant digression on the part of Cesariano ; whereas, it is really a most important illustration of the principles of architecture common to all ancient peoples. It would be unreasonable to expect that we should have in this scheme, applied to the cathedral at Milan, a complete exposition of all the mysteries of the architectural canon, but we have as much as Cesariano dared to reveal, and enough to establish the fundamental principle of the old geometrical system of design.

By the scheme before us, the geometrical figure, forming the basis of the plan of Milan cathedral, is the rhombus or vesica. It is here invisibly introduced into the plan as the mystical comple-

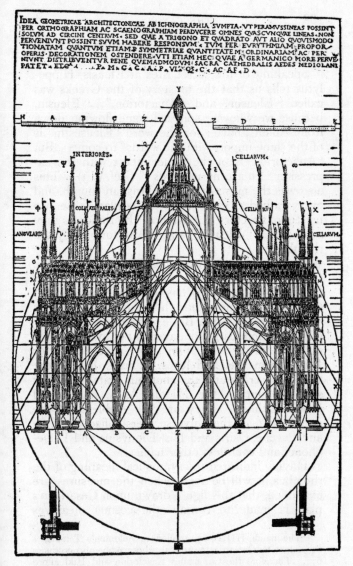

IDEA GEOMETRICAE ARCHITECTONICAE AB ICHNOGRAPHIA SVMPTA·VT PERAMVSSINEAS POSSINT
PER ORTHOGRAPHIAM AC SCAENOGRAPHIAM PERDVCERE OMNES QVASCVNQVAE LINEAS·NON
SOLVM AD CIRCINI CENTRVM·SED QVAE A TRIGONO ET QVADRATO AVT ALIO QVOVISMODO
PERVENIVNT POSSINT SVVM HABERE RESPONSVM·TVM PER EVRYTHMIAM·PROPOR-
TIONATAM QVANTVM ETIAM·P·SYMMETRIAE QVANTITATEM·ORDINARIAM·AC PER
OPERIS·DECORATIONEM OSTENDERE·VTI ETIAM HEC·QVAE A·GERMANICO MORE PERVE-
NIVNT DISTRIBVENTVR PENE QVEMADMODVM·SACRA CATHEDRALIS AEDES MEDIOLANI
PATET·ETC·A·····P·M·G·C·A·P·VI·Q·C·AC AF·D·

FIG. 15.—SECTION OF MILAN CATHEDRAL, FROM THE CUT IN
CESARIANO'S EDITION OF "VITRUVIUS," FOLIO XV, VERSO.

ment of the cross, which is openly and avowedly exhibited in the form of the church.

Speaking of the secret rites at Eleusis, Hippolytus tells us that the mystery of the Greeks was called " Eleusin" and "Anactorion." " Eleusin, because we who are spiritual come flowing down from Adam above ; for the word ' Eleusesthi' is of the same import with the words ' to come.' But ' Anactorion' is of the same import with the expression ' To ascend upwards'" (Ref. v. 3). This also was the mystery of the Christian church, and every cathedral symbolized by its plan those two mysterious factors of existence. By the cross they symbolized " Eleusin," and " Anactorion" by the rhombus.

Anactorion was a word commonly used by the Greeks for a temple. It means the royal house or the king's house, and it has the numerical value of 672, which is 1 more than the value of the Hebrew word Thora, 671, the Bride.[1] She was mystically laid as the foundation or pavement of every church, prepared to received from above Her Spouse or Bridegroom, the Lord Jesus. This is the mystery which the cross and the rhombus united together signified during the Middle Ages, and in all previous times. They are the emblems of the double soul of the universe, personified by Eros and Psyche, Osiris and Isis, Dionysius and Persephone, and countless other names.

Having indicated the symbolical meaning of the rhombus, it will be seen, when the measures are examined, that this figure drawn upon Cesariano's plan is made to contain the cosmic measures

---

[1] The name HIKL, 65, applied to Solomon's Temple, is equivalent by Gematria to Adonai, whose name also produces 671. Therefore the two names Anactorion and Hikl afford another example of the numerical agreement of the Greek and Hebrew languages.

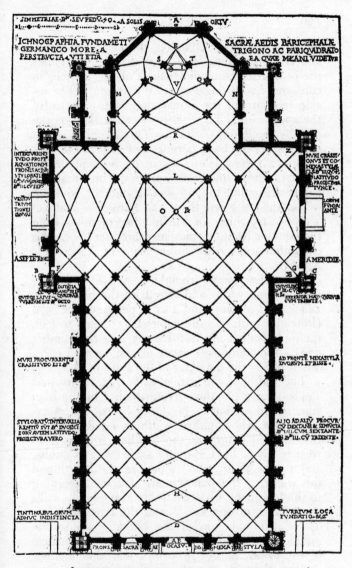

FIG. 16.—PLAN OF MILAN CATHEDRAL, FROM CESARIANO'S
EDITION OF "VITRUVIUS," FOLIO XIIII.

found in the Holy Oblation, the city of Ezekiel, and the New Jerusalem, and that it determines the proportions and dimensions of the church, in conformity with these mystical patterns. The inside measure of the transepts, and the centre of the apse, are fixed by the rhombus, marked on the plan by the letters EFGH. This rhombus is 128 cubits wide, and has a perimeter of 512 (= 128 × 4). Now 512 is the side of a square having a perimeter of 2,048, the diameter of Saturn's orbit; and 512 cubits are equal to 768 feet, a number which is 1 less than the length of the tranverse beam of a cross 1,656 high, or the number of miles from the equator to the tropics, measured on the earth's circumference, and the full measure of this cross is 2,366⅔.

Then the greater rhombus, ABCD, marking the extreme width and length of the building, is 144 × 249⅔ cubits, and has a perimeter of 576 (Pneuma, 576). If the cubits be reduced to feet, the numbers become 216 by 373, and the number 373 is the numerical value of the name Logos. Then 216 is the diameter of the sun's orbit.

The width of the cathedral is 144 cubits, and 144 × 9½ = 1,368, thus giving the height of a man standing in the vesica produced by two intersecting circles, whose united width is 2,368. Again, the internal length of the building from east to west is given by Cesariano as being 250 cubits, and 249¼ × 9½ = 2,368; therefore, the length and the width of the building are decided according to the length of what Sir John Maundeville calls the "Cross of our Lord," and the cross of Ἰησοῦς Χριστός. The height of the building, up to the middle of the figure standing upon the pinnacle of the tower, is 155·79 cubits, and this number multiplied by 9½ = 1,480, so that the three principal dimensions of this great Italian cathedral are derived from the measures of three human bodies, 1,368, 1,480, and 2,368 cubits high respectively.

The nave or ship of the church is 144 cubits, or 216 feet long, and is an appropriate measure for the ark of the sun. Then the length, from the centre of the apse to the western wall, is 235 cubits, the side of the New Jerusalem.

There is the following allusion to the system of geometric proportions in the " Hypnerotomachia," Aldus, 1499, verso of sig. C :

" At length being come to this ancient porch, a worke worthie the looking upon marvellously composed by exquisite rules, and by art nobly beautified, with divers and sundry sorts of cuttings, which did inflame a desire in me to understand and find out the lineaments and practise of the architect. I began in this manner, making a square from the two columns on either side in a perfect sort, in the which I tooke the due proportion of the whole porch.

" A tetragon figure ABCD divided by three lines straight, and three overthwart equally distant one from another will make sixteene quadrats, then adde to the figure as much more in the like proportion, dividing the adjunct you shall finde foure and twenty squares. This figure shall serve of credycels to make the inlepturgie and briefe demonstration that followeth.

" Draw then in the first fygure ABCD two diagons, make also in the same two lines, one straight downe, and the other overthwart, which make foure quadrats mutually intersect.

" Then in the voide over the Isopleures make foure mediane prickes, drawing lines from one to another, and they will make the Rhombus.[1]

[1] In the original the references to the rhombus stand thus : (1) "Item in quella vacua sopra le isopleure facti quatro medi-

"When I had drawn this figure after this
manner I straightway mused with my selfe, what
reason should moove many of our woorkemen in
these dayes eyther to thinke well of themselves, or

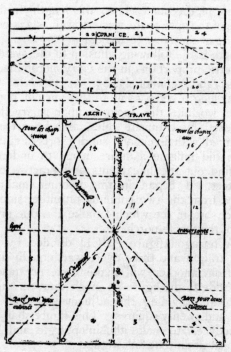

FIG. 17.—DIAGRAM FROM THE "HYPNEROTOMACHIE" (PARIS,
1546), VERSO OF FOLIO 12.

take the art of building in hand, *not knowing what
it is?* Making such groose faults in churches and
great men's houses, defaming arte, and so ignorant,

ani puncti, & da uno ad laltro deducte le linee si constituisce
il Rhombo" (sig. C 1 verso); (2) "Dalla quale removendo
poscia Il rhombo, & gli diagonii" (sig. C 2).

that they seeme as though they could not consider what nature hir selfe dooth teach us in beholding of hir woorkes.

"And what part soever is not agreeable with this principle is foule and nought. For take away *order and rule*, and what thing can any man make, either beautifull to the eye, or of commendable proportion and durable?" (English translation, fol. 18.)

The meaning of the passage is certainly obscure, but the explanation may be suggested thus : The " tetragon figure ABCD " is a square, whose sides are 16, and the "rhombus" of half that width measures 16 × 8. The two combined produce a rectangle 24 × 16, having an area of 384. Now a vesica 384˙225 broad is 666 long, and 384 is the radius of the sun's orbit measured by the tone. The two "diagons" or diagonals, drawn within the square ABCD, form a saltire, the symbol of the microcosm, and their length is nearly 22⅔, therefore by the rule of Vitruvius the corresponding square of the macrocosm would have an area of 512 ($16^2 = 256 \times 2 = 512$). And since a square whose sides are 512 has a perimeter of 2,048, the diameter of Saturn's orbit, the whole figure sets forth the measures of the seven planetary orbits and sphere of the Zodiac, containing the body of Christos in the square 1,480, first by the square and rhombus, the symbols of man and woman, and secondly by the duplication of the square. The four equal "quadrats" made by the cross lines have each an area of 64, and the sum of the numbers from 1 to 64 is 2,080. It will be noticed that the proportion of the rhombus given here is that of a double square, and not 26 : 15 as indicated by Cesariano on the plan of Milan cathedral.

It may have been the contemplation of these mysteries that occasioned the musings of Poliphilus upon those who "take the art of building in hand, not knowing what it is."

The Greeks called their temples by many names besides Anactorion. The word Οἶκος (house), used commonly for the house of man, was also applied to the house of God. It has a numerical value of 370, which, multiplied by 4, produces 1,480, the side of the square contained within the sphere of the Zodiac or the outermost sphere of the universe, inclosed by the Holy Oblation.

The name Ἱερον, again, means properly the Holy Thing or the Holy Place. Its numerical value is 235, which is the length of the side of the New Jerusalem, inclosing the inner orbits of the planets.

The word Naos is spelt in two ways, Νεως, 1,055, Ναος, 321. This, like the Latin and English words Navis and Nave, is the ship of the temple (Ναος = Ναυς). It was that part of the structure which contained the mystical Argo or Ark, having a meaning analogous to the cross. The number 1,055 is the length of a vesica 609 broad, and $194 \times 3\frac{1}{7} = 609$. By transposition the number 321 becomes 312, which is 1 more than the internal width of an ark containing the sun's course measured by the tone. Naos has the same numerical value as Καλός, Beautiful, and 321 is the mean between 320·37 and 322·76, the diameters of the circles which produce the two vesicas 671 and 676 in circumference.

Sekos (Σηκός), the name applied to the cell of a temple, has the value of 498, and 499 is the measure of a cross whose limbs are $249\frac{1}{4}$ ($249\frac{1}{4} \times 9\frac{1}{2} = 2,368$). τὸ πᾶν, the world, is numerically equal to $501 - 2 = 499$.

The name Temenos was given to the precincts of a temple, and it has the value of 670, the numerical equivalent of ὁ κοσμος, the universe.

Further, τό τέμενος yields 1,040, the radius of the sphere of the Zodiac.

Before Christian times a Greek altar was called Bωμός, which yields the number 1,112, which is the circumference of a circle having a diameter of 354, the number of days in the lunar year. As may be seen from ancient vases, the altars of the Greeks were made with horns at their corners, that they might resemble the horned moon. And by Gematria Bomos is equivalent to Zodiakos, 1,112. In the midst of every Christian church around the Omphalos or cross at its centre was the Choros, or choir, set apart for the singers. The name Choros had long been familiar in classical Greece, as applied to certain players who acted a peculiar and important part in the old tragedies. But originally the Choros was a dance by which the earliest worshippers invoked the deity, moving with measured steps around the altar. Theseus is said to have first taught this mystic dance at Athens. And the name Choros yields 1,040, the radius of the zodiacal circle contained within the Holy Oblation. Therefore when the Greek youths and virgins danced round the primitive altar or sacred fire, they sought to reproduce the chorus of the twelve stars, which mark the intervals of the sun's course in his yearly revolution. This simple ritual was the prototype foreshadowing all the elaborate ceremonies in the costly temples of after times, and admirably illustrates the first impulse towards the imitation of the measured harmony of the heavenly bodies, whose circular motions were counterfeited by the choral dance. And the choir (Choros) of the Christian church, "who mystically represent the Cherubim" (Liturgy of St. Chrysostom), sang also in imitation of the celestial music. It has been shown that the Apostles are equivalent to the signs of the Zodiac; and Samuel Lee says that the Church was "signified by the moon and the twelve stars of the Apostles" ("Sol. Temp.," p. 181); and Peter was called by St. Chrysostom "the leader of the Apostolic choir" (ὁ κορυφαῖος τοῦ χοροῦ).

The name given to the Church by the early Christians was the ordinary Greek word for an assembly. Numerically the word Ecclesia has the value of 294, and by Gematria it is equivalent to ἡ Ἀκαδήμεια, which was adopted by Plato as the name of his school, for a vesica formed by two intersecting circles whose united width is 294 is 98 wide; and 98 is the value of the word Μὴν, a month, which by Gematria is equivalent to Ἐλένη, the name of the heroine of the "Iliad," and the Empress of Rome, who is said to have found the true cross at Jerusalem. The moon, or month, was often mentioned by early writers as a symbol of the Church, and St. Helena may be recognized as a personification of it. The vesica was one of the ordinary symbols of the Church, mystically honoured as the spouse of Christ. And St. Helena's discovery of the cross, the complement of the vesica, is a metaphorical way of expressing the nuptial union of the Christos and Ecclesia. If the number 294 be united to 1,480 (Christos) we get 1,774. Now two interlacing triangles whose sides are 1,774 are exactly contained within the orbit of Saturn. This figure, commonly called Solomon's seal, has always been revered by Christians as the symbol of the Trinity—the Father or first person of the Triad being, presumably, implied by the circle of Saturn. And if 1,090, the numerical value of Chronos, be added, the three numbers amount to 2,867, or 1 less than the sum of the numbers obtained from the names of the ten steps of the Cabala :

CHRONOS	.	.	1,090
CHRISTOS	.	.	1,480
ECCLESIA	.	.	294

$\left.\begin{array}{c}1,090\\1,480\\294\end{array}\right\}$ 1,774

2,864 + 3 = 2,867.

Then, 294 is the diameter of a circle having a circumference of 924, the square root of the sun's diameter in miles. And $294\frac{3}{5} \times 10 = 2,946$, the diagonal of the Holy Oblation. These measures seem to have been in the mind of St. Cyril when he says that the Church "is called Catholic because it is throughout the world from one end of the earth to the other; and because it teaches universally and completely one and all the doctrines which ought to come to men's knowledge concerning things both visible and invisible, heavenly and earthly" ("Cat. Lect.," xviii., p. 250). At any rate, such a description could hardly apply to the paltry assembly of Christians who in his day met mostly in holes and corners as advocates of a new and despised mythos.

The basilicas of the Romans were frequently converted into churches by the early Christians. The name was retained, and was often used to designate a church. Βασιλική is numerically equal to 281, which is the amount of the diameter of the moon's orbit, or the sublunary world, divided by

12 thrice, $\dfrac{485,576}{12} = \dfrac{40,464}{12} = \dfrac{3,372}{12} = 281.$

Afterwards the name cathedral was generally applied to the great churches of the west. This word is derived from Καθέδρα, 140, a chair or seat; and ἡ Καθέδρα, that is, the chair, or God's seat, has the numerical value of 148, and 148 is a common measure of the three numbers, 888, 1,480, and 2,368. The word ἕδρα, 110, or ἕδρη, 117, was also applied to an altar or temple. And the number

110 is the measure of the sun's distance, and 116
and a fraction is the diameter of a circle having a
circumference of 360.

The Christians called their altar THUSIASTERION,
1,358, which is the circumference of a circle 432
in diameter.   Now every altar was inscribed with
five crosses, or quincunx, of five points, and if we
multiply 432 by 5 we get 2,160, the number of
miles in the moon's diameter.   And the altar was
connected with the moon both by the Greeks and
Hebrews.   Again, 432 is the circumference of a
circle whose diameter is $137\frac{2}{3}$, which is nearly the
side of a square contained within the Holy Oblation, if the sun's distance be taken at 10.   That
is to say, 137 is equivalent to 1,480.   The number
432 is also the width of the two intersecting circles
which produce the vesica 144 by $249\frac{1}{4}$.   Lastly,
432 is the side of a square having a diagonal of
611, the perimeter of a square inscribed within
the sun's orbit.

The three divisions of a Christian church in its
final development were called Bema, Choros, and
Narthex.

$$\begin{array}{lr}
\text{Βῆμα} . & 51 \\
\text{Χορός} . & 1,040 + 1 \;\}\; \\
\text{Νάρθηξ} & 228 + 1 \;\} \; 1,270 \\
\hline
& 1,319 + 2 = 1,321.
\end{array}$$

They correspond to the Holy of Holies, the Holy
Place, and the Porch of Solomon's Temple, as
indicated on Kircher's cabalistic diagram.   The
sum of the numbers deduced from the three names
is 1,321, and a cross inscribed within a vesica
1,321 long measures (1,321 + 762 =) 2,083, the
side of the Holy Oblation.   The number 51 (Bema)
is the square root of 2,601, or the side of a square
inclosing the body of the Logos crucified on a

cross whose height is equal to the number of miles in the earth's diameter. There is another reason why the Bema or sanctuary, which symbolized Heaven or the Empyreum, may have been so called. For the name Jesus, together with those of his parents on earth, yield 2,601 :

$$
\begin{array}{ll}
\text{Ἰοσὴφ} . & 1,518 + 1 \\
\text{Μαρίαμ} & 192 + 1 \\
\text{Ἰησοῦς} . & 888 + 1 \\
\hline
& 2,598 + 3 = 2,601.
\end{array}
$$

The classical Greeks called the stone from which the Athenians spoke in the Pnyx, the Bema. Choros has the value of 1,040, or 1 and a fraction less than the radius of the sphere of the Zodiac, while 228 (Narthex) multiplied by $9\frac{1}{2}$ produces 2,166, the number of miles in the moon's diameter. With the addition of colel 1,040 and 228 amount to 1,270, or 1 less than the numerical value of Stauros, a cross. The Narthex, or hollow reed by which Prometheus brought down the mystic fire to earth, is peculiarly appropriate to the ideas connected with the third division of a temple or church.

The belief that some mysterious purpose exists in the design of the Egyptian pyramids, although unsupported by the direct testimony of those ancient authors who have alluded to them, may reasonably be held upon various grounds. All we learn from Herodotus is an inaccurate measurement, and the statement that the great pyramid was the tomb of Cheops, erected by him during his lifetime out of despotic vanity, and a desire to perpetuate his memory, if possible, for ever. It has been thought also, that the great pyramid was built as the royal treasury. But assuming that both these objects, as they might have been, were the ostensible motives for its erection, this stupendous fabric may have included less apparent purposes, and given the opportunity to its architects of applying to it whatever ideas prevailed at that time, as to the functions of architecture. That most skilful artificers were employed in its construction is sufficiently attested by the admirable finish and perfection of the masonry. And the marvellous accuracy in fitting and joining the stones favours the idea, that such careful niceties of workmanship must have been applied for some definite reason, which is certainly not that of producing an ornamental effect. Then the peculiarity of the internal arrangements point to the existence of some principle of design, which shows that the builders were governed by some other ideas than those of utility and permanence alone.

If their only object had been to erect a vast heap of well hewn stones to enclose the body and treasures of Cheops, without art or design, the chambers and arrangements of the building would give some evidence of such artlessness in their contrivance. Instead of which, it is well known that the chambers and galleries of the pyramid have been devised upon a system which cannot be accounted for by any simple or obvious reasons. For the intentions of the builders, whatever they may have been, have led them far beyond the ordinary necessities of mere use.

No architect, again, whose object was to produce a beautiful building, would choose a pyramid as a means of accomplishing his end ; therefore beauty cannot be regarded as the motive of his choice. But the pyramidal form must have been advisedly chosen : so, to discover his motive, we must inquire what purpose could be fulfilled architecturally by an unadorned pyramid. The most natural answer seems to be, that apart from its structural fitness, it was selected simply as a geometrical figure. And the existence of the pyramids, the oldest monuments in the world, seems to be a striking confirmation of the statements of the earliest writers, that architecture originally depended upon geometry, and we see in Egypt the first application of that science to building, unaccompanied by the ornaments which were afterwards brought into use. In the hands of geometrical architects the pyramid by its bulk, surface, lines, and angles, would afford the means of recording measures and numbers. For practical purposes, also, the pyramid is a most suitable form for a permanent fabric. For it stands on a solid base, and its sloping sides, rising to a point, prevent water from lodging upon its surface and causing decay. It is much better fitted for such a purpose than a cube, which has a flat top ; moreover, while the latter figure has the greater number of sides, lines, and angles, the pyramid has more points of measurement.

We shall, therefore, conclude that it was the object of the builders, by this simple geometrical figure to set up an enduring monument, exemplifying by its measures and numbers those canonical laws of Egypt, alluded to by Plato, which, it is supposed, were the pattern and source of all our later philosophical and theological systems. It accordingly follows that this remarkable structure is an exact embodiment of the universe, geometrically reduced to a pyramidal form, and exhibiting the true aspect of the cosmic system as it appeared and was known to the Egyptians at the time of its foundation. This view is borne out by the opinion of John Greaves, the old Oxford astronomer, from whose work on "English Weights and Measures" we quote the following: "According to Arabic traditions, one of the pyramids is the sepulchre of Seth . . . and it seems probable that the pyramids are the pillars of Seth. And these pillars of Seth, according to Josephus, were in the very same place where Manetho placed the pillars of Thoth, called Seiread." The words of Josephus respecting these pillars are: " They (the children of Seth) were the inventors of that peculiar sort of wisdom which is concerned with the heavenly bodies and their order. And that their inventions might not be lost before they were sufficiently known, upon Adam's prediction that the world was to be destroyed at one time by the force of fire, and at another time by the violence and quantity of waters, they made two pillars, the one of brick the other of stone; they inscribed their discoveries upon them both, that, in case the pillar of brick should be destroyed by the flood, the pillar of stone might remain, and exhibit those discoveries to mankind; and also inform them that there was another pillar of brick erected by them. Now this remains in the land of Siriad to this day."

Statements of this kind being generally misunderstood at the present time, the subjoined passage taken from another part of the work of Greaves, quoted above, may help to explain the meaning of the tradition. " In the first ages of the world, an obscure way of expressing things was practised by the wise and learned, to whom it seemed good not to expose everything they knew to the eyes of the vulgar, who would not relish such matters that were too sublime for their otherwise disposed thoughts." The latter part of this sentence is an admirable piece of philosophic cant, but as Greaves himself adopted the ancient practice indicated here, it is necessary to receive his statements in a proper spirit. Accordingly, when he quotes with approval the Arabic tradition, he does so, knowing that it does not express the literal truth. He merely repeats it that he may convey the hint that the pyramids were set up for astronomical reasons. Their builders, he says, hoped " by this means to preserve, as long as the world endures, those sciences which their long experience had found out for the good of mankind." And again, he adds, " what is in these pyramids yet undiscovered I know not ; but this, I believe, that what learning is here to be found was also written upon tables, or in books, whose title was ' Inscriptions on the Pillars of Seth.' "

The place where the Pillars of Seth are said to have stood, is called Siriad, which may be taken to mean the place of Anubis, who marked the solstitial or midsummer sun, and it is therefore the region of the abode of the sun. The name Σίριαδ, or Σεῖρεαδ, has the value of 325, and by Gematria it is equivalent to ἔνος, a year. And if 325 be taken as the perimeter of a triangle or pyramid, its sides are $108\frac{1}{3}$, or the sun's distance measured by its own diameter. And $325\frac{1}{2} \times 2 = 651$, which is the diameter of a circle whose circumference is 2,046, the diameter of Saturn's orbit. From these numbers it would appear that the astronomical Pillars of Seth were located in a very appropriate place. And the name of their founder ΣΗΘ (217, the diameter of the sun's orbit) adds further confirmation to the name of the locality. It will also appear that Siriad is a name equally appropriate to the site of the Great Pyramid, and, strange to say, John Greaves seems to have considered it so.

In Arbuthnot's " Tables," published in 1727, the following quotation from Bishop Cumberland appears on p. 68 : " The sides of the base of the Great Pyramid are delivered, on p. 68 of Mr. Greaves' ' Pyramidographia,' to be 693 English feet. For reduction these must be divided by

1·824, which is his length of the Cairo cubit in our foot measure—the quote is 379·934, which is so very little short of 380 Cairo cubits, that I think it is reasonable to believe that the old architects designed just this even number of Egyptian cubits." To this Arbuthnot objects, saying that "the strength of the Bishop's argument *depends chiefly upon* 380 *being a remarkable number, such as an architect would choose for the dimension of the principal part of his fabric.*" The curious fact about this statement is, that both the Bishop and Arbuthnot should consider 380 a "remarkable number." It is needless to say that such a proposition is quite unintelligible to a modern architect, to whom one number is no more remarkable than another. Now Greaves, by bringing out 380 cubits from 693 feet, manages to state two measures of the sun's orbit very nearly. For the diameter of a circle 220 is 691, and the sun's distance, measured by the Tone, or interval between the earth and the moon, is 383.

It has been shown that, according to the system of Cesariano applied to Milan Cathedral the rhombus formed the basis upon which the plan of that church was constructed. And assuming that Cesariano's method was the traditional secret of all ancient builders, it has now to be tried whether any trace of it exists in the design of the Great Pyramid.

Externally the pyramid has but five main external measurements. The length of the side of its square base is $755\frac{2}{3}$ English feet and the diagonal of the base is $1,069\frac{2}{3}$ feet. Its vertical height is $481\frac{1}{3}$ feet. The slope of its sides are $611\frac{4}{5}$ feet and the measure along the angles is $733\frac{9}{10}$ feet.

Since all the Greek writers say that their astronomy and philosophy were derived from Egypt, it is quite reasonable to look for a pre-existing practice

among the Egyptians, similar to that subsequently
found in Greece, Alexandria, or Rome. Having
found that each side of the base of the Great
Pyramid measures 755⅔ feet, there will be nothing
ridiculous in considering what ideas the Greeks, who
wrote the Gospel, connected with the word Petros,
755, a stone. If the text of the Gospel were literally translated, the name Peter would be rendered
"the Stone," for it almost invariably appears as ὁ
Πέτρος, 825. According to the traditions, St. Peter
is said to have been the younger brother of St.
Andrew, the oldest of the Apostles. He was born
three years before the Virgin, and seventeen years

FIG. 18.—THE CUBICAL STONE.

before the Incarnation of Christ. He was the first
Pope of Rome, and held the See for twenty-five
years. He suffered martyrdom in his seventy-sixth
or eighty-sixth year, being crucified along with St.
Paul, on the 29th of June, with his head downwards. He is called Σίμων, 1,100, son of Ἰωνᾶς,
1,061, and Jesus is there made to say, "Thou
shalt be called Κηφᾶς, 729, which is by interpretation a stone (Πέτρος)." The very prominent place
which this apostle holds, both in the Gospel-mythos
and in the Romish Church, must have some explanation. And if he personates that rock (thought
to be impregnable by some) upon which the very
Church itself was founded, we must expect to find
that there is some fundamental truth and mystery

in it. And it is not impossible that the number 755, preserved in the name Petros, may have been the measure of the canonical stone of the old Egyptian priests, handed down by a continuous tradition, and received by the Christians. It was apparently this measure, with all it expressed and concealed, that the old builders sought to give an everlasting permanence in the Great Pyramid.

Assuming that the Egyptians built their pyramid as a symbol of the universe, it may be supposed that they chose the number 755 as the side of the square base for the following reasons. For it is possible to deduce from this square, chiefly by means of the rhombus, an approximate representation of the whole planetary system. No scheme, depending upon a simple geometrical process, can quite accurately measure the universe, because it does not happen to have been constructed upon any such simple principle, therefore the number 755 is more or less a compromise. It must also be assumed that figures corresponding to the temple of Ezekiel and the city of the New Jerusalem, were known to, if not invented by, the pyramid-builders.

To arrive at the numbers intended to be recorded by the architect of any building, it is necessary to know the standard by which it has been set out. What standard was used in the pyramid is unknown. There is, however, we believe, reason for assuming that the standard measure now in use in Great Britain is similar to that which was here employed by the Egyptians.

Now, taking the English foot to be equal to a diameter of the sun, it will be found that the rhombus which contains the square base of the pyramid (755⅔ feet) is 2,065 long, and the number 2,065 is the mean between 2,083, the side of the Holy Oblation, and 2,047, the diameter of

Saturn's orbit. Therefore the extremities of the
rhombus reach to the middle point, between the
sphere of Saturn and the sphere of the Zodiac.
This is simply a practical illustration of the same
geometrical problem which is illustrated by the
peribolus of Ezekiel's temple.

The number 755, found in the name Petros,
may give the clue to the next step. At any rate,
a cubical stone, or hexagon, which measures $755\frac{2}{3}$
feet diagonally from point to point, drawn within

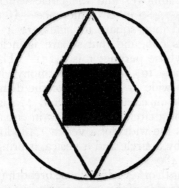

FIG. 19.—THE GREAT PYRAMID ENCLOSED BY A RHOMBUS
INSCRIBED WITHIN THE SPHERE OF THE ZODIAC.

the pyramid, gives by its width the side of a
rhombus which nearly incloses a square of the
same dimensions as the city of Ezekiel—each of
its sides being 416 diameters of the sun; and,
again, the length of another rhombus, which
roughly incloses a square similar to the New
Jerusalem, whose sides are 236 diameters of the
sun. And a third rhombus, drawn within this
last, is 217 on its sides, or the diameter of the
sun's orbit, and also the numerical value of the
name Seth, as it appears in the Septuagint, or
Christian version of the Old Testament. Thus

the whole scheme leads us to the sun's orbit, as its centre, and there is no impropriety, according to the ancient manner of speech, in the Arabians calling the innermost rhombus the tomb of Seth, 217.

A vesica, inclosed within the square 755, contains a Solomon's seal which holds the New Jerusalem within the bases of its two triangles, and these two triangles form a rhombus whose sides are 272, the numerical value of the name Harmonia (wife of Cadmos); and the circle which incloses the seal is 1,480 in circumference. If this circle be inclosed in a square its sides are 471, and its diagonal is 666, and that square is inclosed by a decagon whose perimeter is 2,151. The number 272 appears to be called harmony, because a vesica 272 wide is 471 long, or the diameter of a circle 1,480 in circumference, and 272 is also the diameter of a circle which is 853 in circumference, and 853 is the width of a vesica 1,480 long. That is to say, by a circle and a vesica, it brings out the number 1,480.

The length of a vesica whose breadth (755·76) is equal to the side of the great pyramid, is 1,310, or 1 less than the numerical value of Tetragrammaton.

A rood-cross 756 high can be almost inclosed within the square base of the pyramid; it would, in fact, be four inches too long. Now the extreme measure of this cross is 1,080, the number of miles in the moon's radius; and the numerical equivalent of τό Πνεῦμα Ἅγιον, the Holy Ghost; and it will crucify the lesser man of Vitruvius in a square whose perimeter is 993 (= 248¼ × 4), the numerical value of the name Aphrodite; and the circle inclosing his body is 1,103 in circumference, or 1 more than the height of a cross which will crucify a man in a square whose perimeter is 2,048, the diameter of Saturn's orbit. The name Hiram, the

architect of Solomon's Temple, is translated by
the Seventy Χειράμ, 756.

The diagonals of the base measure 1,069$\frac{2}{3}$, and
a rhombus of this length has a perimeter of 2,468
(= 617·07 × 4), or 2 less than the value of
Macroprosopos, Microprosopos, and Basileia, the
names of the great cabalistic triad.   Moreover, if
the two diagonals be bent into two intersecting
circles, in the Platonic manner, their united width
is 510$\frac{3}{4}$, or very nearly one-quarter of the mean
distance of Saturn's orbit ; and the perimeter
of the rhombus thus produced is 681, or the
length of the sun's orbit, and 680 is the numerical
equivalent of Υἱός, the Son, or second person of
the Christian Trinity.

The sockets cut in the rock to receive the foundation stones at the four corners of the base are
760$\frac{5}{12}$ feet apart.   Therefore, if the lesser man of
Vitruvius be drawn upon the plan, so that his feet
and hands touch their four sockets, his body will
measure diagonally (1,075$\frac{1}{2}$ × 2 =) 2,151 feet, and
2,151 is the number of years in the great month.
The cross required to crucify this figure is 2,314
high, and it is a strange coincidence that a Solomon's seal measuring 2,314 from point to point is
composed of two triangles whose sides are 2,002$\frac{1}{2}$,
or 1$\frac{1}{2}$ less than 2,004, the number out of which
Plato formed his logos and the equivalent of the
names of the four elements in Greek.   The
Hebrew names of the upper triad, or Long-face of
the Cabala, yield 760.

The sides of the core-masonry are 750 feet long
at the base.   Accordingly this square is contained
in a rhombus inscribed within the orbit of Saturn.

The vertical height of the pyramid is 481$\frac{1}{3}$ feet,
and this is the width of a vesica 834·288 long.
From this length we get the exact number of
miles in the equatorial diameter of the earth, for

834·288 multiplied by 9½ produces the measure of
a man 7,925·7 high.

Again, a circle whose diameter is equal to the
vertical height of the pyramid is double the length
of the base, namely, 1,512 feet. Therefore if the
twofold body of the logos, the male having been
separated from the female, were bent into such a
circle, the man above and the woman below, each
semicircular figure would measure 755⅔. It is
certain that the hemispheres were personified in
Egypt by celestial beings who may in some way
be connected with this circle. At any rate the
logos of the Christians was symbolized by the conjoined letters Χῖ, 610, and Ρῶ, 900; and 611 +
901 = 1,512, the circumference of the said circle.

The measure of a cross whose limbs are 481⅓
long is $\left(481\frac{1}{3} \times 2 =\right)$ 962⅔, the numerical equivalent of the word Τέχνη, Art. And 481 is the cir-
cumference of a circle whose diameter is 153,
the side of the square contained within the sun's orbit,
having a perimeter of 612, or 1 less than the
number of precepts in the Hebrew law.

The sloping sides of the pyramid measure 611⅘.
And 611 is nearly the circumference of the sphere
of the Zodiac contained within the Holy Oblation,
if the sun's distance be taken at 10. The name
Zeus has value of 612, and 611 is equivalent to
ΤhΥΡΗ, Thora, the Bride, or Law.

The length from the base to the apex, measured
on the four angles, is 733⁹⁄₁₀ feet. If shown upon
the plan the lines of these angles would indicate
the diagonals of the square in the form of a cross.
And it is curious that the length of a vesica 733·9
broad is 1,271, the numerical value of the Greek
word stauros, a cross.[1]

[1] A saltire whose limbs measure 733·1 may be inscribed
within a square having a perimeter of 2,075, or $\frac{1}{12}$ of the
equatorial circumference of the earth.

From the allusion by Vitruvius (bk. ix., chap. 8) to the Analemma, or diagram for determining the axis of the earth by the equinoctial shadow, we may infer that it was the practice of the builders to set up a figure such as he describes at the foundation of a temple. Accordingly the site of the pyramid may have been chosen at Memphis because they found on constructing the analemma at that latitude (to a scale of one inch to a mile), that a square 2,368 inches set up in the centre of the earth, perpendicular to the horizon, is just contained within the tropics. And when a plan and section of the pyramids are drawn upon the circle 660 feet, or 7,920 inches in diameter, the distance of the south pole below the horizon marks the height of the passage to the Queen's chamber, while the axis of the earth passes through the apex of the great stones over the King's chamber. The length of the equinoctial shadow, from the gnomon, 330 feet high or 3,960 inches, appears to be 192 feet, the shadow at the winter solstice about 454, and that at the summer solstice 33. The Pyramid itself, regarded as a gnomon, casts no shadow on the ground either at the summer solstice or the equinoxes, but at midwinter the shadow measures about 660 feet from the centre. The measurements in this paragraph are only taken from a rough geometrical diagram and are not calculated.

The pavement surrounding the pyramid seems to have measured about 840 feet square, but its full extent does not appear to be ascertainable. The number 840 is numerically equivalent to Microcosmos.

The fact that the cosmic numbers, which may be deduced from the dimensions of the pyramid coffer, measured by the British inch, agree with those of the system which has been applied to the

exterior of the building, is a decided evidence in
favour of the belief, that the standard used by the
Egyptians in setting out the pyramid, is similar to
that now in use in Great Britain. This coincidence,
coupled with the fact that the British quarter
measure is almost exactly a quarter of the contents
of the pyramid chest,[1] may be thought sufficient to
warrant an examination of the chest upon the
hypothesis, that the two standards are practically
identical.

There is no positive evidence that anyone was
ever buried in this sarcophagus, but it is described
as being exactly like the ordinary stone coffins of
the time at which the pyramid is supposed to have
been erected. It may have been the tomb of a
hypothetical king, whose body was supposed to
measure the parts of the world ; that is to say, the
practical embodiment of a structure like that described by Moses in the form of Noah's ark. And,
if we knew all the secrets concealed in the mysterious arrangements of the pyramid, it might be
found that the tomb of the king, earthly or heavenly,
played its part in the order of a symbolical scheme,
reduced possibly to some pictorial figure or mystic
parable capable of being enacted with canonical
ceremonies and initiatory rites. Whatever its use
may have been, the following measurements may
be found worthy of consideration.

The foot having been taken as the unit of
measurement in the main building, the inch becomes the unit for the chest. The outside dimensions of the coffer are 89·62 inches, by 38·5, and
its diagonal is 97½, therefore the perimeter of

---

[1] Magna Charta (A.D. 1215), sect. 35 : "There shall be but
one uniform standard of weights, measures, and manufactures ;
that for corn shall be the London quarter."—Quoted by C.
PIAZZI SMYTH, "Our inheritance in the Great Pyramid,"
p. 161.

a square which would enclose it would be 89·62
× 4 = 358·48. Now, 358 is the number of the
Hebrew name Messiah, and $358\frac{1}{2}$ × 6 = 2,151,
the number of years in a month of the great year.
Moreover, a circle 2,151 in circumference is inclosed by a hexagon whose perimeter is 2,368. A
rhombus described round the square is 244·944, or
say 245 long, and 245 is the numerical equivalent of ADM QDMVN, the supernal Adam or microcosm of the cabala. Further, this rhombus is
surrounded by a circle having a circumference of
769·824, which is the length of the transverse beam
of a rood cross 1,658·076 high, and 2,368·68 in its
total extent. The number of miles in the radius
of the moon's orbit divided by 12 twice is 1,658.

The distance between the tropics measured by
the sun's diameter is 89·48, if the orbit of the sun
be taken at 220 diameters, and the inclination of
the ecliptic at 24 degrees.

The number 89 is the square root of the earth's
diameter in miles $(89^2 = 7,921)$.

The external width of the coffer is 38·5, or
nearly the square root of 1,480 $(38·5^2 = 1,482·25)$.

And it may be contained by a rhombus having
a perimeter of 360·6, and by another 193·824 long,
the latter number being rather more than the
radius of the sphere of the Zodiac, if the sun's distance be taken at 10 (216 : 2,093 : : 20 : : 193·6).

The lid of the coffer, now missing, must have
measured, if it fitted the space provided for it,
81·46 by 34·33 inches. A rhombus described
round it is 140·948 long by 81·33 inches broad,
and has a perimeter of 325·32. Now 325·32 × 2
= 650·64, the diameter of a circle whose circumference is equal to the diameter of Saturn's orbit ;
and 325 is the numerical equivalent of the name
Siriad, already referred to. The diagonal of the
lid is $88\frac{1}{4}$, or the width of the space between the

FIG. 20.—CHRIST'S
BODY IN THE ARK OF
NOAH (MONTANUS).

tropics if the diameter of the sun's orbit be taken at 217. If the sun's orbit and that of Venus be drawn in the centre of the lid to a scale which fixes the sun's distance at 10, the orbit of Venus will be contained in the lid's breadth, and the perimeter of a square 34·33 is 137·32, or the numerical equivalent of the word cabala (QBLH, 137). The perimeter of the lid is 231·62 inches; its area is 2,796 and $\frac{2,796}{6} = 466$.

The inner depth is 34·42, which is the side of a square whose diagonal is 48¾, the square root of 2,368.

Its contents, 72,032, and the solid bulk 70,500 cubic inches, seem to indicate the measure of the sun's diameter in miles, for $72,032 \times 12 = 864,384$ and $\frac{70,500}{12}$ = 846,000, the mean being 855,000.

The inside dimensions of the coffer are 78·06 inches long by 26·81 broad. Supposing it to have been prepared to measure the body of Macrocosmos, as the ark of Noah measures the body of Christ in the diagram of Montanus, then the internal area of the coffin upon which the body would lie measures (78·06 × 26·81 =) 2,092·788, the diameter of the circle containing the square 1,480 within the Holy Oblation. Secondly, a man standing crosswise within a square whose sides are 78·06, would represent the Macrocosm according to the rule of Vitruvius. The diagonal of this square is 110 inches, or the radius of the sun's orbit, and a circle 110 in diameter has a circumference of 345$\frac{5}{9}$, or $\frac{1}{12}$ of the width of the sun's ark, containing the ecliptic measured upon a terrestrial globe. Thirdly, if the microcosm be inclosed within a square whose area is half that of the first, the circle surrounding his body has a circumference of 245$\frac{1}{3}$, or the numerical equivalent of Adam Kadmon. The sides of the smaller square measure 55 inches, or the number of miles in the diameter of the earth divided by 12 twice.

According to the inferences drawn from the measures of the greatest pyramid, it may be supposed that it and the other two were built to symbolize the three persons of the Cabala. In their order the second pyramid would fall to microcosmos, and the measure of its square base is 706$\frac{1}{12}$, and its diagonal 998·67 feet, its vertical height being 472 feet. Now if the microcosm were inclosed within the square base, and crucified upon a rood cross, its height would be 2,151 feet, or the number of years in the great month or Messianic period. By taking the diagonals at 999 feet, and bending them into two circles, after the manner of Plato in the "Timæus," a vesica is formed 666 in circumference. Then 472 feet is the united width of the two circles producing a vesica whose perimeter is equal to $\frac{1}{12}$ of the earth's diameter in miles. It is also one more than the diameter of a circle 1,480 ($471 \times 3\frac{1}{7} = 1,480$).

The fable related by Herodotus, that the third pyramid was built by Rhodopis, the rosy-cheeked (ἡ Ροδῶπις, 1,272), was probably meant to convey that it was dedicated to the Bride, the third person

of the Triad.   At least, the measures of this
pyramid support such a view.   The base is $346\frac{1}{12}$
feet square, and it is $213\frac{2}{3}$ feet high.   The sides
of a rhombus inscribed within the base are equal
to those of the New Jerusalem (199·68), the Bride
of the Apocalypse, while the height, $213\frac{2}{3}$, is the
diameter of a circle 671 in circumference ; and 671
is the numerical equivalent of Thora and Adonai,
the names of the third person of the cabalistic
triad.   The width of the base, $346\frac{1}{12}$, is very
nearly $\frac{1}{12}$ of the width of the sun's ark measured
in miles on a terrestrial globe.   Taking the equatorial circumference at 24,900 miles, the external
width would be $\left(\frac{2,075}{6} =\right) 345\frac{5}{6}$.

The distinguishing measures of the three pyramids seem clearly to agree with the old doctrine of
the Trinity, and if their heights be arranged in a triad :

$$
\begin{array}{lll}
481\frac{1}{3} & 481\frac{1}{3} & 481 \\
472 & \left.\begin{array}{l}472 \\ 213\frac{2}{3}\end{array}\right\}685\frac{2}{3} & 213 \\
\overline{953\frac{1}{3}} & \overline{} & \overline{694} \\
& 1,167 &
\end{array}
$$

the sum of the numbers is 1,167, or $\frac{1}{12}$ of the side
of a square whose area is equal to the surface of
the earth.   The numbers of the second and third
added together give $685\frac{2}{3}$, the diameter of a circle
2,151 in circumference, an appropriate number for
the King and Queen of Heaven.   Then $953\frac{1}{3}$, the
sum of the first and second numbers, with the addition of 2, is the width of a vesica 1,656 long, or the
number of miles from the equator to the tropics,
measured on the earth's circumference.   And 694
is the width of a vesica formed by two intersecting
circles inscribed within the Holy Oblation.

It is well known that Herschel the astronomer
ascertained that the entrance passage of the great

pyramid pointed to that part of the heavens
occupied by the pole star in the year 2,160 or 2,170
B.C. In Herschel's day, this year agreed with the
reputed age of the pyramid, and he consequently
inferred that the passage had been built at this
particular angle to record the date of its erection.
Professor Piazzi Smyth, however, afterwards
calculated that the Pole Star was in the same
position in the year 3,440 B.C., and presumably it
passed the same point at intervals, ages before that.
Whatever the true date may be it is probable that
the Pyramids of Memphis, though less than 10,000
years old, may have been built to preserve the
canon of the Egyptian priests. And Plato's reference to the laws being laid up in the temples,
suggests the conclusion that the pyramids did
actually " fix and exhibit patterns of them," which
became the established traditions of after times,
and never changed.

The Parthenon, like the pyramids, seems to
have illustrated all the astronomical science of the
Greeks. In treating of its geometrical disposition
there is this advantage, that the value of the foot
by which it has been set out has been ascertained
with comparative certainty. For it may be taken
for granted that the width of the top step, as
Mr. Penrose supposes, gave rise to the name
Hecatompedon, and that this measure is 100
Greek, or 101·341 English feet.[1]

A consideration of the value of the names of
the great goddess of Attica, in whose honour the
temple was built, may throw some light upon the
nature of her position among the Greek deities,
and indicate the motives of the builders in making
the design of her temple. Athene is obviously a

---

[1] All the subsequent measures of this temple are given in
Greek feet of this value. Every information with respect to the
temple will be found in Mr. Penrose's "Athenian Architecture."

very complex deity, who embraced in one personification many conceptions, and her house on the Acropolis was probably intended to convey her many-sided character.

As the virgin, mystically born from the forehead of Zeus, the Father, she appears to personate the divine essence in its feminine and immaterial aspect. But it is evident from the various myths related about her, that she was also conceived as a male and androgynous being, thus combining in her person all the powers of creation embodied in the cabalistic triad, and she seems to have been accepted as the cosmic divinity afterwards relegated to the Christian mythos.

The name Athene has the value of 76; it is the square root of 5,776, or half of the sun's distance measured by the earth's diameter. She may therefore be said to represent one part of the twofold principle of life. Again, $76\frac{1}{3}$ is the side of a square whose diagonals measure 216, the diameter of the sun's orbit; and 76, with a fraction added, is also the square root of 5,920, the perimeter of a square whose sides are 1,480 (Christos).

Then her name Athene, the virgin ('Αθήνη Παρθένος) yields 591, and by adding colel to this we get 592, which is the side of a rhombus having a perimeter of 2,368.

Another name under which she was invoked was Athene Polias, goddess of the city, and this has the numerical value of 467, or one more than 466, the height of a cross whose extreme length is 666, and whose transverse beam is 216, the diameter of the sun's orbit. It will be remembered that 666 is the sum of the diagonals of the New Jerusalem, the Heavenly City, of which she seems to have been the goddess.

She was also called Athene Promachos, the avenger; Promachos is numerically equivalent to

1,061, the value of the name Apollo, and 1,061 +
76 = 1,137, which is 1 less than the length of a
vesica 656 broad (Artemis and Messias). And
by adding colel to each name this designation is
equivalent by Gematria to ΔΕΛΦΥΣ, the womb.

But the name which was most commonly applied
to Athene was Pallas, and her statues in the
Parthenon represented her under this image.
Pausanias tells us that the figure was wrought of
gold and ivory, standing erect clad in a long robe
with a Medousa upon her breast. Her helmet was
surmounted by a sphinx, and in one hand she held
a spear, while in the other stood a victory four
cubits high. At her feet lay a shield, and close
beside the spear was a snake, which was supposed
by Pausanias to be Erychthonios. And the birth
of Pandora, the first woman, was depicted on the
pedestal. The height of the statue was 26 cubits,[1]
the number of the mystic Tetragammaton. The
Victory (NIKE, 88), being 4 cubits, is 96 digits
high, or the radius of the sphere of the Zodiac if
the sun's distance be taken at 10, and 88 is the
space between the tropics, measured by the sun's
diameter. All the symbols enumerated by Pausanias are doubtless attributes, appropriate to some
of her many forms. The sphinx, the helmet, the
chiton, the medousa, the spear, the shield, and the
snake being each capable of some explanation.

The name Pallas gives the number 342, which is
the side of a rhombus whose perimeter is 1,368,[2]

---

[1] 26 cubits = 624 digits, and 624 is the length of a vesica
360 broad.

[2]
$$\phi\alpha\lambda\lambda\acute{o}\varsigma \quad . \quad . \quad 831 + 1 = 832$$
$$\kappa\tau\epsilon\acute{\iota}\varsigma \quad . \quad . \quad 535 + 1 = 536$$

$$\overline{1,368}$$

See St. Clement, "Exhortation to the Heathen," p. 32 (Ante-
Nicene Library, vol. iv.). The famous account of the Eleusinian Mysteries occurs in this piece.

and this is the width of a vesica 2,368 long. The statue of Pallas was called Palladium. The most ancient of these mysterious images having been thrown down from Olympus by Zeus at Troy (Τροίη, 488), was set up and worshipped by the Trojans till it was taken by the Greeks and brought to Athens. The figure is said to have been " 3 cubits in height, its legs close together, and holding in its right hand a spear, and in the left a spindle and distaff" (Smith's Dict.). Now three cubits are equal to 54 inches, and 54 is the side of a square whose perimeter is 216, and 54 with a fraction added is the square root of 2,946, the diagonal of the Holy Oblation.

Next to the Palladium the statue of Athene Polias was most highly revered. According to Pausanias (bk. i., ch. 26) the Greeks were accustomed to dedicate this image in that part of each town which was called " the city." Accordingly we may suppose that her statue thus set up symbolized the heavenly city called the Bride, or the New Jerusalem by the Christians. And the extreme length of the Parthenon being about 235 Greek feet, it would appear that this great sanctuary of the goddess was built according to the measure of her city in the sky.

The name Parthenon, the virgin's house, yields 1,095, which is the width of two intersecting circles producing a vesica 365 broad; ὁ Παρθενών has the numerical value of $1,165 - 2 = 1,163$, which is the length of a vesica 671 broad, and 671 is numerically equivalent to Thora, the Hebrew Bride, to whom, in the person of the Virgin Mary, this temple was afterwards dedicated. The word Παρθένος, applied both to Athene and Mary, has the value of 515, which is 1 less than 516, the mean between 512 and 520 ($512 \times 4 = 2,048$ and $520\frac{3}{4} \times 4 = 2,083$). Accordingly, by the name Parthenos the Pagan and Christian virgin symbolized the universe. And we find that the Parthenon, measured on the first step, is inclosed by a rhombus 515·228 long, formed by two intersecting circles whose united width is 891·675, a figure which admirably expresses the significance of the two names in the Greek language, for 891 is the numerical equivalent of Οὐρανός, Heaven.

If the classical temples were designed according to the rule of Vitruvius, so that their measures depended upon the proportions of the human body, we ought to find an illustration of it in the Parthenon. The length of the cell externally, including the antæ, is 165·613 feet, and it is probable that a square inclosing it was intended to contain the lesser of the two pattern-figures. For, if this square be doubled, the larger square, containing the greater man, measures about 234 feet, or nearly the length of the temple measured on the first step. Thus the two main dimensions of the building exemplify the duplication of the square as nearly as the exigencies would admit. The head of the lesser man then lies in the centre of the four pillars of the Opisthodomos, and the phallus falls upon the place chosen for the statue of Pallas. Moreover, the perimeter of the square inclosing his body is 662·452 (165·613 × 4) which is the diameter of a circle 2,081 in circumference. Therefore, with a small addition to the side of the square we get the measure of the Holy Oblation. Then the square surrounding the greater man has a perimeter of 936 (234 × 4), which is the length of a rhombus having a perimeter of 2,160, the number of miles in the moon's diameter.

The measures of the temple, taken on the first step, exclusive of the ledge, are 234·28 by 109·17 feet. The proportions, therefore, are very nearly those of a rood cross. If we suppose 109·17, the extreme breadth of the temple, to be the length of the transverse beam of a cross in the ratio of 28 : 13, its height will be 235·116. If, on the other hand, we suppose the extreme length 234·28 to be the height of a cross, its transverse beam will be 108·77. The first of the two crosses would be contained within the New Jerusalem (235·116), while each would crucify the macrocosm in a square whose sides are equal to a computation of the radius of the sun's orbit.

The rhombus appears to have been similarly applied to the design of the Parthenon, as in the case of the Great Pyramid. For the whole building (234·28 × 109·17 feet) is contained in a rhombus, formed by the intersection of two circles which produce a vesica having a perimeter of 1,023 feet, or the radius of Saturn's orbit.

The perimeter of the top step is 650¼ feet, and is therefore the diameter of a circle whose circumference is equal to the diameter of Saturn's orbit.

The perimeter of the first step, exclusive of the ledge, is 686·9 feet; if the ledge be included we get the diameter of a circle 2,162 in circumference of the number of miles in the moon's diameter.

The number of days in the solar and lunar years has also determined certain of the proportions of the building, for the upper platform is inclosed by a rhombus formed by two intersecting circles 365¼ feet in diameter, or the number of days in the solar year, and the full length of the cell externally is that of a rhombus having a perimeter of 354·6, the number of days in the lunar year.

A rectangle surrounding the cell externally has a perimeter of 471 feet, the diameter of a circle 1,480 in circumference, while the rhombus inclosing it has a perimeter equal to $\frac{1}{12}$ of the number of miles in the earth's diameter.

The external length of the cell exclusive of the antæ is 155·701, and 155·79 × 9·5 = 1,480. Its length from wall to wall above the sill is 155·54, and a vesica 155·468 has a perimeter of 651·228, which is the diameter of a circle 2,046 in circumference, or the mean diameter of Saturn's orbit (651·228 × 3·1,416 = 2,046). And the length between the outer faces of the door-jambs is 155·48, or the distance of the tropics from the equator, measured by the tone.

The internal measures of the cell being 142·2 by 62·17 feet, its proportions are practically those of the "cross of our Lord" described by Sir John Maundeville as being 144 × 63 inches. But Athene being primarily a feminine deity, the builders have made the perimeter of the cell 408·74 feet, and that is the length of a rhombus whose sides are equal to those of the New Jerusalem. In this way the cross and vesica have been mystically combined. The interior of the cell may also be inclosed by a rhombus about $249\frac{1}{4}$ long ($249\frac{1}{4}$ × $9\frac{1}{2}$ = 2,368).

The opisthodomos, the treasury (sometimes called treasuries) was apparently dedicated to the goddess, as the germinating essence, for the diagonals of this chamber measure $75\frac{1}{2}$ feet (Athene, 76). And by giving the measure in the two diagonals, the builders have suggested her double character. For the opisthodomos and naos together must be taken to represent the abode of the deity in the form of the mystical triad. Its perimeter round the cell is 207·484, which is the diameter of a circle 651·9, or the diameter of a circle whose circumference is equal to the diameter of Saturn's orbit. The rhombus inclosing the opisthodomos is a notable one ; those referred to elsewhere seem to have been chosen in all cases on account of the coincidences in their numbers, but this one surrounding the Holy of Holies of the temple is specially worthy of attention. The united width of the circles by which it is produced is 258, or 1 less than the value of Basileia, the third person of the cabalistic triad. The rhombus thus formed has a perimeter of 360·38. The circumferences of the two circles added together amount to 1,081·142, the radius of the moon's diameter, and the numerical equivalent of τὸ πνεῦμα Ἅγιον, the Holy Ghost, who corresponds to Basileia. A cross inscribed within the vesica measures (86 + 149·058 =) 235·058, or nearly the side of the New Jerusalem, the city personified both by Basileia[1] and the Christian bride. A square enclosing the whole figure has a perimeter of (258 × 4 =) 1,032, or the mean radius of a circle between Saturn and the Zodiac. It has been supposed that Hestia, 516, personified this circle, and by Gematria, Parthenos, 515, is equivalent to Hestia. To the old priests looking for numerical harmonies this figure would certainly appear remarkable, and perhaps for this reason the Romans called every diagram such as this vesica 85, being 1 less than 86. And to the architect, seeking a proportion fit for the sanctuary of that goddess, whom they sought to make an image of the universal consonance of nature, such a figure would also appeal.

The length of the naos is 96·78 feet, which

---

[1] Basileia is mentioned in the "Birds" of Aristophanes. She is said to have charge of the thunderbolts of Zeus, and in the play marries the founder of the city in the clouds, which seems to be a pre-Christian version of the City of St. John. It occupied an intermediate position between the earth and the firmament, and was built by 40,000 birds. Now 40,000 is the area of the New Jerusalem ($200^2 = 40,000$). Aristophanes is evidently ridiculing the mystic geometricians in the person of Meton, who offers his services to measure the city.

is the radius of the Zodiac inscribed within the Holy Oblation, if the sun's distance be taken at 10 (108 : 1,046 : : 10 : : 96·80). The diameter of the two circles forming the rhombus which contains the naos is $235\frac{1}{2}$ feet, or the length of the side of the New Jerusalem, and the perimeter of the rhombus thus produced is 471·6, while the perimeter of the vesica inclosing it is 495, or 1 less than the value of the name Malchuth, the bride.

The word Pallas is generally considered to be identical with phallos, and the division of the cell into two parts accords with the idea of the cross, for the front chamber of the temple called naos (the ship or nave), containing the great statue of Pallas, has a perimeter of 317·9, and $317·9 \times 4 = 1,271·6$ the numerical equivalent of stauros, a cross. The statue was said to be 26 cubits or 39 feet high; and 26 multiplied by $9\frac{1}{2}$ produces 247, a number doubly suited to measure this icon of Pallas. Firstly, 247 is the length of the transverse beam of a rood-cross 532 high and 760 over all. Now 760 is the side of a square whose diagonals measure 2,151, the number of years in the great month; and the height 532 is the length of a vesica formed by two circles having a united width of 920·7 and a common diameter of 613·8. The number 532 is the value of the name Atlas, who was fabled to bear up the whole world on his shoulders ; 921 is the numerically equal to the Greek word *canon*, and there were said to be 613 precepts in the Hebrew law. Secondly, by reducing the 26 cubits by a small amount, we find that $25·98 \times 9·5 = 246·792$; and a cross of this height has a transverse beam 114·589, and will consequently crucify the Logos in a circle having a circumference of 360, the number of degrees in the earth's circumference.

Again, then, a circle described round this cross has a circumference equal to the perimeter of the Holy Oblation, if the sun's distance be taken at 10

$$(246.792 \times 3.1,416 = \frac{775.321}{4} = 193.830).$$ And

246.792 cubits are equal to 1,480.752 palms; in like manner the number 25.98 gives the height of the microcosm inclosed in a square, having a perimeter of 1,480.752. Also a vesica 246.792 broad is formed by two intersecting circles whose united width is 740.376, the circumference of a circle inscribed within the New Jerusalem. Lastly, the word Θηρίον, the beast in the Apocalypse whose number was 666, and whose mark was the cross, has the value of 247, and possibly the number 248 mentioned in the cabala ("Greater Holy Assembly," 968) was chosen because it is the mean between 246.792 and 249.264.

The height of the temple from the pavement to the apex of the eastern pediment is 1,025.6 digits, or a large computation of the radius of Saturn's orbit.

From the floor of the peristyle to the apex of the pediment under the cymatium is 226.84 palms, and 226.84 × 9.5 = 2,155 the mean number between 2,151 and 2,160.

The height of the columns and entablature is 176.28 palms, and 176.28 × 9.8 = 1,674.6, or very nearly the side of a square whose diagonals are 2,368.

The four angle-columns being 540.48 digits high, their united height amounts to 2,161.9 digits, or the number of miles in the moon's diameter.

It has been suggested that the area of 10,000 feet attributed to the tent at Delphi is contained within the walls of the cell. Now a parallelogram 150 × 66⅔ feet incloses this area, and is contained within the walls. And if it be supposed that the plan of the Parthenon was set out according to the proportions of Solomon's temple, as given by Laurencio de San Nicolas[1] (1663) on p. 50, and that the length of the Holy Place, and Holy of Holies are 100, and 50 feet respectively, then, their united lengths are 150 feet, agreeing with the length of the parallelogram containing 10,000 square feet. And besides this coincidence it will be found that upon drawing the temple of Solomon according to the above proportions on the plan of the Parthenon, that the division between the Holy Place and the Holy of Holies is marked by the partition between the naos and opisthodomos, and the centre of the opisthodomos, in the middle of the four columns, coincides with the centre of the Holy of Holies of Solomon's temple.

The arrangement of the four columns so exactly agrees with the ciborium of the churches, afterwards raised by the Christian Greeks, that we probably see in the Parthenon the prototype of the arrangements of the Christian Church. There is no doubt that Solomon's temple formed the pattern of the Christian churches, and the ark occupied the centre of the Holy of Holies. Now it is well known that the altar of the first Christian churches placed under the ciborium was in the form of an ark, containing relics of the saints, and was an obvious type of the ark of the Covenant. The four columns were also preserved in the Gothic churches, at the crossing of the nave and transepts.

Another circumstance connecting the plan with this theoretical temple of Solomon is, that the Holy Place, or naos, is 100 feet long, and may have been the true origin of the name Hecatompedon. And when the porch and cruciform additions are added, as shown by Laurencio de

---

[1] "Del Arte y uso de Architectura."

San Nicolas, their total width coincides with the breadth of the top step, and the whole length is 200 feet, which is the side of the cube of the New Jerusalem.

Antiquaries have been a good deal divided in their opinions as to the antiquity of the remains at Stonehenge, for although, perhaps, no one except Inigo Jones ever thought that this ancient structure was a Roman temple, some persons have considered that it might have been set up after the Roman invasion. There is certainly no authentic evidence in existence as to its age. From the nature of the work it might reasonably be judged to belong to the most ancient form of building in the world, for nothing ruder or more primitive can be conceived as the means of inclosing a sacred place for divine worship. As we have no knowledge at all of the early inhabitants of Britain, except what we learn from a few references in late classical authors, it is useless to speculate as to who really were the builders of Stonehenge. We may, in fact, assume anything or nothing. The work has generally been connected with the Druids, who presumably built it, if it is not the work of an earlier race.

Several classical writers have spoken of the British Islands, and appear to have heard some rumours of the customs and character of the people. Diodorus quotes Hecatæus as having said that " The Hyperboreans inhabited an island beyond Gaul, as large as Sicily, in which Apollo was worshipped in a circular temple, considerable for its size and riches." Then Dionysius Periegetes (v. 565, etc.) says that the rites of Dionysus were duly celebrated in the British Islands. And we are told by Strabo that " In an island close to Britain, Ceres and Proserpina are venerated with rites similar to the orgies of Samothrace" (Geog. bk. iv.). The Testimony of Julius Cæsar, who obtained his information at first hand, ought to be strictly veracious and reliable. He declares that the Druids "deemed it unlawful to commit their statutes to writing; though in other matters, whether public or private, *they make use of Greek characters*. They seem to me to follow this method for two reasons: to hide their mysteries from the knowledge of the vulgar: and to exercise the memory of their scholars. . . . They likewise teach many things relating to the stars and their motions, the magnitude of the world and our earth. . . . Mercury is the chief deity with them: of him they have many images, account him the inventor of all arts. . . . Next to him are Apollo, and Mars, and Jupiter, and Minerva. . . . Apollo is their god of physic, Minerva, of works and manufactures: Jove holds empire of heaven, and Mars presides in war. . . . The Gauls fancy themselves to be descended from the god Pluto" ("Gallic Commentaries," bk. vi., ch. 13). We have also the statement of Pomponius Mela, the Roman Geographer (lib. iii., cap. 2), "That the Gauls have their masters of eloquence and wisdom from the Druids. These profess that they know the magnitude and form of the earth and world; they teach many noble persons of their nation *privately*." Finally, Hippolytus (Ref., bk. i., ch. 22) tells us that, "The Celtic Druids investigated to the very highest point the Pythagorean Philosophy."

If all these writers are to be believed, and there is no particular reason to doubt them, we should certainly expect to find that an ancient British or Druidical temple was constructed in a similar manner to those of Greece and Egypt. The statement of Cæsar and the other historians, that the worship of Dionysus, Apollo, Ceres, etc., existed in Britain has been thought to expose the ignorance or credulity of those old writers, but, as a matter of fact, there is nothing surprising in such statements, when it is recognized, that the powers invoked under these names were the gods of all ancient peoples, however they might be called in different places; and the statement of Hecatæus as to the circular temple of Apollo, or the sun, seems to agree very well with the facts which may may be deduced from the measures of Stonehenge.

Mr. Davies ("Mythology and Rites of the British Druids") has given the translation of a poem called the Gododin, supposed to have been written about A.D. 510, by a Briton of Northumbria. The bard describes the massacre of the 360 Britons which took place at Stonehenge in 472. The poem contains several allusions which appear to relate to that structure. The mystical sanctuary which is referred to by the bard is called "The Stone Cell of the Sacred Fire," that is, the ark or coffer of the sun. It is also called "The Great Stone Fence," "The Ark of the World," and "The Circle of the World." And the name *Caer Sidi*, the seat of *Sidi* or Saturn, was applied to it, so that the beings who were worshipped in this mysterious circle appear to be no other than the universal cosmic deities.

Fortunately, Stonehenge, like the Great Pyramid, has been measured by Mr. Petrie, so we are in possession of absolutely trustworthy measurements to work upon.

There will be no great improbability in supposing that we have inherited our present standard measures from our remote ancestors, who built their sanctuary on Salisbury Plain. Consequently it will be assumed, that Stonehenge is set out according to the present standard of British measure. The inside diameter of the outer circle of the temple is given as being 1,167·9 inches. Now the side of a square whose area equals the surface of the earth divided by 12 measures $1,167\frac{1}{2}$ miles, or almost exactly the diameter of the circle.

Again, 1,170 inches is $97\frac{1}{2}$ feet $\left(\frac{1,170}{12} = 97\frac{1}{2}\right)$, therefore the outer circle of stones at Stonehenge will nearly surround an ark of the same size as that in the Great Pyramid, measured by feet instead of inches. And this would appear to be the " stone cell of the sacred fire," or the ark of the sun, whose length measures the limits of the sun's course in the ecliptic. And it is said in the Gododin, " in the circle of the world it was his choice to have Eidiol, the harmonious," Eidiol being the sun, according to Davies.

Then 96·8 is the radius of the sphere of the Zodiac surrounding Saturn's orbit, if the sun's distance be taken at 10. And 1,168 inches $=$ $97\frac{1}{3}$ feet $\div 2 = 48\frac{2}{3}$, the square root of the number 2,368, which may be written in Greek letters as *IESOUS CHRISTOS.*

The only one of the inner circles which is defined is 472·7 inches in diameter; but it is rather irregular, and may very well be taken at 471, which would give it a circumference of 1,480 inches. Mr. Petrie thinks, that this circle may be of later date than other parts of the building.

The arrangement of the smaller stones is rather uncertain, but the inclination of the two upper trilithons, on either side of the altar, appears to be that of the sides of a pentalpha. Accordingly, if a pentalpha touching the trilithons be drawn within a pentagon, having a perimeter of $416\frac{2}{3}$ feet, the sides of the pentalpha will be $132 \times 5 =$ 660[1] feet or 7,920 inches, the number of miles in the earth's diameter.

---

[1] This may possibly be inaccurate.

If the builders of Stonehenge founded their design upon the measures of the ark, which is found in the Great Pyramid, the question arises, whether the Egyptians received their knowledge from the people who built Stonehenge, or whether the latter, as the ingenious Godfrey Higgins supposed, were a colony of Egyptians. If this last opinion be true, it seems strange that a people capable of executing a work, constructed with the utmost science and showing an advanced knowledge of building, should have been content to erect a rude monument like the temple of Stonehenge. But a question of this kind might lead to endless theorizing, which probably could never lead to any satisfactory conclusion.

The Pantheon may be taken as the best remaining example of the classical temples of Rome. From the inscription over the portico we learn that " Having been impiously dedicated of old by Agrippa to Jupiter and all the Gods, it was piously reconsecrated by Pope Boniface the Fourth to the Blessed Virgin and all the Saints." Serlio, the architect, describing it in 1540, says, " Among all the ancient buildings to be seene in Rome, I am of opinion that the Pantheon (for one piece of work alone) is the fayrest, wholest, and best to be understood ; and it is so much the more wonderfull than the rest, because it hath so many members, which are all so correspondent one to another, that whosoever beholdeth it, taketh great pleasure therein, which proceedeth from this, that the excellent workeman, which invented it, chose the perfitest forme, that is, the round forme, whereby it is usually called, Our Lady of the Round ; for within it is as high as it is broad." Further on, he continues: " The widenesse of the whole Temple (that is of the floore within, from one wall to another) is 194 Palmes : and just so much is the height from the floore to the undermost stone of the window above" ("Architettura," bk. iii., ch. iv.). He gives on the margin of the page the length of the old Roman palm by which he measured the Temple. It is divided into twelve fingers, and these again are divided into four minutes. Palladio, about thirty years later, made much more accurate plans, and says that it was made in the form of the world.

Now since the diameter of the sphere of the Zodiac is 193·6, taking the sun's distance at 10, the interior of the Temple would contain the whole world, and the dome being an exact hemisphere surrounding the firmament, it is a literal representation of the vault of heaven. This may account for the remark of Serlio, that of all the temples, it was "the best to be understood."

The reasons for believing that the geometrical principles of design, found in the Gothic cathedrals, formed the secret of the Freemasons, have already been laid before the reader. And it has been supposed that the diagrams of Cesariano applied to the cathedral at Milan, are an exposition of those principles. If those assumptions, therefore, are correct, it is to be expected that a similar system will be found in other mediæval cathedrals built by the Freemasons. Apparently, all the sacred buildings erected in the Middle Ages are alike in this respect, and, as it is easy for anyone to apply Cesariano's system to any cathedral-plan, we shall not tire the reader by giving long descriptions of its application to different churches. It will be enough to draw attention to some of the measures of Westminster Abbey, which is one of the most perfect examples of mediæval building in Europe, and is likely to exhibit the geometrical methods of its builders, as well as any other structure.

The two great churches of London and West-

minster, dedicated to SS. Paul and Peter, were
founded upon the sites of temples of Diana and
Apollo (Dugdale, "History of St. Paul's," p. 3).
And although the good Dugdale was greatly
scandalized at the idolatry of the ancient Lon-
doners, nevertheless, it would appear that the
worshippers of the true God carried on the traditions of their predecessors with tolerable success.
Theophilus Gale tells us that the "canonized
saints are parallel to the pagan demons (Δαίμονες),
as to their origin and formal canonization, so in
like manner in point of office, as mediators between
God and men" ("Court of the Gentiles," vol. iii.,
p. 180). And according to Bochart, "the worshippers of Christ transferred to their saints all the
equipage of the pagan gods; to St. Wolfang, the
hatchet or hooke of Saturne; to Moses, the hornes
of Jupiter Hammon; to St. Peter, the keys of
Janus" (see also Joseph Mede, "Apostasie of the
Latter Times," 1644).

According to Mede and Gale, the dedication of
Christian churches to a particular saint was the
perpetuation of the old pagan practice, which
caused the Athenians to devote the Parthenon to
Pallas Athene. And, just as the measures of the
Greek temple were derived from the numbers of
the names attributed to the goddess, so also we
find that the number 755 (PETROS) seems to
have determined some of the proportions of the
Abbey of Westminster. As Camden and other
old writers have informed us, the idolatrous people
of Westminster worshipped the sun or Apollo;
and it has been already shown, in reference to the
Pyramid, that a stone or hexagon, which measures
755 from point to point, contains the sun's ark
(691 × 115), and a stone or hexagon having a
perimeter of 755 encloses the sun's orbit 217 in
diameter.

Now the great church dedicated by the Christians of Westminster to the canonized and sanctified stone, Petros, 755, measures externally across the transepts about 220 feet. That is to say, if the sun's orbit be drawn with the middle of the cross under the great tower as a centre, the course of the sun would pass the outside limit of the north doorway. Then the external measurement of the wall of the nave appears to be 89½ feet, or the space between the tropics measured by the sun's diameter. And the rhombus, touching the north-west corner of the building, incloses the main part of the church, and has a perimeter of 1,656, the altitude of the ecliptic above the equator measured in miles. Moreover, the rhombus, touching the same point, but drawn horizontally, has a peri-meter of 2,368. A hexagon or cubical stone 755 in circuit marks the outside of the wall of the north transept, while a pentalpa, whose perimeter is 755, seems to determine the inside line of the east wall of the transepts.

If the temple of Solomon be drawn, so that the centre of the Holy of Holies falls upon the middle of the four piers of the great tower, it will be found to cover the space occupied by the choir. The present choir stalls and screen are, of course, modern, but they are in the same place as those shown upon Hollar's plan, engraved in the middle of the seventeenth century.

A rood cross 540 feet high will crucify a man in a square whose perimeter is $(251 \times 4 =)$ 1,004, the interval between the equinoxes; and $540 \times 4 = 2,160$, the number of miles in the moon's diameter. If this cross be drawn so that its centre coincides with the omphalos of the church, its lower end will reach to the western doorway, and the head of the lesser man of Vitruvius, crucified upon it, will fall upon what was presumably the central apsidal chapel in the fourteenth century. The altar occupies the same position, with regard to this figure, as the statue of the Parthenon does to the man, drawn within the square 663.

A square whose sides are 365 set diagonally with its centre on the middle of the great tower incloses Henry VII.'s chapel and touches the western door.

The height of the nave or ship (if it be the same as that of the south transept[1]) is 104⅕ feet, or the height of an ark 1,042 long, and 1,042 is the radius of the Holy Oblation.

From the west wall of the north transept to the apse is 155·79 feet. From the entrance of the choir to the apsidal end of the arcade is 249¼ feet.

It will be noticed that Islip's Chapel forms the corner of a square described round the centre of the building, and this square has a perimeter of 512 feet.

The circuit of the Chapter House internally appears to be 192 feet (24 × 8). And 192·84, besides being the diameter of the sphere of the Zodiac, taking the sun's distance at 10, is the numerical value of the name Mariam. The Chapter House had evidently a peculiarly mystical significance to the old monks, who regularly performed certain offices in it. The name implies that it was the " House of the Head " (Domus Capitis), and from its position here, and the measurement 192, it would seem to inclose the head of the spouse of Christ, laid beside her Lord who mystically occupies the main building. If the Omphalos of her body be taken to fall upon the centre of the cloister garden, which would be its appropriate symbol, the side of the square which would hold her figure stretched crosswise within it would be 512, and

---

[1] See section published in the "Builder," March 7th, 1885.

its perimeter would be 2,048 feet, the diameter of Saturn's orbit. But it may be that this chamber is built to hold the head of a woman whose body is proportionate to it; in that case her body would be 462 feet long, for the house is nearly 58 feet across, and the figure of Vitruvius is 8 heads high. The Chapter House was built in the thirteenth century, when the cult of the Virgin was at its highest popularity among the scholastic theologians, and it is probable that the builders would seek to include in their design the feminine image of the divine power. The Chapter House of Westminster was finished about the year 1260, the date at which the new age of the Holy Ghost was predicted to begin.

The measurements of the abbey have been taken from the plan published in "The Builder" of January 6th, 1894. This is the best plan at present available, but no dimensions being given, the preceding measures are liable to a slight error.

CHAPTER IX.

FREEMASONRY.

"A Mason's Lodge . . . . is a microcosm or picture of the universe."—"Discrepances of Freemasonry," p. 185.

"What is the form of the Lodge?
"A long square.
"How long?
"From east to west.
"How broad?
"Between north and south.
"How deep?
"From the surface of the earth to the centre.
"How high?
"Even as high as the heavens."—"Masonic Ritual," quoted by Dr. Oliver, ibid., p. 209.

IN the traditions and ritual of modern Freemasonry, we have the remains of those philosophical doctrines, which at one time guided the practice of architecture. Whatever uncertainty there may be as to the precise secrets of the old operative masons, it is evident that the rites which are said to have been formulated for the first time in the eighteenth century, were not a brand new invention. For it may be asserted—and this is confirmed by many contemporary evidences—that the establishment of the present forms of initiation and instruction was the attempt of certain mystics of that time, to preserve the ancient secrets of architecture from sinking into the oblivion which was rapidly overtaking the lapsed craft of operative Freemasonry. And the new dilettanti masons seem to have been sufficiently instructed in the mystical traditions, still existing at that time, to compose the degrees in accordance with the old system, so they may be taken as tolerably reliable expositions of the ideas which governed the practice of their predecessors.

Building was not the only art or science which had its symbolical secrets, but the Freemasons depended entirely upon the Church for their support, consequently, when the Reformation began to discourage the secret discipline as a part of the teaching of theology, masons of the old instructed kind were no longer employed to build the churches. The disuse of symbolical architecture, however, does not seem to have come about till after the time of Sir Christopher Wren, for it is known that he was the master of an operative lodge, and that Freemasons were employed in building St. Paul's, the last of the old cathedrals. We are told that " The highest or last stone on the top of the Lantern was laid by the hands of the surveyor's son, Christopher Wren, deputed by his father, in the presence of that excellent artificer, Mr. Strong, his son, and other *Free* and *Accepted Masons* chiefly employed in the execution of the work." (" Parentalia," p. 293.)

The coming to light of all sorts of mystical knowledge that had been carefully concealed in previous times, is one of the noticeable features of the seventeenth and eighteenth centuries. But it is a mistake to suppose that for this reason these centuries were peculiarly given to mysticism, on the contrary, the appearance in the seventeenth century of Rosicrucian, Hermetic, and Masonic Societies was a sign of decadence, and the premonition of the final extinction of the esoteric traditions of antiquity. As long as the secret doctrines of masonry were received as the vital inspiration of the craft, no one heard anything about them, and the same thing applies to theology itself. In fact the mysteries, which in the past were only spoken in secret and never written, became faintly heard when their power had practically ceased.

It is not to be expected that a society, whose secrets were communicated orally, should have records to prove the nature of its mysteries, therefore it is to the monuments, which the mediæval masons have everywhere left behind them, that we must look for the evidence of their practical methods; while the ritual, however doubtful its antiquity may be, is the best and only surviving instance of those mystical initiations which prevailed in the pagan world. All intelligent masons agree that, notwithstanding the alterations which may have been made to the ceremonies during the eighteenth century, certain forms of initiation in use from time immemorial were required " to make a mason." In the Lansdowne manuscript (1560), it is said, "These be all the charges . . . read at the making of a mason" (Mackenzie's " Cyclop."). But the ancient ritual may well have been a comparatively simple affair, when it is understood that the chief business of an operative mason was to learn the principles of his craft. And it is obvious that this would have to be done in some more practical way than by a purely symbolical ceremony, which was quite sufficient, however, for the theoretic masons of the last century. And it is probable that all the modern degrees were an attempt to reduce to a ceremonial order some of the practices actually forming a part of the ancient architectural methods of design. It would be manifestly inexpedient that the profounder secrets of theology should be intrusted to young and ignorant apprentices, so that there would naturally arise a practical necessity for progressive degrees of instruction, leading up to the full knowledge of the esoteric rules which constituted the architectural canon.

The early Freemasons, being the ecclesiastical workmen, were authorized by the Pope, who was regarded as their head. They were exempted from taxation, and had other privileges; and "the papal briefs, which protected them, alleged that such immunities were given them after the example of Hiram, King of Tyre, when he sent artisans to King Solomon for the purpose of building the temple at Jerusalem." At that time many of the masters were bishops and abbots, while the monks worked as journeymen in the different crafts.

Although there is no direct documentary evidence giving a straightforward explanation of the Masonic mysteries, there are various traditions which profess to give an account of the origin and purpose of the craft. Modern masons, who do not understand the symbolical mode of communication, regard these traditions as worthless fictions, deserving no serious consideration. We venture, however, to take another view of the case, and an analysis of the following quotation from a document, published in the " Gentleman's Magazine " (June, 1815), will show that the statements of the old masons, like those of the priests, were published in the form of grotesque historical allegory, for the sole purpose, apparently, of deceiving those who were considered to be unfit to appreciate the simple truth.

" Good Breetheren and Fellowes : Our purpose is to tell you how and in what manner this worthy science of Masonrye was begunne. . . . For there be seaven liberall sciences, of the which seaven it is one of them. And the names of the seaven scyences bene these; first is Grammere : and it teacheth man to speake truly and write truly. And

the second is Rethorike; and teacheth a man to
speak faire in subtill termes.   And the third is
Dialectyke ; and teacheth a man for to discern
and know truth from false.   And the fourth is
Arithmeticke ; and teacheth a man for to reckon
and to accompte all manner of numbers.   And the
fifth is called Geometrie ; and that teacheth Mett
and Measure of earth, and all other things ; *of the
which science is called Masonrye.*   And the sixth
science is called Musicke ; and that teacheth a
man of songe, and voice of tongue, and orgaine,
harpe, and trompe.   And the seaventh science is
called Astronomye; and that teacheth a man the
course of the sunn, moone, and stars.

   " How that these worthy sciences were first
begonne I shall tell you.   Before Noyes Floode,
there was a man called Lameche, as it is written
in the Byble, in the fourth chapter of Genesis: and
this Lameche had two wives, and the one height
Ada and the other height Sella : by his first wife
Ada he gott two sons, and that one Jabell and
thother Tuball, and by that other wife Sella he
got a son and a daughter.   All these children
founden the beginning of all the sciences in the
world.   And this elder son Jabell found the
science of Geometrie, and he departed flocks of
sheepe and lambs of the field, and first wrought
house of stone and tree, as is noted in the chapter
above said.   And his brother Tubal found the
science of Musicke, songe of tongue, harpe and
orgaine.   And the third son, Tuball Cain, found
smithcraft of gold, silver, and copper, iron and
steel : and the daughter found the crafte of Weav-
inge.   And these children knew well that God
would take vengeance for synn, either by fire or
by water ; wherefore they writt their science that
they had found in two pillars of stone, that they
might be found after Noyes Floode.   And that

one stone was marble, for that would not bren with
fire ; and that other stone was clepped laterns,
and would not drown in noe water.

"Our intent is to tell you trulie, and in what
manner these stones were found, that these
sciences were written in. The Greet Hemarynes
that was Cubys son, the which Cub was Sem's
son, that was Noys son. This Hemarynes afterwards was called Harmes, the father of wise men ;
he found one of the two pillars of stone, and found the
science written here, and he taught it to other men.
And at the making of the tower of Babylon, there
was Masonry first made much of. And the Kinge
of Babylon, that height Nemrothe, was a Mason
himself. . . . And this was the first tyme that
ever Mason had any charge of his science.

"Moreover, when Abraham and Sara his wife
went into Egypt, there he taught the seaven
sciences to the Egiptians, and he had a worthy
Scoller that height Ewclyde, and he learned right
well, and was a master of all the VII sciences
liberall. And in his days it befell, that the lond
and the estates of the realme had so many sonnes
. . . . and they had not competent livehode to
find with their children . . . . And they did crye
through all the realme, if there were any man
that could informe them, that he should come to
them. . . .

"After that this crye was made, then came this
worthy clarke Ewclyde, and said to the Kinge
and to all his great lords, ' If yee will take me
your children to governe, and to teach them one
of the seaven Scyences, wherewith they may live
honestly as gentlemen should, under a condition
that yee will grant me and them a commission,
that I may have power to rule them after the
manner that the science ought to be ruled ! And
that the kinge and all his counsell granted to him

anone, and sealed their commission,' . . . And
thus was the scyence grounded there : and that
worthy Mr Ewclide gave it the name of geometrie. And now it is called through all this land
Masonrye."

It is first to be noticed, that Masonry is said to
be identical with geometry, the fifth of the sciences,
which teaches the measure of the earth. This
definition is to be found in all the old accounts of
the craft, and whatever else may be mythical in
these histories, this at least may be taken literally.
As heretofore, it will be found that the numbers of
names play the same part in the Masonic parables
as in the case of other mystical writings.

It has been previously suggested that the
cabalistic process of Gematria was practised by
other peoples besides the Hebrews and Greeks,
and the English Freemasons seem to have applied
that system of numbers to the names used in their
science.

In the preceding document we are told that
Lameche was the father of Masonry. Now, in
the Greek, Λάμεχ has the numerical value of 676,
the square of 26. And 26, the number of Tetragammaton, was also in England the number of
letters in the alphabet, which (according to the
book of Yetsirah), together with the Sephiroth,
are the foundation of all things. And the word
Masonrye has the value of 676, supposing the
English letters to have the same value as the
Hebrew ; while the more modern spelling of the
word, without the final e, gives it the value of 671
—the number of the Bride—and confirms the Ionic
tendency of English Masonry. In corroboration
of this, Vitruvius (bk. i., ch. ii.) says that architecture consists of order, arrangement, and eco-
nomy. These names are given in Greek (τάξις,
διάθεσις, οἰκονομία), and are numerically equal to

1,351. If colel be added we get 1,352, which is
the measure of a cross whose limbs are each 676
long. Again, the name Lameche treated in the
same way gives the number 89, which is the square
root of the earth's diameter in miles $(89^2 = 7,921)$.
And Lameche was, in the order of the patriarchal
giants, the ninth from Adam, and corresponds to
the step Yesod of the Cabala. In this capacity
he may be said to be the symbol of the generative
power of the sun, for the distance between the
tropics, or the limit of the solar path, is $89\frac{1}{2}$ diameters of the sun. And Lameche, with his two
wives (Ada, 6, and Sella, 366), complete a triad
$(89 + 6 + 366)$ numerically equal to 461, which
is 1 less than the height of a cross whose area
measures a rood of 40 perches or 660 feet or
7,920 inches in length. In Hebrew the name
Lamech (LMK) has the value of 90, which is the
side of a rhombus having a perimeter of 360,
while Tubal Cain (TUBL QIN) yields 1,248 which
is the width of a vesica 2,163 long, or the number
of miles in the moon's diameter, and may symbolize
the Tone. The numbers of the five names, deducting colel from each, amount to 1,003, or 1
more than 1,002, the limb of the cross described
by Plato [1] in the " Timæus."

Tubal, it is said, founded the science of Musicke,
384, the number of Plutarch's soul of the world,
and the measure of the sun's distance computed
by the tone. And Tubal Cain yields $1,183 =$
$(469 + 714)$; he is called the first worker in
metals, and the value of his name is one less than
the half of the number, 2,368 $(1,184 \times 2)$.

It would take too long to discuss all the numbers
which occur in the piece, but it may be noticed
that the name Noye yields 135, or the vertical

---

[1] According to the tradition Plato had been instructed in
Masonry, and was claimed as an ancient brother.

height of the tropic above the equator on a globe 660 in diameter. Hemarynes has the numerical value of 616, the number of the beast according to some of the manuscripts of the Apocalypse. Then Nemroth yields 735, which is the width of a vesica 1,275 long, and 1,275 is the height of a cross, which will crucify a man in a square whose perimeter is 2,368. Ewclyde appears to be brought in to show that the Greeks were fully instructed in Masonry. His name yields 69, and the sum of the numbers from 1 to 68 is 2,346, so that 69 may stand for 2,368.

It is possible, also, that there is an arcanum hidden beneath this account of the seven sciences, for the sum of the numbers deduced from the English names given here is 5,261, which divided by 7 gives 751, but 5,261 may also be taken as the perimeter of a square inclosing a rhombus whose width is 758. Now if 2 be taken from 758 and added to 751, the numbers become 753 and 756, the one being the diameter of a circle whose circumference is 2,368, and the other being the height of rood cross whose extreme measure is 1,080. These Scyences, 676, therefore involved the knowledge of Jesus Christ, who personated the cosmos mystically embodied in the measures of His cross. The same sciences are dealt with at some length in the cosmographical treatise called "The Mirrour of the Worlde," translated by Caxton, and published by him in the year 1480. To Christians who were fond of numerical analogies, the year whose number corresponded with the name of Christos would be a notable one, and this cosmic work—the only book printed in England in that year—was probably considered suitable to the occasion. And the word "Scyences" having the same numerical value as "Masonrye," namely, 676, they are by Gematria equivalent to one another, and are appropriately introduced into the parable to illustrate the meaning of the Masonic craft.

In the treatise of Vitruvius there are certain rules laid down as to the proportions of columns for the practical guidance of architects. These rules are said to have been derived from the writings and monuments of the Greeks. No Greek treatise on architecture exists at the present day, nor is there any exact uniformity in the proportions of the columns of Greek temples. The rules must, therefore, be taken independently upon their own merits. There is reason to believe that this method of measuring columns is connected with the mystical practice of architecture set forth here as obscurely as elsewhere. Although modern architects no longer proportion their buildings according to a scale of modules, as Vitruvius directs, that system has only been dropt within comparatively recent times. Alberti, whose book on building is the next in point of age to that of Vitruvius, lived nearly 1,500 years after his master, nevertheless he scrupulously advocated the same principles, and the other architects of the Renascence followed in his steps. It may be concluded, therefore, that the later architects had good reasons for accepting these rules, and for continuing to use them.

We are told by Vitruvius (bk. iv., ch. i.), that there are three sorts of columns, the Doric, Ionic, and Corinthian. The names and proportions connected with these three columns have evidently been assigned with a mystical purpose, as an analysis of their numbers will show. The Doric was the oldest column, and was first made of the proportion of six to one, in imitation of the body of a man, as it is said, whose foot was found to be the sixth part of his height. Then they made the

Ionic column according to the proportion of a woman, and made its height eight times its thickness. Lastly, Kallimachos invented a still more slender and graceful proportion for the Corinthian column in imitation of the slim figure of a young virgin. "Thus two orders were invented, one of a masculine character without ornament, the other bearing a character which resembled the delicacy, ornament, and proportion of a female."

These three columns have the greatest architectural importance, for they are the distinguishing features of the three great types of design applied to all classical temples. They apparently symbolize the Macrocosm, the Microcosm, and the Bride or Virgin of the Cabala, the three personifications of the architectural canon.

The Doric column, if it signified the Macrocosm, would be designed as the emblem of the original cause of all things, and according to the mystical account of Vitruvius it is to be conceived as a type of the upper Triad of the Cabala, set forth by the father, Hellen, 123, his wife, Orseis, 588, and Doros, 1,174, their son.

The original proportion of the Doric column being six to one, the ratio of Noah's ark, it was said to have been based upon the human form. In the Greek language, Κίων Δωρικός (Doric column) is equivalent to the number 2,084, the side of the Holy Oblation. It was also called Κίων Δώριας, 2,003, or 1 less than the number produced from the four elements described by Plato in the "Timæus," and from ὁ κίων Δώριας we get 2,073, or $\frac{1}{12}$ of the earth's circumference in miles. The name Δῶρος yields 1,174, and this is the length of a rhombus whose width is 677, which is 1 more than the square of 26, and 1 less than the length of the sun's orbit. The Doric column, therefore, may be said to be the symbol of the generative

power of the universe, expressed by the sun, which
of all the celestial bodies most conspicuously
appears to measure the whole extent of the cosmic
system.

The method of measuring the proportion of a
column is described by Vitruvius in bk. iii., ch. iii.,
where we are told that the thickness of a column
is to be 2 modules, and this has always been the
received principle among architects. Each module
was further divided into 30 parts, so that the thickness of every column, no matter what its size may
be, is always a measure of 60 parts, and those
parts form the basis of a proportionate scale of
measurement throughout the building. Now every
Doric column whose height is 6 times its thickness, is 360 parts high, or the number of degrees
in the circumference of any circle—the sun's orbit
for instance—or the earth's circumference.[1] And
these 2 modules have also a symbolical import, as
the foundation upon which every column was
supposed to stand.

The numerical value of the name Doros, and
those of his father and mother, when added together amount to 1,885 (Δῶρος, 1,174, Ἕλλην, 123,
Ὄρσηις, 588), which is the perimeter of a rhombus

---

[1] The architects of the Renascence considered that the most
perfect proportions had been realized in the Temple of "Jupiter
Stator" in the Forum at Rome. The height of the Order is
given at 762·91 parts. Now a square 763 is enclosed by a
rhombus inscribed within the Holy Oblation. The height of
the shaft being 606⅓ parts is very nearly the circumference of
the zodiac, taking the sun's distance at 10. Then the height
of the column and architrave is 649·83, or nearly the diameter
of a circle whose circumference is equal to the diameter of
Saturn's orbit. If the Pattern-temples described by Vitruvius,
and the designs published by Alberti, Serlio, Vignola, Palladio,
and other architects of the sixteenth century be computed in
the same way, it will be found that they also are illustrations of
the harmonious order of the universe, accepted as the canon
of beauty by all the artists of antiquity.

whose sides are 471, the diameter of a circle 1,480
in circumference. The number 1,885 is also the
sum of the diagonals of a square whose sides are
666. According to Vitruvius, Hellen and Orseis
reigned over Achaia, 613, and Peloponnesos, 913,
both names yielding mystical numbers already
discussed. The name Hellen and that of his wife
Orseis, are numerically equal to 711, or 2 more
than the side of a square whose diagonals measure
2,004; while 588 + 1,174 = 1,762, or the circumference of a circle 532 in diameter. Now the
length of a vesica 532 broad is 921, the value of
the name Κανών (Canon).

The invention of the Ionic column is ascribed
by Vitruvius to the Asiatic colony of 13 cities,
founded by Ion, 860, the son of Xouthos, 709, and
Chreousa, 796. When the Ionians were about to
build a temple to Artemis and "seeking a new
proportion, they used the female figure as the
standard." Modern philologists have frequently
derived the word Ionic from the Oriental Yoni,
whose symbol is the vesica. The Ionic was the
most ancient form of Greek philosophy, and was
introduced by Thales, celebrated for his observations of the Lesser Bear, Κυνόσουρα, 1,311. By
Gematria, Cynosoura is equivalent to Tetragrammaton, and she is the feminine of the two.[1]   A
rhombus—the Ionic symbol—which is 1,311 long,
is 756 broad, and this is the height of a cross
whose extreme measure is 1,080, the number of
miles in the moon's radius, and the numerical value
of τὸ Πνεῦμα Ἅγιον, the Holy Ghost of the Christians.
By adding colel to 248, the value of the name of
the first Ionic philosopher, we get 249, and $294\frac{1}{4}$ ×
$9\frac{1}{2}$ = 2,368. Again the sum of the numbers of the

---

[1] Arctos, the Great or masculine Bear, has the value of 691,
the length of the sun's orbit ($220 \times 3\frac{1}{7} = 691$).

name Ion, and those of his father and mother,
when colel is added to each, amounts to 2,368.

$$\left.\begin{array}{r} 709 + 1 \\ 796 + 1 \\ 860 + 1 \end{array}\right\} 1,658$$

$$2,365 + 3 = 2,368.$$

The design of the Ionic column is primarily
distinguished by its double character, marked by
the two spiral volutes of its capital. It would
seem that the Greeks connected this number,
2,368, not only with the feminine symbolism of
the number 2, associated specially with the Ionic
column, but that it was also regarded as an emblem
of the masculo-feminine potency of the Logos.
For the number 2 may express cabalistically both
the second step and the second person of the
great Triad, composed of the six steps intermediate
between the first Triad and the tenth step. Therefore the Ionic system includes the two first principles of life, joined together in the person of the
Microcosm or Logos, who in a manner epitomized
all the philosophy of the ancients. Moses appears
to have been, like Thales, an Ionic philosopher,
for the numerical value of his name signifies the
period of the equinoxes, which divide the year into
two parts ($345\frac{1}{2} \times 2 = 691$, the length of the sun's
orbit measuring the space of the year), and 345 is
the diameter of a circle whose circumference
is equal to the number of miles in the moon's
radius—the moon being the feminine of the two
great lights of the heavens. And he attributed the
creation of the world to the twofold Deity called
the Elohim.

And just as the universe was built by a twofold
agency, so the temple of Solomon, designed in

imitation of the greater world, was built by the
two kings, Solomon and Hiram. The walls of
Troy were also built by Apollo and Poseidon.
Kadmos and Harmonia built the city of Thebes;
the Aloadae, Otos and Ephialtes, are said to have
founded the city Aloeum; and the invention of
brick building was attributed to the two brothers,
Euryalos and Hyperbios. Thus the creative
powers were commonly symbolized in a double
form, and are identical with the two intersecting
circles of the Ionic vesica, and are reproduced in
the two volutes of the Ionic capital.

It is said that 8 letters were added in later
times to the primitive Greek alphabet of Kadmos,
consisting of 16 letters. The 8 Ionic letters were
$\zeta, \eta, \theta, \xi, \varphi, \chi, \psi, \omega$, and the numerical value amounts
to 2,684, which is the perimeter of a rhombus
whose sides are 671, the number of the Hebrew
name, Thora or Adonai, the bride, who corresponds to the feminine part of the Logos, and
appropriately embodies all the feminine attributes
of the number 2.

The name Ion, the founder of the Ionic race,
having the value of 860, further emphasizes this
connection between the Ionic cultus and the
Cabalistic Spouse, for a vesica 496 (Malchuth) is
860 long.

The numerical value of Κίων Ἰωνικός is $2,040 + 2$
$= 2,042$, which is nearly the diameter of Saturn's
orbit.

The proportion of the Ionic column was at first
made 8 times its thickness, making its height 480
modules ($60 \times 8 = 480$) and 480 is the width of a
vesica 831 long. It was also made of the proportion of $8\frac{1}{2}$ to 1, which gives it a height of 510
modules, which is about the side of a rhombus
whose perimeter is equal to the diameter of Saturn's
orbit ($510 \times 4 = 2,040$). But the most usual height

for this column, although it is not mentioned by Vitruvius, is 9 times its thickness, which produces 540 modules, or the side of a rhombus whose perimeter is 2,160, the number of miles in the moon's diameter.

The account of the accident which suggested to Kallimachos the hint for composing a new capital is well known to every one. John Shute, an English architect of the sixteenth century, was evidently pleased with the story, and, as it stands in his book, it has more freshness and simplicity than the barer narrative of the Roman writer, so we shall repeat the legend in his works. "After that, in the citie of Corinthe was buried a certaine maiden, after whose burial her nourishe (who lamented much her death) knowing her delightes to have bene in prettye cuppes, and such like conceytes in her lifetime with many other thinges, appertayninge only to the pleasure of the eye, toke them and broke them, and put them in a littell preatie baskette, and did sette the basket on her grave, and covered the basket with a square pavinge stone. That done, with weping teares she sayde, 'Let pleasure go wyth pleasure,' and so the nourishe departed. It chanced, that the basket was set upon a certain roote of an herbe called acanthus, in frenche Brankursine, or Beare fote with us, now in the spring time of the yeare, when every roote spreadeth fourth his leaves in the increasing, they did ronne up by the sides of the basket, until they could rise no higher for the stone that covered the basket, which, being square, and castinge his foure corners over the sydes of of the rounde basket, constrained the branches of the herbe to draw downwardes againe with a certaine compasse, and so drew to the fashion that Vitruvius calleth Voluta. . . . In this citie one Callimachus, an excellent architectur, passinge or going thereby, regarding the beawtifull worke of nature," devised a column, and set a capital upon it in imitation of the tomb which he had seen.   This story is generally supposed to be no more than an idle fancy, invented or repeated by Vitruvius. Nevertheless the circumstances related here are probably an indication of the ideas which the classical architects associated with the third order of columns.   Although this pillar is called Corinthian, it might appropriately be called Æolic, and represent the third division of the Greek race, since the names Doric and Ionic were given to the preceding orders.

Supposing that these three columns symbolize the three cabalistic powers, then the Corinthian order must be identical with the tenth step, and third person of the Trinity.   Aiolos, 381, appears in the "Odyssey" as the god of the winds, which seems to correspond with the pneuma, breath, or spirit of the Christian Trinity.   The word Anemos, wind, has the value of 366, or the number of days in the year, and 381 (Aiolos) is the length of a vesica 220 broad, or the diameter of the sun's orbit.   Thus, by the circle of the year, by the winds, which the old cosmographers placed round the world, by the sun's orbit enclosed by the city of the bride, they associated the third column with the centre of the universe, and its flowering capital is a beautiful emblem of the fertile earth.   There was also a mystery in the Tomb of the Virgin that will be touched upon further on.

The name Korinthios yields the number 539, which is the side of a rhombus having a perimeter of 2,156, the mean between the numbers 2,151 and 2,160—the first being the number of years in the great month, and the second the number of miles in the moon's diameter.   Kallimachos, the

artificer, who is said to have first made a column
of this form, has the numerical value of 1,002, or
$\frac{1}{12}$ of the length of the equinox when the sun's
course is measured on the earth's circumference,
and contained in an ark. The number 1,002 is
also the diagonal of a square 709, and the length
of one of the strips of Plato's cross, composed of
the four elements.

The proportions of this column are omitted by
Vitruvius, but its height is generally about 10 times
its thickness, and is therefore 600 parts ($60 \times 10 =$
600). Now 600 is the numerical equivalent of the
word cosmos.

The two pillars, Jachin and Boaz, in the porch
of Solomon's temple, were supposed to exemplify
the Hebrew proportions of columns. The position
of these pillars decides their primary significance.
From Villalpanda's plan, it will be seen that they
flank the two chambers on either side of the porch
and are intended to symbolize the double portion
of the Triad, represented by the whole Temple.
Their names, Strength and Stability, are analogous
to the names of the two beings, Kratos, 691
(Strength), and Bia, 13 (Force), who appear in the
play of Æschylus as the male and female powers,
who bind or crucify Prometheus. They represent
the twofold element of creation.

Jachin in Hebrew has the value of 735 (IHKN)
or counting the final " n " at 50 the number is 85.
Boaz, again, yields 79 (BOZ). Now 735 is the
width of a vesica 1,275 long, and 1,275 is the
height of a cross which crucifies a man in a square
whose perimeter is 2,368. And $85\frac{1}{4}$ is $\frac{1}{12}$ of the
radius of Saturn's orbit, measured by the sun's
diameter.

Then 79, the value of Boaz, is the square root
of 6,241, which is the perimeter of a triangle whose
sides are 2,080. And $79\frac{1}{2}$ is the side of a rhombus

having a perimeter of 318. Again, $735 + 79 = 814$, which is the circumference of a circle having a diameter of 259, which is the numerical equivalent of Basileia, the Bride, or third person of the cabalistic triad. And $814 + 2 = 816$, which is the length of a vesica whose width is 471, the diameter of a circle 1,480 in circumference.

It is obvious that these two mystical columns are analogous to the pillars of Hermes and Seth, set up to record the astronomical science of their time. The height of each shaft was 18 cubits, its girth 12 cubits, and the chapter 5 cubits. They were cast in brass by HIRM (Hiram), or 255, an admirable number, for a square whose sides are 255 has a diagonal of 360 and a perimeter of 1,020, the radius of Saturn's orbit; and the measures which he cunningly ascribed to these canonical pillars are no less significant than this.

Since their circumference is exactly specified, we find their diameter, reduced to inches, to be $68\frac{3}{4}$, a number probably chosen because the sum of the numbers from 1 to $68 = 2,346$, or nearly 2,368. Accordingly, if the shafts be laid side by side, they occupy an area of 324 by $137\frac{1}{2}$ inches, having a perimeter of 923, or nearly the square root of the sun's diameter in miles. Then, if the chapiters be added, the rectangle enclosing them becomes $(324 + 900 =)$ 414 by $137\frac{1}{2}$, and its perimeter is 1,103 or the height of a rood cross which will crucify a man in a square with a circuit equal to the diameter of Saturn's orbit. The rhombus which encloses the two pillars is 652 long, or nearly the diameter of a circle whose circumference is equal to the diameter of Saturn's orbit. Again, the circumference of each shaft being 216 inches, we get the measure of the diameter of the sun's orbit. And a square enclosing the pillars has a perimeter of 1,656 (414

× 4), the number of miles from the equator to the tropics.

Thus the Hebrews established a standard measure of the planetary system, by which the Freemasons ever afterwards instructed their fellows and masters in the mysteries of the craft.

CHAPTER X.

MUSIC OF THE SPHERES.

*" From whence proceed these sounds, so strong and yet so sweet,
that fill my ears?*

*" The melody which you hear, and which, though composed in
unequal time, is nevertheless divided into regular harmony, is
effected by the impulse and motion of the spheres. . . . The ears
of mankind, filled with these sounds, have become deaf . . . . and
cannot comprehend them, just as you cannot look directly upon
the sun, because your sight and sense are overcome by his beams."*
—CICERO's " Vision of Scipio."

THE theory of ancient music seems to have been
constructed from a study of the harmonic relations
existing between the parts of the universe; and
the musical canon, like that of architecture, was
probably based upon certain symmetrical conson-
ances, discovered in the proportions of the planets,
and the intervals between their orbits. Yet none
of the ancient rules of harmony, which are now
intelligible, can be directly or simply traced to the
known ratios of the planetary orbits. But all the
ancient expositions of the science of music are
very obscure, and give the reader the impresssion
that, as in the case of other arts, there is something
behind their obvious statements which the writers
did not choose to disclose.

For instance, Vitruvius (bk. v., ch. 4), after
stating that music is an abstruse science, difficult
to understand, and requiring many Greek words in
its explanation, says, "There are three sorts of
modulation, the enharmonic (ἁρμονίαν), the chro-

matic (χρῶμα), and the diatonic (διάτονον), so called
by the Greeks." From the numbers deduced
from these Greek words, it may be reasonably
assumed that they have been introduced into the
text for mystical reasons; for we find *Harmonia*
yields 272, *Chroma*, 1,541, and *Diatonos*, 705; and
272 is the width of a vesica 471 long, and 471
is the diameter of a circle having a circumference
of 1,480 (a square whose sides are 471 has a
diagonal of 666), and 272 is the diameter of a
circle having a circumference of 854, which is the
width of a vesica 1,480 long. It may be therefore
supposed that the word harmonia implies the
number 1,480. Then 1,540 is the length of a vesica
888 long, so that the word chroma may be taken
to indicate the number 888. Diatonos, again, has
the value of 705, which is in round numbers the
side of a square whose diagonals are 999; and a
vesica formed of two circles 999 in circumference
has a perimeter of 666, which may be supposed to
be the number intended to be expressed by this
name. We therefore get from the names given to
the three kinds of harmony the numbers 2,046,
1,480, and 2,093, as the supposed basis of the
harmonic system, and they are, apparently, used
here by Vitruvius, as the received canonical
measures summarizing the principal dimensions of
the universe.

The three numbers, 2,368, 1,480, and 888 are
in the ratio of 6 : 10 : 16, being divisible by 148.
Now, if the sun's distance be taken at 10, the order
of the planets is very nearly in the following proportion : ☿ 4, ♀ 7, ☉ 10, ♂ 16, ♃ 52, ♄ 97. Therefore the numbers 10 and 16 agree with the ratios
of the sun and Mars, while the number 6 falls
between Mercury and Venus; that is to say, 2,368
may represent the planet Mars, 1,480 the sun, and
888 the two inner planets Mercury and Venus.

Thus the whole three are analogous to the cabalistic triad, according to the Pythagorean theory. For the first person was said to be male, the second person female, and the third person comprised the union of both. Pythagoras sometimes regarded the sun as the central fire of the universe, in which case it may have a feminine sense. These proportions probably formed the harmonic canon of the architects, and it may be concluded that they were known to Vitruvius.

A theory of music is said to have been invented by Pythagoras, who said that numbers were the principles and elements of all things, and composed the harmonic proportions of the whole world. To him the rhythmic treatment of numbers was music, and he declared that "without numbers all measures, weights, and art itself, would fall to the ground." And music was the art of composing, and reconciling contrary and discordant things, according to the harmony of the world, called by the Greeks ὁ κοσμος, 670. It is also said that the system of Pythagoras was reduced to certain "harmonical canons, or rules found out by reason."

The assertion that the planets in their revolutions round the earth uttered certain sounds differing according to their respective "magnitude, celerity and local distance," was commonly made by the Greeks. Thus Saturn, the farthest planet, was said to give the gravest note, while the moon, which is the nearest, gave the sharpest. "These sounds of the seven planets, and the sphere of the fixed stars, together with that above us, are the nine Muses, and their joint symphony is called Mnemosyne." Pliny (bk. iii., ch. 22) says, "Saturn moveth by the Doric tone : Mercury by Pthongus, Jupiter by Phrygian and the rest likewise." The Pythragorean harmony consisted of three concords, called Diapente, Diatessaron, and Diapason. The

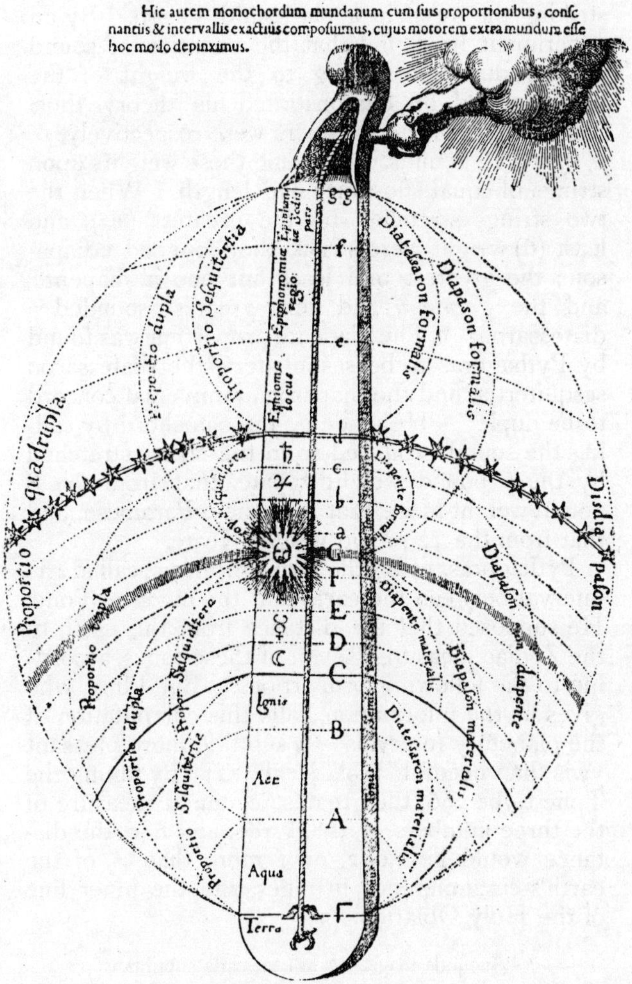
Hic autem monochordum mundanum cum suis proportionibus, consc
nantiis & intervallis exactiùs composuimus, cujus motorem extra mundum esse
hoc modo depinximus.
Proportio quadrupla
Proportio dupla
Proportio Sesquitertia
Diatessaron formalis
Diapason formalis
Disdiapason
Proportio dupla
Proportio Sesquialtera
Diapente formalis
Diapente materialis
Diapason materialis
Diapason cum diapente
Diatessaron materialis
Proportio Sesquitertia
Ignis
Aer
Aqua
Terra
gg
f
e
d
c
b
a
G
F
E
D
C
B
A
Γ

FIG. 21.—THE COSMIC HARMONY. FROM ROBERT FLUDD'S "UTRIUSQUE COSMI HISTORIA," P. 90.

discovery of these concords is said to have been
made by Pythagoras, on hearing the hammers
striking the anvil in a blacksmith's shop. By an
experiment he found that the variation of sound
was produced according to the weight of the
hammer, and he demonstrated his theory thus.
The weights of the hammers were respectively, 6,
8, 9, and 12 pounds. He hung these weights upon
strings of equal substance and length. When the
two strings stretched by the greatest (12), and
least (6) weight were struck, they sounded a diapason; the greatest and least but one a diapente,
and the greatest, and next greatest sounded a
diatessaron. " The diapente proportion was found
by Pythagoras to be sesquialtera, the diatessaron
sesquitertia, and the diapason or universal concord
to be duple." He made up the octochord by calling the sound produced from the string stretched
by the 6 pound weight Hyate, that from the 8
pound weight Mese, that from the 9 Paramese, and
that from the 12 pound weight Neate.

Pythagoras, using the terms of music, called the
interval between the earth and the moon a Tone.
He supposed that the distance from the earth to
the Zodiac measured seven of these tones, according to the following proportions. But Pliny, who
gives us the information, calls this computation of
the planetary intervals " a subtiltie more pleasant
ywis than needful "[1] (bk. ii., ch. 22). By taking the
Tone to be 296, the greatest common measure of
the three numbers, 2,368, 1,480, and 886, the distance would be 2,072, or 1 more than $\frac{1}{12}$ of the
earth's circumference in miles, and the inner line
of the Holy Oblation.

---

[1] " Jucunda magis, quam necessaria subtilitate."

Zodiac.

♄	1½	444
♃	½	148
♂	½	148
☉	1	296
♀	1½	444
☿	½	148
☽	½	148
⊕	1	296

2,072

Although Vitruvius does not show how the theory of music which he introduces into his treatise is to be applied to architecture, it is certain that some method of harmonic proportion was known to, and practised by, the Greek architects. We are told by Serlio, who wrote in 1537, that there were seven quadrangular proportions generally used in architecture. " The first figure is a perfect square of four equal sides, and four right angles. The second figure is a sesquiquarta, that is, a square and a quarter (5 : 4). The third figure is a sesquitertia, that is, a square and a third (being of the proportion of 4 : 3, it is the diatessaron). The fourth figure is of the proportion called diagonea, because its length is equal to the diagonal of the square ; it is irrational, there being no simple way of finding out this proportion from the fractional part of a square. The fifth figure is called sesquialtera, that is, a square and a half (it is of the proportion of 3 : 2, or diapente). The sixth figure is called superbipartiens tertias, that is a square and two thirds added. The seventh and last figure is called dupla, and is formed of two squares joined together" (this is the proportion of 2 : 1, or diapason).

Serlio, like Vitruvius, suggests no way of applying these proportions, but it may be, that by taking some number as the measure of the square, a series of proportions are derived, which when distributed throughout a building would give an harmonic result. Thus, if the sides of the square measured 592, and its perimeter 2,368, the six numbers produced according to the above ratios would be 640, 789$\frac{1}{3}$, 833, 888, 996$\frac{2}{3}$, and 1,184.

Another series of harmonic proportions may be derived from the divisions of a circle, divided according to the figure given by Cesariano (Vitruvius, p. 11).

Nearly all the old philosophers devised an harmonic theory with respect to the universe, and the practice continued till the old mode of philosophizing died out. Kepler (1596), in order to demonstrate the Platonic doctrine, that the universe was formed of the five regular solids, proposed the following rule. "The earth is a circle, the measurer of all. Round it describe a dodecahedron; the circle inclosing this will be Mars. Round Mars describe a tetrahedron; the sphere inclosing this will be Jupiter. Describe a cube round Jupiter; the sphere containing this will be Saturn. Now inscribe in the earth an icosohedron; the circle inscribed in it will be Venus. Inscribe an octohedron in Venus; the circle inscribed in it will be Mercury" ("Mysterium Cosmographicum," 1596).

This rule cannot be taken seriously as a real statement of the proportions of the cosmos, for it bears no real resemblance to the ratios published by Copernicus in the beginning of the sixteenth century. Yet Kepler was very proud of his formula, and said he valued it more than the Electorate of Saxony. It was also approved by those two eminent authorities, Tycho and Galileo, who evidently understood it. Kepler himself never gives the least hint of how his precious rule is to be interpreted. The subjoined explanation is submitted as a possible solution of its meaning. The earth, he says, is the mensor, or measurer of all, therefore everything depends upon the first step. The diameter of the earth is taken to be 660, that is, $\frac{7,920}{12}$; and instead of taking the five figures as solids, they are assumed to be so many regular plane polygons of 4, 6, 8, 12, and 2c sides respectively. The construction of the figure is consequently extremely easy. The twelve-sided figure enclosing the earth is contained by a circle $684\frac{2}{5}$ in diameter, whose circumference is 2,151. This is the circle of Mars. The square described round Mars is enclosed by a circle with a radius of 488, and a circumference of 3,067; this is the circle of Jupiter. The hexagon described round Jupiter is enclosed by a circle whose diameter is 1,120; and this is the circle of Saturn. The twenty-sided polygon inscribed within the earth contains a circle with a diameter of 651, and a circumference of 2,046; this is the circle of Venus. The octagon inscribed within Venus contains a circle whose diameter is 596; this is the circle of Mercury.

It will be seen at once that the relative proportions of these circles have no agreement with the orbits of the planets whose names they bear; but every circle, either in its diameter or circumference, represents a cosmic measure. The circle of Mars has a circumference of 2,151; and according to Plato's distribution of the five solids in the "Timæus," the dodecahedron represents the Zodiac; and 2,151 being the number of years in the great month, this may properly symbolize the Zodiacal circle. A hexagon described round this circle has a perimeter of 2,368. The radius of the circle called Jupiter is 488, the square root of the moon's distance from the earth in miles; the circumference of the same circle is the perimeter of the square which incloses the sun's orbit measured by the tone, and is inclosed by a rhombus inscribed within the Holy Oblation. The circle assigned to Saturn has a diameter of 1,120, which is the height of a rood cross which crucifies a man contained in a square having a perimeter equal to the side of the Holy Oblation. The circumference of the circle of Venus is equal to the diameter of Saturn's orbit, measured by the sun's diameter. The circle called Mercury has a diameter of 596, which is the circumference of Saturn's orbit if the sun's distance be taken at 10, and it may be taken for 592, the side of a square having a perimeter of 2,368. In Kepler's figure in the "Harmonices Mundi," he allows three lines to each circle, which seems to imply that a certain latitude is to be allowed in the geometry.

Probably, therefore, this mystical diagram symbolically reveals the astronomical measures secretly applied to theology, and seems to be intended to illustrate the harmony which was supposed to exist between the sun, the fixed stars, and the intervening planets, likened, by Kepler, to the Father, the Son, and the Holy Ghost. It seems to exemplify Kepler's attitude to all astronomical problems, and to be a result of the old searching after symmetry and harmony in the order of the heavens. For the three laws formulated by him could only have been discovered by a mind intent upon finding harmonic relations of this kind. And he evidently devoted his life to this search. It was music and philosophy which really interested Kepler, rather than the patient and careful observation of nature which occupied his friend Tycho. And although he used Tycho's observations he never seriously pursued any of these natural inquiries as an end, but rather, like the ancients, he tried to use them as a means to artistic expression. He stands as one of the last astronomers of the old type, and gives us a valuable insight into the practice of the earlier school, who combined astronomy with the doctrines of philosophy.

Another ingenious contrivance of the old philosophers was the magic square. The curious results produced from the combination of numbers in these squares would naturally appeal to the mind, when first discovered, as presenting an analogy to that harmony and symmetry which they discovered, or sought to discover, in all creation. The admiration for these numerical wonders was probably genuine among the philosophers, but the magical properties attributed to them by the priests could only have been believed in by an ignorant and superstitious populace. Cornelius Agrippa describes seven of these squares. " It is affirmed," he says, "by magicians, that there are certain sacred tables of the planets endowed with many and very great virtues of the heavens, inasmuch as they represent that divine order of celestial numbers which can no other way be expressed than by the marks of numbers and characters. The first of them is assigned to Saturn, and consists of a square of three, containing the particular numbers of nine, and in every line, three every way and through each diameter (diagonal), making fifteen. Now the whole sum of the numbers is forty-five. Each number represents an intelligency for good, or a spirit for bad. Out of the same numbers is drawn the seal, or character, which should be engraved on a plate of lead. If this be done with a fortunate Saturn it is a safeguard to births and bringing forth, but if it be done with an unfortunate Saturn, it hinders buildings, plantings, and the like, and casts a man from honours and dignities."

The number 45, deduced from this square, is in round numbers the square root of Saturn's orbit. And if the numbers of the square be read from right to left in the three rows, we get 294, 753, and 618, all of which are mystical numbers, already discussed. 294 is the numerical equivalent for Ecclesia, the Church, 753 is the diameter of a circle whose circumference is 2,368, and 618 is the numerical equivalent of ΙΗΣ, etc. By reading it perpendicularly other numbers are obtained, which have also mystical meanings.

The number of circles in the universe, counting from the earth to the empyreum is 15.

4	9	2
3	5	7
8	1	6

"The second is called the table of Jupiter, which consists of a quaternion drawn into itself, containing 16 particular numbers, and in every line and diameter 4, making 34. Now the sum of all is 136. . . . They say that if it be impressed on a silver plate with Jupiter ruling it conduces to riches, favour, love, and peace. To dissolve enchantments it should be engraven on coral."

The number 34 is the square root of 1,156, the width of a vesica 2,004 long, while 136·9 is the side of a square inscribed within the Holy Oblation taking the sun's distance at 10; it is therefore equivalent to the number 1,480.

"The third table belongs to Mars, which is made of a square of 5 containing 25 numbers, and of these in every side and diameter 5, which make 65, and the sum of all is 325. . . . These, with

Mars being fortunate, being engraved on an iron plate or sword, make a man potent in war and judgments, but if it be engraven with Mars being unfortunate, on a plate of red brass, it hinders buildings, and causes discords."

The numbers 5, 25, 65, and 325 are all discussed in the course of this work, and the meanings attributed to them are found in some of the attributes of the planet Mars.

" The fourth tablet is of the sun, and is made of a square of 6, and contains 36 numbers, whereof 6 on every side and diameter, produce 111, and the sum of all is 666. . . . This being engraven on a golden plate, renders him who wears it renowned and amiable, and equals a man to kings and princes . . . but with an unfortunate sun it makes a tyrant."

The numbers of this square are all curiously appropriate to the sun, whose ark has been shown to measure 666 of its diameters. Again, 666 is the diameter of a circle 2,093 in circumference, and 2,093 is $9\frac{1}{2}$ times the diameter of the sun's orbit as well as the diameter of the circle containing the square whose sides are 1,480,—the measure of the body of Christos.

" The fifth table is of Venus, consisting of a square of 7 drawn into itself, namely, of 49 numbers, whereof 7 on each side and diameter make 175, and the sum of all is 1,225. This being engraven on a silver plate, Venus being fortunate procureth concord and love, and endeth strife, . . . and conduceth to the cure of all melancholy distempers. . . . But if it be formed upon brass with an unfortunate Venus, it produceth the contrary."

In round numbers 49 is the square root of 2,368. And 1,225 is the measure of a cross whose limbs are $612\frac{1}{2}$ long.

" The sixth table is of Mercury, resulting from

the square of 8 drawn into itself, containing 64 numbers, whereof 8 on every side and by both diameters make 260, and the sum of all, 2,080. . . . If it be with Mercury being fortunate, engraven upon silver or tin or yellow brass, or be writ upon virgin parchment, it renders the bearer grateful and fortunate . . . *and conduceth to the memory . . . and understanding of occult things.*"

The numbers produced by this square are perhaps the most remarkable of the seven, and this seems to be suggested by the comment of Cornelius Agrippa. The number 2,080, thus associated with Hermes, connects this god with the Holy Oblation and confirms the opinion of the Gnostics, that he was identical with Christos. The number 64 is the numerical equivalent of the word Aletheia, Truth. And 260 is, besides being 10 times 26, the diameter of a circle whose area is equal to that of a square whose sides are 231.

" The seventh table is of the moon, of a square of 9 multiplied into itself, having 81 numbers, in every side and diameter 9, producing 369, and the sum of all is 3,321. . . This fortunate moon being engraven on silver renders the bearer amiable, pleasant, honoured, and without malice. But if it be an unfortunate moon, engraven on a plate of lead, wherever it shall be buried it makes that place unfortunate."

The moon was the accepted symbol of the sublunary world, containing the four elements, and the four elements were attributed to the body of the Logos. Now, $81 \times 9\frac{1}{2} = 769$, and 769 is the length of the transverse beam of a cross whose extreme measure is 2,368. Again, 369 is 1 less than 370, the side of a square whose perimeter is 1,480 ("Occult Philosophy," bk. ii., ch. 22).

Another way by which the ancients appear to have concealed mystical and cosmic numbers was

in the words and names written on their charms
and sigils. The inscriptions on these mysterious
gems are very often unreadable, and bear upon
them unknown names and words without meaning.
It is probable, therefore, that they were intended
to be read as numbers, and thus conveyed a meaning appropriate to the symbolical devices which
they accompanied. In Kircher's "Arithmologia"
(p. 220), there is a Solomon's seal inscribed within
a circle, containing a square divided into 25 smaller
squares, with a letter in each. The letters are

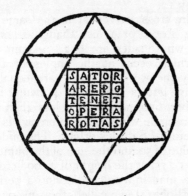

FIG. 22.—SIGIL FROM KIRCHER'S "ARITHMOLOGIA."

arranged so as to read "Sator Arepo Tenet Opera
Rotas," which has the look of a Latin epigram,
but it is apparently untranslatable. We know
that the priests sometimes converted Roman letters
into Greek, so as to obtain numbers from them, as
for instance in the "Œdipus Egyptiacus" (tom. ii.,
par. i., p. 219), where various Latin words are
written in Greek letters which bring out the
number 666. If we give the letters of this seal
the value of their Greek equivalents, we get 25
numbers, which may be read in various ways.
The five letters on the four sides of the square

form the word Sator, the "Sower," or backwards "Rotas," wheels. This word, written in Greek letters, has the numerical value of 671, the number of Thora, the Hebrew Bride, and $\delta\ \varkappa\acute{o}\sigma\mu o\varsigma = 670$. Then the sum of the numbers forming the perimeter of the square is 2,084, or the length of the side of the Holy Oblation. The two middle rows of letters make up the word "Tenet," read vertically and horizontally, and the numerical value of this word written in Greek letters is 660, or the number of miles in the diameter of the earth divided by 12.

A saltire-cross arrived at in the same way has the value 1,060, or 1 less than the length of a rhombus whose sides are 612. Again, the four letters, which occur at the angles of the cross formed by the word "Tenet," are equal to 360, and the five letters forming a quincunx bring out the number 650, which is 1 less than the diameter of a circle whose circumference is equal to the diameter of Saturn's orbit. The middle letter has the value of 50, and the sum of the numbers from 1 to 50 is 1,275, or the height of a rood cross which crucifies a man in a square having a perimeter of 2,368. Eliphaz Levi called this mystic seal the "Great Arcanum," and in his version of the diagram, a man and woman occupy the two interlacing triangles. The figure illustrates the following passage from the "Lesser Holy Assembly" (par. 720), "So also here, when the Male is joined to the Female, they both constitute one complete body, and all the universe is in a state of happiness because all things receive blessing from their perfect body. And this is an arcanum."

The number five had a peculiar significance to the Pythagoreans and Christian Cabalists. The Greeks are said to have regarded the pentalpha as the symbol of the Microcosm, and to have written

the word Ὑγίεα, 419 (Health), at its five points.[1]
Caramuel, in a curious work on architecture (1678),
gives the figure of a pentalpha, which not only has
the letters of the word Hygeia written round the
pentagon at its centre, but also the word Jesus.
Now, if a pentalpha be inscribed within the Holy
Oblation, the perimeter of the pentagon at its
centre measures 2,368.[2] And a pentalpha whose
sides measure 418⅗, a fraction less than the
numerical equivalent of Hygeia, has a perimeter
of (418⅗ × 5 =) 2,093, the side of the Holy Oblation
containing the crucified body of CHRISTOS. And

FIG. 23.—PENTALPHA FROM C. AGRIPPA'S "OCCULT PHILO-
SOPHY," BK. III., CH. 31.

419 is the diagonal of a square whose sides are 296,
the greatest common measure of the three numbers
888, 1,480, and 2,368. And a pentalpha whose
sides are 296 has a perimeter of 1,480.

The mystic word ABRACADABRA was said to have
great power as a charm. Kircher derives it from
Abraxas, 365. According to the Greek valuation
of the letters it has the value of 216, the diameter
of the sun's orbit measured by its own diameter.
When written in the form of a triangle, each side
having 11 letters, the numerical equivalent of the
3 sides is 443 (216 + 216 + 11), the number of

[1] Kircher's "Arithmologia," p. 217.
[2] Not calculated.

the name ὁ λογος. The sum of all the letters arranged thus is 1,197, which is the length of a vesica 691 broad, and 691 is the length of the sun's orbit ($220 \times 3\frac{1}{7} = 691$). The number 1,197 is also the circumference of a circle having a diameter of 381, the width of a vesica whose length is equal to $\frac{1}{12}$ of the earth's diameter.

By counting the letters according to the Hebrew valuations, ABRACADABRA yields the number 416, which is the side of Ezekiel's city, and the length of a rhombus 240 wide. A cross drawn within this rhombus measures 656, the numerical equivalent of the name Messias.

CHAPTER XI.

RITUAL.

"Now I know that the mysteries of the gnosis are a laughing-stock to many, especially when not patched up with sophistical figurative language. And the few are at first startled at them; *as when light is suddenly brought into a convivial party in the dark. Subsequently, on getting used and accustomed, and trained to reasoning, as if gladdened and exulting for delight, they* [*praise*] *the Lord."*—"Selections from the Prophetic Scriptures," ch. xxxv., Ante-Nicene Library, vol. xxiv.

BEFORE entering upon the details of the ancient mystic rites, perhaps a word ought to be said on the virtue of modesty. Tertullian, justly admired for the enthusiastic eloquence of his writings, calls "modesty the flower of manners, the honour of our bodies, the grace of the sexes, the integrity of the blood, the guarantee of our race, the basis of sanctity, the pre-indication of every good disposition." We can hardly doubt the sincerity of the man who bestows such praise upon this virtue, or refuse to regard him as a modest man. Yet neither can we suppose that our British matron in these days would sanction Tertullian's treatises "On Baptism," "The Soul," "The Ascetic's Mantle," or "The Strain of Jonah," were the good lady capable of understanding them. It is not that he fails to cover religiously every naked thought with the symbolical cloak of shame, exactly as she would demand, but there is that in his argument which would inevitably revolt a nine-teenth century champion of modesty. For now we demand a theme which can be uttered simply, and without all the elaborate toilet of a shameful thing. And herein lies one of the differences between the feeling of the ancients and our own.

Brought up as we all are in the nineteenth century, it seems at first sight shocking that they should have argued by analogies which appear so impossible to our minds. Not that they had no sense of decorum, but there is something in their attitude of mind towards certain matters which divides them from us. It is almost incredible that, underlying the beautiful legend of Cupid and Psyche as told by Apuleius, or the marvellous parable of the crucified Christ, there should be a hidden meaning of which it is impossible to speak.

All this leads us to search into the root and origin of that shame, which all mankind possess, but in different degrees. It must have been a feeling akin to our own, which caused the primitive theologists to hide from view the spirit of their dogma, and to establish an inviolable secrecy around their mysteries. For they made it sometimes shameful even to utter the name of God. From this, doubtless, a purely superstitious feeling of modesty arose, but it seems that shame is a spontaneous impulse peculiar to man, for the beasts have none of it; and it is more than an artificial sense fostered originally by priests and taught by women to their children. In fact, it is a higher faculty developed by the increased sensitiveness of men over the brute animals. And it arises plainly from natural reasons, which it would be immodest to mention.

Of this shame the Greeks seem to have had the least of all civilized people. And they were at once the most refined, cultivated, and accomplished race who have ever lived in this world. We learn from Plutarch, that Lycurgus ordered the Spartan

virgins "to go naked, as well as the young men,"
and to dance and sing in their presence, at certain
solemn feasts and sacrifices. "And though it may
appear strange," he says, "that virgins should
appear thus naked in public, yet, as the strictest
modesty was preserved, there was nothing of
indecency in it; but it accustomed them to an
innocent simplicity." At Sparta this practice
formed a part of the noble cultivation of the body,
which gave that people their great physical strength
and beauty. We see that, although Plutarch here
speaks of modesty, it is something rather different
from ours.

Again, the religious rite described by Aristophanes, in the "Acharnians" (v. 241), sounds
strange in nineteenth century ears : "Use no ill-
omened words. Let the basket-bearer advance
a little forward. Let Xanthias set up the phallus
erect." But to the Greek, who walked naked in
the sun, this was a most natural, and in no sense
an immodest proceeding. The same absence of
shame existed in Rome, where unabashed virgins
and matrons were accustomed to hang garlands on
the effigy of Priapus,[1] standing in the midst of his
garden. For the good Priapus, with his homely
bucolic grin, was regarded by the old Roman with
a peculiar veneration, which was a mixture of
affection and buffoonery, not always or necessarily
the expression of indecency or unseemliness, but
rather the remnant of the crude but chaste impulse,
which moved the simple rural population to gather
in worship round the undisguised Phallus, as the
emblem of the generative powers of Nature.

It was ever the function of ancient art to ingeniously cover the naked truth, and to veil the
primitive nudity with other and perhaps seemlier

[1] See St. Augustine, "City of God," bk. vii., ch. xxi.-xxiv.

forms. And so it was that naked Hermes gradually disappeared from the market place, and crude old Priapus was decked with no more garlands in ladies' gardens. Then the Cross, the old symbol of Egypt was brought forth from the secrecy of mysterious orgies, and was displayed more and more openly. It not only replaced the old Hermes at cross-roads, and in the middle of the town, but was conspicuously seen as the central object in every new temple. The cross was chosen as a fitting emblem to express the same fundamental principle of creation which had been denoted by the earlier figures. Consequently, in the Middle Ages, when the glorification of the Cross reached its height, we find the pious monk kneeling in adoration of the Logos, or devoutly kissing his crucifix in simple faith and knowledge, but without shame.

Thus it is plain that, while all the ancients knew and experienced a certain feeling of modesty, the sense of it to which our forefathers, the Puritans, first gave expression, is a peculiarly modern feeling. The Puritans were very obviously absurd people, and the reformation with which they were connected, was an ignorant movement from the beginning, notwithstanding the fact that it may have been a tendency towards better things. Yet those Puritans, whom it is so easy to ridicule, have so far influenced the generations immediately preceding our own, that it has become difficult to decide whether ours is a worthier feeling of modesty than that of our ancestors. In their revolt against the old pagan doctrines of the church, as something indecent and repulsive, they rose up and destroyed the old images and ecclesiastical symbols, to such purpose, that we believe there does not exist in England a rood cross, dating from a time previous to the Reformation. This idol seems to have been especially shameful in their eyes. The Scottish covenanters were horrified at the very sight of a cross—their feelings being like those of old Philip Stubbes towards the May-pole, when he called it a "Stinkying idoll."[1] The only thing we do not understand is, how, when they rejected the Cross they retained the Christ, for the two are so inseparably connected to a modern mind, that the aversion to the one would naturally apply to the other.

The ritual of all the pagan cults has been so effectually destroyed by their successors, that there does not exist a single vestige of the ceremonial rites with which the Greeks and Romans invoked their deities. All the offices and ritual appertaining to the worship of the virgin Athene in the Parthenon, or Apollo at Delphi, are now lost and forgotten. A few hymns addressed to the old gods have come down to us, but there is not a trace of the ceremonial order observed in the ordinary temple services of the pagan cults, and there remain only a few references to the sacred rites enacted in the celebration of the initiatory mysteries at Eleusis and elsewhere.[2] We possess,

---

[1] Thomas Gale, "Another sort of Papist Idols," etc.

[2] Of the religious mysteries of Pagan Rome very little is now known. St. Augustine ("De Civitate Dei," lib. vii., cap. 34) tells us, on the authority of Varro, that some books were discovered by a man who was ploughing the land near the grave of Numa. These books contained the secret knowledge underlying the theology instituted by Numa, and that, according to St. Augustine, was too infamous even to be retained as the mystery of the priesthood, from which it would appear that it was very bad indeed. Numa, it was said, feared to publish the books on account of their singular contents; nor did he dare to burn them, for fear of devils; so as a compromise he buried them in the earth. The senate ultimately obtained possession of them; but although they thus discovered the shameful nature of their ancestral religion, they were afraid to overturn it. Nevertheless that the revelation of the ancient

however, a masonic ritual, possibly of great antiquity, and the canonical offices of the Jewish and Christian churches; both of which were formulated in classical times.

The Liturgy of the Christians introduced so many of the rites previously established as a part of the Greek mysteries, that the correspondence between the two must be acknowledged by every one acquainted with the ceremonies of both systems. The two great Sacraments of the Christian church were mystical rites, having a hidden or esoteric meaning, secretly performed after an elaborate and exacting preparation. The mysterious nature of the faith is distinctly set forth by Origen, as follows: "Since he [Celsus] frequently calls the Christian doctrine a secret system, we must confute him on this point also, since almost the entire world is better acquainted with what Christians preach than with the favourite opinions of philosophers. For who is ignorant of the statement that Jesus was born of a virgin, and that He was crucified, and that His resurrection is an article of faith among many, and that a general judgment is announced to come, in which the wicked are to be punished according to their

mysteries might be lost for ever, they ordered the books to be burnt.

Lactantius gives another account of the finding of Numa's books ("Divine Institutes," bk. i., chap. 22). He says that Numa was the first to establish pontiffs, priests, salii, and augurs among the Romans. "But though he deceived others he did not deceive himself. For after many years, in the consulship of Cornelius and Bebius, in a field belonging to the Scribe Petilius, under the Janiculum, two stone chests were found by men who were digging, in one of which was the body of Numa, in the other seven books in Latin, respecting the law of the pontiffs, and the same number written in Greek respecting systems of philosophy, in which he not only annulled the religious rites which he himself had instituted, but all others also."

deserts, and the righteous to be duly rewarded? And yet the *mystery of the resurrection, not being understood,* is made a subject of ridicule among unbelievers. In these circumstances, to speak of the Christian doctrine as a *secret* system, is altogether absurd. But that there should be certain doctrines not made known to the multitude, which are [revealed] after the exoteric ones have been taught, is not a peculiarity of Christianity alone, but also of philosophic systems, in which certain truths are exoteric and others esoteric. Some of the hearers of Pythagoras were content with his *ipse dixit;* while others were taught in secret those doctrines which were not deemed fit to be communicated to profane and insufficiently prepared ears. Moreover, all the mysteries that are celebrated everywhere throughout Greece and barbarian countries, although held in secret have no discredit thrown upon them, so that it is vain that he endeavours to caluminate the secret doctrines of Christianity, seeing he does not correctly understand its nature." ("Against Celsus," bk. i., ch. 7.)

Origen, in the above quotation, complains that the misconceptions concerning the Christian faith arose from the mystery of the resurrection not being properly understood. It is therefore necessary to make sure that the meaning of the great events of Christ's life are known to us before inquiring into those rites which merely commemorated or typically represented them.

The resurrection, the immediate consequence of the crucifixion, offered by analogy the joyful prospect of a future life according to the revelation of the mysteries. For the crucifixion of Christ, like the "unspeakable mystery of the Eleusinian rites," [1] was the great cosmic love-scene, hyper-

[1] See Hippolytus, quoted below, on p. 60.

bolically portrayed as a symbol of the conjunction
or marriage of the heaven and the earth ; it
exhibited the natural powers of the universe in the
act of begetting, and afforded a sight of God and
Nature in the very pangs and embracements of
love. It presented to the eye an image of the
actual germination, which recurs in regular order
every spring.

The vernal equinox had been the occasion when
the impregnation of the world was annually celebrated for centuries before the Christians began to
commemorate the Crucifixion on Good Friday and
the Resurrection on Easter Day. To the old
Pagans this stupendous consummation had been
the humanizing of the natural powers of omni-
potence, infinity, and eternity, which could only
be conceived by some concrete figure, and it
brought home to them by analogy the love of God
for the earth and the hope of life through death.
To the Christian a similar vision was set forth in
the Passion of Christ described in the Gospel.
For when the light of the sun was quenched,
amidst thunder and lightning and other strange
portents, we must imagine the earth quivering and
shaking at the awful moment when the spirit
of God descended upon her. All this was simply
man, the microcosm, arguing from the lesser to
the greater, and attributing to the unknown powers
above and beyond him, a grander and more sublime
version of his own miniature powers of creation.
The experienced knew something of this, and
bowed down without superstition or delusion
before the symbol of a mighty transaction, too
great and deep for their comprehension.

The supposed analogy between the creative
functions of God and man supplied the basis of
the principal ritualistic ceremonies of antiquity,
and constituted the culminating revelation dis-

closed to the initiate at the celebration of the mysteries. In the case of the Greeks, Hebrews, and Christians, the great feast of the year was a commemoration of this fact, and in each case was celebrated at the vernal equinox. The pious Greeks were quite as careful to guard the secrets of paganism as the Christians were with respect to the doctrines of the Church; our knowledge of the Eleusinian and other mysteries is chiefly confined to the accounts of the Fathers, who, being the supporters of a rival system, give us a very perverted and inadequate description of them.[1]

In his "Exhortation to the Heathen" St. Clement, who had been initiated, has made some instructive allusions to the old mystic feasts, which may be profitably studied.[2] But notwithstanding the lack of precise information as to the details of the ancient mysteries, we know that the rites of

---

[1] All the rival religious sects, ancient and modern, have accused each other of worshipping false gods. The Sibyl, whose gods were no better than those of other people, thus reproves the Greeks:

"Why trustest thou, O Greece, to princely men?
Why to the dead dost offer empty gifts?
Thou offerest to idols; this error who suggested,
That thou shouldst leave the presence of the mighty God,
And make these offerings?"
        LACTANTIUS, "Divine Institutes," bk. i., ch. xv.

The Christian fathers administered similar rebukes to those who upheld the theology of the Sibylline books, and the Reformers hurled even more violent reproaches at their fellow-Christians, who continued to maintain the practises of the early church. These sectarian squabbles are both unseemly and absurd in themselves, but their value to outsiders is enormous, for whenever people quarrel they become indiscreet, and the result is that we learn more of the hidden doctrines of the priests from these foolish theological disputes than from any other source.

[2] Among modern writers, the "Great Dionysiak Myth," by Mr. Robert Brown, jun., will also be found instructive on this subject.

baptism and the Eucharist were perpetuated by the Christians from similar ordinances forming a part of the pagan ritual, and the parallel between the dramatic shows representing the life of Orpheus or Dionysus enacted in Greece and the symbolical scene of the Mass is complete. In both cases the acts of the drama unfolded the meaning of the theological mystery by means of imitative ceremonies, and the initiations were so arranged that the ignorant neophytes were gradually instructed in the hidden truths, which were concealed under the characters and events of the mythos.

Although it is unknown how the pagan neophyte was prepared and instructed, so as to be able to understand the ceremonial acts which he was finally to witness, there are extant a set of lectures delivered by St. Cyril of Jerusalem, which furnish us with an outline of the teaching accorded to the Christian before he was allowed to participate in the Rites and Mysteries of his religion. Unless those lectures were accompanied, as doubtless they were, with further oral instructions, there does not seem to have been much necessity for keeping them secret. Nevertheless, the following address to the reader is found at the beginning of the book. "These catechetical lectures thou mayest put into the hands of Candidates for Baptism and Baptized believers, but by no means of Catechumens, nor of any others, who are not Christians; as thou shalt answer to the Lord. And if thou take a copy of them, write this in the beginning, as in the sight of the Lord."

The lectures were delivered with closed doors, in the evening during Lent. The candidates were baptized on Easter eve, and afterwards partook of the Eucharistic feast. The final instruction is contained in the last four lectures, delivered to the baptized in Easter week. St. Silvia ("Pilgrimage to the Holy Places," p. 76, Palestine Pilgrim Text Soc.) has vividly portrayed the scene of a Christian initiation in her time. She says, "The doors are shut lest any catechumen should find his way in. And while the bishop is arguing about and expounding the details, so loud are the voices of those applauding, that they are heard outside the church. For truly all the mysteries are made so plain that there is no one but is moved by the things that he hears thus expounded." The following passage from the Sixth Lecture of St. Cyril is an instance of how they were addressed : "To hear the Gospel is allowed to all : but the *glory* of the Gospel is set apart for them that are truly Christ's. Therefore our Lord spake in parables to them who were not able to hear ; but to his disciples he expounded them privately : for the brightness of Glory is for the Illuminated, but blindness for the unbelievers. These mysteries which the Church now speaks to thee who art removed from the catechumens, it is not the custom to speak to the Gentiles : for to a Gentile we speak not the mysteries concerning the Father, and Son, and the Holy Spirit, nor before catechumens do we discourse plainly about mysteries ; but many things many times we speak in a covert manner, that *the faithful who know* may understand, and that those who know not may receive no hurt." (Lect. vi., 29.)

In the early Church, infant baptism was unknown ; the ceremony being consciously undergone by those who had come to years of discretion as a symbolical rite, which raised them from ignorance to a knowledge and participation in the deeper mysteries of the Church, and its elaborate ritual was only second in importance to that of the Mass, and was properly the prelude to the Eucharistic feast. It seems, however, to have been performed as a complete ordinance, having much the same significance as the higher mystery. In primitive times it consisted in the immersion of the body into the sea, a river, or fountain, but in St. Cyril's time it was the custom among the Christians to anoint the baptized person with chrism or oil before entering the water. St. Cyril says, " when ye were stripped ye were annointed with exorcised oil, from the very hairs of your head to your feet. . . . After those things ye were led to the holy pool of Divine baptism, as Christ was carried from the cross to the Sepulchre. . . . And descended three times into the water, and ascended again " (Lect. xx.). He further says that the three immersions refer to the three days passed by Christ in the " womb of the Earth," for " at the self-same moment ye died and were born ; and that water of salvation was at once your grave and your mother."

Besides its other mysteries the Baptismal ritual exhibits a cosmic significance in the names and words used in the performance of the rite. The word *Baptismos* (baptism) has the value of 903, which is 1 more than the side of a square having a diagonal of 1,275, the height of a cross which will crucify a man in a square having a perimeter of 2,368 ; and a rhombus 902·77 long has a perimeter of $2,083\frac{1}{3}$, the length of the side of the Holy Oblation.

Sometimes the neophyte was anointed twice, first with oil ('EΛAION, 166), and afterwards with chrism (MΥPON, 660). The esoteric meaning of this double unction is obvious, but it is remarkable that the two words may symbolize by their numbers the Sun and the Earth, for $166\frac{1}{2}$ is the side of a rhombus having a perimeter of 666, and 660 is $\frac{1}{12}$ of the Earth's diameter in miles. And 660+166 = 826, which is the diagonal of a square whose area is equal to a circle 660 in diameter. Again,

826 is the side of a rhombus whose perimeter is 3,307, which is the height of a cross having a transverse beam 1,075 long; it will, therefore, crucify the figure of the Logos, whose body measures $(1,075 \times 2 =)$ 2,150. The circle surrounding the figure has a circumference of 3,378, or the number of miles in the diameter of the moon's orbit divided by 12 twice.

The Baptistry of the early Basilicas (as at Torcello) was built at the west end of the church, occupying a position corresponding to that of the Holy Sepulchre in the church at Jerusalem. It was generally a detached structure, and supposing the whole church to be an emblem of the ten steps comprised in the cabalistic diagram, the Baptistry appropriately typifies the tenth step, which was a personification of the great mother Earth, or the heavenly spouse of the Logos, called the Holy Ghost.

The Eucharist, as the supreme mystery of the church, was the last ceremony of initiation, and constituted the final enlightenment of the Christian neophyte. In the early Church it was a secret orgy, celebrated at night, like the Greek mysteries. No unbelievers, Gentiles, or Catechumens, were admitted. As everybody knows, it was analogous to the Jewish feast of the Passover, and commemorated the Paschal Supper, partaken of by Christ and his disciples on the eve of his betrayal.

On the 14th day of the month of Nisan (March), the Hebrews killed a lamb, which was roasted and eaten by each family with certain observances, among which were the eating of unleavened cakes and the drinking of four cups of wine. According to Lightfoot the Jews called the third of these cups the "cup of blessing," and he says that it was this cup which Jesus blessed at his last Passover. The novelty, therefore, of the Christian rite chiefly

lay in their dispensing with the slaughter of the
lamb, a ceremony which had doubtless become
obsolete when the sun passed from the sign of the
Ram. Both Jews and Christians were alike in
symbolically commemorating the act of salvation
by the death of a victim, the only difference being
that the Christians, in the bloodless sacrifice,
assumed that the death of Christos was mystically
enacted at every celebration of the Mass, when
the faithful, according to St. Cyril, tasted the body
and drank the blood of their Saviour. " Judge not
the matter by taste," he says, " but from faith
be fully assured without misgiving, that thou
hast been vouchsafed the Body and Blood of
Christ."

While the ceremonies of the Pagan mysteries
and the Jewish Paschal feast account for the institution of the Christian Eucharist, its more immediate
prototype was the Last Supper of Christ and his
disciples described in the Gospel. The language
and words used on this occasion were considered
of so great importance that they were incorporated,
word for word, into the liturgy of Mass, and were
understood to convey the true meaning and purpose of this mystic feast. That these words should
have been chosen with the utmost care by the
compilers of the Gospel may be taken for granted,
and if there is any truth in what has been said
about the numerical value of names, it is to be
expected that here, if anywhere, the application of
that system would be clearly manifest.

In St. Mark's Gospel (xiv. 22) the description
of the supper is given thus : " And as they did
eat, Jesus took bread, and blessed, and brake it,
and gave to them, and said, Take, eat; this is my
body. And he took the cup, and when he had
given thanks he gave it to them ; and they all
drank of it. And he said unto them, This is my

blood of the [new] testament, which is shed for many. Verily I say unto you, I will drink no more of the fruit of the vine, until that day that I drink it new in the kingdom of God."

In the first place it is said that he took bread, the element which signified his body. In the original the word ΑΡΤΟΣ (bread) has the value of 671,[1] and is, therefore, by the Gematria equivalent to Thora and Adonai, the names of the third person of the Cabalistic Triad, here synonymous with the Holy Ghost, the spouse, or feminine aspect of the Logos. And the word ΣΩΜΑ (body) yields the number 1,041, or the radius of the sphere of the Zodiac contained within the Holy Oblation ($1,041\frac{1}{2} \times 2 = 2,083$). This measure may be taken as an emblem of the vital essence, or spirit of life, surrounding the whole material universe, and exhibits the bride by a figure, analogous to the Greek Aphrodite Ourania. Next, it is said, " He took the cup," which figuratively stands also for the wine which was in it. The Greek word used here for cup is ΠΟΤΗΡΙΟΝ, and it is numerically equal to 688, which is the diameter of a circle having a circumference of 2,162, the number of miles in the moon's diameter. By this it may be supposed that the sublunary world is intended, from the four elements of which the body of the Logos was compounded, in the shape of a cross, the masculine emblem. Then ΑΙΜΑ

---

[1] The fact that ἄρτος yields 671 may explain the sarcastic remark of the puritanical Gale, that, " The great sacrifice which the sons of Antichrist so much adore is that of their Masse, or Hostie, as they call it, wherein they sacrifice and eat their Breaden God, in commemoration, as they fancie, of Christ's sacrifice on the crosse . . . which is a piece of idolatrie so monstrous that Averroes himself abhorred it, crying out that he had rather his soul should be with the philosophers than with such as did eat their God" ("Court of the Gentiles," vol. iii., p. 200).

(blood) yields 52, the square root of 2,704, the perimeter of a rhombus whose sides are 676.

Again, the sides of the two interlacing triangles, forming a Solomon's Seal within the Holy Oblation, measure 1,805·4, and the names of the two elements, with the addition of the article, amount to 1,803.

ὁ ἄρτος (the bread) . . 741 + 2
τό ποτήριον (the cup) . . 1,058 + 2

1,799 + 4 = 1,803.

The two names synonymous with those are :

τό σῶμα (the body) . . 1,411
τό αἷμα (the blood) . . 422

1,833

and the Holy Oblation, when the sun's distance is taken at 10, measures 192·9 (216 : 2,083·3 : : 10 : : 192·9).   Now 192·9 × 9·5 = 1,832·5.

By the Bread and the Cup, therefore, we see the symbols of the masculine and feminine powers of the universe commingled together.   And thus the Christian philosophers, like their predecessors, typically celebrated the marriage of the cosmic powers, which every spring revivify the earth, causing her to bring forth her yearly fruits.

In the Greek Church the Oblation, or Host was marked with a cross, having the inscription, "ʼΙΗΣΟΥΣ ΧΡΙΣΤΟΣ ΝΙΚΑ" (Jesus Christ conquers) abbreviated in the four corners thus :

FIG. 24.—ROCK'S "HIERURGIA," P. 208.

The number of letters retained is six, agreeing with
the six members of the body of the Cabalistic
Logos, and their numerical value being 1,080, or
the number of miles in the radius of the moon, it
exhibits a figure of the sublunary world composed
of the four elements. Another method of marking
the oblation was with 2 *Chis* crossing one another,
The letter, *Chi*, having the value of 600, the two
together yield 1,200, and a vesica 1,200 broad, is
2,080 long, or the side of the Holy Oblation,
therefore this device upon the offering may be
said to signify the figure of Christos, extended
crosswise throughout the whole universe. The
offering or oblation was also called *Anaphora*,
which is a combination of the two words, ἀνά, 52,
and φορά, 671. The conjunction of the two numbers
is presumably intentional. In Hebrew the word
Ben (son) yields 52, which is moreover the square
root of 2,704, the perimeter of the rhombus whose
sides are 676.

The Seventy apply the word ΑΠΑΡΧΗ, 790, to
the Holy Oblation, and 789$\frac{1}{3}$ is the width of a
vesica formed by two intersecting circles, whose
united width is 2,368, which appropriately identified the offering, or victim, with the Messiah,
Jesus Christ, whose body was mystically encompassed by the figure of Ezekiel. The word
Anaphora, again, has the value of 723, which is a
fraction more than the length of a rhombus whose
sides are 416$\frac{2}{3}$. Now the city in the centre of
the Holy Oblation has been shown to measure
416$\frac{2}{3}$ on each of its sides, so this rhombus may be
taken as a secret emblem of the same figure.

Not only were the elements of the mass symbolical, but every detail of the ritual, the vestments
of the celebrant, the utensils and furnishing of the
altar, had each their meaning, and convey some
circumstance in the Passion of Christ.   In the

"Book of Ceremonies" or "Rationale," drawn up by Cranmer in 1542, we are told that "the Amice, as touching the mystery, signifies the veil with which the Jews covered the face of Christ when they buffeted him."

"The Albe, as touching the mystery, manifests the white garment wherewith Herod clothed Christ in mockery when he sent him to Pilate."

"The Girdle, as touching the mystery, signifies the scourge with which Christ was scourged." It was also said to be the cord by which he was bound in the garden.

"The Stole, as touching the mystery, signifies the ropes or bands with which Christ was bound to the pillar, when he was scourged."

"The Maniple, or Phanon, admonisheth him of ghostly strength," and was also said to be the cord which bound him to the pillar.

The Chasuble signified the seamless garment, or purple robe.

The altar represented the cross; the chalice the Sepulchre of Christ; the paten the stone rolled to the door of the sepulchre; and the altar cloths, the corporal, and pall symbolized "the linen in which the body of Christ was shrouded."

Each gesture[1] and act of the priests during the

---

[1] "I have often read in books of magicians, and their works and experiments, certain and, as they seemed to me, ridiculous gesturings . . . but after I did more seriously examine the matter, then I did presently understand that they were not the compacts of divels, *but that there lay in them the reason of numbers*, by which the ancients did by the various bending forward and backward their hands and fingers represent numbers, by whose gesturings the magicians did silently signifie words unknown by sound. . . . The rites whereof Martianus makes mention of in his Arithmetick, saying, The fingers of the Virgin were moved all manner of ways, who after she went in, did by expressing 717 numbers with her bended fingers call upon

celebration was also imitative of the events of the Passion, and had an esoteric import. By taking three steps back from the altar, and humbling himself before beginning the mass, the celebrant expressed the prostration of Christ in the Garden.

" Ascending to the altar, the priest kisseth the middle of it, because the altar signifies the Church."

" The Gospel was read at the north end of the altar to signify that Satan's Kingdom (seated in the north, Lev. i. 14) is destroyed."

The offerings were signed five times to signify Christ's five wounds, and the Host and Chalice were signed three times, to denote the three hours which Christ hung on the Cross.

The uncovering of the chalice, and signing it three times with the Host, indicate the rending the veil of the Temple.

The laying down of the Host upon the corporal, and then covering the chalice again, signified the descent from the Cross, and the silence which followed denoted Christ's period in the grave. The Host, divided into three parts, signified the dividing of the Body into hands, side, and feet.

The particle of the Host, put into the chalice, symbolized the "re-uniting of our Saviour's Body and Soul" (W. Turner, "Hist. of all Religions," 1625, pp. 263-264).

The ceremonial acts just enumerated follow

Jupiter. But that these things may be the better understood, I shall bring something out of Beda who saith, When thou sayest one, bend in the little finger on thy left hand, and set it in the middle of the Palme; when thou sayest two, etc." (Cornelius Agrippa, "Occult Philosophy," bk. ii., ch. xiv). The number 717 mentioned here is the height of a rood cross, which would crucify the Logos in a square equal to the New Jerusalem ; and the square inclosing the cross has a perimeter of 2,868, the sum of the numbers obtained from the Hebrew names of the ten steps of the cabala. It is also width of a vesica produced by two circles, whose united breadth is 2,151. Again, the value of Μαριαμ ἡ παρθενος, the Virgin Mary, is 715 + 2 = 717.

the order of the office as performed in the Latin
Church, but they by no means exhaust the mysteries of this profoundly symbolic rite.

In the Church of Rome the mass was called
missa, for no very obvious reason, but if the letters
of the word are computed, according to the Hebrew
valuations, its numerical value is 651, or the
diameter of the circle having a circumference
equal to the diameter of Saturn's orbit ; being
equivalent by Gematria to *Teletai*, mystic rites,
and to *Episteme*, science, it may fitly represent the
nature of the knowledge communicated to the
initiate who was allowed to partake of the feast
with an instructed and enlightened mind.

The baptismal rite, as already pointed out, was
performed in a chamber at the west end of the
church, but the Eucharist was offered at the altar
in the east, within the bema or sanctuary. By
referring to the plan of the Basilica of Torcello, it
will be seen that the church, according to the
practice of the time, has a threefold termination,
and supposing the church to represent the cabalistic diagram, this triple arrangement would correspond to the three upper steps.

The east end of the Gothic churches was built
in the form of a tau cross, the western half of the
church being of a long rectangular shape, resembling Noah's Ark, which is probably connected
with the name, ship, or nave, given to this part of
the building. Therefore the east end of the church
exhibits the symbol of the Macrocosm or Father,
who is the antithesis of the Bride, allocated to the
west.   While the choir or CHOROS, 1,040, between
the two, figuratively contained the seven circles of
the planets, with the body of Christ in the midst
of them.   That this threefold arrangement of the
Christian church agrees with the pattern of a
masonic lodge, may be shown from an examination

of an old "Tracing Board," preserved at the
Masonic Hall, Great Queen Street.

In the working of a masonic degree the symbolical lodge is not the room in which the ceremony is performed, but the emblematic design
which is painted upon a movable board and laid
upon the floor. As the initiate advances the lodge
changes its character, and in every degree he finds
a new board before him, the symbolic devices
upon it being appropriate to each step in the
ritual. The particular specimen before us is not
more than a hundred years old, but it was probably
designed according to a traditional plan handed
down from remote times. On one side it shows a
lodge of the first and second degrees, and on the
other, that of the third degree. The proportion
of the Board is very nearly in the ratio of $3 : 1$,
that is to say, it is composed of three squares laid
in a row, and is consequently of the same proportion as the floor of the tabernacle.

The events enacted in the Masonic ritual are, of
course, supposed to take place at the building of
Solomon's Temple, and in the first degree the
apprentice enters into the porch, which is symbolized on the lodge board by the two Pillars with a
doorway between them. It has been said that the
Temple of Solomon is figuratively set forth in
every church, and if, as we have supposed, the
Temple followed the pattern of the Cabalistic
diagram, then the apprentice, being brought into
the porch, which has been identified with the
tenth step, must symbolically ascend from the
earth to the highest heaven. At first the candidate
only sees half of the board, for he is admitted no
farther than the porch or sublunary world.

In the next degree as a fellow craft, he enters
into the holy place of the Temple, when, the other
half of the tracing board being unfolded, he sees a

" Point within a circle" bounded by two parallel
lines, denoting the universe, the ladder expressing
the intervals between the planetary orbits, and the
sun, moon, and seven stars completing the
number of the heavenly bodies.   It has already
been shown that the six steps, intermediate between
the tenth and the third, were referred by cabalists
to the Logos, or the second person of the triad.
Accordingly the fellow craft sees in these emblems
on the floor a figure of the Microcosm whose
body occupies the region between the moon and
the zodiac.   The choir in the middle of a church
corresponds to the tracing board of a fellow craft's
lodge.

For the third degree the tracing board is turned
over, and the candidate is confronted with the half
open coffin. He has passed through the elements
as an embryo, traversed the planetary orbits as a
man, and now having left the material world
behind, he enters the empyreum or three hypothetical circles which surround the zodiac.   The
Holy of Holies of the Temple was supposed to
symbolize this region, corresponding to the three
upper steps of the Cabala under the name of the
Macrocosm or Father.   So the initiate now
personates Father Hiram, the master builder of
Solomon, whose spirit in death ascends to the
spheres of Heaven, which the ancients supposed
to be the dwelling place of souls.   Thus the
masonic ritual epitomizes, in its three stages, the
whole compass of existence, both cosmic and
human.   The apprentice personates the man in
his embryonic or antenatal period, the fellow craft
represents him in the flesh, while the master's
death allegorically signifies the transmission of the
soul to the starry fluid of the Empyreum, from
which it re-issues into a new sphere of life, in
another incarnation.   The fitness of the altar, as a

place for celebrating the mystical rite of the
Eucharist, or the passing of the spirit to its new
body, will now be apparent.

The emblematic order of the tracing board may
be compared with the disposition of a Christian
church, described by that truly instructed mason,
Dr. Oliver ("Discrepancies," p. 103). The diagram
represents the six square sides of a cube, laid in
the form of a cross, each square having a suitable
name, taken from the New Testament.

'Αγάπη, 93
(1 John iv. 16)
LOVE.

Χαρις, 911			'Ελπις, 325			Πιστις, 800
(Heb. vi. 19)		(Heb. vi. 19)		(Heb. xi. 1)
CHARITY.			HOPE.			FAITH.

'Αληθεια, 64
(Eph. iv. 15)
TRUTH.

Διακονια, 166
(Acts xi. 29)
RELIEF.

He explains that " in the progress of a Christain
from this world to a better, he first enters as a
catechumen at the *narthex*, or ante-temple in the
west, under the assurance of relief from worldly
trouble ; presses forward into the *naos* or church
militant, where dwelleth Truth ; and having at
length advanced, by the practice of Christian
charity, through the gates of Faith and Hope, he
enters by the *portæ sanctæ* into the *bema*, chancel
or choir, the Church Triumphant," the sanctuary
of Love. When the numbers are examined, the
meaning is made still clearer. First, the number
93 ascribed to the chancel gives the height of a

man 888 high $(93\frac{1}{2} \times 9\frac{1}{2} = 888)$.   Then the triad,
composed of the transepts and sanctuary, amounts
to $(93 + 800 + 911 =)$ 1,804 or 1 less than the
side of a triangle inscribed within the Holy Oblation.
Secondly, to the middle point, at the crossing of
the transepts and nave, is assigned the number
325, and the cross, whose limbs are $325\frac{1}{2}$, measures
651.   If we add to this 64, we get 389, or 1 less
than the number of *polis*, a city, and the side of a
rhombus 676 feet long.   These two middle names,
applied to the church " Militant," represent the
stauros and *omphalos* in the centre of the world.
Thirdly, the number of the porch is 166, or 1
more than the side of a rhombus whose perimeter
is 660, the diameter of the earth.   Lastly, the sum
of the six numbers is $2,359 + 6 = 2,365$, which
is apparently intended for 2,368, Jesus Christ.

A further connection between the three degrees,
and the " Church Expectant, the Church Militant,
and the Church Triumphant " is noticed by Oliver.
A mason's lodge is theoretically supported by
three pillars, called in Hebrew, DBR (wisdom),
OTZ (strength), and GMR (beauty).   The numerical value of the three names is 426, the side
of a square inclosed by a rhombus whose sides are
671.   Now, besides being the numerical equivalent
of the English word masonry, 671 is numerically
equal to Thorah, the law (" Discrepancies," pp.
104 and 188).

Geometrically, the measures of the tracing-
board fully bear out the statements in the ritual,
that the lodge is as long as the east is from the
west, and as broad as the north is from the south,
and as high as the heavens.   It measures externally about $64 \times 21\frac{1}{4}$ inches, and seems to have
been ingeniously contrived to include all the
canonical numbers of the universe.   For the vesica,
which contains the board, is $48\frac{2}{3}$ wide, the square

root of 2,368. Then the perimeter is $170\frac{1}{2}$ inches, or $\frac{1}{12}$ of the diameter of Saturn's orbit measured by the sun's diameter $\left(\dfrac{2,046}{12} = 170\frac{1}{2}\right)$.

Again, the perimeter of the inner line of the denticulated border is 155·79, and 155·79 × 9·5 = 1,480.

Thus indirectly the numbers 2,368, 2,046, and 1,480 are obtained in a very simple way.

Further, the number 64 implies the measure of the Holy Oblation, for the sum of the numbers from 1 to 64 = 2,080. Also 64 inches are equal to 192 barleycorns, and 192 is the numerical equivalent of the name *Mariam*.

The area of the space inclosed by the border is (60 × 18 =) 1,080 inches, or the number of miles in the moon's radius, and the numerical equivalent of *To Pneuma Hagion*, the Holy Ghost.

The rhombus which contains the board has a perimeter of 231 inches, which is also the circuit of the lid of the pyramid-coffer.

The hexagon which surrounds the board has a perimeter of 691, or the length of the sun's orbit.

If the board be inclosed by a Solomon's Seal, the measure of the interlacing triangles from point to point is 384 barleycorns, or the amount of the sun's distance measured by the tone.

Then if the lesser Man of Vitruvius be drawn within a square equal to the length of the board, the perimeter of the square is 768 barleycorns, and a vesica 768 long is 443 broad, or the numerical value of ὁ λόγος, the word. The square containing the greater man, being double the last, has a perimeter of 365 inches.

If a circle 14·2 inches in diameter be drawn in the middle of the tracing board, to represent the orbit of Saturn—that is, 2,046 divided by 12 twice—it will appear to be supported by the two pillars, Jachin and Boaz, and the two globes placed upon these columns may have had their origin from this circumstance.

The mutilated and contorted body of Hiram was often shown lying in the coffins, depicted on tracing boards of the third degree. In the present instance the length of the coffin is $48\frac{2}{3}$ inches, or the square root of 2,368, which implies that Hiram was a personification of Jesus Christ. It is impossible to discuss the Masonic legend here, since the masons, unlike the Christian priests, still perform their ceremonies in secret, but all who are initiated know that the import of Hiram's death is exactly analogous to that of Christos, and that the third degree is symbolically similar to the Eucharistic rite, which in the early Church was enacted with the same secrecy and mystery as is still observed in the raising of a master mason.

CHAPTER XII.

GEOGRAPHY.

"God did, in a manner, tie up the Church of the Jews to Types, Figures, and Similitudes . . . . yea . . . . as it seems to me the whole Land of Canaan, the place of their lot to dwell in, was to them a Ceremonial or a Figure. Their Land was a Type of Heaven."—BUNYAN'S "Solomon's Temple," p. 4.

IT would appear that the same system of cosmic imitation which was applied to the temple was extended on a larger scale to countries and cities, and even to the whole inhabitable world. Strabo, the oldest classical writer on geography whose work has survived to our time, says, "in its figure the habitable earth resembles a chlamys or soldier's cloak." He computes its breadth to be under 30,000 stadia, and its length at 70,000, thus the length of the habitable earth is above twice its breadth. Now the Greek word *chlamys* has the numerical value of 1,271, and consequently by Gematria it is equivalent to *stauros*, a cross, and the proportions of a rood cross being in the ratio of 28 : 13, its length is rather more than double its breadth. However, if the length of such a cross were 70,000, its transverse beam would measure 32,500, so that the measurements only approximate those of the rood cross. Still the use of the word *chlamys*, and the entirely arbitrary limit to the inhabitable space of the world suggests a mystical intention on Strabo's part.[1]

[1] The symbol of the world has been for centuries a cross within a circle, and the name *mundus* has the value of 406,

Kosmas, an Egyptian monk of the sixth century, in his "Christian Topography" tried to prove that the earth was a rectangle, whose length was more than twice its breadth. Ephorus, again, appears to have divided the world saltire-wise, after the image of the Microcosm, for he says, "if the whole celestial and terrestrial globe were divided into four parts, the Indians would possess that towards the east, the Ethiopians towards the south, the Kelts towards the west, and the Scythians towards the north" (Strabo, bk. i., ch. 28). Thus it seems evident that the ancient geographers mapped out the world, according to some of the canonical forms which have been described in the preceding pages.

But not only was the whole earth conceived as an illustration of the Canon law, but every country was seemingly made to conform to the same hypothetical standard — Palestine, for instance, being regarded by the Jews and Christians as the Canonical land, while a similar idea guided the Greeks in assigning a mystical significance to the various regions and cities of their country. The word Canaan applied to the Holy Land seems to have some connection with the word canon. In Greek, κανών [1] is derived from κάννα or κάννη, a reed, and meant a measuring rod or carpenter's rule. The Hebrew word for a reed is QNH (Kanah), and

the equivalent of THV, Tau, and the diameter of a circle whose circumference is 1,276, the height of a rood cross which will crucify a man in a square having a perimeter of 2,368. Accordingly, when we see the cruciform figure drawn upon Ebstorf's map (p. 316), we can perhaps understand the intention of Strabo when he said that the habitable earth was in shape like a soldier's cloak (Chlamys, 1,271).

[1] The word ὀφθαλμός, the eye, is equivalent by Gematria to Kanon, and it is said in the Talmud, that "the world is like the eyeball of a man: the white is the ocean which surrounds the world, the black is the world itself, the pupil is Jerusalem, and the image of the pupil is the Temple."

is presumably of kindred origin. Numerically QNH is equivalent to 155, and this number denotes its purport as a symbol. For, by the proportions of Cesariano's lesser figure, $155\frac{4}{5}$ measures the phallus of a man, who is 1,480 high, that is, of a man stretched crosswise within the Holy Oblation. And the land of Canaan, or Palestine, measures from Dan to Beersheba about 155 miles. The Hebrew name KNAAN yields 840, a number already discussed under the name Microcosmos. The Seventy translate Canaanites, Φοινικες or Phœnicians, and in Greek Canaan was called XNA, which has the value of 651, the diameter of a circle having a circumference of 2,046, the diameter of Saturn's orbit. All these numbers obviously agree in defining the Holy Land as a Microcosm, or lesser image of the world.

The Greek word KANΩN, 921, favours a similar interpretation, for $96.8 \times 9.5 = 919.6$, or 1 and a fraction less than 921 ; and 96.8 is the radius of the circle containing the square 1,480, taking the sun's distance at 10. The word would therefore mean the rule, or scale, which measures the universe by the figure of a man. Menasseh Ben Israel ("Conciliator," vol. ii., p. 115) says, that the body has 248 members, 365 nerves, and 307 bones ; those three numbers amount to 920, and sum up all the philosophy of the Hebrew law in a man's body. For the Mosaic Tables were written in two columns, 306 words on the one side, and 307 on the other, the whole number of words being 613.[1] By transposition 921 may be converted

[1] And, "It is written" (Exod. iii. 5), "This is my name, and this is my memorial." "My name," together with *Yeho*, amounts numerically to 365 ; *Vah*, together with "my memorial," amounts to 248. Here we have the number 613 in the "Holy One—blessed be He !" ("Talmudic Miscell.," p. 325). This division of the Law into 613 precepts was called *Theriog* (THRIG) a name which has the numerical value of 613.

into 912, the numerical equivalent of the name Prometheus. So the *Radius*, or rod, was like the hollow reed (*narthex*), which " has shown itself a teacher of every art" (Æschylus). Otherwise transposed, the three numerals become 219, the diameter of the sun's orbit; or again, 192, the side of the Holy Oblation if the sun's distance be taken at 10 (216 : 2,083$\frac{1}{3}$: : 10 : : 192·9).

Analogous to the narthex of Prometheus was the Syrinx, or Pipe of Pan. The story of its origin is told by Longus as follows : " This Syrinx, the musicke whereof hath been from Pan recounted always so excellent, was not at the first an instrument, but was a faire young maide, of favour and feature most singular & perfect, wel loved she to chaunt foorth hir laies, with grace most wonderful, and harmonie right pleasant. . . . Pan frequently at this time frequented the fields and pastures . . . & hearing the wonderful and variable notes she sang, drew neere unto the place, and seeing that as wel with excellent cunning, as with most rare and piercing beautie she was replenished, he boldly stept to hir, because he was a god, & praied at hir hands the thing he most desired. . . . But Syrinx nothing regarding these amorous offers, scoffed rather at his shape. . . . The god, angry at her disdainful usage, intended to take hir by force, but shee preventing his fraud by flight, endeavoured to escape, & he still pursued her. And feeling herself in thend to be greatly wearied, she suddenly got at last among the reeds, and therein creeping from place to place wound herself out of sight. But Pan, enraged with greater vehemencie than before, in that he could not overtaike hir, cutte down the reeds in haste, in minde to seek & sue after her, and not finding anything else besides the marshes, for that she was utterly vanished . . . and sorrowing greatly for the Nymph, whome he

knewe to have beene converted into a reede, hee
cropped the same reede also from the place, and

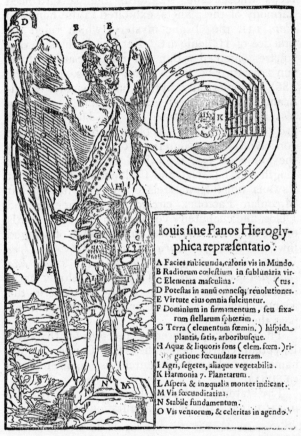

Iouis fiue Panos Hierogly-
phica repræfentatio.

A Facies rubicunda, caloris vis in Mundo.
B Radiorum cœleftium in fublunaria vir-
C Elementa mafculina.   (tus.
D Poteftas in annũ omncſq; reuolutiones.
E Virtute eius omnia fulciuntur.
F Dominium in firmamentum, feu fixa-
    rum ftellarum fphœram.
G Terra (elementum fœmin.) hifpida
    plantis, fatis, arboribufque.
H Aquæ & liquoris fons (elem. fœm.) ri-
    gatione fœcundans terram.
I Agri, fegetes, aliaque vegetabilia.
K Harmonia 7. Planetarum.
L Afpera & inæqualia montes indicant.
M Vis fœcunditatiua.
N Stabile fundamentum.
O Vis ventorum, & celeritas in agendo.

FIG. 25.—TO ΠΑΝ, THE UNIVERSE. FROM KIRCHER'S "ŒDIPUS,"
TOM. II., PARS I. P. 204.

thereof framed in seven quills his arcificial and
excellent pipe, the most sweete and delicate instrument of any other, the pleasantnes whereof record-

X

ing yet the melody of hir from whence it came"
("Daphnis and Chloe," bk. ii.).[1] The Pipe of
reeds whose tune set forth the seven-voiced
harmony of the planets, exhibited in the hands of
Pan, 131, the cosmic mystery, which ruled the
practice of Hellenic art. For 132 is the side of a
square contained within the orbit of Saturn, if the
sun's distance be taken at 10 (220 : 2,046 :: 10 ::
186). Numerically Syrinx has a similar significance, 773 (Σῦριγξ) being 1 and a fraction
less than the perimeter of the Holy Oblation
(193·6 × 4 = 774·4). Apollo's Lyre was likewise
conceived as a counterpart of this, *Lyra* having
the value of 531, the width of a vesica whose
length is 921 (κανων), and Callimachus relates that
"swans, tuneful minstrels of the god, having left
Mæonian Pactolus, circled *seven* times around
Delos, and chaunted over Leto in childbirth, birds
of the muses as they are, most tuneful of winged
fowl. *Hence afterward the boy fitted to the lyre
just so many strings, as the times the swans had
chaunted over her throes*" (Hymn to Delos, v. 250).
And again he says, "Thee, fragrant Asterie, the
islands circle round about, and, as it were, encompass thee with a choir."

The Greeks apparently recognized that the
Egyptian Osiris personified the Canon, for his
name, according to Plutarch, is equal to 920
(ΎΣΙΡΙΣ).

The statement of Gale (Court of Gent., vol. iii.,
p. 216), that "the Jews, in imitation of the Pytha-

---

[1] Compare this with the exposition of the Myth in Bacon's
"Advancement of Learning," bk. ii., ch. xiii. "The two en-
signs which Pan bears in his hands, do point, the one at
Harmony, the other at Empiry: for the Pipe of Seven Reeds
doth evidently demonstrate the consent and harmony, or discordant concord of Nature, which is caused by the motion of
the seven wandring stars : for there are no errors or manifest
expiations in heaven save those of the Seven Planets."

gorean Institutes, made the Cabala their Codex or Canon-law," has already been quoted, and its accuracy with respect to the geographical distribution of Palestine and Jerusalem appears to be amply verified. The land of Hellas seems to have been fancifully treated by the poets in the same way. Accordingly, if the cabalistic diagram be drawn upon the map of Greece, so that the summit or "crown" falls upon Mount Olympus, and the "foundation" upon the extremity of Mount Tainaros, it will be seen that Delphi roughly marks the centre of the figure, while the eastern boundary passes through Athens, and just as Canaan is 155·79 miles long, so Greece, from Olympus to Tainaros, measures $249\frac{1}{4}$ miles ($249\frac{1}{4} \times 9\frac{1}{2} = 2,368$). The Island of Crete, to the south-east, will supply the tenth step, which is detached from the main figure like an island.

Because Homer and the Greek poets allude to Olympus as the dwelling-place of the gods, people of the present day suppose that the Greeks were credulous enough to believe that if any one climbed to the top of that mountain he would probably surprise the immortal gods in council, or become an enraptured listener to the divine choir of the muses. Whether even the clod-pate, who had spent his life in an Arcadian ditch, believed such stories, it would be difficult nowadays to ascertain, but the ease with which our learned men are able to impute such credulity to the crafty Homer and his readers, is a touching indication of that childlike faith of their own, which is one of the marvels of the age.

But if, instead of regarding the Greek poets as being filled with a strange and improbable superstition—which is belied both by the skill and ingenuity of their writings, and by the testimony of the oldest critics—we suppose that geography

supplied a means of setting forth the mysteries of
the Canon, we may find a reason for their otherwise unaccountable fables.   For, assuming that
Olympus was the crown of the Cabala, it becomes
at once evident how it might be figuratively considered as the region of the Empyreum, and the
habitation of the gods.

Olympus was the most northern of the two
other peaks, Ossa and Pelion, which were generally associated with it.   It is generally called
makros by Homer, and, together with the other
two, was evidently viewed by the poets as an
emblem of Macrocosmos, the triad at the summit
of the diagram.

The numbers of the three names are *Olympos*,
890, *Ossa*, 471, and *Pelion*, 248.   By Gematria
Olympus is equivalent to *Ouranos*, 891, Heaven ;
and 471, the number of the name Ossa, is the
diameter of a circle whose circumference is 1,480,
the side of the square enclosed by the sphere of
the Zodiac ; and, if 1 and a fraction be added
to 248, the numerical equivalent to the name
Pelion, we get the number 2,368, for $249\frac{1}{4} \times 9\frac{1}{2}$
= 2,368.   Then the sum of the three numbers is
1,609, which is the circumference of a circle 512
in diameter ($512 \times 4 = 2,048$).   The legend that
the timber for the ship Argo was hewn on Mount
Pelion further indicates its meaning and place in
the triad.

Athens, by its position, ought to have the significance of the fifth step in the diagram, and
would symbolize one of the two cabalistic laws.
For this reason, apparently, Athene was selected
as the goddess of the city, since one of her chief
characteristics was her personification of the
number 5, her mysterious birth from the forehead
of Zeus expressing this idea.   The name Ἀθῆναι
has the value of 79, the square root of 6,241, a

number which is the perimeter of a triangle whose sides are 2,080, the side of the Holy Oblation. The number 79 and a fraction is also the diameter of a circle whose circumference is $249\frac{1}{4}$, the mystic measure of the body of a man 2,368 high ($249\frac{1}{4} \times 9\frac{1}{2} = 2,368$).

The site of Delphi, the metropolis or canonical city of Greece, was said to have been determined from its being the place where the two eagles of Zeus met. These had been sent, the one from the East and the other from the West, and alighted at the middle point, or navel of the world. According to the Cabala, they would represent the emanations from the fourth and fifth steps. The name Delphi has an obvious connection with *Delphys*, the womb, and its numerical value is 619. When this number is read backwards it becomes 916, the product of $96\cdot45 \times 9\frac{1}{2}$; again $169 \times 4 = 676$; otherwise transposed it becomes 691, the length of the sun's orbit. Finally 619 is the sum of the numbers of the two names, *Helios*, 318, and *Selene*, 301, the sun and the moon. This combination of the male and female powers of the universe was expressed in the Temple of Apollo by the Cleft in the rock, and the Tripod, which stood over it. The two eagles, the two mythical architects, Trophonios and Agamedes,[1] with other indications of duality all bring us to the *omphalos* and *stauros*, symbolically united at this place. The two latter words have the numerical value of 1,271, the length of the diagonals of a square whose sides are equal to the radius of Saturn's orbit, if the sun's distance be taken at 10; and their conjunction at the middle of the earth clearly exemplifies

---

[1] The names Triphonios and Agamedes yield the numbers 2,100 and 265, and, by adding colel to each, we get 2,367, or 1 less than 2,368.

the geographical application of the microcosmic theory.

The whole arrangement of the Temple resembled that of the Jews, with the great altar (βωμός) of sacrifice in the court before the door. Its name, Pythion, has the same value as Delphi, namely, 619. This was from Pytho (Πυθώ) the original name of the place. Numerically, *Pytho* yields 1,288, which is 1 less than the diagonal of a square whose sides are 912½, consequently its perimeter is 3,650, the distance of Saturn's orbit measured by the Tone. The Tripod, upon which the priestess sat who delivered the oracles, stood in the innermost sanctuary of the Temple, called Τό Ἄντρον, 941 (the cave), Ἄδυτον, 825 (adytum), or Μυχός, 1,310 (recess). Of these numbers the first with the addition of colel is the diagonal of a square whose sides are 666; the second is the diagonal of a square whose area is equal to that of a circle 660 in diameter, and 825 being the numerical equivalent of ὁ πέτρος, the stone, may account for the curious legend that the Holy of Holies of Solomon's Temple was built upon a stone, which was the foundation of the world; the third number is the numerical equivalent of *Tetragrammaton*, and *anthropos* (a man).

The ninth Step, or the "Foundation," we have supposed to be represented by the promontory of Tainaros, which yields 732, or 1 less than the width of a vesica whose length is 1,271 (*stauros*). There was a cave on this promontory which was said to be the entrance to Hell, and Hercules brought the dog, Cerberus, through it in his twelfth Labour. Tainaros being regarded as the entrance to Hades implied its cabalistic position, for the ninth Step leads directly through the channel to the tenth, a hieroglyph of the underworld, which is thus connected to the main figure, like an island.

Crete, lying to the south of the mainland, bears a perfect analogy to the tenth Step, and the traditions related about it accord with such an interpretation. Ναϭός, an island, has the numerical value of 521, which is the side of a rhombus having a perimeter of 2,084, the side of the Holy Oblation. The most celebrated monument of Crete, the famous Labyrinth of Dædalus, at once connects it with the cosmos of which it was theoretically the centre, and the seven concentric walls are an obvious illustration of the seven circles of the planets. The Hebrew Malchuth (the tenth Step) was a personification of the umbilicus, or cardinal points meeting at the middle of the world; and we find that in Crete the women were the heads of the family, the children taking their names from their mothers, and not from their fathers (Herod. bk. i., 173).

The name Κρήτη has the value of 436, and if this be taken as the measure of a cardinal cross, the length of each limb will be 218, the diameter of the sun's orbit; and a square [1] surrounding such a cross (218 × 4) has a perimeter of 872, the numerical equivalent of λαβύρινθος, the labyrinth. Ὁ λαβύρινθος, again, yields 942, the diagonal of a square whose sides are 666. Further, 435 and a fraction is the diameter of a circle 1,368 in circumference, and 1,368 is the side of a rhombus 2,368 long.

The legends of Minos, the law giver, who on his death became the judge of the shades in Hades, all point to his being King of Crete, regarded as an image of the world. By Gematria Minos is equivalent to Macroprosopos, the Long Face of the Cabala. He was the father of Deucalion and Ariadne. Deucalion, as we have seen,

---

[1] The diagonals of a square enclosing the sun's orbit (218⅓) measure (309½ × 2 =) 619.

was regarded by the writer of the Clementine
Homilies as a mythical double of Noah, and the
statement that he was born in Crete must have
the same origin as that of Hippolytus, who declared
that the Ark of Noah rested on Mount Cardu, or
Cardo, that is, the middle of the world.   The
Greeks evidently implied the same thing when
they said that Deucalion's Ark rested on Mount
Parnassus, at Delphi, another omphalos, where the
Temple of Apollo with its mystic cave, and the
subterranean prison of the Minotaur[1] in Crete
express the same idea.   The reader may be
reminded that the Ark was a symbol analogous to
the cross. Ariadne, Deucalion's sister, appears
to personify the cosmos, and in the Iliad (bk.
xviii., v. 590) Dædalus is said to have wrought
her a dancing-place ($\chi o \rho \acute{o} \varsigma$) in Gnossus, which
must refer to the Labyrinth that symbolized the
circling dance of the Planets.   The name Ariadne
has the value of 174, which is $\frac{1}{12}$ of 2,083, the
side of the Holy Oblation $\left(\frac{2,083}{12} = 173\frac{7}{12} \right)$.

The fact that Apollo was worshipped both at
Delphi and Crete seems to suggest that the
Pythagorean doctrine concerning the sun may
have determined the choice of the omphalos, as
the great seat of sun worship. The statues of
Apollo, standing on the navel-stone, also point to
a similar motive.

The treatment of cities appears to have followed
the same cosmic distribution as that of the whole
country. Ambrosius Leo, a writer at the beginning of the sixteenth century, has accompanied

---

[1] This monstrous creature, half man, half bull, confined in
the centre of the Labyrinth, or world, is probably a grotesque
personification of the omphalos and stauros, for his name
Minotauros, 1,971, is equivalent by Gematria to *Phallos*, 831,
and *Delphys*, 1,139 (831 + 1,139 = 1,970).

his description of the city of Nola with some mysterious diagrams, which apparently refer to the geometrical measurement of ancient cities. These diagrams are supplied without explanation, as is usual in the case of mystical figures only intended for the instructed.

Boissardo has published an ideal arrangement

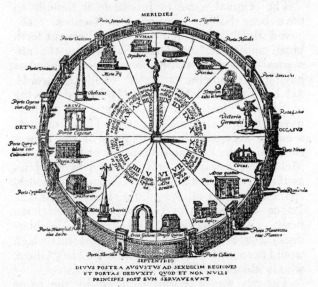

FIG. 26.—CITY OF ROME. FROM BOISSARDO'S "TOPOGRAPHIA ROMÆ," 1597.

of the city of Rome on a geometrical plan, and shows the development of the city by means of three different diagrams, having four, eight and six-teen gates and towers, corresponding to the number of the winds. He has so arranged the number of the division of the circle on plan c (fig. 26), that an appropriate building falls into each of the twelve spaces. From this it may be concluded, that the site of a great temple, or public building was chosen so that, if possible, it might conform to the mystical scheme of the town, and stand in its proper relation to its surroundings. In order to illustrate this, we shall now examine in detail the distribution of the city of Jerusalem, the metropolis of the Canonical land of the Hebrews and Christians.

The original name of Jerusalem is thought to have been Salem, mentioned in Gen. xiv. 18: "And Melchizedeck King of *Salem* brought forth bread and wine." SHLM (Salem) has the numerical value of 370, or the width of a rhombus having a perimeter of 1,480. And the words, MLKI-TzDQ MLK SHLM (Melchizedek, King of Salem), yield 754, the diameter of a circle having a circumference of 2,368. These numbers seem to accord with the opinions of the fathers concerning the king and the priest of this city, for Melchizedeck was not only regarded by the Jews as the Messiah, but the early Christians variously spoke of him as an Angel, the Holy Ghost, the Logos, or the Son of God appearing in human flesh. By Gematria MLKI-TzDQ (Melchizedeck), 294, is equivalent to Ecclesia, a fact which would account for his being called the Holy Ghost, who is identical with the spouse of Christ.

The city was afterwards known by the name Jebus, and its inhabitants as Jebusites. From this name we derive the number 318, which is the diameter of the two circles forming a vesica 666 in perimeter. The Greeks gave the number 318 to *Helios*, the sun, and by transposition 318 becomes 831.

IRVShLIM (Jerusalem), again, yields 1,156, which is the width of a vesica 2,004 long, and 2,004 is the measure of the cross composed of the four elements described by Plato in the "Timæus."

Josephus (vii. 2) makes one of the Greek

names Σολυμα, 741, and adds ιερο[ν], producing Ἱεροσολυμα, 926, the Holy Soluma. The number 741 is the circumference of a circle described within the New Jerusalem, that is, with a diameter of 236, while 926 is nearly the square root of the sun's diameter in miles. In the New Testament we find the name of Jerusalem as Ἱερουσαλήμ, 864, which is the length of a rhombus 374⅖ broad, or very nearly the length of the side of the city of Ezekiel, and a rhombus whose sides are 216, the diameter of the sun's orbit, has a perimeter of 864.

Bearing in mind that Jerusalem occupies an analogous position in the land of Canaan to that of Delphi in Greece, we see that the numbers attributed to the names of the Jewish metropolis, or *omphalos*, are singularly appropriate to the city, which was said to be the central point of the world.

We have the testimony of Vitruvius, that ancient cities like the Temples were laid out round the cardo or cross, for he tells us that the area enclosed within the walls of a city should be planned so as to exclude the winds, which are reckoned as being four, eight, or sixteen in number. " To find and lay down their situation, we proceed as follows : Let a marble slab be fixed in the centre of the space enclosed by the walls . . . . and erect a gnomon in its centre . . . . and mark off the divisions or regions of the winds, etc." ("Vit.," bk. i. c. 6). This method explained by Vitruvius for disposing the streets to dissipate the violence of the winds, is apparently a mystical artifice to obscure the meaning of the passage, for no city was ever built on such a plan, and if it were, it is extremely doubtful if such an arrangement would have the effect claimed for it. But when he proceeds to give the measures of the earth according

to Eratosthenes, who ascertained from the sun's
shadow at the Equinox that the circuit of the
earth was 252,000 stadia, a quarter, an eighth, or
a sixteenth part of which was occupied by each
wind, the natural inference to be drawn from
these remarks is, that in planning a city it was
customary to begin by describing the earth's circumference round the centre, and marking upon it
the points of the compass. This supposition is
confirmed by the plan of the city of Nola already
alluded to. The ancient city is there shown to be
surrounded by a circular wall, 660 paces in
diameter, and 2,074 paces in circumference. The
circuit of the citadel is given at 924 paces, the
square root of the sun's diameter in miles. The
circular wall, which is exactly $\frac{1}{12}$ of the earth's
magnitude measured by miles, is divided into
twelve equal parts by so many turrets.

There are also evidences which seem to justify
the assumption, that the same practice was adopted
by the Jews in setting out Jerusalem. Accordingly, on examining the plan of the city to discover
upon what principle it is laid out, and whether the
sacred places have any relation to the cosmic
scheme, the first measurement we find suggesting
such a connection is the distance between the
Serpent pool in the west (called also Upper Gibon),
and the Church of the Ascension on the Mount of
Olives in the east. From the north-west corner
of the Pool of the Serpent to the eastern boundary
of the Church of the Ascension is a distance of
7,920 feet, or the number of miles in the diameter
of the earth. If a meridian line be drawn between
these two points, passing through the Golden
Gate and the Holy Sepulchre, its centre will fall
upon the Acra, or Acropolis. And a circle 7,920
feet in diameter described from this centre, will
represent the earth's circumference to a scale of

one foot to a mile. If this circle be divided according to the method described by Vitruvius in his account of the analemma (bk. ix., ch. 6), the latitude of Jerusalem being 31°, the axis of the earth will be found to pass through the Damascus gate, while the whole city will lie within the space of the Tropics or the path of the sun. In fact the south-east angle of the Haram wall nearly touches the line of the southern tropic.

Next, if a rood cross of the proportions of 28 : 13 be drawn with its centre upon the Acra, or the centre of the world, so that it may bear upon it the crucified figure of Christos within the square 1,480, the base of the cross will stand upon the Garden of Gethsemane, while the top will reach to the most western point of the city wall. There are also the foundations of an older wall a little to the south, which show that the old western boundary had been fixed at exactly the same distance from the middle of the city. The head of Christos crucified in this manner falls upon the site of the Holy Sepulchre Church, which is built upon Golgotha, the Place of the Skull; and as the Jews personified the Logos under the name of Adam, it is probable that the chapel called the " Skull of Adam" included within the church was introduced there in reference to this fact.

The Sepulchre is itself apparently 1,046½ feet from the middle of the city, that is, a distance equal to the radius of a circle containing a square whose sides measure 1,480 feet.

Jerusalem being in the possession of three peoples professing a distinct religious system, and having holy places peculiar to their cult, it is necessary to treat the Jewish sites captured by the Mohammedans and the precincts of the Holy Sepulchre separately. Nevertheless, the sanctity which had first been extended to the various places by the Jews was preserved afterwards both by the Christians and Mohammedans, who avowedly founded their religion upon the law of Moses. The difficulty of dealing with the city when in the hands of the Jews, lies in the fact that there are no essentially Jewish remains now in existence to work upon. The accounts of the buildings and disposition of the city found in the scriptures and in the gospels are all we have to guide us as to the appearance of ancient Jerusalem. From these sources, however, it is evident that the rabbis regarded their metropolis as an image of the cabalistic diagram, the castle of Goliath and the western extremity of the city being the place of the Macrocosm ; the acra and the haram area, which is said to have contained Solomon's temple, being apportioned to the Microcosm, while the valley of Jehoshophat and the Mount of Olives fall to the Bride. The Jewish way of looking at the city would therefore accord with the orientation of the Temple. But in the Middle Ages, when the Christians built their temples facing the west instead of the east, this was reversed, and, if this be remembered, much confusion will be avoided in reading the descriptions of the city written by later pilgrims from the west.

Now from the Golden Gate to the extremity of the western wall is a distance of about 3,600 feet, therefore the diagram covering the city, being of the ratio of $26:15$, is 2,076 feet broad, or $\frac{1}{12}$ of the circumference of the earth in miles. The citadel occupies the place of the third step, while the site of the Holy Sepulchre falls on the point called Daath, 474, or knowledge, by the Cabalists. It is the place marked by the head of Microcosmos, which again affords a reason for calling the place Golgotha, the skull. " In three hollow places of the skull the brain is contained." " In the third cavity

Daath, knowledge, is contained and dwelleth." [1]
Further, by Gematria Golgotha is equivalent to
Daath, for BGVLGLTHA = 475 or GVLGTHA
= 473, therefore by adding or deducting colel in
either case we get 474 = DOTH. The stables of
Solomon stand on the eighth Step, and the Golden
Gate on the ninth. The sixth Step, Beauty, lies
outside the Haram enclosure, to the east of the
Acra. The valley of Kedron, called also Tophet
or Hinnon, was identified with Hades, and seems
to have been always associated with the ideas connected with the tenth Step. Here is found the
garden of Gethsemane, called in Arabic "the place
of incarnation," the Church of the Tomb of the
Virgin, and the Tombs of Jehoshophat, Absalom,
Zachariah, and St. James. Towards the south
is the pool of Siloam, and the Virgin's well.

The holy places of Jerusalem being thus
included within the circumference of the earth, the
city and its precincts are an exact microcosm.
That it was regarded as such, and that Christ was
accepted as a personification of the old microcosmic
deity of the Greeks, is made clearly manifest by a
thirteenth-century geographer, who has left us a
map of the world (exhibited in the King's Library
of the British Museum), in which the figure of
Jesus is expanded, in the form of a cross like the
macrocosm of Cesariano. His body, symbolically
comprising the whole world, is depicted by its
extremities only, his head in the east, his two
hands in the north and south, and his feet in the
west.

In this map we see a literal presentation of the
crucified Logos, unobscured by the metaphorical
disguise of the customary fables; for it was thus

[1] See Cabala, "Greater Holy Assembly," ch. xxvii., On the
Brain of Microprosopus, p. 180.

" He stretched out His hands on the cross, that
He might encompass the ends of the world," and
" wrought salvation in the middle of the earth." [1]
St. Augustine, who knew this well, explains the
mystery not less surely but more cautiously; he
says, " the first letters of the words North, South,
East and West in Greek form the word Adam.
Adam is, therefore, the type of all nations. But
these Greek letters, being taken according to the
value of their numbers, make 46. Our Lord did
of Adam receive a body; and he did in three days
raise it up" (On St. John, ii. 20). Now the
points of the compass are called:

North	Ἄρκτος	691		691 + 1
West	Δύσις	814	1,274	814 + 1
East	Ἀνατολή	460		460 + 1
South	Μεσημβρία	406		

$$2,371 - 3 = 2,368.$$

$$1,965 + 3 = 1,968.$$

Their numerical values amount to 2,371, or, by
deducting colel from three of the names, 2,368
(*Iesous Christos*). Accordingly the four quarters
of the world are a visible emblem of Adam, and
Christ; and we find that *Staurosis*, 2,211 (crucifixion), is equivalent by Gematria to εἷς, δύο, τρεῖς,
and τετράς, the names of the Greek numerals 1, 2,
3, 4. Moreover, the breadth of a vesica 2,210
long is 1,275, which is the height of a rood cross
which will crucify a man in a square having a
perimeter of 2,368. And 2,211 is the sum of the
two numbers 1,101 (Macroprosopos) and 1,110
(Microprosopos). Again, the sum of the numbers
from 1 to 46 is 1,081, the radius of the moon and
the symbol of the four elements of which the body
of the Logos was made. So the verity of the
symbolic crucifixion is as skilfully and unmistak-

[1] St. Cyril, "Cat. Lect.," xiii. 28.

ably adumbrated by the words of St. Augustine as by the map of the geographer.

Bearing in mind the primitive ideas of theology, it becomes at once apparent why the Greeks, Jews and Christians chose to consider their country and metropolis to be in the middle of the world.[1] For we see in this monkish map that Jerusalem is built over the centre of Christ's body, thereby acquiring its reputed sanctity ; and the symbol, by which this Christian priest has notified the mystery of the holy city, would be quite as appropriate to Heliopolis, Babylon, and Delphi, as Jerusalem. Within the four square walls there is drawn the figure of Christos issuing from an oblong tomb, intended to represent the Holy Sepulchre or *omphalos* of the world. Nor does his piety allow him to omit the cross, for by the addition of the two soldiers[2] still asleep outside the sarcophagus, the mystic triad is ingeniously included in the composition. In the Hereford map the walls of Jerusalem are made round, in the image of the navel, while the cross stands up outside the walls. Thus we distinctly see why the writers of the Gospel selected the centre of the world wherein to lay the scene of the crucifixion, the central feature and climax of their parable.

The actual navel-stone of Jerusalem is not shown in the Acra or centre of the city, but in the middle of the Church of the Holy Sepulchre—the reason of this probably being, that the Chris-

---

[1] "The land of Israel is situated in the centre of the world, and Jerusalem in the centre of the land of Israel, and the Temple in the centre of Jerusalem, and the Holy of Holies in the centre of the Temple, and the foundation-stone on which the world was founded is situated in front of the ark."— HERSHON, "Talmudic Miscellany," p. 300.

[2] The two soldiers are representatives of the Armies (Tzabaoth) mentioned in the Cabala. "Lesser Holy Assembly," ch. xxii., pars. 740, 741, and 742 (Mathers).

tians preferred to especially consecrate a place of their own when they succeeded the Jews. Accordingly we find that the navel-stone marks the centre of Christ's body, if crucified on a rood cross inscribed within the circle of the earth, 7,920 feet in diameter.

We further see from Ebstorf's map that the Christian Paradise corresponds to the head of Macrocosmos (831), and the three first steps of the Cabalistic Diagram. According to Hippolytus (Ref., bk. v., ch. iv.) the Nasseni "suppose that man, as far as the head only, is Paradise." The "man" being Adam ('Αδαμας, 247), the Macrocosm, or as shown on the map, Christos.[1]

All the holy places of Jerusalem, as well as those of the greater world being associated with the parts of the human body, it was probably for this reason, that the footprints of Jesus were shown in the Church of the Ascension, where the feet of the Macrocosm appear on the map.

Like the travels of Pausanias, the diaries of the pilgrims who journeyed to Jerusalem in the early days of the Church are most valuable records of antiquity, revealing the spirit of the old world, interpreting naturally and unfeignedly its own conceptions, without any of the effort and learned affectation required by a modern traveller to adjust a new mind to an old subject. For every quotation and observation they make is a valuable criticism, and to the instructed, it is overwhelmingly evident, that the saintly pilgrims of the Middle Ages saw a very different parable in the sites and episodes of the Gospel than that which is discernible to one of Mr. Cook's tourists. An old

---

[1] In a mediæval map of Jerusalem Solomon's Temple stands in Paradise, Golgotha in the middle of the world, and the Holy Sepulchre in the west occupies the place of the Bride. To a Jew, however, the order was exactly reversed.

pilgrimage forms a summary of the sacred histories, where legends often derive as much point from their situation as from any other cause.

The descriptions of these pious travellers are so ample, that we are left in no doubt as to the general significance of the holy places, and so systematically do the localities appear to have been fixed, that since the Land of Canaan, Jerusalem, and the churches or cathedrals were all microcosms, exactly delineated, it was possible to assign every event of Christ's passion to its proper place in the world, in the city and in the Temple. Accordingly we find in the churches, as at Chartres, a labyrinth with Jerusalem in its centre, just as the corresponding place in the city itself was also called Jerusalem. At Durham there is the Galilee Chapel at the west, corresponding to the Galilee on the Mount of Olives.[1] Elsewhere we find a calvarium, golden and beautiful gates, but whether the places were marked or not, they could be located by measurement, and any mediæval Christian could make a pilgrimage round his cathedral, to all intents and purposes, as though he were in Jerusalem.

[1] "On the other side of the Church (of the Ascension) is the chapel where our Lord Jesus Christ first appeared to the Apostles after his resurrection, and it is called Galilee, as he said to the Apostles, 'After I am risen again, I will go before you unto Galilee.'" (Saewulf's Travels.) He also mentions "the Galilee of Mount Sion." Sir John Maundeville says, "After Mount Olivet is the Mount of Galilee, where the Apostles assembled when Mary Magdalene came and told them of Christ's ascension. And there between Mount Olivet and the Mount of Galilee is a church where the angel foretold our Lady of her death." He also mentions (ch. viii.) "a deep cave under the rock, which is called the Galilee of our Lord, where St. Peter hid himself when he had forsaken our Lord." Again, in the "City of Jerusalem," it is said, "in this Church (of the Ascension) is the place where Holy Mary died in Galilee."

It was this mystical order that Eusebius seems
to have had in his mind, when describing the
Basilica of Constantine with its threefold division,
agreeing with the cabalistic diagram. The Sepulchre, or cave in the west, he says, marking the
place of the Macrocosm was joined to an open
court, "paved with shining stones," in which was
the navel of the world. Next to this was the
Martyrium, its apse standing over Golgotha, where
a hemisphere was "girt with 12 pillars, according
to the number of the Apostles of the Saviour"—
these are of course the 12 signs of the Zodiac,
surrounding the body of Christos crucified in their
midst. And the vestibule, or atrium in the east
was the appointed symbol of the Bride.

It is recorded by an anonymous pilgrim who
visited the Church of the Holy Sepulchre in the
Middle Ages, that "in the midst of the choir
is the middle of the world, where our Lord was
laid, when Nicodemus took him down from the
cross." A similar statement occurs in the "Citez
de Jherusalem": "Near to the Holy Sepulchre,
that is to say, in the choir where is *the compass of
our Lord*, is also the place where Nicodemus and
Joseph of Arimathæa placed his blessed body"
(Capt. Conder's trans., p. 34). Again we learn
from Theoderich, the pilgrim, that "about the
middle of the choir [of the Church of the Holy
Sepulchre] there is a small open altar of great
sanctity, on the flooring whereof is marked a cross
inscribed in a circle, which signifies that on this
spot Joseph and Nicodemus laid our Lord's body,
in order to wash it, after they had taken it down
from the cross."

The "cross inscribed in a circle" probably refers
to the figure of the Microcosm stretched within the
sphere of the Zodiac. And supposing the lesser
man of Vitruvius be drawn within that circle, the

sun's distance being taken at 10,[1] his head will
occupy the space between the high altar and the
front line of the Iconostasis, so that it is entirely
enclosed within the sanctuary, or apse, which
Eusebius has called the κεφάλαιον, the place of
the head. The top of the head also marks the
attitude of the pole above the horizon, according
to the latitude of Jerusalem. And a line drawn
southwards at right angles to the axis of the church
from the crown of the head touches the eastern
extremity of the Chapel of the Skull of Adam,
thereby implying that Adam's Skull is no other
than that of the hypothetical Man, or Microcosm
whose body was made to measure the universe.

Without having the exact dimensions to work
upon it would be hazardous to say more about
this pre-eminently important church, but it is to be
hoped that the deficiency with respect to the
measures will be supplied.

According to Eusebius, when Constantine projected the building of his Basilica, he discovered a
" mound of Venus" raised over the Saviour's tomb
(" Life of Constantine"). The earliest travellers
describe the Sepulchre as being a separate structure surrounded by pillars enclosed by a circular
wall, having the entrance facing the east. Its
position in the present building corresponds to the
narthex, or baptistry of a primitive church, or the
porch of Solomon's Temple. The name *Anastasis*,
Resurrection, has the value of 963, and is equivalent by Gematria to τέχνη, art.

The account of Bernard the wise is that the
four principal churches in Jerusalem were " connected with each other by walls ; one to the east,

---

[1] The only available plan of this church (that of the Ordnance
Survey) gives no measurements. But by taking the sun's distance as being equal to ten English feet, the result will be approximately accurate.

which contains the Mount of Calvary and the
place in which the Cross of our Lord was found,
and is called the Basilica of Constantine; another
to the south, a third to the west, in the middle of
which is the Sepulchre of our Lord, having nine
columns in its circuit. . . . Between the aforesaid
four churches is a parvis without roof, the walls of
which shine with gold, and the pavement is laid
with very precious stone; and in the middle four
chains, coming from each of the four churches,
join in a point which is said to be the middle of
the world."[1]   Bernard is the only pilgrim who
mentioned these four "chains," but they are
doubtless the cross-lines of the cardinal points or
quarters.   The same adherence to the canonical
pattern seems to have made the priests declare
that it was on this spot that Adam was formed,
and that here Abraham prepared to sacrifice Isaac.
Here also Jacob saw the mystic Ladder.   Even
the horn, wherewith David was anointed, was seen
here, as was also in after times "the banquet hall
(*missorium*), where the head of John the Baptist
was brought before Herod the King."   Here
again is displayed the "hole in which it is known
that the cross was fixed; into which hole pilgrims,
out of the love and respect which they bear to
Him that was crucified, are wont to plunge their
head and face," and close by, in a little shrine,
was the "cup of our Lord which Arculf touched

[1] "At the head of the Church of the Holy Sepulchre, in the
wall outside, not far from the place of Calvary, is the place
called Compas, which our Lord Jesus Christ himself signified
and measured with his own hand as the middle of the world,
according to the words of the Psalmist, 'For God is my King
of old, working salvation in the midst of the earth' (Psalm
lxxiv. 12).   But some say that that is the place where our
Lord Jesus Christ first appeared to Mary Magdalène, while she
sought Him weeping, and thought He had been a gardener, as
is related in the Gospel."   (Saewulf's "Travels.")

and kissed through a hole in the covering." In the same place stood the pillar to which Christ was bound, and which at midday at the summer solstice cast no shadow, because it was in the centre of the world. These are a few of the things that happened and were seen at this site, but many more are mentioned by the pious pilgrims, whose works may be consulted.[1]

It was apparently for similar reasons that the Druids held their great festival "at a consecrated place in the territories of the Carnutes, *whose country is supposed to be in the middle of Gaul*" (Cæsar, Gallic Com., bk. vi., c. 13), and as the institution is said to have come originally from Britain, there was probably a correspondingly holy place in the centre of our island. In Christian times the *omphalos* of England appears to have been reckoned in Lichfield, in the county of Staffordshire.

We learn from Camden that "the people whereof as living in the heart of England, are called in Bede *Angli mediterranei* . . . it lies from south to north, almost in the form of a rhombus, being broad in the middle, but narrow and contracted towards the ends." Bede calls it Licidfield, which Rouse of Warwick renders "a field of carcasses," and tells us that many Christians suffered martyrdom there. According to some authorities the number of the martyrs was 888, the diameter of the circle enclosing the New Jerusalem, which is in the middle of the universe. "This worde Lichefelde," says Lydgate, who described the slaughter by the *paynyms*, "by interpretation, is . . . a felde that lyeth full of bodyes dead," while the manner in which Amphibalus was put to death, suggesting the ritualistic ceremonies

[1] See the publications of the Palestine Pilgrim Text Society.

of a pagan sacrifice, is no doubt related with a mystical intention. One of the "paynyms," he continues ("Life and Passion of St. Alban and St. Amphibalus"),

> "Like a bocher (butcher) persed his entrayles,
> This homycyde that ranne afore the route
> Raffe his *navylle*, and toke out his bowelles,
> And at a stake whiche that stode without
> Tyed like ropes evyn rounde about,
> And with a scurge the martyr he gan make
> In cercle wyse to go aboute the stake."

Then they threw swords, daggers, spears, and knives at him, but "ever the more again they did malign, the more they found him gracious and benign."

Kircher ("Œdipus," tom. ii., pars ii., p. 358), has depicted the Microcosm standing in the midst of the planets with his body cut open, so that the intestines are seen in a spiral coil encircling the navel. It is an ugly simile; but it seems that the ancients derived the idea of the Labyrinth from the tortuous winding of the entrails round the *omphalos*, and they were likened to the orbits of the planets surrounding the earth, or navel of the universe.

Delos is said to have been visited by Theseus on his return from Crete, where he had slain the Minotaur; "and having sacrificed to Apollo, and dedicated in the temple the image of Aphrodite, which Ariadne had given him, he danced with the young Athenians a dance that in memory of him is still preserved among the inhabitants of Delos, and which by its various turnings and involutions imitated the intricate windings of the Labyrinth. And this dance, as Dicæarchus writes, is called among the Delians the Crane. This he danced round the Ceratonian altar, so called from its being built entirely of horns; and these were

taken only from the left side of the head"
(Plutarch's "Theseus"). This dance has probably
an anatomical as well as an astral significance, and
the speech in the Hymn of Callimachus in reference to the navel at Delphi appears to have a
similar meaning; "nor yet hath died the huge
serpent, but still that monster with dreadful jaws,
creeping down from Plistus, enwreaths snowy
Parnassus with *nine coils*" ("Hymn to Delos,"
v. 92).

In Lydgate's poem the coiling of the entrails
of Amphibalus round the stake seems to be an
obvious imitation of the circling of the planets
round the pole, whose emblem was the serpent
Draco, and it is probable that the entrails were
used for some such reason as this, in the old sacri-
ficial rites. Amphibalus, the "cloak" of St. Alban,
takes the second place in the legend, and it must
be borne in mind that Christ's death on Golgotha
was the prototype of all the martyrdoms of the
Saints. It is therefore natural that the "cloak"
of the first English martyr to Christianity should
be sacrificed at Lichfield, called by Bede mediter-
ranean, or in the centre of the world.

Now taking a point a little to the south of Lichfield as a centre, we find that the circumference
of a circle 220 miles in diameter passes through
London. And London has the numerical value
of 924, the square root of the sun's diameter in
miles. Stephanus in his "Book of Cities" calls it
Λινδόνιον, which yields 344, the diameter of a circle
1,081 in circumference (Camden).

Again, if the sphere of the Zodiac be drawn
within the Holy Oblation with the same centre,
and taking a furlong to be equivalent to the sun's
diameter, the square enclosing the body of Christos
passes through the city of York in the north, and
through Stonehenge in the south. The square of

the Holy Oblation passes through Canterbury and the Isle of Wight; whether the name of " Wight," a man, has any reference to this fact, or that the right hand of a man inscribed within a circle 2,368 in diameter touches the " Isle of Man," has any connection with its name, we have no idea.

Supposing Lichfield to have been the navel of England, it may be that the singular revels anciently celebrated at Coventry, lying about twenty-five miles to the south-east, had a phallic origin. Camden derives the name from *Conventus*, a convent, and, amongst other things, says that their Cross for beauty and workmanship is inferior to few in England. Its height appears to have been 57 feet ($57 \times 9\frac{1}{2} = 541$, the side of a rhombus having a perimeter equal to the moon's diameter). The annual procession in memory of Godiva, represented by a naked figure riding on horseback, was still continued in Camden's time, and several of the old mystery plays enacted by the trade guilds are yet extant. One of these, published by Sharp, is a dramatized life of Noah, a subject which entirely accords with the nature of the place.

In pre-Christian times the great city in the middle of England was Caerleon, or the city of Legions. It was the seat of an Archflamen, along with London and York. But when the new cult was established the two archbishops were confined to the north and south.

The finding of the true cross has a personal interest for Englishmen, for (if Jeffrey of Monmouth spoke the truth) St. Helena, who surpassed all the ladies of her time in beauty and skill in music, was the daughter of King Cole of Colchester. It is true that Colchester is not the only city named as her birth-place, but its claims are certainly as good as those of any other. Jeffrey calls it " Kaercolvin, id est Colecestriae " (lib. v., cap. 6), and when that name is resolved into a number, its relation to the true cross may be explained thus : 401 is 1 less than the breadth of a vesica formed by two intersecting circles whose united width is 1,206, which is the side of a rhombus inscribed within the Holy Oblation containing the cruciform body of Christos. Helena yields 96, and 96·8 is the radius of Holy Oblation if the sun's distance be taken at 10. Again, the name of her son Constantine (Κωνσταντινος), the first Christian emperor, has the value of 2,051, or about the diameter of Saturn's orbit, while 2,051 + 98 ('Ελενη) = 2,149 + 2 = 2,151. In Latin, Constantinus yields 378, the side of a rhombus having a perimeter of ($377\frac{5}{8}$ × 4 =) 1,510, the numerical equivalent of Χι, Ρω, ☧, the Labarum or standard fashioned as the emblem of Constantine's vision. Finally, 378 (Constantinus) + 96 (Helena) = 474, the number of the name Golgotha, where the cross was discovered in the year A.D. 326 ($325\frac{1}{2}$ × 2 = 651).

According to the traditions the cross was made of the wood of the Tree of Paradise ; and we see on Ebstorf's map that Paradise is situated beside the head of Christ or Macrocosmos, and the tree stands between Adam and Eve, the central feature of a triad evidently corresponding to the first three steps of the Cabala.

We are told that Adam, who died at the age of 930 years, was buried with a branch of the Tree of Paradise in his mouth. This branch took root and grew to be a tree, and, having incorporated the body of Adam in its stem, they say that for this reason Adam's head is always shown on the upright beam of the cross on old crucifixes. Afterwards Noah carried it through the flood in the Ark. It was next brought to Jerusalem with the

other materials of which the temple was built.
But no place could be found for it in the building,
so it lay on the ground unregarded except by the
careless people, who scraped their muddy feet upon
it; till the Queen of Sheba, passing that way,
saw it, wiped it with her own clothes, and adored
it.   After that, it seems to have taken root
again, for "they show a place encircled by walls
near Jerusalem, where it is said the tree grew from
which the Holy Cross was made" (Abbot Daniel).
Then on Golgotha, and in a garden (St. Cyril, Cat.
Lect. XIII., 8) the salvation of mankind having
been achieved, the cross, as in former times, lay
neglected for 293 years, when the devotion of St.
Helena drew attention to it again.

A simple geometrical demonstration is all that
is required to disclose the verity of the tradition.
For the distance from the navel-stone in the
centre of the Holy Sepulchre Church to the place
of the invention is about 200 feet.   And, since
it has been shown that the said stone coincides
with the navel of the Microcosm crucified on a rood
cross inscribed within the circumference of the
earth, it will be at once apparent how St. Helena
came to find the cross just at the spot where the
chapel stands to commemorate it (see the Ordnance
Survey of the Church of the Holy Sepulchre).

The old artists, who were piously instructed in
the Ecclesiastical Tradition, always represented
St. Helena and the cross according to the mystic
sense.   That the theoretical treatment was still
known in the sixteenth century is attested by one
of the most beautiful pictures in the world—that of
Paolo Caliari (National Gallery, No. 1041).   The
artist has depicted the invention as a visionary
revelation merely, but he has taken care that the
mystery of the true cross is presented with significant accuracy.

Countries and cities appear to have been named upon the same microcosmic principle as the world itself. *Hellas* has the value of 266, which is the diameter of a circle, whose area is equal to the square of the New Jerusalem.

Latium, the country of the Latins, yields 1,047, the radius of the circle containing the square 1,480.

Roma has the value of 311, the side of a rhombus 540 long, and $540 \times 4 = 2,160$. According to the Greek valuation of the letters it is equal to 941, and 942 is the diagonal of a square whose sides are 666. The statements of Francis Potter and the Puritans seem to show that they knew this.

The number of a name might even assist in the making of history. At least the writer of the " Acts of the Apostles " (xi. 26) was probably not ignorant that *Antiocheia* had the value of 1,047, when he said " the disciples were called Christians first in Antioch." Nor could a more suitable place than this be found in the whole world in which to give a name to the followers of Christos, 1,480.

CHAPTER XIII.

RHETORIC.

" Ten are the Numbers, as are the Sephiroth, and twenty-two [1] *the letters ; these are the foundation of all things."*—CABALA, Yetsirah."

"Against order is against reason."—" Recognitions of Clement," bk. iii., ch. xxxiv.

HISTORY, it has been said, has two eyes, Chronology and Geography. Having already touched upon historical phenomena in relation to the latter science, we shall now briefly treat of the epochs and sequence of time, as viewed by old historians. Strauchius (" Chronology," p. 2), says that "the chronologer disposeth times, and gives certain characters of them ; the historian records things done and fills up the spaces, which the other leaves empty. . . . Yea, Scaliger (" Proleg. in Euseb.") makes chronology to be the *soul* of history, and to excel it as much as the soul doth the body." He adds further, that " it assumes most of its principles out of astronomy." According to these authorities history is made a mere accessory to chronology, and occupies a place exactly the reverse of that which we are accustomed to give it at the present day. For, according to them, the times must be first established, and then a series of events found to fit them. That chronology did actually affect the composition of ancient history seems to be indis-

[1] 10 + 22 = 32, which is the square root of 1,024, the radius of Saturn's orbit.

putable, and there is every reason to believe that the eminent Scaliger was not mistaken in exalting chronology as the guiding spirit of history.[1]

It is well known that the epochs and cycles of the ancients were arranged according to a canonical system. Ptolemy's chronological canon of the Ptolemaic dynasty is still extant, and Plutarch ("Life of Solon," p. 307, Edin., 1763), speaking of Solon's interview with Crœsus, says that he cannot reject it as fictitious because it does not agree with "some chronological canons, which thousands have endeavoured to regulate, and yet to this day could never bring the different accounts to any agreement." It is, moreover, clearly evident that the period reckoned from the creation of the world to the birth of Christ belongs to the category of canonical or artificial computations referred to by Plutarch. This imaginary cycle is so obviously fictitious that modern churchmen, committed as they are to a literal acceptance of the Scriptures, rather than support the reality of this epoch prefer the ignominious and absurd alternative of believing the history while rejecting the dates. If Strauchius be correct these semi-believers are leaning on the more shadowy support of the two, for he says "in relating matters of fact History pretends to no demonstrations : but Chronology produces the firmest that are." And this must necessarily be so, if the history of the world from the creation to the birth of Christ is an ingeniously compiled chronicle, relating in canonical order events appro-

---

[1] A distinction ought to be made between sacred and profane history—as, for instance, between the works of Homer or Moses and, say, those of Thucydides or writers who aimed at veracity simply. When Pythagoras went down into Hell, he found Homer's soul hung upon a tree, surrounded by serpents, as a punishment for his having related fabulous stories about the gods (DIOGENES LAERTES, "Life of Pythagoras"). He does not seem to have noticed the soul of Moses.

priate to the numbers of the years determined by the length of the cycle.

Upwards of fifty different computations of this important epoch have been made by Christian chronologers (Strauchius, p. 166), who reckon the interval at from 3,760 to 6,484 years. When the chief of these reckonings are severally examined, it would seem that the chronological canon was constructed in accordance with the fundamental doctrines of the Cabala, explained in the case of the other arts. For the three persons of the Triad representing the whole scheme of creation from the firmament to the earth symbolize, in the period of time occupied by the events of the Old Testament, the mediating powers by which the emanation of God or germ of life descended from heaven, and became incarnate on earth in the body of Jesus Christ. And since the exposition of the Cabala is easily effected by numbers, the computation of the years in any cycle was a simple means of mystically supplying a measurement, which conveyed to the philosophers a representation of the three symbolic persons. Consequently it is necessary to resolve the period into three terms, so that a proper number falls to each person, the result of the varying length of the cycle being that the symbolical meaning of the events will be capable of a variable interpretation.

According to Strauchius (p. 166), the Greeks constituted the period from the creation of the world to the birth of Christ at 5,598 years. Now the three obvious numbers appropriate to the persons of the Cabala, which may be deduced from 5,598 are 2,368, 2,151, and 1,080 (2,368+2,151+1,080 = 5,599). These numbers, as already explained, accurately describe the three parts of the universe, the Empyrean, the Zodiac together with the planets, and the Sublunary, or elementary world.

The Constantinopolitans and Alexandrians counted 5,508 years as the canonical period. And this number is made up of 2,368, 2,093, and 1,047—the first being, as before, the numerical equivalent of Jesus Christ, the second the diameter of the circle containing the square 1,480 (Christos), and the third number, being the radius of the same circle, applies to the feminine half of the Logos.

The cycle of the Æthiopic church is 9 less than the preceding, so that the numbers become 2,368, $2,083\frac{1}{3}$, and $1,046\frac{1}{2}$. The only difference is that the Holy Oblation signifying Christ is indicated by the mean number $2,083\frac{1}{3}$, instead of 2,093.

In our English Bible the cycle is set down at 4,004 years. This is a late calculation made by Archbishop Ussher in the seventeenth century, but it was evidently adopted by the English Church for sound theological reasons. The three numbers into which the period may be resolved are 2,083, 1480, and 441. Consequently we get the dimensions of the universe as measured by the bodies of the Macrocosm and the Microcosm in their due relation to each other (or nearly so), while the number of the third person is the measure of a cross drawn within the sun's orbit ($220 \times 2 = 440$). This is a most instructive triad, well worthy of consideration as manifesting the hidden doctrine. The first and second persons exhibit the duplication of the square illustrated by the figures of Cesariano, and the sun's orbit, being the emblem of the new Jerusalem or city of the sun, marks the *omphalos* and *stauros* in the middle of the world.[1]

---

[1] A vesica 441 broad is 766 long, and a square whose sides are 766 has a diagonal of 1,083, the radius of the moon; and such a square is contained within a rhombus inscribed in the Holy Oblation, so that every attribute of the Bride or Holy Ghost are implied by the number 441. The Hebrew word,

Scaliger's number is 3,949 years, which produces 2,083, 1,480, and 386. The last number is
the side of a rhombus whose length is 670, the
numerical equivalent of ὁ κόσμος, and 1 less than
that of Adonai and Thorah, the Hebrew names of
Malchuth, the Bride.

Haynlinus chose the number 3,963, the number
of miles in the earth's radius. Taking the first
and second numbers, as before, to be 2,083 and
1,480, the third is 400, which is the length of a
rhombus having a perimeter of 924, the square
root of the number of miles in the sun's diameter.

Even the reckoning of the Jews brings out a
mystical triad, for 3,760 may be divided into
2,083, 1,480, and 197—the twelfth of 2,368 being
$197\frac{1}{3}$.

Strauchius, on p. 382, gives the following quotation from the Roman Martyrology published by
the authority of Pope Gregory XIII., and publicly
read every year on Christmas Day: "In the
5,199th year from the creation of the world, when
God created Heaven and Earth; and the 2,957th
after the Deluge; the 2,015th from the birth of
Abraham; 1,510th from Moses, and the time of
the Israelites leaving Egypt; and 1,032nd from
the time of David's being anointed king; in the
65th annual week of Daniel; in the 194th
Olympiad; in the 752nd year since the building
of Rome; in the 42nd year of the Emperor
Octavius Augustus, when the whole world was
blessed with peace; in the 6th Age of the world;
Jesus Christ, Eternal God, and Son of the Eternal
Father, conceived from the Holy Ghost, was born
of the Virgin Mary in Bethlehem of Judæa." The
entire cycle of 5,199 years may be divided into
2,368, 2,083, and 748—the last number being the

AMTн, truth, τὸ ἀγαθόν, the good, and ὁ λόγος (deducting
colel), the word, yield 441.

side of a square contained in a rhombus inscribed within the orbit of Saturn. But, leaving the other numbers, the remarkable fact in the preceding passage is the striking numerical coincidence in the years according to the reckonings of Greece and Rome. Counting by the Greek chronology, Christ was born in the 194th Olympiad. Now 193·6 is the side of the Holy Oblation, if the sun's distance be taken at 10 : and 194 Olympiads are 776 (= 194 × 4) years ; and the transverse beam of a rood cross 776 high is 360, the number of degrees in the earth's circumference. Then, counting by the Roman chronology, the year 752 from the founding of the city is 1 less than the diameter of a circle 2,368 in circumference. This curious coincidence, occurring at a time when the sun had passed into a new sign of the Zodiac, and when consequently a new Messiah was required, strangely confirms, by the appearance of the Gospel, the suggested influence of chronology upon history.

Christ (supposing him to have been a real personage) was not the only claimant to the honour of personifying the Logos. The fathers give accounts of similar pretensions on the part of Marcus, Basilides, Marcion, and others, while the introduction of the cults of Abraxas, 365, and Mithras, 360, at Rome may be attributed to some such cause as this.

The only rival of Jesus alluded to in the New Testament is Σίμων ὁ Μάγος (Simon Magus),[1] whose

---

[1] "There was one John, a day-baptist, who was also, according to the method of combination, the forerunner of our Lord Jesus ; and as the Lord had 12 *apostles, bearing the number of the* 12 *months* of the sun, so also he [John] had 30 chief men, fulfilling the monthly reckoning of the moon, in which number was a certain woman called Helena, that not even this might be without a dispensational significance. For a woman, being half a man, made up the imperfect number of the tria-

name, when colel is deducted from the three
words, yields 1,481, or 1 more than Christos. He
declared himself to be a personification of the
Father (*Simon*, 1,100 = *Macroprosopos*, 1,101),
and showed himself among the Jews as Christ,
"not in the flesh, but in appearance; and after
this, as the Holy Ghost, of whom Christ had
promised that he should be sent as the Comforter"
(St. Cyril, Lect. VI.). We are also told that
Claudius set up a statue to him inscribed "To
Simon, the Holy God" (*Ibid.*).

In the third century Manes, a Persian, also pro-
claimed himself to be a personification of the Holy
Ghost—or Logos, for Manes in Persian means
speech. He appears to have healed the sick, and
performed wonders like Simon Magus and the
rest. He was worshipped by disciples, persecuted
by other Christian sects, and like the gentle
Christos, was taken prisoner, condemned as a
malefactor, and having been flayed alive, consum-
mated his martyrdom with every accompaniment
of infamy (St. Cyril of Jerusalem, Cat. Lect. VI.,
20-31).

Again, the impersonation of the Holy Ghost by
a woman of the thirteenth century appears to be
due to chronological reasons. A fondness for the
worship of the Virgin was characteristic of the
theology of this century, and it resulted in the
introduction of the doctrine of transubstantiation
decreed 1,215 (by transposition 2151), besides
the addition of new offices especially addressed to
the Mother of God.

It was declared by various mystics that a Third
Age was to succeed those of the Father and the

contad; as also in the case of the moon, whose revolution does
not make the complete course of the month. But of these
thirty, the first and the most esteemed by John was Simon"
("Clementine Homilies," ch. xxiii., Hom. ii.).

Son, which were past. The Age of the Father, or the old law, they considered to have lasted till the first century, when the Logos was incarnated in the body of Jesus, and there was not wanting a woman in the thirteenth century, Wilhelmina by name, who undertook to personate the Holy Ghost. Her doctrine was that "all that had happened to Christ during His appearance upon earth in the human nature, was to be exactly renewed in her person, or rather in that of the Holy Ghost, which was united to her." She died at Milan, says Mosheim, "in the most fragrant odour of sanctity, and her memory was not only held in the highest veneration by her numerous followers and the ignorant multitude, but was also honoured with religious worship both in public and private" ("Eccles. Hist.," p. 349).

These opinions, according to Guillaume de St. Amour, were first propagated in the year 1200, although Joachim's "Everlasting Gospel," which named the year 1260 as the beginning of the New Age, was not published till 1254. The reason of the appearance of these prophecies was probably due to the fact that, according to the theory of mystical numbers, the year 1200 was remarkable because a vesica 1,201 broad is 2,083 long, and 2,083 being the size of the Holy Oblation enclosing the sphere of the Zodiac, that number was the symbol of the Holy Spirit. Again, 1,200 is also the length of a vesica 692 broad, and 691 is the length of the sun's orbit, which is enclosed in the New Jerusalem, the city of the Bride. In the same way the year 1239 would be remarkable, for 1,239 is the side of a vesica 2,151 long, or the number of years in the great month which symbolized the feminine aspect of the Logos, corresponding to the Holy Ghost. And 1,246 is the width of a vesica 2,160 long, the number of miles in the

moon's diameter, and consequently a symbol of
the elements, the emblem of the Bride. The
number 1,260 is not so easily accounted for, unless
it be that it is composed of the figures 2,160
transposed.

In the ecclesiastical computation of time there
are two great cycles observed, one of the sun and
one of the moon. The Lunar cycle is composed of
235 lunations of nineteen solar years, and by it the
golden number of the calendar is adjusted. The
solar cycle consists of a period of twenty-eight
years, and determines the changes of the Dominical
letter. It is assumed that the precession of the
equinoxes or great year [1] constituted the third
cycle during one month of which the Messiah was
supposed to rule.

The commemoration of the saints in the calendar
afforded another means of chronicling the doctrine
of theology with respect to numbers. For the
feasts, dedicated to the spirits or souls of the holy
persons canonized by the church, appear to be
distributed in a numerical order throughout the
circle of the year, to symbolize the choir of saints
who filled the sphere of heaven.

The Puritans have shown (Gale, " Court of the
Gentiles," vol. iii., p. 184, etc.) that the invocation
of saints was instituted by the Christians in imitation of the rites with which the pagans honoured
their demons (spirits). [2]   It was thought that when

[1] The precessional cycle, like other hidden matters, was
brought to light by Copernicus. (Vincent Wing, "Harmonicon
Celeste," 1651, p. 60.)

[2] "As the Pagans had their Holy-dayes dedicated to their
Demons, so also sacred *Hymnes*, whereby they sung their
praises . . . . So Bacchus had his τραγωδιας, Tragedies, and
κωμωδιας, Comedies: the former so called from the sacrificing
a *goat*, the latter, in that they were sung in *Villages*, answer-
ably to the Popish wake-songs. . . . And are not those Hymnes,
which the sons of Antichrist sing to their Canonised Saints on

the golden race of men died they became spirits (demons) " kindly, haunting earth, guardians of mortal men, who, I ween," as Hesiod says, " watch both the decisions of justice and harsh deeds, going to and fro everywhere over the earth, having wrapt themselves in mist, givers of riches as they are : and this is a kingly function which they have" ("Works and Days," v., 109). Plato, in the "Cratylus," calls these spirits mediators between gods and men. And according to both, they are the souls or spirits of departed heroes, who dwell and move about the intermediate space between the gods and mortals.

To go deeper into the matter we must consider what theories the old philosophers had about the soul. Cicero has preserved some of the ancient notions in the " Vision of Scipio," who is brought in a dream to the abode of the shades. He is there instructed by the spirit of Africanus his father, as to the nature of the place and the condition of souls after death, and is informed that " 'a soul has been supplied to them [men] from those eternal fires which you call constellations and stars . . . and the assembly of those who have lived before, and who, having been released from their bodies inhabit that place which thou beholdest.' Now the place my father spoke of was a radiant circle of dazzling brightness amid the flaming bodies you, as you have learned from the Greeks, term the Milky Way. . . . All things," he continues, "are connected by nine circles or rather spheres : the outermost of which is heaven,

their Holy-dayes, an exact ὑπόκρισις, or *Imitamen* of these Pagan Hymnes? . . . . The Pagans also had their Playes which were a part of those solemnities they performed to their Demons . . . . and as Antichrist has his Canonic *Playes* and *Dayes*, so also his *Images, Crosses, Reliques,* and other *Idol-representations* of his Saints."

and comprehends all the rest, inhabited by that all-powerful God who bounds and controls the others ; and in this sphere reside the original principles of those endless revolutions which the planets perform . . ." which as I was gazing at in amazement I said as I recovered myself : From whence proceed these sounds so strong and yet so sweet that fill my ears ? "The melody," replied he, which you hear, and which, though composed in unequal time is nevertheless divided into regular harmony, is effected by the impulse and motion of the spheres themselves which by a happy temper of sharp and grave notes regularly produces various harmonic effects."

From the preceding quotation Cicero makes it clear that the souls of men descend to the earth from the "constellations or stars," and then after death ascend to the circle of dazzling brightness, which the Greeks call the Milky Way, that is, to the place from whence they came. But Plato speaks of demons or spirits, who are "intermediate between the divine and the mortal," and who can be no other than the seven planets encircling the earth and filling the interval between it and heaven.

The action of the soul in its passage through the planets is obscurely referred to by Macrobius in his commentary on Scipio's dream (ch. xii.). "The soul, therefore, falling with this first weight, from the Zodiac and Milky Way into each of the subject spheres is not only clothed with the accession of a luminous body but produces the particular motions which it is to exercise in the respective orbs, etc." It is also explained by Porphyry ("Cave of the Nymphs," par. 11), that souls descending in generation enter through the "gate" of Cancer, the northern Tropic on their way to an earthly body, and, on their release at death, they ascend through

Capricorn the southern tropic, on their way back
to heaven.

Those hymns to which Gale draws attention
were probably sung in allusion to the celestial
music of the spheres, representing the demons,
who convey the souls of men down to earth and
from thence to heaven. Origen has a passage of
like purport. "Celsus," he says, "too agreeably
to the opinion of Plato, asserts that souls can make
their way to and from the earth through the
planets; while Moses, our most ancient prophet,
says that a divine vision was presented to the view
of our prophet Jacob,—a ladder stretching to
heaven, and the angels of God ascending and descending upon it, and the Lord supported upon its
top—obscurely pointing, by this matter of the
ladder, either to the same truths which Plato had
in view, or to something greater than these."

The number of saints commemorated in the
calendar of the English Church has varied with
the changes of opinion and jurisdiction which
have occurred at different times. In the Prayer
Book, as published in the reign of James II., in
the year 1680, the holy days and festivals, including
52 Sundays, amount to 81; then there are 16
vigils, the 40 days of Lent, the 12 Ember days,
the 3 Rogation days, and lastly, all the Fridays
in the year, to which are added "3 solemn
days," with appointed services. Consequently,
all the days devoted to religious exercises are
207, which is the diameter of a circle having a
circumference of 651, which in its turn is the
diameter of Saturn's orbit. Again, the total
number of saints named in the calendar is 93,
which is the radius of Saturn's orbit if the sun's
distance be taken at 10 (220 : 2,046 :: 10 :: 93),
and $93.8 \times 9.5 = 891$ (*ouranos*).

But the system seems to have been carried

further, as a closer examination of the calendar will show. According to the usage of the English church the ecclesiastical year begins on the first Sunday of Advent, which falls in the current year upon the 29th of November, 1896. Consequently, St. Andrew's Day, fixed for the 30th of November, is observed on the second day of the year. Now St. Andrew, who was said to have been crucified on a cross saltirewise, like the second figure of Cesariano, is an obvious personification of the Microcosm, and may be appropriately symbolized by the number 2.[1] The square of 30 is 900, and if 1 and a fraction be added we get the side of a square whose diagonal is 1,275.

St. Thomas's Day (December 21st) falls upon the 23rd day of the year. This apostle is called in the Gospel, Didymus, the Twin, being regarded as the twin-brother of Christ. In the apocryphal Gospel, "The Acts of the Holy Apostle Thomas," when the disciples were sent out to all the corners of the earth to preach, it fell to the lot of Thomas to go to India. At first he was unwilling to go owing to weakness of the flesh, but his brother Christ sold him to a merchant, who had been sent by the King of India to buy a carpenter.

Sir John Maundeville, in the thirteenth century, speaks of India as the Antipodes: "The Londes of Prestre John, Emperour of Ynde ben undre us," he says, "and thei han there the day, whan wee have the nyghte" (ch. xvii.). The southern hemisphere seems to have been fancifully conceived as a cup by the ancients. According to the legends, the Holy Grail was preserved in India by Prestre John, and the diagram of a chalice given by Greaves ("English Weights and

[1] The days of the month upon which the feasts of the saints are fixed must be considered as well as the days of the year, especially as the day of the year yields a variable number.

Measures ") seems to disclose its esoteric meaning. It is drawn as a hollow hemisphere or bowl
set upon a stem with the twenty-four hour-circles
of the earth marked upon it, and is consequently
a symbol of the under world. In some of the
earliest crucifixes a chalice is shown at the feet
of the Saviour. On turning to Cesariano's Macrocosm it will be seen that the four points of the
compass are clearly distinguished upon it. The
head and hands are enclosed by three circles,
and the feet by a vesica, the three upper points
representing the upper hemisphere or the male,
the lower hemisphere being the emblem of the
female.

In the order of the apostles Thomas stands
seventh according to St. Matthew (ch. x.). Therefore supposing St. Peter to correspond to the sign
of the fishes, Thomas would represent the Virgin,
or seventh month of the year, when the sun enters
the lower hemisphere at the autumnal equinox.

Thomas was also called Judas, 685, and Ἰούδας
Θωμας = 1,735, or 1 more than Dionysos, who
also made a famous expedition into India.

Thus, the two brothers, Christ and Thomas
(δίδυμοι), symbolize the male and female powers
of the Logos. In the English calendar the feast
of St. Thomas is the sixth in order, which again
connects it with the double potency.

The Epiphany occurs in the 6th week, and
39th day of the year. This festival signified the
manifestation of Christ, and in Greek *Epiphaneia*
yields 662 + 1 = 663, which is the diameter of a
circle having a circumference equal to the side of
the Holy Oblation. And the 39th day may stand
for the number $38\frac{1}{2}$, which is the square root of
1,480, while the 6th week probably refers to the
6 cabalistic steps, of which the body of the Microcosm is composed.

The Purification of the Blessed Virgin falls in the 10th week on the 66th day of the year. Now the number 10 is the cabalistic equivalent of the Bride, and 66 is the diameter of a circle 207 in circumference, while $207\frac{1}{3}$ is in its turn the diameter of a circle 651 in circumference, which is the diameter of a third circle whose circumference is 2,046, the diameter of Saturn's orbit.

The Annunciation of Mary falls in the 17th week, on the 117th day of the year. The number 17 is treated on p.   , and 117 is the diameter of a circle whose circumference is 367, the numerical equivalent of the word Venus.

The Invention of the Cross is commemorated in the 23rd week, and the 158th day of the year. And 158 is the diameter of a circle having a circumference of 496, the numerical equivalent of Malchuth, who personified the earth and sublunary world symbolized by the cross $\oplus$. Again, $158 \times 9\frac{1}{2} = 1,501$, and a cross inscribed in a vesica 1,501 long measures $(1,501 + 866 =)$ 2,368.

St. Mary the Magdalen is commemorated in the 34th week, and the 236th day of the year. And $34^2 = 1,156$, the side of a vesica 2,004 long, while 236 is the side of the New Jerusalem.

Lammas day falls in the 36th week, on the 246th day of the year. Now the sum of the numbers from 1 to 36 amounts to 666, and 246 is the diameter of a circle 773 in circumference, and 773 is the perimeter of the Holy Oblation if the sun's distance be taken at 10.

In the same week, the Transfiguration is commemorated on the 251st day of the year. And 251 is the diameter of a circle 788 in circumference, and $789\frac{1}{3}$ is the width of a vesica formed by two circles whose united width is 2,368.

The Name of Jesus[1] falls on the following day in the same week. And 252 is the length of a vesica 146 long, which is the width of the circles forming a vesica 48⅔ broad, or the square root of '2,368.

Holy Cross day is celebrated in the 42nd week and 290th day of the year. And $290 \times 3\frac{1}{7} = 911$.

All Saints' day occurs in the 49th week and the 338th day of the year. Now 48⅔ is the square root of 2,368, and 338, besides being the limb of a cross which measures 676 $(338 \times 2 = 676)$, is the diameter of a circle having a circumference of 1,062. (*See* Apollo.)

The feast of St. Catherine falls on the 361st day of the year, and 361 is the width of a vesica formed by two circles whose united width is 1,083, the radius of the moon. Ἡκατερινα yields 495, or ⅛th of the earth's radius, so the wheel of St. Catherine may be regarded as a symbol of the earth surrounded by the circles of the four elements.

Although chronology has been said to be the soul of history, there is yet another source from which literary composition received an inspiration corresponding to the divine afflatus breathed into the nostrils of Adam at his creation. For the structure of the law was like that of a man having a body and soul, the written word or Scriptures

---

[1] When Truth appeared to Marcus, the Gnostic, it is said that she "opened her mouth, and uttered a word. That word was a name, and the name was this one which we do know and speak of, viz., Christ Jesus. . . . This which thou knowest and seemest to possess, is not an ancient name. For thou possessest the sound of it merely, whilst thou art ignorant of its power. *For Jesus* (Ἰησοῦς) *is a name arithmetically symbolical,* consisting of six letters, *and is known* by all those *that belong to the called.*" (Irenæus, "Against Heresies," bk. i., ch. xiv.)

corresponding to the body, and the Tradition or
unwritten word to the soul. Now since the
written Law, as we all know, can only be interpreted by the oral tradition, it is highly important
that this spirit, which is said to vivify and impart
meaning to the letter, should be sought for and
studied. Perhaps to make the analogy between
the soul and the body more complete, the old
philosophers always kept the oral law a secret, so
that its operation was conducted invisibly and
inscrutably like its counterpart in nature. At any
rate the mysteries, which it unfolded to those who
knew it, have never been communicated to the
outer world.

The oral tradition of the Hebrews was also
double, being called Masorah and Cabala, or that
which was delivered and that which was received.
Now these two are presumably the Logos and
Psyche of the Greeks, or the double soul, which
was supposed to exist in the body of every man.
In a passage quoted by Menasseh Ben Israel
("Conciliator," vol. i., p. 207) it is said that angels,
in descending to the elemental world, incorporate
themselves with the law. The whole section is
purposely obscure, but the words associating the
soul of the law with the descent of angels to the
sublunary world, are clear enough. According to
R. Isaac Abarbanel, the name Elohim denotes
"the relation between the creative power that
bestows, and his creatures that receive; it is likewise applied to those created beings who by
means of their official situation, bestow on others
who receive. Hence angels are called Elohim, as
they are the divine instruments to bestow his
blessings on the world." Cornelius Agrippa
("Occult Philosophy," p. 215) mentions ten orders
of the blessed, with ten archangels, corresponding
to one of the cabalistic steps and one of the celes-

tial spheres, viz., Primum Mobile, Zodiac, Saturn, Jupiter, Mars, Sun, Venus, Mercury, Moon, and the elementary world.

We also learn from the Talmud, that "the distance from the earth to the firmament is 500 years journey, and so it is from each successive firmament to the next throughout the series of the seven heavens.[1] ' Now as I beheld the living creatures, behold one wheel upon the earth by the living creatures' (Ezek. i. 15). Rabbi Eleazar says, *it was an angel who stood upon the earth, and his head reached to the living creatures.* It is recorded in a Mishna that his name is Sandalphon, who towers above his fellow-angels to a height of 500 years' journey: he stands behind the chariot and binds crowns on the head of his creator." In the liturgy of the Feast of Tabernacles, it is said, that Sandalphon gathers in his hands the prayers of Israel, and, forming a wreath of them, he adjures it to ascend as an orb for the head of the Supreme King of Kings." (Hershon's "Talmudic Miscellany," p.

---

[1] To account for Moses having omitted to mention the creation of the planets or the angels, Bishop Wilkins quotes Mr. Wright and other authorities, as follows: "'Tis not the endeavour of Moses, or the Prophets, to discover any Mathematical or Philosophical subtilties, but rather to accommodate themselves to vulgar capacities, and ordinary speech, *as nurses are wont to use to their Infants.* . . . But 'tis certain (saith *Calvin*) that his purpose is to treat only of the visible form of the world, and those parts of it, which might be most easily understood by the Ignorant and Ruder sort of people, and therefore we are not to expect the discovery of any Natural Secret.   As for more hidden arts, they must be looked for elsewhere ; the Holy Ghost did here intend to instruct all without exception. . . . And therefore too, *Aquinas* observes, that he writes nothing of the Air, because that being invisible, the People knew not whether there were any such Body or no.   And for this reason St. *Jerom* also thinks, that there is nothing exprest concerning the creation of Angels because the rude and ignorant Vulgar were not so capable of apprehending their Natures" ("Discovery of a New World," 1684, p. 22, by John Wilkins, Bishop of Chester).

250).   The height of Sandalphon would be (500 ×
8 =) 4,000 years' journey, or 1 more than 3,999.
See p. 370.

Again, Plato's description of Eros (Love),
exactly agrees with this angel of the Hebrews.
" These spirits (δαίμονες) or intermediate powers,"
he says, " are many and diverse, and one of them
is Eros (Love).   He is a great spirit, and like all
spirits he is intermediate between the divine and
mortal. . . . He interprets between gods and men,
conveying and taking across the prayers and sacrifices of men, and to men the commands and replies
of the Gods ; he is the mediator who spans the
chasm which divides them, and therefore in him
all is bound together, and through him the arts of
the prophet and the priest, their sacrifices and
mysteries, and charms and all prophecy and incantation find their way.   For God mingles not with
man ; but through Eros all intercourse and converse of God with man, whether awake or asleep,
is carried on."   (Symposium.)

One of the difficulties which the theology of the
ancients attempted to explain was the problem of
human generation.   Having assumed that man
was a twofold being with a soul and a body, and
that his soul was a scintillation of the divine essence
derived from the sphere of the fixed stars or Milky
Way, it was necessary to suggest the means by
which the immortal soul reached its earthly dwelling.   For this purpose the ten cabalistic steps,
personified by Eros, Sandalphon, or Macroprosopus, were devised, and afforded the hypothetical
ladder by which souls descended to the elemental
world.   The five books of the Law written according to this mystical hypothesis, imitated by its
symbolical composition the order of creation.   But
the Mosaic method of philosophizing will perhaps
be made clearer by the testimony of numbers.

The Law was said to have been first written on a roll by Moses himself, from the B(*beth*) of *Brashith*, the first letter of the first word in Genesis to the L (*lamed*) of *Isral*, the last letter of the last word in Deuteronomy ("Talmud, Treatise, Bava bathra," ch. i., fol. 15). Thus the whole fabric of the law is included between these two letters. Now the numerical value of Beth is 2, and that of Lamed is 30; and $2 + 30 = 32$, which is the square root of 1,024, the radius of Saturn's orbit. Again, the two words *Brashith*, 913, and *Isral*, 541, express the twofold principle corresponding to Masorah and Cabala, whilst $913 + 541 = 1,454$, or one less than the value of Adam Kadmon, the celestial Adam or Macroprosopus, who in one sense comprehends the whole ten steps of the diagram in his body, and conveyed the spirit of life to the earth.

Since it was supposed that the generation of the world was accomplished after the manner of men, we must conceive the Macrocosm or celestial Adam stretched within the sphere of the Zodiac, so that the centre of his body (the phallus) coincides with the centre of the universe occupied by the earth and the elements. And since the earth was philosophically considered to be the mother or receptive power in the planetary system, she was figuratively said to have conceived and brought forth the primæval man, the earth-born Adam, the son of the supernal Adam. Thus, according to the Hebrews, the race of mortals was produced ; and the spirit of life having been implanted in the body of the First Man he transmitted it through Eve to all subsequent generations.

In the "Phædrus" of Plato, a treatise very apposite to the present inquiry, Socrates says, "The method of the Art of Rhetoric is in a manner the same as that of medicine. *Phædrus.* How

so? *Socrates*. In both it is requisite that nature
should be thoroughly investigated, the nature of
the body in the one, and the nature of the soul
in the other." Let us literally follow the advice
of Plato in investigating the progress of a human
soul as far as our natural powers of observation
will carry us. As far as human science can trace
it the human soul in its passage through life exists
in at least three distinct habitations, and in each
case under very different circumstances. Beyond
this, it may be said, that nothing else is positively
known. The germ of life, which ultimately becomes a human creature, first exists in the body
of the man, whom we call its father. In the act
of coition it is transmitted to the womb of the
woman, whom we call its mother; and in the third
stage of its known existence it is born into the
world where, as a man or woman, it remains till
death.

Although some philosophers supposed that at
the death of the body the soul evaporated and
ceased to exist, it was generally held as a reasonable hypothesis grounded upon the analogy of its
progressive existence, that the soul continued to
live after death, and by returning to the stars from
whence it came completed the cycle of its being.

The first abode occupied by the soul in its
mundane state is thus referred to in the New
Testament: "And as I may so say, Levi also,
who receiveth tithes, payed tithes in Abraham.
For he was yet in the loins of his father when
Melchisedec met him" (Heb. vii. 9, 10). The
transition from the first abode to the second
constitutes the soul's first death and birth. The
Greek initiate into the mysteries, having figuratively passed through the region of Hades, was
called διφυής, twice-born; and it was by the analogy
borne by the first dissolution to the last, that the

ancients argued their doctrine of immortality. The evidence and hope of the resurrection was commonly demonstrated by the rising again of the Phœnix after complete decay. St. Cyril of Jerusalem says that God, knowing man's unbelief, had provided the Phœnix to disclose his purpose. "This bird," as Clement writes, and as many more relate, "the only one of its race, going to the land of the Egyptians at revolutions of 500 years, shows forth the resurrection ; and this, not in desert places, lest the mystery which comes to pass should remain unknown, but in a notable city, that men might even handle what they disbelieve. For it makes itself a nest of frankincense and myrrh and other spices, and entering into this when its years are fulfilled, it evidently dies and moulders away. Then from the mouldering flesh of the dead a worm springs, and this worm when grown large is transformed into a bird, etc." (Cat. Lect. xviii.). The Phœnix is only another image of the Christ, whose crucifixion, burial and descent into Hell, and ultimate resurrection illustrate in another way the same order of nature.

The next stage of the soul's existence, when it reaches its second abode, is its period in the womb, the dark and gloomy place through which it was doomed to pass in its appointed course ; when, in the symbolical language of the Greeks, it makes its descent into Hades. An ample description of the regions of Tartarus is given by Plato in the "Phædo." "One of the chasms of the earth," he says, "is exceedingly large, and perforated through the entire earth, and is that which Homer speaks of, 'very far off, where is the most profound abyss beneath the earth,' which elsewhere both he and many other poets have called Tartaros. For into this chasm all rivers flow together, and from it flow out again." Plato, who always "moralized" his

fables, pretended (for the benefit of the populace)
that the *wicked* souls who were hurled into Tartaros
perished and never came out again. " But those
who are found to have lived an eminently holy life,
these are they, who, being freed and set at large
from these regions in the earth, as from a prison,
arrive at the pure abode above, and dwell in the
upper parts of the earth." [1]

The Christian idea of Hades did not differ from
that of Homer and Plato, as it is said of Christ in
the Epistle to the Ephesians: " Now that He
ascended, what is it but that he also descended first
into the lower parts of the earth ? " (ch. iv. 9):
and the following extract from Tertullian is to the
same purpose. " By ourselves the lower regions
are not supposed to be a bare cavity, nor some
subterranean sewer, but a vast deep space in the
interior of the earth, and a concealed recess in its
very bowels; inasmuch as we read that Christ in
His death spent three days in the heart of the
earth (Matt. xii. 40), that is, in the secret inner
recess which is hidden in the earth . . . therefore
keep at arm's length those who are too proud to
believe that the souls of the faithful deserve a
place in the lower regions. Those persons who
are 'servants above their Lord, and disciples
above their Master,' would no doubt spurn to
receive the comfort of the resurrection, if they
must expect it in Abraham's bosom " ("De Anima,"
cap. lv.).

The allusion above to Abraham's bosom is as
important as it is peculiar, since this expression

---

[1] In concluding the passage, that no one may be deceived,
he adds, "To affirm positively, indeed, that these things are as
I have described them, does not become a man of sense; that,
however, this or something of the kind takes place with respect
to our souls and their habitations—since our soul is certainly
immortal—this appears to be most fitting to be believed."

denotes in the Gospel the place prepared for the
reception of virtuous souls. Now everybody
knows that "there was a certain rich man, which
was clothed in purple and fine linen, and fared
sumptuously every day ; and there was a certain
beggar named Lazarus, who was laid at his gate,
full of sores, and desiring to be fed with the crumbs
which fell from the rich man's table : moreover the
dogs came and licked his sores. And it came to
pass that the beggar died, and was carried by the
angels [1] into Abraham's bosom : the rich man also
died and was buried : and in hell he lift up his
eyes, being in torments, and seeth Abraham afar
off, and Lazarus in his bosom. And he cried and
said, Father Abraham, have mercy on me, and
send Lazarus, that he may dip the tip of his finger
in water, and cool my tongue ; for I am tormented
in this flame," and so on (Luke, xvi. 19-24).

The word κόλπος, euphemistically translated
"bosom" in the text, means the womb. In a
previous chapter of the same treatise, Tertullian,
affirming the corporeal nature of the soul in hell,
draws attention to the fact that Lazarus is said to
have a finger and the rich man a tongue. Accordingly it may be supposed that Abraham's bosom
was also attached to a body. Now when Plato in
the "Phædo" is describing the parts and structure
of the earth it is evident that he is mystically
referring to a woman's body, the centre of which is
called by him Hades, and it may be concluded
that the κόλπος,[2] or "bosom" of Abraham, belongs to

---

[1] In the "Selections from the Prophetic Scriptures," the
soul is said to enter the womb, "introduced by one of the
angels who preside over generation" ("Ante-Nicene Library,"
vol. xxiv., p. 131).

[2] ὁ κόλπος Ἀβραάμ (Abraham's bosom) has the numerical
value of 685 (70 + 470 + 145), the diameter of a circle whose
circumference is 2,151, the number of years in the great month.
Ἀδης (Hell) yields 213, the diameter of a circle having a cir-

the same mystical body. We must consequently assume that the body of a woman was supposed by the philosophers to extend in an opposite direction to that of the Macrocosm in the manner depicted by Eliphas Levi, and the generative attributes thus meeting together in the middle of the universe explains the conjunction of the *omphalos* and *stauros* at the earth's centre. These two figures commonly symbolized by a Solomon's Seal will also represent the double soul of the law, Masorah and Cabala, the part of the man being to deliver, the part of the woman to receive.

On issuing from the womb, provided with a substantial body, the soul begins the third term of its mundane life as a man. Of its waxing and waning upon earth it is hardly necessary to speak. But to the philosophers the sacredness of the body consisted in its being the receptacle or temple of a spark of the vital essence which they called God, for such they considered to be the soul of man. And the human creature having reached the full limit of his development was endowed with the supreme faculty of transmitting a portion of the soul within him, and thereby rendering himself immortal by adding a new link in the continuous chain of life whose beginning was in heaven.

This much at least was knowledge : and those ascertained facts set forth in symbols and parables constituted the gnosis imparted to initiates at the celebration of the mysteries. The attainment of immortality wherein a man could reproduce himself by sending forth a new born soul into the depths of futurity was regarded as the utmost function of manhood, and since the man gave up his soul and the woman gave it back nourished

cumference of 671, the numerical equivalent of Thorah and Adonai, the Bride. The patriarch must, of course, be considered to be androgynous.

with her blood and covered with her flesh, they looked upon this act as a work of sacrifice, as well as an imperative duty.

Tertullian tells us more than once that all souls flow from Adam.[1] For the chain of life was conceived like a series of threads which followed backwards from son to father converge and meet in the first thread generated by the earth-born Adam. So when the body, worn out with age, succumbed at last to death, it was honoured with funeral rites, enacted in imitation of that former parting at the gates of Hades. Such was the meaning of the Egyptian ceremonies bestowed upon their dead, for by the analogy of the soul's entrance into the world or body, with faith and hope they argued its exit into another, and looked forward to the completion of the full span of life when carried by the seven spirits, demons, angels, or wanderers (πλανῆται) they should ascend to the firmament and join the everlasting choir of the stars. Or, as Origen puts it, " we hope, after the troubles and struggles which we suffer here, to reach the highest heavens, and receiving, agreeably to the teaching of Jesus, the fountains of water that spring up unto eternal life, and being filled with the rivers of knowledge, shall be united with those waters that are said to be above the heavens, and which praise His name. As many of us as praise Him shall not be carried about by the revolution of the heaven, but shall be ever engaged in the contemplation of the invisible

[1] That this was the doctrine of the mysteries is evident from the following speech of Pythagoras, who appears in Lucian's dialogue reincarnated in a cock. "How this soul of mine, which came originally from Apollo, flew down to earth and got into a human body as a punishment for its crimes it would be tedious to recount : besides those are things which it is neither lawful for me to tell or you to hear" ("The Cock and the Cobbler").

things of God" ("Against Celsus," bk. vi., ch. xx.).

The custom of burying the dead in a contracted position (the knees being drawn up to the head) once practised by the ancient Peruvians and Egyptians still prevails in certain parts of Africa. "Some writers have expressed the opinion that the object of burying a person in this position was to imitate that of a child in the womb of its mother, so that the man or woman's entrance into another world should to some extent resemble that of their entrance into this world" (H. N. Hutchinson, "Prehistoric Man," p. 209).

The process of creation may be expressed by inscribing the cabalistic diagram in the upper hemisphere, so that the apex or crown reaches to the Milky Way, while the tenth step will coincide with the earth. By this means the ladder for the descent of the soul may be reduced to specific measures, determining the sizes of the figures of which it is composed. Geometrically, the symbols of the three persons of the triad are, firstly, a pyramid or triangle; secondly, a cube or hexagon, a circle, or a saltire; thirdly, a vesica or rhombus, or a cross.

ΠΥΡΑΜΙΣ	831	
ΚΥΒΟΣ	692	} 1,174
ΡΟΜΒΟΣ	482	

$$\overline{ 2,005 }$$

The manner of ascertaining their relative sizes may be illustrated thus. The numerical value of the name Macrocosmos is 831. Now, if the first three steps be relegated to a triangle having a perimeter of 832·5, the base of the triangle will be 386·5 and its sides 222·9 (386·5 : 222·9 : : 26 : 15). And since the steps from 1 to 9 are arranged in a

figure of the proportion of 26 : 15 the distance from
the first to the ninth step will be 670 (ὁ κόσμος). By
adding a rhombus, whose sides are 222·9, to represent the Bride who occupies the tenth step, the
diagram is complete and it only remains to depict
upon it the figures of the persons. In the Zohar
we are told that Macroprosopos is only represented
by his head, which is fully described in the " Lesser
Holy Assembly." Now, if the greater man of
Cesariano be drawn so as to occupy the entire
extent of the diagram, his head will be found to
be contained within the triangle formed by the first
three steps which properly belong to him. The
height of his body measures 892·9, which is 1 and
a fraction more than the value of *Ouranos*, Heaven,
the Father of the Gods, according to Hesiod.

Another notable fact respecting the height of
Macrocosmos in the diagram is that a rood-
cross 892 high will crucify a man in a square
having a perimeter of 1,656, the distance of the
tropics from the equator measured on the earth's
circumference; and its extreme length is 1,274¾,
or the height of a cross which will crucify a man
in a square having a perimeter of 2,368.

Then, if a circle be described round his body,
and a square inscribed within it, we obtain a square
whose sides are 630. When the figure of the
Microcosm is stretched within its four corners, the
lines indicating the emanations from the second
and third steps mark his forehead with a cross by
their intersection.[1]

The sides of the rhombus denoting the Bride
are 222·9 or in a round number 223, the numerical

---

[1] This point is called Däath, knowledge, and it is said in the
" Lesser Holy Assembly" (chap. xx., par. 709-710): "The
masculine power is extended through Däath; and the Assemblies
and Conclaves are filled. It commenceth from the beginning
of the skull, etc."

equivalent of the word "Ἀιδης, Hades, which has
been shown to be synonymous with the earth or
womb. The circle inscribed within the rhombus
has a diameter of 193·2 or nearly that of the Zodiac
if the sun's distance be taken at 10. The distance
from the first to the tenth step is 781·4, the
numerical equivalent of the word *Sophia*, wisdom,
while the circumference of the circle including the
whole diagram ($892 \times 3\frac{1}{7}$) is 2,803, which by transposition becomes 2,083, the side of the Holy
Oblation.

That the pictures of the Christian Trinity were
founded upon this diagram it is impossible to
doubt. There is one in the National Gallery
(No. 1478) by Giovanni Mansueti, in which the
cabalistic symbolism is very plainly discernible.
The persons of the Great Triad are depicted in
the ordinary canonical manner. The Father is
seated with Christ on the Cross in front of Him,
the Dove appearing to proceed from the Father
to the Son. Mary the Magdalene is represented
upon the ground clasping the foot of the Cross
and evidently personifying the tenth step. Mary
the Virgin and St. John stand on either side, while
the full number of the ten steps are completed in
the persons of other saints.

With the preceding description in his mind, the
reader will perhaps more clearly understand the
following passage from the " Lesser Holy Assembly " concerning the members of Microprosopos. " 734. The Male is extended in right and
left, through the inheritance which he receiveth
(*i. e.*, from the second and third steps). 735. But
whensoever the colours are mingled together then
is He called Tiphereth, and the whole body is
formed into a tree (the Autz-Ha-Chaiim, or Tree
of Life),[1] great and strong, and fair and beautiful,

[1] Tiphereth, Beauty, is the sixth step. It marks the centre

Dan. iv. 11. 737. His arms are right and left.
In the right arm is Chesed, life; in the left is
Geburah, death. 738. Through Däath are His
inner parts formed, and they fill the Assemblies
and Conclaves, as we have said. 739. For thus
is it written: 'And through Däath shall the Conclaves be filled.' 740. Afterwards is his body
extended into two thighs, et intra hæc continentur
duo renes, duo testiculi masculini. 741. Omne
enim oleum, et dignitas, et vis masculi e toto cor-
pore in istis congregatur; nam omnes exercitus,
qui prodeunt ab iis, omnes prodeunt et morantur
in orificio membri genitalis. 742. And therefore
are they called Tzabaoth, the Armies; and they
are Victory (the seventh step) and Glory (the
eighth). For Beauty is Tetragrammaton, but
Victory and Glory are the armies; hence cometh
that name, Tetragrammaton Tzabaoth. 743.
Membrum masculi est extremitas totius corporis,
et vocatur yesod, fundamentum; et hic est gradus
ille qui mitigat fœminam. For every desire of
the male is toward the female. 744. Per hoc
fundamentum ille ingreditur in fœminam; in locum
qui vocatur Tzion et Jerusalem. Nam hic est
locus tegendus fœminæ, et in uxore vocatur uterus.
745. And hence is Tetragrammaton Tzabaoth
called Yesod, the Foundation (the ninth step).
Also it is written Ps. cxxxii. 13: 'Since Tetragrammaton hath chosen Tzion to be a habitation
for himself, He hath desired her.' 746. When
Matronitha, the mother, is separated and conjoined
with the King face to face in the excellence of the
Sabbath, all things become one body. 747. And
then the Holy One—blessed be He!—sitteth on
His throne, and all things are called the Complete

of the figure, and is consequently the place occupied by the
phallos of Macrocosmos and the *omphalos* of Microcosmos.
Astronomically it is the sun.

Name, the Holy Name. Blessed be His Name for ever, and unto the ages of the ages! 748. All these words have I kept back unto this day, which is crowned by them for the world to come." Such is said to have been the dying revelation of Rabbi Schimeon in which he unfolded, with passing breath and in an ecstasy of joy, the inmost verity of the Hebrew Law.

Since the ten steps of the diagram astronomically represent the radius or interval between the firmament and the earth, the tenth step being assigned to the world in the middle of the universe, it is necessary to repeat the figure twice in order to span the diameter of the sphere. In that case the two figures, the one occupying the upper hemisphere and the other the lower, provide a ladder by which souls descending to the earth may return to heaven; and by thus completing the diagram there is presented a perfect image of the double soul of the world, shadowing forth the two laws, Masorah and Cabala, by the male power above and the female below, and likewise the two trees, the one of knowledge, the other of life, the two testaments, the old and new, comprehending the mystic cycle of birth, death, and resurrection. The man belonging to the upper hemisphere may be conceived standing upright in the midst of the spheres with his feet upon the earth, like the figure of the Macrocosm in Caxton's " Mirror of the World." He is there shown in the circle four times repeated, thus producing the four arms of a cross. All four have their feet upon the earth, so that the figure in the lower hemisphere stands head downwards. But the two bodies may also be stretched into a semicircle with their arms extended like those figures of the Egyptians, so that the man occupies half the circumference of the Zodiac from Aries to Virgo, and the woman the lower half from Libra to Pisces. In astrology the signs are alternately male and female, so that when distributed to the various members of the body they comprise the two-fold Microcosm, the King and the Bride.

Several writers have shown that the symbols of the Hebrew alphabet, from Aleph to Yod, correspond to the ten cabalistic steps. The Greeks also distributed the 24 letters of their alphabet to the members of the human body. Now the circumference of the world has been from time immemorial divided into 24 hour-circles, and if the double figure, just described, be bent into a circle composed of 24 steps, each of these may be identified with a letter of the alphabet. In Kircher's representation of the diagram (p. 51) each of the 22 Hebrew letters is assigned to one of the "canals" through which the soul flows from step to step, but there is good reason for believing that the letters were associated with the steps themselves in the order which we shall now endeavour to explain.

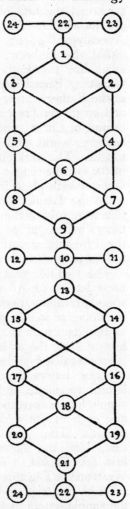

FIG. 27.—THE CABALISTIC ORDER AS FAR AS THE TWENTY-FOURTH STEP.

Grammar, the first of the seven sciences which governed the arts of antiquity, is derived from γράμμα, a letter. According to Brocardo ("On the Apocalypse," p. 167, translated by James Sanford, 1582), the Hebrew, Greek, and Latin alphabets symbolize the Father, the Son, and the Holy Ghost. "Because ye olde Testament and worke of the Father was wrytten in the Hebrew tongue : and so the Hebrew alphabet continued unto the coming of Christ : and there *according to a certayne order* ye worke doth end wrytten in ye Hebrew tongue. The worke of the Sonne ensueth wrytten in the Greeke tongue : . . . ye worke of the Holy Ghost taketh place in ye Lord's second cominge, while the Latine tonge doth declare the eventes that were told of things to come, and openeth the things written in ye Lawe, in ye Gosple, and in the Prophets, repeating all mysteries in ye two former tongues from the beginning."

The tradition that the Elohim taught the Hebrew letters to Adam is of course a figure of speech, meaning, perhaps, that as all the parts of the universe were represented by the letters, and as the stars were considered to be the manifestation of God, the alphabet might be said to have been revealed from heaven. The number of the Hebrew letters is 22, consisting of 3 mother-letters, 12 simple, and 7 double. Each of the 12 simple letters corresponds to a sign of the Zodiac, and each of the 7 double letters to one of the planets. The 3 mother-letters are *Aleph*, the first, *Mem*, the thirteenth, and *Shin*, the twenty-first (*see* Cabala, "Yetsirah," translated by Dr. Westcott). The three divisions appear to denote the cabalistic triad, corresponding to Macrocosmos, the simple letters to Microcosmos, and the double letters to the Bride. By computing their respective numerical values, they yield the following numbers :

The 3 mother-letters (empyreum) . 341
 „ 12 simple letters (zodiac) . 445 ⎫
 „ 7 double letters (planets) . 709 ⎭ 1,154
                                      ——
                                    1,495

The sum of the 3 mother-letters is 341, and the length of a vesica 341 broad is 592, which is the width of a rhombus having a perimeter of 2,368 ; and 341 multiplied by 3 produces 1,023, the radius of Saturn's orbit. Then the width of a vesica 445 broad is 771, the perimeter of the Holy Oblation taking the sun's distance at 10 (216 : 2,083·3 : : 20 : 192·9). The third number, 709, is the length of a vesica, which will contain a rhombus whose sides are equal to those of the New Jerusalem. It is also the side of a square whose diagonals measure 2,004, the value of the names of the four elements in Greek, and 710 is the numerical equivalent of *Pneuma Hagion*, the Holy Ghost. Lastly if the two parts of the body of the Microcosm are united we get the number (445 + 709 =) 1,154, or the length of a vesica 666 broad.

In their elaborate " refutations " of the Gnostic heresies, the Fathers reveal, that the Greeks divided and distinguished their letters in much the same manner as the Hebrews, but no complete exposition of their system exists. In a treatise, " Against all Heresies," attributed to Tertullian (ch. v.), it is said : " After these there were not wanting a Marcus and Colarbasus, composing a novel heresy out of the Greek alphabet. For they affirm, that without those letters *Truth* cannot be found : nay more, *that in those letters the whole plenitude and perfection of truth is comprised :* for this was why Christ said, ' I am the Alpha and the Omega.' "[1]

[1] This is the Colarbasus who, according to Hippolytus

At the beginning of the sixteenth century Cornelius Agrippa says that "the vowels in the Greek tongue, viz., α ε η ι ο υ ω answer to the seven planets, β γ δ ζ κ λ μ ν π ρ σ τ are attributed to the 12 signs of the Zodiac, the other five, θ ξ φ χ ψ, represent the four elements, and the Spirit of the world. Amongst the Latine there is the same signification of them. For the five vowels, A E I O U, and J and V consonants, are ascribed to the seven planets; but the consonants, B C D F G L M N P R S T, are answerable to the twelve signs. The rest, viz., K Q X Z, make four elements. H, the aspiration, represents the Spirit of the World. Y, because it is a Greek word, and not a Latine character, and serving only to Greek words, follows the nature of its idiome" ("Occult Philosophy," bk. i., ch. 74).

Again we know from Manilius that the Roman astrologers located the signs of the Zodiac throughout the members of the body, and Marcus similarly ascribed two of the 24 letters to each of the 12 divisions, that the body, being a type of the alphabet as well as the universe, might serve as a rule for literary art.

According to Manilius.		According to Irenæus.	
Head	♈	Head . . .	A Ω
Neck	♉	Neck . . .	B Ψ
Arms and Shoulders	♊	Shoulders .	Γ X

("Ref.," bk. iv., ch. xiii.), "as if, having propounded great conclusions, and supposed things worthy of reason . . . . attempts to explain religion by measures and numbers." Now the number deduced from A καὶ Ω is 832 (φαλλός). In the Apocalypse, where the statement occurs, it is written in some manuscripts, τὸ Ἄλφα, καὶ τὸ Ὠμέγα (902 + 31 + 1219 =) 2152, or even Ἄλφα καὶ Ω (532 + 31 + 800 =) 1363 + 3 = 1366 (φαλλός κτείς), and 532 + 800 = 1332 ÷ 2 = 666. Again, A 1 + Ω 800 = 801, which Irenæus tells us is equivalent by Gematria to περιστερά, the Dove or Holy Ghost, and 800 is the perimeter of the new Jerusalem (200 × 4 = 800).

According to Manilius.		According to Irenæus.		
Breast	♋	Breast . .	Δ	Φ
Shoulder-blades . .	♌	Diaphragm .	E	Υ
Flank	♍	Belly . . .	Z	T
Buttocks	♎	Genitalia .	H	Σ
Groin	♏	Thighs . .	Θ	P
Thighs	♐	Knees . .	I	Π
Knees	♑	Shins . . .	K	O
Legs	♒	Ankles . .	Λ	Ξ
Feet	♓	Feet . . .	M	N

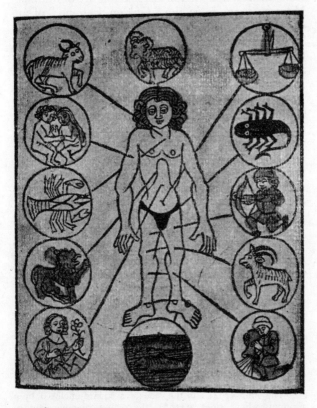

FIG. 28.—THE MICROCOSM ACCORDING TO THE ASTROLOGERS.
FROM AN ALMANAC OF THE FIFTEENTH CENTURY.

B B

The total value of the 24 letters is 3,999, so the
body to which they are assigned may be symbolically expressed by the three measures 2,093, 1,480
and 426,[1] whose sum is 3,999.   Further, taking
the proportions of a human figure to be 6 : 1
a body 3,999 high is 666½ broad.   These numbers
shadowing forth the figure of Christ and his Bride,
suggest a reason for the name, Truth ('Αλήθεια),
being bestowed upon the visionary figure of Marcus.
Mention is made in the " Golden Legend " of an
early rite practised at the dedication of a church.
The letters of the alphabet were inscribed on the
floor in the form of a cross, which was no doubt
an obscure way of indicating the body of the
Microcosm.

The symbolical association of the body with
letters, the elements of words and the basis of
literature, discloses the last aspect of the canon to
which we shall allude, namely, that application of
it which was called Rhetoric.   From its derivation
the second of the seven sciences seems to have
meant what the Hebrews called Cabala, or Tradition, the word Ῥητορική, 616, coming from Ῥήτρη,
516, an unwritten or oral law.   Thus the traditional
laws of Lycurgus were called Ῥῆτραι, 511 ; and
Rhetoric may be taken to mean the unwritten law
or canon of speech which supplied the means of
effecting an exact analogy between a set oration
and the order of the universe—the conformity of
any work to that order making it " canonical."
It is probably due to the objections of the Puritans
that the art of Rhetoric is no longer taught, and
that the methods of its former professors have
passed into oblivion.   Plato, however, has made
the old manner of oratorical composition the subject

[1] The number 426 is the side of a square enclosed by a
rhombus whose sides are 671, the numerical equivalent of
Adonai the Bride, or third person of the Triad.

of discussion in the " Phædrus." Socrates is there made to say, after inquiring whether the sentences in a speech are written in any express order, " but this, at least, I think you will allow that every speech ought to be put together like a living creature, with a body of its own, so as neither to be without head nor without feet, but to have both middle and extremities ;" and again, " All great arts require a subtle and speculative research into the law of nature. . . . But do you think it possible rightly to understand the nature of the soul, without understanding the nature of the universe ? "

In the " Recognitions " of Clement, who lived in the Apostolic age and was a companion and disciple of St. Peter, the rhetorical manner of speech is alluded to more than once. In the twenty-first chapter (bk. i.), speaking of the postponement of his debate with Simon Magus, the apostle says, " I believe that it has been done by the providence of God for your advantage : that I may be able in this interval of seven days to expound to you the method of our faith without any distraction, and the *order continuously* according to the tradition of the true Prophet, who alone knows the past as it was, the present as it is, and the future as it shall be : which things were indeed *plainly spoken* by Him, but *not plainly written :*[1] so much so that they

[1] " Our prophets did know of greater things than any in the Scriptures, but which they did not commit to writing. Ezekiel, *e.g.*, received a roll, written within and without, in which were contained 'lamentations,' and 'songs,' and 'denunciations ;' but at the command of the Logos he swallowed the book in order that its contents might not be written, and so made known to unworthy persons. John also is recorded to have seen and done a similar thing. Nay, Paul even heard 'unspeakable words, which it is not lawful for a man to utter.' And it is related of Jesus, who was greater than all those, that He conversed with His disciples in private, and especially in their secret retreats, concerning the Gospel of God ; but the words which he uttered have not been preserved, because it

cannot be understood without an expounder."
And in the twenty-fourth chapter (bk. iii.), he declares that "the teaching of all doctrine has a
certain order and there are some things which must
be delivered first, others in the second place, and
others in the third, and so all in their order : and
if those things be delivered in their order, they
become plain : but if they be brought forward out
of order they will seem to be spoken against reason.
And therefore order is to be observed above all
things, if we seek for the purpose of finding what
we seek. For he who enters rightly upon the
road will observe the second place in due order,
and from the second will more easily find the third ;
and the further he proceeds so much the more will
the way of knowledge become open to him even
till he arrive at the City of Truth."

Lord Bacon has also left some dark hints on the
mystic or *traditional* teaching of Rhetoric. In the
"Advancement of Learning" (bk. ii., ch. 2), he
says, " Let us now come to the doctrine concerning
the Method of Speech. This hath been handled
as a part of Logick, so it hath found a place in
Rhetorick by the name of Disposition. But the
placing of it as a part of the Train of other Arts,
hath been the cause that many things which refer
unto it, and are useful to be known, are preter-
missed : wherefore we thought good to constitute a
substantial and principal doctrine touching *Method*,
which by a general name we call the *wisdom of
Tradition*. . . .

" Wherefore let the first difference of Method be
set down to be either Magistral or Initiative ;
neither do we understand the word *initiative*, as if
this should lay the groundwork, the other raise the

appeared to the evangelists that they could not be adequately
conveyed to the multitude in writing or in speech " (Origen,
" Against Celsus," Bk. vi., ch. 6).

perfect building of sciences ; but in a far different sense (borrowing the word from sacred ceremonies), we call that *Initiative Method* which discloses and unveils the mysteries of knowledges. . . . The one delivers popular science fit for learners ; the other, sciences as to the sons of science . . . and we call it *Traditionem lampadis*, the Delivery of the Lamp, or the method bequeathed to the Sons of Sapience.

"Another diversity of Method followeth. . . . In this both these methods agree, that they separate the vulgar auditors from the select. . . . Let therefore the distinction of them be this, that the one is an exoterical, or revealed ; the other an acroamatical, or concealed method. For the same difference the ancients specially observed in publishing books. . . . So the Acroamatic Method was in use with the writers of former ages . . . that by the intricate envelopings of *Delivery*, the profane and vulgar may be removed from the secrets of sciences ; and they only admitted which had either acquired the interpretation of parables by tradition from their teachers ; or by the sharpness and subtilty of their own wit, could pierce the veil."

On the same subject Theophilus Gale asserts, "that the majestie of the Scripture style was the original idea and exemplar of that sublimitie of speech or Rhetorick, in use amongst the heathens, we may conjecture from the consideration of those particular Canons which are given by Pagan Rhetoricians or observed in their choicest pieces of oratorie ; but nowhere to be found in such a degree of perfection as in the sacred scriptures. The most ancient piece of Rhetorick or oratorie commended and practised by Heathen masters of speech consisted in the right framing and application of Metaphors, Allegories, and other Symbolick images, sensible forms and similitudes, whereby the Ancients were wont to paint forth or give lively

colours to their *more choice* and *hidden* notions and
things. And the great Canon on which they
founded this artificial mode of expressing things
was this : ' Sensible formes are but imitates of In-
telligibles ' " ("Court of the Gentiles," vol. i., p.
382).

The most careless reader who has merely turned
over the leaves of a few old books cannot have
failed to notice the striking difference between
them and the works of the present day. The
reason for this manifest diversity seems to be that
nowadays the old canon of rhetoric, which pre-
scribed the order of a discourse, has ceased to be
used in literary composition. And since the preceding quotations refer to the existence of a definite
rule determining the symbolic form of a speech we
shall now endeavour to show more specifically what
that canon was and how it was applied.

Each letter of the Hebrew or Phœnician alphabet
has a symbol corresponding to it. Nothing appears
to be known of these primitive symbols now but
their names ; however, in the twenty-two trump
cards of the Tarot we possess a series of hieroglyphs corresponding to the letters of the Hebrew
alphabet. The origin of these twenty-two cards is
dubious, but it has been surmized that they are of
Egyptian extraction. In any case they were connected with the Hebrew letters in the fifteenth
century, specimens of that date being still extant,
and they certainly represent an authentic and fundamental version of the ideas formerly associated
with the primitive alphabet believed to be of
Phœnician origin.[1]

---

[1] " The Phœnicians who came with Cadmus . . . . introduced . . . . amongst other things letters, with which, as I
conceive, the Greeks were unacquainted. These were at first
such as the Phœnicians themselves indiscriminately use ; in
process of time, however, they were changed both in sound and

Since the ten steps and the twenty-two letters
are said to be the foundation of all things (Yetsirah)
by arranging the letters progressively according to
the order of the diagram, we get a continuous
sequence of hieroglyphs following the downward
and upward course of the soul as it enters and
leaves a body on the earth.   A glance at the
figure (p. 365) will explain the disposition of the
letters.   They agree with the order of the steps as
far as the tenth, then the eleventh and twelfth are
added to mark the two equinoctial points on the
horizon or equator.   The thirteenth step corresponds to the first of the ten lower steps, the last
of which is the twenty-second.   To complete the
cycle two more steps are required, as in the case of
the eleventh and twelfth, making altogether twenty-
four, the final number of the Greek letters.   These
symbols recurring in regular order may be compared to a circle of twenty-four divisions corresponding to the meridians of the earth's circum-

form. . . . I myself have seen in the temple of the Ismenian
Apollo at Thebes, in Bœotia, these Cadmean letters inscribed
upon some tripods" (Herod. v. 58; see also Diod., v. 24;
Plin. v. 12, vii. 56; "Tacit.," Ann., xi. 14; and Euseb., "Chron.,"
can. i. 13).   The similarity between the Phœnician, Greek, and
Hebrew alphabets will be evident upon a reference to Rawlinson's "History of Phœnicia" (p. 379).   Mr. Rawlinson observes
that the people who invented letters have left us no literature—
the Sanchoniathon being only known in a Greek translation,
and the inscriptions being few and of limited range.   But he
does not notice what is even more curious, that the Hebrews,
whose alphabet (according to the traditions) was far older than
that of the Phœnicians, have left neither inscriptions nor docu-
ments of any antiquity.   The MSS. of the Hebrew Bible begin
to appear about the tenth century A.D.   There is exhibited in
the British Museum the cast of a single stone, found at Jerusalem, in the valley of Jehoshaphat, and inscribed with what
are presumed to be the local characters.   The date of the inscription, however, is unknown.   Mr. Rawlinson does not say
whether it is from this source that the "old Hebrew letters"
printed in his table are taken.

ference or to an endless chain capable of infinite extension, and any literary composition might be constructed to set forth the sequence of ideas thus established. In fact the rhetorical canon enabled the poet or philosopher to inspire his work with an invisible spirit in the semblance of that which also animated the universal scheme of nature, and gave his writing an allegorical sense hidden from the vulgar or uninstructed reader.

The upper half of the diagram symbolized the germ of life in its descent or fall, the lower half the ascent or resurrection—the two together embodying the entire compass of human existence. The great canonical works of the Greeks and Christians appear to be arranged in accordance with this division. The Old Testament in describing the events from the generation of the world to the incarnation of Christ metaphorically illustrates the "fall" of the soul from heaven to earth, the deity of the Hebrew writers being conceived as residing in heaven. But in the second of the two Testaments God becomes incarnate upon earth and, as Athanasius says ("Incarnation of Jesus Christ"), "What Adam brought down from heaven to earth [1] Christ carried up from earth to heaven." In this aspect the Iliad and the Odyssey accord with the Christian Testaments, for the epic of the Trojan war affords an exact parallel to the mystical history of the scriptures. The Greek heroes who set sail against Troy (the sublunary world) are, like the patriarchs, incarnations of the sephiroth.[2] Their encounter with the Trojans,

---

[1] According to Origen, "the soul of our Saviour was the same that was in Adam" (Preface to Henry More's Works, p. xxiii). And we learn from the Talmud that "after Adam sinned his soul passed into David, and the latter having sinned it passed into the Messiah" (Hershon's "Miscell.," p. 325).

[2] Metrodorus of Lampsacus, who died B.C. 464, declared

and subsequent introduction into the "city" in the wooden horse represent the soul on its way to earth ; the dispersal of the armies (*Tzabaoth*) with the voyage of Odysseus and his descent into Hell symbolize the second stage of the allegory.

The Egyptian "Book of the Dead," as compiled in the Turin manuscript of the Ptolemaic period, consists of twenty-two books and apparently follows the same symbolical order as the works of the Greeks ; and above all, Dante's "Divine Comedy," the great epic of the middle ages, is a conspicuous illustration of the mystical *rhetre* or tradition of antiquity. In fact, wherever we find in ancient art a series of designs or parts making up a whole work, it will appear on examination that the order of the divisions is canonical. Such are books of emblems from the hieroglyphs of Horapollo and the Icones of Philostratus downwards. In itineraries like that of Pausanias or Sir John Mandeville, or in the description of cities like the Mirabilia Romæ the same mystical rule seems to be observed. Whenever there is a sequence in the painted or sculptured ornaments of a temple they are disposed in like order. The verses and stanzas of the old poets, the paragraphs and chapters of the prose writers may be devised with similar purpose, so that the allegory may be expressed with all the manifold resources of pictorial, plastic, or literary art.

To fully substantiate so sweeping a generalization would of course require nothing less than

"that neither Hera, nor Athene, or Zeus are what those persons suppose who consecrate to them sacred enclosures and groves, but are parts of Nature and certain arrangements of the Elements." And he said that Hector, Achilles, Agamemnon, with Helen and Paris were merely allegorical creations, and never had any real existence (Tatian, "Address to the Greeks," ch. xxi.). Plato, Eratosthenes, Strabo, and presumably all but the ignorant and vulgar were of the same opinion.

a whole volume of evidence in its support instead
of the few isolated notes which must conclude our
investigations for the present.   However, having
something further to say on the subject, we hope
that a final judgment may be postponed, till the
question receives a more adequate and systematic
treatment.

Francis Roberts ("Key of the Bible," 1649)
gives certain rules for the gaining of scripture-
knowledge.   On page 34, he advises "the prudent
use of *Logick*, for orderly and methodical resolu-
tion of the text, and the subservient helps of other
Arts as *Rhetorick, Natural Philosophy*, etc., without which it is impossible satisfactorily to interpret
the scriptures.   For, as Ambrose well observes,
'though Penmen of Scripture wrote not according
to Art . . . yet they that have written of Art,
have found an Art in their writings.'"   The Jews
divided the Old Testament like the Iliad into
twenty-four books, and these again had a threefold
division corresponding to the three persons of the
great triad of the cabala.   The Law, consisting of
five books and fifty-four [1] sections (*siderim*) or
"orders," constitutes the first division.   The Prophets, or second division, included the following
eight works :—Joshua, Judges, Samuel, and Kings,
together with Isaiah, Jeremiah, Ezekiel, and the
Twelve minor Prophets.   The third division, called
the Writings (*Hagiographa*) was composed of the
eleven remaining books, namely, Ruth, Psalms,
Job, Proverbs, Ecclesiastes, Song of Songs,
Lamentations, Daniel, Esther, Ezra (with Nehe-
miah), and Chronicles.   In the Articles of the
English Church these are the twenty-four books
which are named as canonical, but they follow a
different order.   According to Josephus and St.

[1] The sum of the numbers from 1 to 54 is 1,485.

Cyril, however, the canon consisted of only twenty-two books. Thus it would appear to be impossible to make the twenty-two or twenty-four books agree with a set order unless their hieroglyphic meaning were capable of being transferred from one symbol to another. But although this might be done, we find that amongst Christians the sequence of the books was one of the secrets imparted to initiates at their preparation for baptism. In his fourth lecture St. Cyril enumerates them in what was evidently their esoteric order, by which their true symbolic significance could be ascertained, and it may be accepted as the traditional order having the authority of the Church.

In treating the cabalistic steps we have heretofore considered that they represented the elements, the Zodiac with the seven planets, and the Primum Mobile ; but the celestial circles may be extended by the addition of nine angelic spheres, while each of the four elements may be counted separately, thus making twenty-two circles or steps. One of the engravings by De Bry in Fludd's " Microcosmi Historia " (p. 93) thus illustrates the soul's progress through the universe. The germ is depicted as a winged head surrounded by luminous rays like a star. It is shown to descend through the twenty-two spheres to the body of Adam drawn in microcosmic fashion upon the earth. Again, on page 219 of the same work, the ascent of the soul from earth to heaven is depicted in the form of a spiral having twenty-two rings, with the Hebrew letters inscribed upon them, and a similar arrangement of the celestial spheres. Therefore the centre of the universe may be computed at the twenty-second step as well as the tenth.

Rhetoric was the art of saying one thing and meaning another. And it was practised with so much subtilty by old writers that in a treatise

HEBREW AND CHALDEE ALPHABET, WITH THE HIEROGLYPHS CORRESPONDING TO THE LETTERS.

St. Cyril's Canon	Roman equivalent	The Hebrew Letters, their names and significations		The Symbols of the Tarot	The ten steps of the Cabala	EMP.
1. Genesis	A	*Aleph*, ox	Mother	The Juggler	Crown	
2. Exodus	B	*Beth*, house	☽	The High Priestess	Wisdom	✳
3. Leviticus	G	*Gimel*, camel	♀	The Empress	Understanding	♄
4. Numbers	D	*Daleth*, door	♃	The Emperor	Mercy	♃
5. Deuteronomy	H	*He*, window	♈	The Pope	Strength	♂
6. Joshua	V	*Vau*, peg	♉	The Lovers	Beauty	☉
7. Ruth	Z	*Zayin*, sword	♊	The Chariot	Victory	☉ ♀
8. Judges	CH	*Cheth*, enclosure	♋	Justice	Splendour	☿
9. Kings	T	*Teth*, serpent	♌	The Hermit	Foundation	☽
10. Chronicles	I	*Yod*, hand	♍	The Wheel of Fortune	Bride	⊕
11. Esdras	K	*Caph*, palm		Strength.		
12. Esther	L	*Lamed*, ox-goad	♎	The Hanged Man.		
13. Job	M	*Menn*, water	Mother	Death.		
14. Psalms	N	*Nun*, fish	♏	Temperance.		
15. Proverbs	S	*Samekh*, prop	♐	The Devil.		
16. Ecclesiastes	O	*Ayin*, eye	♑	The Lightning-struck Tower.		
17. Song of Songs	P	*Pe*, mouth	♒	The Stars.		
18. Twelve Prophets	Tz	*Tzaddi*, fishing-hook		The Moon.		
19. Esaias	Q	*Qoph*, back of the head	♓	The Sun.		
20. Jeremaias	R	*Resh*, head		The Judgment.		
21. Ezekiel	SH	*Shin*, tooth	Mother	The Mate.		
22. Daniel	TH	*Tau*, cross	☉	The World.		

before us the tropes and figures of speech are distinguished in ninety-four different ways. So it is not always easy to follow the metaphorical allusions. No one, of course, can readily perceive the affinity between the divisions of a canonical work and the twenty-two hieroglyphs without first committing the latter to memory. Then comes the most serious difficulty—that of discerning the various meanings of each. An explicit interpretation of them does not exist, but the " Tarot," by Papus, and the remarks on the subject by Eliphaz Levi may be referred to.

God has ever been the supreme symbol of human nescience ; for by that name there is suggested all that we do not know concerning the remote cause of things. Accordingly, " one thinks He is made of fire. . . . The Epicureans that He is idle and inactive and so to speak a nobody in human affairs. Then the Stoics represent Him as placed outside the world whirling round this huge mass from without like a potter; while the Platonists place Him within the world, as a pilot is in the ship he steers." Other conceptions even more curious and barbarous than these will at once occur to each of us. In fact we begin to doubt whether the fool who said in his heart " there is no God," was after all so much worse than the many who have made assertions to the contrary.

But though no one does, or ever did, know anything about the gods, the more one studies the ancient scriptures the more one sees that this very lack of knowledge made theology the one theme which allowed unlimited scope for the imagination or humour of the artist. No absurdities were too grotesque to apply to a god and no humour too broad. Hyperbole was the sanctioned vehicle of expression ; poets and artists vying with each other in the gross monstrosity as well as the sublimity of their productions. But all this is wasted upon the serious people who nowadays monopolize religion, for they neither admire the delicacy and art in the handling of a difficult subject, nor laugh at the cruder caricature of a coarser wit.

And since the gods are but the reflex of their creators, what more natural than that the fortune-tellers and mountebanks for whom the Tarot was designed should have regarded the maker of heaven and earth as a juggler, and the feat of creation as an inexplicable trick? With this apt conceit the series of the twenty-two symbols begins; and from it we derive some of the ideas connected with the number *one*. By some type or emblem the first division of a canonical work ought to express a suggestion of the primary principle. This is obviously done in the book of Genesis, wherein the manifestation of the deity, the creation of the world and its history for 2,368 years,[1] are obscurely set forth.

Briefly, the first hieroglyph represents the be-ginning and first cause of things—in Nature the universal life, in persons the god, king, chief, father or generator, in astronomy the empyreum, in geometry a point, and so on, with a similar figure appropriate to each of the arts and sciences.

In his preface to the Cabala, Mr. Mathers com-plains of the shameful suppression in modern times of all references to the feminine principle in theo-logy. At an earlier period they were less reticent. So the histories include a female Pope,[2] who per-

---

[1] See F. Roberts, "Key of the Bible," 1649, p. 9.

[2] The inclusion of Pope Joan in the order of the Popes seems to be accounted for by chronological reasons. In the list of Ciaconius (tom. i., fol. 626), under the name of John VIII., she follows Leo IV., who died in 855, and was the 105th Pope in order. Pope Joan, therefore was the 106th. Now 106 is the diameter of a circle 333 in circumference, and

sonifies the number *two* in the Tarot. She is the
Vicar of Christ in his feminine capacity. In the
Pythagorean system the number one was generally
considered to be male, the number two female, and
the number three the union of both, thus making
the second person of the Triad a woman; and
from an old English homily for Trinity Sunday
we learn that "the fourme of the Trinity was
founden in man, that was Adam our forefadir, of
earth oon personne, and Eve of Adam the seconde
personne; and of them both was the thirde person" (Strutt's "Manners and Customs," vol. iii.,
p. 176; see Oliver's "Pythag. Triangle," p. 98).
But the number two was sometimes regarded as a
masculine power as in the case of the second step
in the Cabala, where it refers to the Logos or the
emanation of the male. The Mohammedan idea
of the Christian Trinity is thus expressed in the
fourth chapter of the Koran, "Jesus (the son of
Mary) is the apostle of God and his Word, which
he conveyed into Mary, and a spirit proceeding
from Him." As representing the double potency
in creation, the second hieroglyph signifies the
feminine essence of life.

The departure of the children of Israel out of
Egypt, the crossing of the Red Sea and the
wandering in the desert may be interpreted as an
image of the transition of the soul, the Israelites
being likened to the stars or germs of life in the
firmament (see Sir W. Drummond, "Œdipus

333 is the diagonal of the New Jerusalem, emblem of the
Bride. And the circumference of a circle 855 in diameter is
equal to the perimeter of a rhombus, whose sides are $671\frac{3}{4}$, or
the numerical equivalent of Thorah and Adonai. Like St.
Helena this famous lady was said to have been an English
girl. And in the guise of a priest she lived many years with a
reputation for great learning, and for a time also for piety
(*see* Boccaccio, "De Mulieribus Claris," 1539, p. 73).

Judaicus," and Gerald Massey, "Book of Beginnings").

The upper Triad is completed by the *third* hieroglyph, which is represented in the Tarot by the Empress, for the Christians usually assigned a feminine personification to the third person of the Trinity. She corresponds to Mary the Virgin as contrasted with Mary the Magdalen,[1] who belongs to the tenth step. These three steps typify God (*Macrocosmos*, 831) as the Father and Husband of the universe, as Philo says.

The exposition of the Law (Thorah) in Leviticus makes that book appropriate to the number three.

The fourth card of the Tarot bears upon it the figure of an Emperor seated on a throne. And *Daleth*, the letter whose numerical equivalent is 4, signifies a door or the womb. This hieroglyph added to the Triad represent the material terms of creation.

From these two is generated the fifth power personified in the Tarot by the Pope, who is the earthly substitute or vicar of the Logos. The Spirit of the world, says Cornelius Agrippa, was called the quintessence, that is, the fifth essence, which existed above the four elements and pervaded the Æther or planetary system (bk. i., ch. xiv).

In his "Address to the Greeks" (ch. xii.), Tatian says "we recognize two varieties of spirit, one of which is called the soul (ψυχή), but the other is greater than the soul [viz., *Logos*, see ch. vii., *ibid.*], an image and likeness of God : both existed in the first man." The number six represented the mingling together of these two. It is an emblem of Psyche, whose marriage is so beautifully portrayed by Apuleius in the *sixth* chapter of

---

[1] Bacon says that the ancients conceived matter as a courtezan ("Advancement of Learning," bk. ii., ch. 13).

the "Golden Ass." In the order of progression
the number six marks the time of conception, and
if we count nine for the months of gestation, the
the period of birth would be fulfilled at the fourteenth step. It was perhaps for this reason that
the sonnet was composed of 14 lines, embracing
the complete cycle of human life. The steps from
1 to 5 are also a complete cycle, whence probably
Moses chose this number for the books of the Law.
Again, the 6 steps of the Cabala from the third to
the tenth make up the body of Microcosmos, and
he is evidently personified by Joshua, whose name
is written 'Iησοῦς, Jesus by Josephus and the Seventy
(IHSHO, Joshua, yields 385 and a vesica 384·2
broad is 666 long).

The next two symbols are too obscure to be
explained briefly. A reference to the ninth step
is quoted on page 363. In the ninth book of the
" Book of the Dead " (Turin MS.), the soul of the
deceased comes to the Ark of Osiris and the Hill
of Bat.[1] Now, if the reader will turn to the
diagram on page 365 he will see that the ninth
step forms one of the extremities of a cross whose
centre is in the tenth. Hippolytus tells us that
Noah's Ark was turned round upon Mount Kardu
(cardo) towards the four cardinal points of the
world, and "finally stood towards the East. We
say, moreover, that that was a sign of the Cross.
And the ark was a symbol of the Christ who was
expected " (" Ante-Nicene Library," vol. vi., p.
495). An examination of the tenth hieroglyph of
the Tarot makes this clearer; for the Wheel of
Fortune is an obvious representation of the planets
revolving round the navel or centre of the world.
On the right a dog ascends, and on the left an
ape descends, while a sphinx surmounts the wheel

[1] Described on p. 136.

in the middle. Her twofold body, the hinder parts being those of a lion, seem to refer to the fact that she sits on the horizon between the upper and lower hemisphere; the figures on either side are apparently personifications of the eleventh and twelfth steps or the equinoxes. The name Σφίγξ (Sphinx) has the value of 773, or the perimeter of the Holy Oblation taking the sun's distance at 10. St. Clement ("Miscell.," bk. v., ch. 8), says, "The sphinx is not the comprehension of the universe, and the revolution of the world, according to the poet Aratus. . . . But it is better to regard it as the Ether, which holds together and presses all things." By gematria Sphinx is equivalent to Syrinx, the pipe of seven reeds shown in the hand of Pan (fig. 25). And doubtless her well-known riddle, whose answer was a Man, mystically adumbrated the Microcosm whose body is measured by the number 773. Or can it be a purely accidental coincidence that the name of Œdipus (ὁ οἰδίπους, the swollen-footed) should have the value of $514 + 2 = 516$, the side of a rhombus whose perimeter is equal to the mean diameter of the spheres of Saturn and the Zodiac?

The Hebrew word ODN (Eden) has the same numerical value, and must be regarded as an analogous place in biblical mythology. The Mount of Purgatory, described by Dante, had 7 terraces, the Terrestrial Paradise being at its summit. It is, of course, an image of the 7 planetary orbits surrounding the earth which stands in the diagram intermediate between Heaven, the upper hemisphere, and Hell, the lower; and Botticelli's design seems to show that he conceived it in this cosmic sense.

Sir John Maundeville speaks of a "well" in the *middle place* of Paradise that cast out four floods [marking the cardinal points]. And "many great Lords," he says, "have assayed with great will many times for to passe by those rivers with full great companies : but they might not speed in their voyage : and many died from weariness of rowing against so strong waves," etc. Sir John, who wrote with the authority of the Pope, was a good cabalist, and did not forget that the tenth step was an emblem of the Bride.

The cross in the centre of the world also represents the Elements, or the universal matter, out of which the body of the Logos was compounded ; and the incarnation of the soul upon earth was symbolized among Christians by Jesus and his earthly parents, Joseph and Mary. Their names have the value of $2,598 + 3 = 2,601$, which is the side of a square enclosing the Microcosm crucified on a rood-cross inscribed within the earth's circumference.

The suggestion that Noah's Ark is shadowed forth in the cardinal cross, dividing the sublunary world, is corroborated by the value of the names of Noah and his sons, to whom the earth was said to have been apportioned.[1] The numbers are NCh 58, ShM 340, ChM 48, and IPhTh $490 = 936$, or the length of a rhombus having a perimeter of 2,160, the number of miles in the moon's diameter. Again, $933\frac{1}{3}$ is the diagonal of a square whose sides are 660; while 938 is the width of a rhombus whose length is 1,626, the numerical equivalent of *Tetractys*, the sacred emblem of the Pythagoreans, which was synonymous with the Tetragrammaton of the Jews. It is further remarkable that a

---

[1] The names of the five earliest races of men mentioned by Hesiod are derived from the minerals of which the earth is largely composed, viz., gold, silver, brass, earth, and iron. The sum of their numbers is $3968 - 5 = 3963$, which is the exact radius of the earth at the equator.

cross inscribed in a vesica 938 long measures
1,480.

In St. Cyril's Canon the Book of Chronicles,
called in Hebrew the "words of days,"[1] has the
10th place. It begins with the generation of the
sons of Adam and gives a recapitulation of the
events narrated in the previous books. By the
philosophic method of addition 10 is reduced to 1
(1 + 0 = 1). Therefore the history in the tenth
book is the going-back to the beginning and
original starting point. And the incarnation of the
soul being accomplished in Adam and his successors, the genealogy of Chronicles fitly expresses
man's birth and heritage of the earth down to
the time of its composition.

The symbols of the tenth step, referring as they
do to the universe, the elements, and the earth, are
very numerous. For instance, as the genetrix or
mother of men, the earth was conceived as a loom.
For she as the woman was said to weave the
purple web of flesh with which the soul is invested
as with a garment. So Persephone "is represented by Orpheus as weaving a web, and the
heavens are called by the ancients a veil, in consequence of being, as it were, the vestment of the
celestial gods" (Porphyry, "Cave of the Nymphs").
By poets, priests, and craftsmen she was idealized
in countless forms as the emblem of productive
Art. And for this reason apparently Plato in the
tenth book of the "Republic" pictured Necessity
as a spinster bearing a mighty distaff having 7
whorls, corresponding to the planetary orbits. With
her three daughters, the Fates, who correspond to
the 11th, 12th, and 13th steps, she seems to be an
image similar to the Wheel of Fortune in the Tarot.

The adventures of Odysseus in the 10th book of

---

[1] DBRI, 216, HIMIM, 665. Now 216 + 665 = 881.

the Odyssey include his coming to the Hall of Circe, 158 (× 3⅐ = 496). There he receives from Hermes the plant *Moly*, 1270, to enable him to withstand the magic arts of the enchantress. This herb was said to have a black root and a white (milky) blossom ; by gematria it is equivalent to *Stauros*.

The 11th and 12th steps, marking the two points on the horizon, may be taken to be the two poles, the two equinoxes or solstices. And the 12th book of the Odyssey relates how Odysseus passes the monsters *Scylla*, 688, and *Charybdis*, 1,317,[1] which appear to be hyperbolical personifications of these ; for 688 + 1,317 = 2,005, or the internal width of an ark whose outer measure is 2,083. In the " Book of the Dead " it is at the 11th chapter that the soul of the deceased reaches the *Hall of the Two Laws*, so it is possible that they also refer to these positive and negative symbols. The 12th card of the Tarot plainly sets forth one aspect of the hieroglyph. A man is represented hanging head-downwards from a beam resting upon two trees, each having 6 lopped branches. Now since the earth turns once upon its axis every 24 hours, the 12th hour divides the day from the night; accordingly, when the soul has passed the 12th step it metaphorically enters the lower hemisphere. This is indicated by the man hanging head downwards. The writer of the book of Esther (the 12th on St. Cyril's list) makes use of this very metaphor. For the hanging of the malefactor, Haman, and the release of the just Mordecai through the intercession of Queen Esther[2] is the Old Testament type of the crucifixion—the gallows of the Hanged Man of the Tarot being a foreshadowing of the cross and the 12 disciples.

---

[1] 688 × 3⅐ = 2,162, and 1,317 is the width of an ark 7,902 long, the polar diameter of the earth.

[2] ASThR = 661.

The five hieroglyphs, the 9th, 10th, 11th, 12th, and 13th, occupying the middle and extremities of the cross, may be all connected with the world, or Malchuth ; thus Odysseus makes his descent into Hades in the 11th book of the Odyssey.   But the 13th is essentially the symbol of the lower hemisphere, corresponding in the underworld to the first step above.   It is called " Death " in the Tarot, and has the signification of a woman.   Its hieroglyphic meaning is adumbrated in the Book of Job—a treatise so greatly admired by the old theologians that it was considered the masterpiece of the Old Testament.   The name Job means " the assailed " in Hebrew, and has the value of 19 ; so it is equivalent by gematria to Eve.   At this point the soul has crossed the line, so to speak, and enters the threshold of death, or Hell ; and when depicting the exaggerated trials and dangers of the passage the ancients placed no limits upon their imagination, as when the old artists delighted to paint the agonies of Christ on the cross and all the cruelties of the Passion.   So we find upon the 13th card of the Tarot a grisly skeleton remorselessly cutting off human heads and hands with a scythe.

From a statement in the " Court of the Gentiles " we gather that the Book of Job was the oldest *dialogue* ever written, and that its form had a symbolic meaning.   Job, it is said, is the respondent in the dispute, and his three friends the assailants. So when wrestling with his adversaries, and argument is met by argument, we are to admire the patient persistency of the pious Job and to wonder as he justifies himself against the attacks of his opponents, undauntedly pushing a fresh argument again and again till they are at last put to silence.

The Rabbis declared that the disease from which the patient one suffered was elephantiasis.

Another figure by which this step may be expressed is signified by St. Augustine in the *thirteenth* chapter of the first book of the "City of God": "Aye, but many Christians (say they) were led into captivity : this indeed had been a lamentable case, if they had been led into some place where they could not possibly have found their God. But for comforts in captivity, the Scriptures have store : the three children were in bondage : so was Daniel, so were others of the Prophets : but they never wanted God their comforter. No more did He here abandon His faithful ; being under the command of barbarous men, who forsook not His Prophet being even in the belly of a beast. This now they with whom we are to deal, had rather scorn than believe, yet of that fable in their own books they are fully persuaded, namely, that that same excellent harper Arion of Methymna, being cast overboard, was taken up on a dolphin's back, and so borne safe to land. Is our history of Jonas more incredible than this ? yes, because it is more admirable ; and it is more admirable, because more powerful" (*compare with the* 13*th book of the same work*).

Sir John Maundeville describes the country of Job in the *fourteenth* chapter of his "Travels," and so carries us a step further than St. Cyril. He says that Job was a paynim, but served God well "after his Law," and that in his land "there ben Hills where men getten great plenty of Manna . . . this Mana is clept Bread of Angels." In the Tarot a winged figure is shown to pour liquid from one vessel into another. The moral inculcated is Temperance. It is difficult to speak otherwise than metaphorically with respect to this hieroglyph, but the manna and the pouring-out of the liquid are both types of the mystery, which are again expressed by the Psalms, the figurative swan-song when the gates of Hades are passed. The Fathers called the Psalter an epitome of the Scriptures, and its order appears to follow the rule we are now attempting to explain. Luther's commentary on the first twenty-two Psalms is as instructive as the more extensive work of St. Augustine, and shows that this early reformer had no desire to depart from the ancient Canon of the Church.

The 15th step completes the upper Triad in the underworld, and is represented by the Devil, who is simply Macrocosmos in the lower hemisphere. The received manner of depicting the evil one was after the fashion of Pan (fig. 25) ; and it is extremely curious that the numerical values of the names applied to him are identical with those of the good deity. Thus *Satanas* yields 753, the diameter of a circle whose circumference is 2,368 ; *Antichristos*, 1,841, when read backwards makes 1,481, but 193·6, the diameter of the Holy Oblation multiplied by 9·5, produces 1,839·2 ; again *Ophis*, the Serpent, is equivalent by Gematria to *Sophia*, wisdom ; and THLI, dragon, and AMTH, truth, have each the same numerical value, and are equal by Gematria to *To agathon*, the good. It would be difficult to find an instance more clearly manifesting the profundity of the old philosophy than this.

Passing over the intermediate hieroglyphs for the present we shall only refer to the 22nd, or last of the series. It is symbolized by the cross, and is a repetition of the 10th step. The letter Tau with which it is associated, like *chi*, the 22nd letter of the Greek alphabet, was originally a cross ; and its numerical value (THV = 406) [1] is the diameter of a circle whose circumference is 1,276, the height of a rood cross which will crucify a man in a square having a perimeter of

[1] A rhombus whose sides are 406 has a perimeter of 1,626, the numerical equivalent of *Tetractys*.

2,368. In Fludd's " Historia Microcosmi," p. 114, there is an engraving of Macrocosmos, whose body is obviously disposed in the form of a cross like the letter Tau ; and underneath it is written, " Hence we conclude that the veritable, genuine, and visible figure of the outer man is a *true representation of the cross of Christ.*" [1] It is also noteworthy that the 10th Roman numeral, X, is a cross in the form of a saltire.

By gematria THV is equivalent to Εὐα, 406, Eve, and the 22nd card of the Tarot displays the figure of a woman enclosed by a vesica, surrounded by the four beasts of the Evangelists, which are the four corner signs of the Zodiac, in the form which has been ascribed to the New Jerusalem. In the Apocalypse, whose chapters correspond with the canonical symbols, the City of the Bride is described in the 21st [2] and 22nd chapters. The last design of the Tarot, called " The World," depicts that image of Thorah, [3] the Law, under which she appeared in heaven as a " woman clothed with the sun, and the moon under her feet, and upon her head a crown of 12 stars," or as the Christian counterpart of her classic prototype Helen, the daughter of Zeus, ever adored as the feminine ideal of beauty, love, and nature by all old artists, and glorified by the priest as the virgin, bride, and mother, who sets forth the three phases of womanhood exhibited in the threefold sequence of the Cabala.

Pythagoras defined the soul as being composed

---

[1] " Hinc etiam elicimus, quod vera, genuina atque visibilis hominis externi figura *veram crucis Christi effigiem* repraesentet." See fig. 8, p. 54, of the present volume.

[2] The 22nd card is numbered 21, the 21st card being unnumbered.

[3] Thorah means "gate," and is similar to the Greek θύρα, which yields 510, or the side of a rhombus having a perimeter equal to the diameter of Saturn's orbit.

of νοῦς, φρήν, and θυμός, understanding, reason, and anger, whose numbers amount to 2,097 — 3 = 2,094, the diameter of the zodiac. His doctrine that the soul must pass through the bodies of various animals before attaining perfection probably refers to its supposed passage into the signs and constellations, most of which are figured as beasts of some kind He himself said that "he

FIG. 29.—ASTRONOMICAL HIEROGLYPH OF THE 22ND, 23RD, AND 24TH STEPS, CALLED CIRCULUS LACTEUS, HYGINUS, 1488.

should again return from the other world and converse with men after the expiration of 207 [1] years" (Diogenes Laertius, "Life of Pythagoras"). Accordingly, by the spirit of the world on the 22nd card, the artist has intimated that the cycle of life has been completed; the soul has traversed the whole circle of the universe, and, as a small

[1] $207 \times 3\frac{1}{7} = 681 \times 3\frac{1}{7} = 2,047$, the diameter of Saturn's orbit, which is surrounded by the twelve beasts of the zodiac.

drop merges into a greater, it is assimilated into the sphere of infinity.

The application of the order of ideas which we have attempted to describe may be seen in a short piece like the Apostles' Creed, forming a part of the avowedly canonical ritual of the English Common Prayer. The tradition, according to Ambrose, is that the twelve Apostles assembled together and made the creed, each of them inserting an article. It thus acquired a cosmic significance from being an image of the zodiacal circle. Although it was unknown to the Greeks, it was greatly esteemed in the Western Church. It was called the symbolum, and was secretly preserved *unwritten*, being one of the mysteries communicated to the baptized at their initiation. In the English Church it is printed with only three sections, and these manifestly correspond to the Cabalistic Triad, or the Persons of the Trinity, whom the initiated in the early Church secretly confessed as the all-embracing summary of their faith. The subdivisions of the Prayer-book are marked thus, ¶, and the Creed occupies the 13th division in the Morning Prayer, and the 9th in the Evening Prayer, or, counting from the beginning, the 34th. Now it has been shown that the steps from the 9th to the 13th typify the Zodiac, since they comprise the centre and extremities of the mundane cross, or "cosmic wheel. And if the diagram (p. 365) be continued and another link added to the chain, the 34th step corresponds to the 10th and 22nd, each of which is an emblem of the world.

In this way much light will be thrown upon old books if they be studied in connexion with this order. St. Cyril's lectures and other patristic commentaries, the old allegories and romances which puzzle everyone now, from Apuleius to

Spenser, or even the scenes of " Hamlet," may be redeemed from obscurity, and often an unexpected meaning will be imparted to the barest platitude when the reference to the symbol is perceived.

The divisions of the New Testament, according to St. Cyril, amount to 26, the number of the Tetragrammaton. He omits the Apocalypse just as other early canons are without the Epistle to the Hebrews. The authorship of the four versions of the life of Christ being attributed to persons typifying the four corner signs of the Zodiac, the Man, the Lion, the Bull, and the Eagle, the astronomical sense of the parable is disclosed. And the name $εὐαγγέλιον$, 577, the " good news," appears to have been chosen with the same mystical intention, for a Solomon's seal whose sides are 577·2 is enclosed by a circle 666 in diameter and 2,093 in circumference. It has already been shown (pp. 56-57) that these numbers supply the key to the cosmic aspect of the Christian theology, and suggest the true nature of the Microcosmic Man personified in the Gospels by the Saviour.

Biblos, 314, the first word of the New Testament, has a similar meaning, since a vesica 314 wide is formed by two intersecting circles whose united width is 942, the diagonal of a square whose sides are 666. And both these names are indirectly equivalent to *Paradosis*, TRADITION, whose numerical value is 666.

The numbers 137 deduced from QBLH, Cabala, has the same import as 1480, for the square contained within the zodiac, if the sun's distance be taken at 10, is 136·9 ; and ZHR, Zohar, the name of the principal cabalistic treatise, yields 212, the diameter of a circle 666 in circumference.

Of the morality which the philosophers attempted to combine with their theological myths we have said nothing, because very often it is only an irrelevant accessory. Besides, a treatise on the subject is a superfluity nowadays, the moral features of religion have become so exceedingly popular that everyone knows how to be good, if no one wishes to be so. Morals, of course, are merely customs (*mores*). Each code is a local and temporal affair, constructed to suit the exigencies of the time and place, and no more states the law finally and absolutely than any one of the extant theologies states the true nature of the deity. Still the attempt to demonstrate (however unsuccessfully) that a moral, or rather a beneficent purpose is involved in the operations of nature, will always touch a chord deep-rooted in our hearts. And if there is any analogy between the soul of man and the soul of the universe, the moral sense, which is undoubtedly though strangely manifested in each of us, must have its counterpart in the Logos or soul of all.

We have not tried to defend the priests for having deceived the multitude, or to uphold their doctrines now or in the past. Nor have we sought to make an idol of antiquity. But in looking back we see the same mad, foolish, credulous, and incredible world, which is here to-day, with its infinite capacity for being tricked and imposed upon, for establishing and supporting the absurdest institutions ; while, in extenuation of their guilt, it must be conceded that the saner could hardly bequeath their wisdom to a populace, which in all ages has persistently declined to inherit it. As for the enlightened amongst ourselves who conscientiously suppose that the ancients were children, and patronize them as such, we imagine that the slightest acquaintance with the works of both must make it conclusively apparent who the children are.

In conclusion, this essay to explain the legend

on the door-post of Plato's school, "LET NONE
IGNORANT OF GEOMETRY ENTER HERE," may fitly
close in the Master's words. It seems that he fore-
saw that the geometrical tradition of the academy
was passing into oblivion and would some day be
utterly forgotten. Such apparently was his meaning when he composed the Prediction of Thamus,
whose fulfilment has been most curiously accomplished. When the Egyptian Theuth invented the
alphabet he showed it to King Thamus, declaring
that the knowledge of letters would be an incentive
to wisdom and a medicine for memory. But the
king replied, "Most ingenious Theuth, one person is able to give birth to art, another to judge
of what amount of detriment or advantage it
will be to those who use it, and now you, as
being the father of letters, out of fondness have
attributed to them just the contrary effect to that
which they will have. For this invention will produce forgetfulness in the minds of those who learn
it through the neglect of memory, for that through
trusting to writing they will remember outwardly
by means of foreign marks, and not inwardly by
means of their own faculties. . . . For hearing
many things through your means WITHOUT IN-
STRUCTION they will appear to know a great deal,
although they are for the most part ignorant, and
will become troublesome associates, through thinking themselves wise instead of being so."

> "*Gemetré the seventhe syens hyt ysse*
> *That con deperte falshed from trewthe y-wys.*"

THE END.

INDEX.

CHISWICK PRESS:—CHARLES WHITTINGHAM AND CO.
TOOKS COURT, CHANCERY LANE, LONDON.

fructus inter folia